The Construal of Spatial Meaning

EXPLORATIONS IN LANGUAGE AND SPACE

Series editor
Emile van der Zee, University of Lincoln

Published
1 Representing Direction in Language and Space
Edited by Emile van der Zee and Jon Slack

2 Functional Features in Language and Space
Insights from Perception, Categorization, and Development
Edited by Laura A. Carlson and Emile van der Zee

3 Spatial Language and Dialogue
Edited by Kenny R. Coventry, Thora Tenbrink, and John A. Bateman

4 The Spatial Foundations of Cognition and Language
Edited by Kelly S. Mix, Linda B. Smith, and Michael Gasser

5 Interpreting Motion
Grounded Representations for Spatial Language
Inderjeet Mani and James Pustejovsky

6 Motion Encoding in Language and Space
Edited by Mila Vulchanova and Emile van der Zee

7 The Construal of Spatial Meaning
Windows into Conceptual Space
Edited by Carita Paradis, Jean Hudson, and Ulf Magnusson

In preparation
Representing Space in Cognition
Interrelations of behaviour, language, and formal models
Edited by Thora Tenbrink, Jan Wiener, and Christophe Claramunt

The Construal of Spatial Meaning: Windows into Conceptual Space

Edited by

CARITA PARADIS, JEAN HUDSON,
and ULF MAGNUSSON

OXFORD
UNIVERSITY PRESS

OXFORD
UNIVERSITY PRESS

Great Clarendon Street, Oxford, OX2 6DP,
United Kingdom

Oxford University Press is a department of the University of Oxford.
It furthers the University's objective of excellence in research, scholarship,
and education by publishing worldwide. Oxford is a registered trade mark of
Oxford University Press in the UK and in certain other countries

First Edition published in 2013

Impression: 1

British Library Cataloguing in Publication Data

Data available

ISBN 978–0–19–964163–5

Printed by the MPG Printgroup, UK

Contents

Preface

The idea for this book has its origin in a theme session on Space and Language at the first SALC (Scandinavian Association for Language and Cognition)* conference which was held in Lund, Sweden, in December 2007. We would like to express our gratitude to the series editor, Emile van der Zee, for encouraging us to collect the articles that make up this volume, many, though not all, of which were presented at the conference.

We are indebted to a number of reviewers, who have generously provided insightful comments in their various fields of expertise. Our thanks on this score go to: Liliana Albertazzi, David Barner, Sven Bertel, Niclas Burenhult, Soonja Choi, Carlos Cornejo, Seana Coulson, Östen Dahl, René Dirven, Małgorzata Fabiszak, Nancy Franklin, Marianne Gullberg, Iraide Ibarretxe-Antuñano, Steven Jones, David A. Leavens, Ulf Liszkowski, David McNeill, Diane Pecher, Günter Radden, Chris Sinha, Dan Slobin, Göran Sonesson, Jürgen Streeck, Jan Svanlund, Ida Toivonen, Graeme Trousdale, Joost van de Weijer, Phyllis Wilcox, and Jordan Zlatev.

Last but not least, we would like to thank the editorial team at OUP, in particular Julia Steer, for patient and friendly guidance throughout the preparation of this volume.

Carita Paradis
Jean Hudson
Ulf Magnusson

---

* At the time of the conference: The Swedish Association for Language and Cognition.

Notes on Contributors

PER DURST-ANDERSEN is a professor at Copenhagen Business School and the director of the Centre for Language, Cognition, and Mentality. In 1992 he wrote *Mental Grammar. Russian Aspect and Related Issues*, which laid the foundation for his cognitive theory of language and communication. He has published on verb typology, aspect, mood and modality, case, syntactic typology, pragmatics, and semiotics. In *Linguistic Supertypes. A Cognitive–Semiotic Theory of Human Communication* 2011, he breaks down the wall between language and communication.

PETER GÄRDENFORS is Professor of Cognitive Science at Lund University. His main current research concerns applications of conceptual spaces and the evolution of cognition. Among his publications are *Knowledge in Flux* (1988), *Conceptual Spaces* (2000), *How Homo Became Sapiens* (2003), and *The Dynamics of Thought* (2005).

RAYMOND W. GIBBS, JR is Professor of Psychology at the University of California, Santa Cruz, and is author of several books, including *The Poetics of Mind: Figurative Thought, Language and Understanding* (1994), and *Embodiment and Cognitive Science* (2006), as well as editor of the *Cambridge Handbook of Metaphor and Thought* (2008) and the journal *Metaphor and Symbol*.

ANNE-KATHARINA HARR studied French and German language and literature from 2000 to 2007 at the Ludwig-Maximilians-University in Munich and at the University of Paris 5. She carried out her doctoral thesis under the supervision of Katrin Lindner (University of Munich) and Maya Hickmann (University of Paris 8 and CNRS). Her main research interests are first and second language acquisition and bilingualism. She currently participates in several international projects and is a lecturer at the University of Munich.

MAYA HICKMANN received her PhD from the University of Chicago in 1982. She was a member of the Max Planck Institute for Psycholinguistics from 1982 to 1992, and since then of several CNRS laboratories in France within the areas of Psychology and Linguistics. She is currently Research Director in the Laboratoire Structures Formelles du Langage (CNRS and Université de Paris 8). Her research mainly focuses on the role of structural vs functional and universal vs language-specific determinants in first and second language acquisition.

KENNETH HOLMQVIST is the manager of the Humanities laboratory at Lund University and an expert on eye-tracking methodology. His previous research interest concerned computational models of cognitive semantics, stressing the visual and attentional properties of the underlying representations (image schemata). In

1996 he founded an eye-tracking laboratory that has now grown to become a centre for interdisciplinary research (www.humlab.lu.se), and the focus of his research has moved towards methods of measuring cognition through vision. He is the author of *Eye Tracking: a Comprehensive Guide to Methods and Measures.*

JANA HOLSANOVA is Associate Professor in Cognitive Science at Lund University. She works as a senior researcher at the Linnaeus Centre for Cognition, Communication, and Learning, focusing on cognitive processes underlying language use, picture viewing, and mental imagery. In her work, she uses eye-tracking methodology along with simultaneous or retrospective verbal protocols. Her recent book, *Discourse, Vision, and Cognition*, explores the relationship between language, eye movements, and cognition, and brings together discourse analysis with cognitively oriented behavioural research.

HENRIK HOVMARK is Associate Professor at the University of Copenhagen, and received his PhD in 2007 for a thesis on the expression of spatial meaning in Danish, with a special emphasis on the relationship between language, culture, and cognition, and drawing on dialectal data. Since 2002 he has been working in the Dialectology Section at the University of Copenhagen as a researcher and editor for the Dictionary of Danish Insular Dialects. He has previously worked as an editor at the Danish Society for Language and Literature and at Gyldendal Publishers.

JEAN HUDSON is Professor of English Linguistics at Malmö University, Sweden. The focus of her research efforts is on the empirical investigation of spontaneous speech data in the search for insights into the relationship between language and cognition. She is currently investigating prepositional usage within the general framework of construction grammar.

ROGER JOHANSSON is a PhD student in Cognitive Science at Lund University. His PhD project is entitled 'The existence and use of mental images'. The project is funded by The Swedish Research Council and is integrated into the Linnaeus Centre for Cognition, Communication, and Learning at Lund. His main interests are in spatial cognition, mental imagery, and the relationship between language and mental models of spatiality. He specializes in experimental research using eye-tracking methods.

MARLENE JOHANSSON FALCK received her PhD in English Linguistics from Luleå University of Technology in 2005. She is currently a researcher in the Department of Language Studies, Umeå University. Her contribution to this volume was written when she was a post-doctoral fellow in the Department of Psychology, University of California, Santa Cruz. Her research interests are in the fields of cognitive linguistics, corpus linguistics, and psycholinguistics. She is especially interested in metaphor, spatial language, and cognition.

KRISTIINA JOKINEN is Adjunct Professor and Project Manager at the University of Helsinki, Finland and Visiting Professor of Intelligent User Interfaces at the University of Tartu, Estonia. She received her PhD at UMIST, Manchester, UK, and worked for four years in Japan as JSPS Research Fellow at Nara Institute of Science and Technology, and as Invited Researcher at ATR (Advanced Telecommunications Research Laboratories) in Kyoto. In Finland she has played a leading role in several academic and industrial research projects concerning natural language interactive systems, spoken dialogue management, and multimodality. Her current interests focus on human non-verbal communication, gestures, and facial expressions. She has authored numerous papers and conference publications, and her book, *Constructive Dialogue Management—Speech Interaction and Rational Agents*, was published in 2009. She is the secretary of SIGDial, the ACL/ISCA Special Interest Group for Discourse and Dialogue.

ULF MAGNUSSON is Emeritus Professor of English at Luleå University of Technology, Sweden, and previously held posts as Professor of English and University Lecturer at Högskolan Kristianstad, Sweden. Before then he had a long career as a senior upper secondary school teacher of English and French. Magnusson's interests are mainly in English lexicography, metaphor, and cognitive linguistics.

LILIANA MARTINEZ is a PhD student in the Department of Modern Languages at the Norwegian University of Science and Technology, Trondheim. Her research interests are in the field of categorization and linguistic encoding of motion. She is currently working on a dissertation on the semantics of motion verbs.

OLE NEDERGAARD THOMSEN has a PhD in general linguistics from the University of Copenhagen (1992). Researcher at Copenhagen Business School, Centre for Language, Cognition, and Mentality, where he works with Prof. Søren Brier within the transdisciplinary theory 'Cybersemiotics', developing a model of human 'total communication'. Other research interests are in Danish, linguistic typology, language change, incorporation, ergativity (Greenlandic, Dyirbal), direct-inverse languages (Mapudungun), functional discourse grammar and pragmatics, integral linguistics (Coseriu), distributed language theory, evolution of human communication, and Peircean semiotics.

CARITA PARADIS is Professor of English Linguistics at the Centre for Languages and Literature at Lund University in Sweden. Her main research interests concern meaning in the broad sense. She specializes in lexical semantics and the modelling of meaning within the Cognitive Linguistics framework. She combines corpus methods and experimental methods in her work.

JOHAN PEDERSEN holds a PhD in Spanish Linguistics and is Associate Professor in Spanish Language and Linguistics at the Department of English, Germanic and Romance Studies, University of Copenhagen, Denmark. His primary research interests are Spanish grammar, syntax and semantics, contrastive linguistics, language typology, corpus linguistics, general linguistics, and historical linguistics. He is Spanish Linguistics editor of the journal *Revue Romane*.

MARCUS PERLMAN received his PhD in Psychology from the University of California, Santa Cruz where he is also a postdoctoral fellow. He also works at the Gorilla Foundation in Woodside, California. He is interested in embodied cognition, speech communication, and comparative cognition.

NICLA ROSSINI is a research fellow and External Professor of Non-Verbal Communication at the University of Eastern Piedmont (Italy), and lecturer on Multimodal Communication and Video Analysis at the University of Luxembourg. She has authored several articles on the role of gesture and language. Her research interests include the ontogenetic and phylogenetic origin of gesture and its relation to language, as well as issues in face-to-face and written cross-cultural communication and mediation.

INGRID RUMMO is Lecturer in Estonian as a Foreign Language at the University of Tartu, Estonia. She was awarded her Master's degree at the University of Tartu, for a thesis on 'Teaching and Development of Foreign Language Skills Using Possibilities of Interactive Technology', in 2001. She worked from 2004–6 as a teacher of Estonian for the EU institutions in Brussels and is currently focused on her PhD studies. Her research interests are conversation and Patau syndrome, chromosomal abnormalities, multimodal (including non-verbal) communication, language, sign languages and neurocognition. The main methods she uses at present are conversation and discourse analysis.

VIKTOR SMITH is Associate Professor at Copenhagen Business School, Centre for Language, Cognition, and Mentality. His main research focus is the lexicon as the key elements of any manifestation of the complex socio-cognitive mechanism, human language, and a versatile tool for interacting with and, indeed, shaping the world (e.g. when generating innovative product ideas, navigating through clashing and converging legal orders, or crystallizing scientific paradigms). In his latest research, he addresses words and language in the wider context of multimodal interplay with other carriers of communicational content (images, colours, sensory impressions).

SILVI TENJES is Associate Professor of Estonian as a Foreign Language at the University of Tartu, Estonia. She focuses on discourse studies, human cognition, and linguistics, and her main research projects concern hand gestures, linguistic aspects of communicative processes, structure of multimodal communication, and choices of communication strategies. She is the head of the Research Group on Multimodal Communication at the University of Tartu and she was, from 2006–9, the project coordinator for Estonia in the Nordic research network on 'Place, Mediated Discourse and Embodied Interaction: PlaceME'. She has published on hand gestures and speech, space and metaphor, and interaction and discourse. Her current research focuses on multimodal communication and communicative strategies, sensory-motor mechanisms, and movement.

ELENA TRIBUSHININA received her PhD in Cognitive Linguistics at the University of Leiden, the Netherlands, in 2008. She then worked as a postdoctoral researcher at the University of Antwerp, Belgium. At present, she is an assistant professor at Utrecht Institute of Linguistics, the Netherlands. Her current research interests lie in the acquisition of adjectives and degree adverbs by Dutch- and Russian-speaking children.

MARK TUTTON was awarded his PhD in Linguistics in 2010 by the University of New South Wales and Université Charles de Gaulle (Lille 3). His PhD thesis examines how speakers of English and French use speech and gesture to communicate the fixed locations of objects in different spatial scenes. His research interests include how speakers of different languages express spatial semantics in speech and gesture, and the roles played by co-speech gestures in social interaction.

MILA VULCHANOVA is a professor at the Department of Modern Languages, the Norwegian University of Science and Technology, Trondheim, Norway. She holds a PhD in Theoretical Linguistics. Her main research interests include the interface of language and cognition, experimental research, lexical semantics, diachronic linguistics, and formal approaches to grammar.

MASSIMO WARGLIEN is Professor of Behavioural Economics at the Advanced School of Economics of the Ca' Foscari University of Venice. His current work concerns economics and language, the semantics of action, mental models of games, and neural network models of interactive learning. His most recent papers have been published in *Science*, *Proceedings of the National Academy of Sciences*, *Games and Economic Behaviour*, and *Physica A*.

CAROLINE WILLNERS is a researcher in linguistics at the Centre for Languages and Literature at Lund University in Sweden. She has a background in language technology and corpus linguistics, which has provided useful tools in her research in lexical semantics in general and antonymy in particular. Lately she has shifted to psycho- and neurolinguistic methods in her study of antonyms as well as synonyms. She is also interested in language acquisition, dyslexia, and writing aids. Apart from her research position at the university, she develops writing aids for people with reading and writing disabilities at Oribi AB, Sweden.

1

Windows In: Empirical Evidence of Construals of Spatial Meaning

CARITA PARADIS, JEAN HUDSON
and ULF MAGNUSSON

1.1 Introduction

In the domain of interactions between language and cognition, SPACE and expressions of SPACE in languages are prominent topics of scientific inquiry. In spite of the extremely rich flora of investigation that we have seen in the recent past, the topic is far from being exhaustively researched. On the contrary, it has yet to offer many new developments and new knowledge, partly thanks to theoretical development in the area of language and cognition, and partly due to developments of new empirical techniques and computational facilities. As the title of this volume indicates, the centre of gravity is at the interface between theoretical and empirical development and progress.

The research reported in this volume is all carried out within the broad framework of Cognitive Linguistics, reflecting the main ideas of the theory as well as its point of departure in *Space Grammar* (Langacker 1982). Cognitive Linguistics is not monolithic, but holds a wide variety of research topics and empirical methods. Central to the framework, however, is that our conceptual and linguistic structures are physically, socially, and cognitively grounded. Geeraerts and Cuyckens (2007) select three fundamental tenets: (i) the primacy of semantics in linguistic analysis, (ii) the encyclopaedic nature of linguistic meaning, and (iii) the perspectival nature of linguistic meaning. 'Specifically, language is a way of organizing knowledge that reflects the needs, interests and experiences of individuals and cultures' (2007: 5).

Our interest in the topic is inclusive rather than restricted in that we take linguistics to encompass both verbal and non-verbal communication systems. Knowledge is obtained in physical space and thought of as reflecting inner (mental) space. The contributions reflect the multidisciplinary character of the study of SPACE. At the heart of all of them is the relation between physical space and mental space as it is expressed in human communication. Alluding to the title of Johansson, Holsanova, and Holmqvist's contribution to this volume,

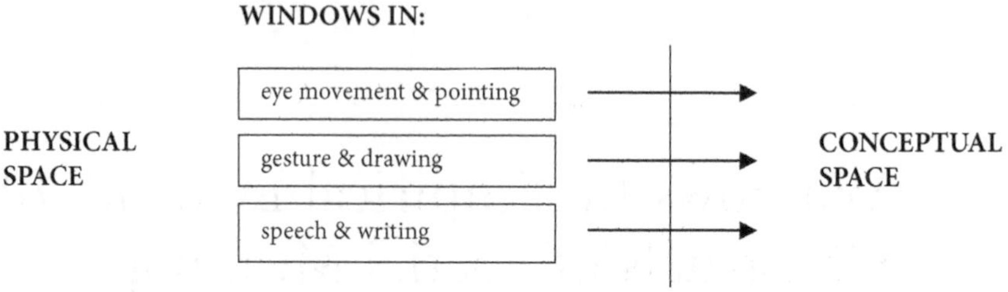

WINDOWS IN:

PHYSICAL SPACE	eye movement & pointing ⟶	CONCEPTUAL SPACE
	gesture & drawing ⟶	
	speech & writing ⟶	

FIG. 1.1. Windows into conceptual space

we have organized the contributions on the basis of a spatial metaphor of a window through which we as analysts are able to get a glimpse of inner space. Eye movement, pointing, gesture, drawing, speech, and writing are all such windows. To reflect the empirical focus of the contributions, we introduce them in order along a cline of 'windows in', starting with what we interpret as the most fundamental and basic means of expression: eye movement and pointing, through gesture and drawing, to speech and writing (Figure 1.1).

Not only does the figure reflect the different 'windows in' and the types of data used by the authors in this volume, but it also reflects the development of human communication, both ontogenetically and phylogenetically:

Specifically, pointing is based on humans' natural tendency to follow the gaze direction of others to external targets, and pantomiming is based on humans' natural tendency to interpret the actions of others intentionally. This naturalness makes these gestures good candidates as an intermediate step between ape communication and linguistic conventions. [...] Conventional languages (first signed and then vocal) thus arose by piggybacking on these already understood gestures, substituting for the naturalness of pointing and pantomiming a shared (and mutually known to be shared) social learning history.

(Tomasello 2008: 9)

Besides being a reflection of the data used and the types of windows in, Figure 1.1 is also a representation of the organizational structure of the book, with a starting point in the types of data investigated by its contributors in the search for a better understanding of the relationship between physical and conceptual space.

1.2   Eye Movement and Pointing

The volume opens with an argument in favour of eye-tracking methodology in the study of 'inner space' imagery. In *Using eye movements and spoken discourse as windows to inner space*, Roger Johansson, Jana Holsanova, and Kenneth Holmqvist offer an overview of the current mental imagery debate and an extensive account of mental imagery research. Imagery is the mental counterpart of an experience that resembles that of perceiving a scene or an event without direct sensory stimulation. Mental imagery is activated when people are engaged in activities such as remembering, planning, and problem solving. The authors focus on their own 'inner space' studies, where they demonstrate that there is spatial correspondence between eye movement and the perception of scenes during the visualization of pictures and spoken scene descriptions. They discuss advantages as well as disadvantages of eye-tracking methodology and relate the discussion to current theories of mental imagery, perception, and mental simulation.

Peter Gärdenfors' and Massimo Warglien's contribution is concerned with the development of semantic space in childhood. Meanings of expressions reside neither solely in the world nor solely in people's minds, but develop through 'meetings of minds' in communication. In pointing, meetings of minds occur when people perceive that they align their attention in physical space, and in verbal communication, when they perceive that they are aligned in mental space. In *The development of semantic space for pointing and verbal communication*, the authors identify a developmental sequence of pointing: imperative pointing, emotional declarative pointing, goal-directed declarative pointing, pointing in combination with words, and, finally, (detached) language. They conclude that the development from pointing to verbal communication is a transitional phase from pointing in physical space using pointing gestures to pointing in mental space using language. Thus, children acquire ever more sophisticated skills, as increasing cognitive complexity is achieved through the expansion of semantic space, generating a continuum from physical to mental spaces, which enables them to take part in more complex communication.

1.3   Gesture and Drawing

A substantial amount of psycholinguistic research has demonstrated the importance of embodied simulations in the understanding of literal language about space and movement. Several recent projects have shown how embodied simulations are also relevant to understanding certain forms of metaphorical language. The study by Marcus Perlman and Raymond Gibbs, *Drawing motion that isn't there: pscholinguistic evidence on the spatial basis of metaphorical motion verbs*, extends this work to show that speakers have definite, generally consistent intuitions about the spatial meanings of metaphorical motion verbs. They have investigated participants' interpretation of metaphorical (*John ran through the presentation*) and physical (*John ran through the neighbourhood*) motion expressions using the novel technique of asking people to read sentences and draw a line within a circle indicating the motion of the action depicted in each sentence. There was significant overlap in intuitions about the direction of motion for the metaphorical and physical readings of the sentences. These results are not congruent with earlier hypotheses that metaphorical verb meanings are highly abstract and unstructured, compared to the meanings of concrete, physical motion verbs. On the contrary, it seems that metaphorical motion verbs are interpreted in specific, embodied ways that enable people to draw motion that really does not exist.

The rest of the contributions in this section have their empirical base in the study of gesture. In *Differential use of dominant and non-dominant hands: a window on referential and non-referential functions*, Nicla Rossini distinguishes between 'planning' gestures and 'referential' gestures in videographs of map-task activities with blocked visibility. The speakers giving route directions to listeners behind a screen use the dominant hand for referential functions, while the weak hand is used for self-regulatory and/or other psycho-pragmatic functions. Previous studies have largely focused on the communicativeness of gestures, while neglecting the self-directional role of language. Rossini's results are consistent with the view that speech and gesture share the same cognitive, psychological, and ontogenetic origins, and that they interact in handling language functions. The map-task data indicate that gestures can serve self-regulatory and planning functions even before they become communicative and interactive.

In the next chapter, *Embodied interaction and semiotic categorization communicative gestures of a girl with Patav syndrome*, Kristina Jokinen, Silvi Tenjes, and Ingrid Rummo probe the extent to which gestures and body posture can replace speech in the construal of meaning. Using video data, the authors analyse how a seventeen year-old girl, called L, with the mosaic variant of Patau syndrome uses hand gestures and situational information to communicate. L understands everyday questions, but her speech is disturbed due to motor dysphasia and she can produce no speech beyond the vocalization of a few concepts important to her. She extracts intricate information through gestures and body postures and is also able to impart meaning with hand gestures in communication situations. She asks questions primarily in order to move the conversation in a direction that suits her needs, and she also realizes that the others would understand her more easily if her gestures could be translated into spoken words. As one of the first studies on the communicative behaviour of people with Patau syndrome, it not only contributes to explaining the communicative capability of people with this diagnosis, but also shows how our ability to form symbolic concepts and understand meanings is reliant not so much on a spoken language as on the cognitive capacity to observe and interact with the surrounding world.

The last chapter in this section, *Describing adjacency along the lateral axis: the complement roles of speech and gesture*, is concerned with gestures accompanying the use of the preposition *next to*, which encodes the adjacency of two objects but is neutral as far as directional information is concerned. Mark Tutton has carried out a filmed experiment in which one participant is asked to describe objects and their locations in a picture of a living room, while the other has to identify the correct picture from a given selection. The relation between locative expressions and coverbal gestures during their question and answer sequences is the focal point of the investigation. When using *next to*, the speakers frequently use gesture to express left and right directional information which is not lexically encoded elsewhere in the utterance.

Since the provision of directional information is pivotal to the successful description of object location in stimulus pictures, the author concludes that these gestures are intended to communicate directional information to addressees.

1.4 Speech and Writing

We now move on from primarily non-verbal data to verbal stimuli and objects of study, beginning with a focus on SPACE through two kinds of mental spaces: first-order perceptual space and second-order conceptual space. In *Toward a cognitive-semiotic typology of motion verbs*, Per Durst-Andersen, Viktor Smith, and Ole Nedergaard Thomsen use evidence from Danish, English, and Russian to provide an experientially-founded typology of motion verbs which is sensitive to subtle differences within typologically similar manner languages. The framework assumes that we experience situations primarily through mental pictures organized as figure–ground–manner–path configurations which form the basis for cognitive interpretations. The authors treat states and activities as simple situations, since they are captured in one single picture. States are stable pictures and activities unstable. Processes and events are complex situations composed of simple ones: an activity and a state are related to one another by the relational concepts *purpose* and *causation*, respectively. Thus, the proposed framework makes it possible to distinguish motion events from motion in a wider sense and shows that it is necessary to distinguish two types of figure: a primary and a secondary figure, and two types of manner: manner of existence and manner of activity. It provides a basis for describing and explaining not only already observed differences between languages, but also differences that have been left unnoticed—for example, important differences between languages which have been classified as manner languages.

The next chapter continues on the theme of encoding motion. In *A basic level for the encoding of biological motion*, Mila Vulchanova and Liliana Martinez contribute to the modelling of manner of biological motion in language by proposing a new and more fine-grained typology of features to account for the composition of the category of 'manner'. They propose that meanings of lexical items are organized in a prototypical fashion round the default settings of parameters for the individual types and manner of biological motion, at three levels of specificity: basic level expressions (*walk, run, crawl, climb*), superordinates (*go, come, move*), and specific manner verbs (*gallop, scurry, jog, pace, saunter*). The study reports on an exploratory elicitation experiment where native speakers of Bulgarian, English, and Norwegian were asked to describe what is going on in video clips. The experiment was designed to test the authors' assumption about speakers' preferences for the level of specificity, the prediction being that basic level expressions will be the preferred category. The outcome indicates that the participants do indeed favour basic level expressions for a wide range of biological motion. While there are strong similarities across the three languages, there are also differences relating to the boundaries between superordinate and subordinate expression types.

A third contribution on the encoding of motion focuses on adverbs. Henrik Hovmark's contribution, *Danish directional adverbs: ways of profiling a motion event*, is a corpus-based study of directional adverbs, such as *op* 'up', *ned* 'down', and *ud* 'out'. Danish is a typical satellite-framed language according to Talmy's (2000) framework, but what makes Danish special is that it has a rich system of directional expressions, which provide the geometric information of the path in motion events. The directional adverbs are satellites which form part of a syntagm consisting of 'verb + directional adverb + prepositional phrase': for example, *han kørte / ud / til lufthavnen* 'he went by car / out / to the airport'. The directional adverbs come in three flavours: a zero-form (*ud-Ø*), a form with a derivative -*e*-suffix (*ud-e*), and a third form with a prepositional -*ad*-suffix ('-wards'). Each of these adverbs profiles different aspects of the motion event, namely a dynamic event, a static event, and a procedural event respectively. Hovmark shows how the different forms of directional adverbs in Danish are used to construe spatial meaning by coding information about the geometric properties of the path in a motion event.

In *How German and French children express voluntary motion*, Anne-Katharina Harr and Maya Hickmann examine how children of four, six, and ten years of age develop expressions for voluntary motion events involving up/down/across paths and how Manner and Path are encoded across the two typologically different languages. German is a satellite-framed language typically encoding Manner in the main verb (*klettern* 'climb') and Path in verbal satellites such as prepositions and particles (*runter* 'down'). French, on the other hand, is a verb-framed language typically encoding Path in the main verb (*descendre* 'descend') and Manner in more complex ways such as prepositional phrases (*à quatre patte* 'on all fours') or gerunds (*en glissant* 'by sliding'). The experiments show that while, overall, both language groups showed a common progression towards including expressions of both Manner and Path in their descriptions of the motion events, the two groups differed considerably in their response patterns: German speakers of all ages frequently encoded both Manner and Path in their descriptions, while the responses by the French speakers most frequently focused on Path. On the basis of these results, the authors conclude that both general cognitive factors and language-specific properties determine how children learn to construct the semantics of space.

The next chapter, Marlene Johansson Falck's *Narrow paths, difficult roads, and long ways: travel through space and metaphorical meaning*, is concerned with the spatial concepts associated with artefacts on the ground meant for travelling along, more specifically *paths*, *roads*, and *ways*. The author shows that these artefacts give rise to embodied experiences of travel through physical space, as in *the path was barely wide enough, badly kept, branches low across it*, and that they are equally embodied when extended to abstract metaphorical space, as in *the path through the undergrowth of arguments and data is not a very straight or a very clear one*. In a detailed corpus analysis, the author finds first, coherent ways in which sentences including these terms are generally structured; second, differences between *path, road*, and *way* sentences at a more specific level of abstraction; and third, similarities between non-metaphorical and metaphorical sentences with the same item (e.g. non-metaphorical *path* and metaphorical *path*). The image-schematic structures of these experiences create coherence in word use. Differences between paths, roads, and ways, and hence between journeys along these, lead to variation in spatial metaphorical meaning. The analysis suggests that human conceptualization processes operate in a more specific way than suggested in previous versions of conceptual metaphor theory, which does not reveal in what different ways artefacts and actions connected with different kinds of travel through space help us to structure the language and logic of that travel.

Johan Pedersen has a different take on *way*. In *The way-construction and cross-linguistic variation in syntax: implications for typological theory*, he presents a cross-linguistic analysis of the English *way*-construction and other complex predicate constructions. By means of a parallel corpus study of English, German, French, and Spanish, Pedersen shows that there are systematic differences in the way argument structure is organized, beyond the binary distinction of verb-frame and satellite-frame. In discussing the implications of this approach for typological theory, he concludes that typological distinctions made on the basis of lexicalization patterns are superficial, and not fundamental, while distinctions made on the basis of parameter setting lack complexity and are too focused on grammatical form. In some languages, lexical constructions have a central role in the clausal organization of argument structure, while schematic constructions correspondingly play a more secondary role. Pedersen concludes that fundamental typological distinctions should be based on the relative importance of constructional and lexical constraints in the clausal organization of argument structure.

The last two chapters in the volume focus on observations concerning adjectives, albeit from widely different perspectives. Elena Tribushinina's contribution, *Spatial adjectives in Dutch child language: towards a usage-based model of adjective acquisition*, tests the predictions of three hypotheses about the acquisition of spatial adjectives such as *large, tall*, and *long*—the semantic feature hypothesis, the haphazard example hypothesis, and the best exemplar hypothesis—against longitudinal Dutch data from the CHILDES database. Her results suggest that none of the existing hypotheses can fully handle this naturalistic longitudinal data. Tribushinina proposes an alternative usage-based approach to accommodate the shortcomings of the three existing models, which states that children store specific adjective–noun pairings from the input and start by reproducing these prefabs with the same communicative function as in the language they hear around them. This explains why the relative frequencies of spatial adjectives in child speech reflect child-directed speech. After having stored a critical mass of exemplars, toddlers start generalizing over the specific instances. This stage is characterized by the formation of abstract semantic categories and by overgeneralization (combinability) errors.

Finally, in *Negation and approximation of antonymic meanings as configuration construals in* SPACE, Carita Paradis and Caroline Willners investigate native speakers' interpretations of negation in combination with BOUNDED antonymic adjectival meanings (e.g. 'closed', 'true') and also in relation to their interpretations of the approximating degree modifier 'almost' in Swedish. In an online judgment experiment, participants were asked to assess test sentences such as 'The door to the kitchen was not closed', in which 'not closed' is the test item. The task of the participants was to make a judgment of the test item on a scale with the end points 'non-existent' and 'maximal' in response to the trigger question 'How was the gap?'. The results of the investigation were then related to a similar study by the same authors (2006), which includes 'not' with UNBOUNDED SCALE meanings (e.g. 'narrow') 'long', and in relation to 'fairly'. On the basis of these behavioural data, they propose that 'not' is a degree modifier and like all other degree modifiers it operates on configurational structures. While the results for the UNBOUNDED meanings are very robust across all test items, the BOUNDED meanings are much more volatile and adaptive to alternative scalar interpretations. The implication of the results is that the negator is best seen as a pragmatically-motivated configuration construal of a SPACE structure.

The exploration of language and space continues. With this volume we offer a collection of some of the latest findings gleaned through empirical research and hope that it will provide inspiration for further investigation as ever more sophisticated tools of analysis and theoretical insights are developed.

2

Using Eye Movements and Spoken Discourse as Windows to Inner Space

ROGER JOHANSSON, JANA HOLSANOVA,
and KENNETH HOLMQVIST

2.1 Introduction

The ability to visualize things and events has played a very important role in the evolution of human cognition (e.g. Zlatev et al. 2005). We do, for instance, not only use language when we are trying to describe a thrilling event. We also use gestures, draw sketches, imitate voices, and engage our whole body to re-enact this event. The intent of this multimodal way of delivering the message is to enable the listener to form a mental image of what it was like to perceive the things depicted in the described event (Holsanova et al. 2008). Experiences of having mental images are apparent in a lot of everyday situations. We 'see' images when we mentally recreate experiences, when we plan future events, when we solve problems, when we retrieve information about physical properties or relationships, when we read an absorbing novel, or when we use metaphorical language. Finke (1989: 2) describes imagery as 'the mental invention of an experience that at least in some respects resembles the experience of actually perceiving an object or an event either in conjunction with, or in the absence of, direct sensory stimulation'. In popular terms, mental imagery is often referred to as 'seeing something in the mind's eye'.

Mental imagery has for a long time been very hard to study. However, with present day eye-tracking technology, a new window has been opened to understanding the mind.

2.1.1 Purpose

The purpose of this chapter is to show how eye-tracking methodology can be used as a direct link between physical space and conceptual space: both from a theoretical point of view—the existence (or not) of internal image representations, and from an applied point of view—the usage of an 'inner space' in thinking, reasoning, and communication.

First, we introduce the reader to the mental imagery debate. Second, we summarize studies on mental imagery in different areas of research. Third, we focus on our studies, described in Johansson et al. (2005, 2006), where we developed a method to study 'inner space', and showed that eye movements do to a high degree reflect spatiality during verbal reports of both pictures and spoken scene descriptions. Fourth, we discuss theoretical implications, advantages, and limitations of this methodology and relate them to current theories of mental imagery, perception, and mental simulation. Fifth, we mention relevant application areas and show how our method can be used in thinking, reasoning, and communication.

2.1.2   Mental imagery debate

The existence of image representations in our brain is an old philosophical question that has been one of the most debated questions of human cognition (see Pylyshyn 2002; Kosslyn et al. 2006). The debate is, however, often misunderstood. No one debates the actual experience of mental imagery. What the 'imagery debate' is all about is what format the internal representation takes in the brain. The crucial question is whether we really do have an 'inner space' in our brain; that is, whether points in an internal representational space correspond to points on objects seen in the external world. An inner space would make it possible to represent internal images of a depictive format. These depictive representations are not considered to share all of the properties of what they depict (e.g. less detail), only some (e.g. spatial extension). On the one hand, there is much empirical evidence in favour of internal image representations (e.g. Finke 1989; Kosslyn et al. 2006). On the other hand, the existence of internal image representations has been heavily criticized from propositional accounts, which claim that there are no such things as internal images or an inner space in the brain. According to these accounts, all our mental representations are propositional and have the same functional nature (e.g. Pylyshyn 2002).

Historically, representations in the brain have been very hard to study. But with the scientific approach from 'cognitive psychology' a large body of experiments started to appear in the early 1970s. For example, in the classic experiments of 'mental rotation' (Shepard and Metzler 1971) and 'mental scanning' (Kosslyn 1973), it was shown that time increases with the distance of a mental scanning, or with the degree of mental rotation. These results were taken as strong support for internal image representations. However, the interpretations of these kinds of experiments were then in the 1980s heavily criticized. The main criticism was that these results appeared because the participants were either induced by the task itself or because of 'tacit knowledge': knowing how you 'should' behave in a certain situation (e.g. Pylyshyn 2002). In this strand of criticism the results of mental scanning-experiments were considered only 'epiphenomenal' and not related to the scanning of an internal image representation. In the 1990s neuroscience studies started to appear which were sensitive neither to task-induced demands nor to tacit knowledge. These studies used brain-mapping technologies like fMRI and PET to study activation in brain regions. The main results from neuroscience in support of internal image representations are the following: first, early visual cortex has been found to be topographically organized and can preserve geometrical structure from the retina (Kosslyn et al. 1995); and second, it has also been shown that perception and imagery to a very high degree share the same neural machinery in the brain (e.g. Ganis et al. 2004). Alongside neuroscience studies, certain studies in the late 1990s found a close relation between eye movements and visualized scenes (Brandt and Stark 1997; Holsanova et al. 1999), which was a starting point for researchers to use eye-tracking technology as a method to study mental imagery (e.g. Spivey and Geng 2001; Laeng and Teodorescu 2002; Johansson et al. 2005, 2006).

Apart from the debate concerning the existence of image representations there is also an important discussion about 'when', 'how', and 'why' we use mental imagery in certain situations, and what 'role' it has in thinking and reasoning (e.g. Markman et al. 2009).

2.2   Eye-tracking Studies of Mental Imagery

2.2.1   Mental imagery and scene perception

A growing body of research suggests that there is a close relation between eye movements and inner space. Brandt and Stark (1997) showed that spontaneous eye movements occurred during visual imagery and that these eye movements closely reflected the content and spatial relations of the original picture or scene. The participants were first introduced to a simple visual grid pattern that they were to memorize, and afterwards they were asked to imagine the pattern. The unique scanpaths established during the viewing of a pattern spontaneously reappeared when the participants later imagined the same pattern. Laeng and Teodorescu (2001) replicated the study by Brandt and Stark (1997), and also showed that participants who fixed their gaze centrally during the initial scene perception phase produced comparable results, spontaneously, during the imagery phase (i.e. re-capitulation of similar scanpaths). They also showed that participants free to explore a pattern during perception, when required to maintain central fixation during the imagery phase, exhibited a decreased ability to recall the pattern. Holsanova et al. (1999) found striking similarities between participants' eye movement patterns when they looked at a complex picture (a natural real-life scene) and their eye movements when they later looked at a whiteboard and described this scene from memory.

2.2.2   Mental imagery and scene description

A similar eye movement effect has also been found for spatial relations that are verbally described. Demarais and Cohen (1998) demonstrated that participants who solved spoken syllogisms containing the words 'left' and 'right' exhibited more horizontal eye movements, and syllogisms containing 'above' and 'below' exhibited more vertical eye movements. Spivey and Geng (2001) extended Demarais' and Cohen's experiments and showed that participants who listened to a spatial scene description, and who were instructed to imagine it, tended to make eye movements in the same directions as indicated in the described scene.

In Johansson et al. (2005, 2006) we extended the previous studies by using stimuli of high complexity. The participants in these studies either inspected a complex picture or listened to a verbal scene description. The picture consisted of many objects with rich detail and clear spatial relations (Figure 2.7) and the scene description used several complex spatial relations (like *at the centre, at the top, between, above, in front of, to the far right, on top of, below, to the left of*). Afterwards, while looking at a blank whiteboard, they orally described the picture or retold the scene description. The results showed that the eye movements of the participants to a very high degree 'painted the scene' on the blank whiteboard during their visualizations. Furthermore, it was found that the effect was equally strong irrespective of whether the original elicitation was spoken or visual. These experiments strongly suggest that eye movements do reflect spatial positions from an inner space.

2.2.3   Mental imagery and problem solving

Apart from studies of scene inspections and verbal descriptions, eye movements reflecting inner space have also been observed in other contexts and situations. The investigation of mental images in problem solving goes back to the experiments on mental rotation conducted by Shepard and Metzler (1971). Hegarty (1992) studied how people understand physical systems from diagrams. Understanding systems such as machines includes an understanding of how the parts move and constrain each other's movements to achieve the function of the system. In order to achieve this type of understanding from a static diagram, people have to imagine how the objects move and to 'mentally animate' the static structure. Thanks to eye tracking methodology, it is possible to observe and analyse diagram comprehension as an active process of knowledge construction.

Yoon and Narayanan (2004a, b) conducted eye-tracking studies of mechanical problem solving from cross-sectional diagrams of devices. The results revealed that successful problem solvers and unsuccessful ones allocated their visual attention differently among the critical components of the devices. These findings throw light on effective diagrammatic reasoning strategies and suggest ideas for the design of information displays that support causal reasoning. Huber and Kirst (2004) reported similar findings for participants who were mentally tracking a moving object, and Matlock and Richardson (2004) demonstrated that the effect is also present for fictive motion sentences (e.g. *the road runs through the desert*). Additionally, de'Sperati (2003) has shown that eye movements form curved trajectories during mental rotation tasks and circular motion imagery.

Bertel (2007), and Freksa and Bertel (2007) investigated cognitive processes during diagrammatic problem solving. They argue that eye movement data can help us to analyse which problem parts are attended to at which moment and which mental reasoning strategies are employed. The study shows differences in problem-solving styles and provides evidence for distinct problem-solving phases. Eye movement data can be used as an input for a robust and dynamic modelling of attentional shifts (Bertel et al. 2006; Schultheis 2007).

2.2.4   Mental imagery and time perception

In a recent study of time statements (Polunin et al. 2008) it was reported that eye movements correspond with the movement along a timeline. For example, participants who imagined an event that happened last week moved their eyes further to the left on a 'mental timeline' and further to the right when they imagined an event that was supposed to happen in the future.

2.3   Eye Tracking and Verbal Protocols as Methods to Study 'Inner Space'

Current research (as established in Section 2) has found a close relation between eye movements and mental imagery, and eye-tracking methodology has become a very important tool in the study of human cognition. However, the relationship between eye movements and inner space is far from unproblematic and easy to study. For example, what spatial and temporal criteria are needed for an eye movement for us to be able to claim that it corresponds with an object in a mental image (which we cannot see)?

Therefore, the methodology behind our studies in Johansson et al. (2005, 2006) and Holsanova (2001), where we combined eye tracking with spoken discourse, will be used as a walkthrough to describe necessary and important issues that have to be taken into consideration. Holsanova (2001) studied picture viewing and picture descriptions in order to explore the relationship between language, eye movements, and cognition. She developed a method for synchronizing verbal and visual data, used them as two windows to the mind, and showed how overt verbal and visual protocols can, in concert, elucidate covert mental processes (cf. Holsanova 2008, 2011). In Johansson et al. (2006) two studies were carried out: (1) a study with twelve participants who listened to a pre-recorded spoken scene description while looking at a whiteboard and later retold it from memory, and (2) a study with another twelve participants who were asked to look at a complex picture for a while and then describe it from memory while looking at a whiteboard.

The eye tracker used in both experiments was an SMI iView X infrared pupil and corneal reflex imaging system, sampling data at 50 Hz. The eye tracker consisted of a bicycle helmet with scene camera and eye camera. With magnetic head tracking, the helmet allowed the participant freedom of motion of the head.

The auditory stimulus consisted of a pre-recorded spoken scene description (2 minutes and 6 seconds long), which was told in a normal tempo by a male voice (not by one of the experiment leaders). The picture (Figure 2.7) was a children's book illustration by Sven Nordqvist (1990). The blank whiteboard used in both experiments was 657 mm in height and 960 mm in width, and the participants in both experiments were seated in front of it at a distance of 150 cm. The analysis of the eye data was done with an eye-tracking analysis program developed by SMI, *iView for Windows*, which can trace the participant's eye movements over time.

Throughout, to conceal the true nature of the experiment, participants were told that the experiment concerned pupil dilation during the retelling of descriptions held in memory. It was explained that the participants' eyes would be filmed, but nothing was said about the experimenters knowing in which directions they were looking. They were asked to keep their eyes open so that their pupils could be filmed, and to look only at the whiteboard in front of them so that varying light conditions beyond the board would not disturb the pupil dilation measurements.

The participants were never told to visualize, to use mental imagery, or to move their eyes in any part of the experiments. The major instruction in the four experiments was to 'describe from memory'.

Post-test interviews revealed that no participant had comprehended the true nature of the experiment. Neither imagery nor eye movements were part of their guesses as to what was studied.

2.3.1 Listening and retelling

In the first study, twelve participants—six female and six male students at Lund University—listened to a pre-recorded spoken scene description and later retold it from memory. The time between the listening-phase and the retelling-phase was about 40 seconds. The retelling typically lasted for approximately 1 to 2 minutes.

The goal of this study was to extend the previous findings (Demarais and Cohen 1998; Spivey and Geng 2001; Spivey et al. 2000) in two respects. First, instead of only studying simple directions, as in the previous studies, we focused on complex spatial relations expressed in a coherent scene description (expressions like *at the centre, at the top, between, above, in front of, to the far right, on top of, below, to the left of*). Second, apart from measuring eye movements only during a listening phase, we added a retelling phase where the subjects were asked to freely retell the described scene from memory. Eye movements were measured during both phases. To our knowledge, these aspects had not been studied before. The pre-recorded description was the following (here translated into English):[1]

Imagine a two dimensional picture. At the centre of the picture, there is a large green spruce. At the top of the spruce a bird is sitting. To the left of the spruce and to the far left in the picture there is a yellow house with a black tin roof and white corners. The house has a chimney on which a bird is sitting. To the right of the large spruce and to the far right in the picture, there is a tree, which is as high as the spruce. The leaves of the tree are coloured in yellow and red. Above the tree, at the top of the picture, a bird is flying. Between the spruce and the tree, there is a man in blue overalls, who is raking leaves. In front of the spruce, the house, the tree and the man, i.e. below them in the picture, there is a long red fence, which runs from the picture's left side to the picture's right side. At the left side of the picture, a bike is leaning towards the fence, and just to the right of the bike there is a yellow mailbox. On top of the mailbox a cat is sleeping. In front of the fence, i.e. below the fence in the picture, there is a road, which leads from the picture's left side to the picture's right side. On the road, to the right of the mailbox and the bike, a black-haired girl is bouncing a ball. To the right of the girl, a boy wearing a red cap is sitting and watching her. To the far right on the road a lady wearing a big red hat is walking with books under her arm. To the left of her, on the road, a bird is eating a worm.

Spatial schematics for the objects in the pre-recorded description can be seen in Figure 2.1. The experiment consisted of two main phases, one listening phase in which the subjects listened to the verbal description, and one retelling phase in which the participants retold the description they had listened to in their own words. Eye movements were recorded both while subjects listened to the spoken description and while they retold it.

2.3.2   Eye movement correspondence

As it is possible that participants could imagine a scene either using the whole whiteboard or only a certain part of it, it would be unsound to define actual

---

[1] The initial verb in Swedish was 'Föreställ dig...' which is neutral to the modality (image or word) of thinking.

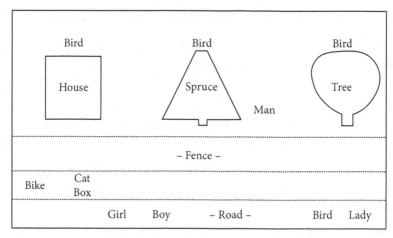

FIG. 2.1. Spatial schematics for the objects in the pre-recorded description

physical coordinates of objects on the whiteboard, as Brandt and Stark (1997) and Laeng and Teodorescu (2001) did. Instead, we developed a method to analyse the relative position of an eye movement compared to the overall structure of each participant's individual gaze pattern—spatial correspondence. Additionally, we needed to relate participants' eye movements to an appropriate point in time to ensure temporal correspondence between objects which are mentioned verbally and fixations which reflect imagery of those objects. The methodology described in the next section covers how these issues were addressed.

2.3.3   Eye–voice latencies and measuring eye movement characteristics

The temporal criteria for the occurrence of a fixation (to ensure that it concerns the same object that is mentioned verbally) may be referred to as the eye–voice latency. Figure 2.2 shows four examples of how the eye movements of one participant are represented in iView over four successive points in time during the description (circles represent fixations, lines represent saccades).

In a study of simultaneous descriptions of the same stimulus picture, Holsanova (2001) found that eye–voice latencies, i.e. the time from when an object is mentioned until the eye moves to the corresponding location, typically range between 2 and 4 seconds. In the listening phase of the spoken elicitation experiment eye movements can only occur *after* an object is mentioned. Alternatively, during the retelling phase in the spoken elicitation experiment, or while describing the picture, eye movements may actually *precede* the mentioning of an object. That is, sometimes some participants first move their eyes to a new position and then start talking about that object, while others start talking about an object and then move their eyes to the new location.

A.   B.

C.   D.

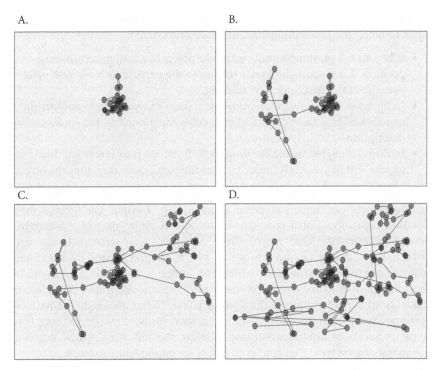

FIG. 2.2. iView analysis of the first 67 seconds for one participant listening to the verbal scene description. (A) 0–19 s. Spruce and bird on top. (B) 19–32 s. The house to the left of the spruce with bird on top of chimney. (C) 32–52 s. The tree to the right of the house and the spruce. (D) 52–67 s. The man between the spruce and the tree, and the fence in front of them running from left to right

On average, the voice–eye latency was 2.1 seconds while listening to the description and 0.29 seconds during the retelling of it. The maximum value over all participants was 5 seconds. Therefore, a 5-second limit was chosen for both before and after the verbal onset of an object.

Apart from the temporal criterion in relation to the description, it is also necessary to define a minimum threshold for the saccadic amplitude (the distance of the eye movement between two fixations) to be considered an actual movement from one imagined object to another. Since scanpaths during imagery are idiosyncratic, this threshold is not easy to define. However, in line with Zangemeister and Liman (2007) the threshold was set to 1.1°, that is all saccades below this threshold were not considered to be an actual movement to a new area in the 'mental image' (this represents about 1 cm on the whiteboard).

Eye movements of the participants were then scored as correct or incorrect according to either of two forms of spatial correspondence coding: global correspondence or local correspondence. Global correspondence was considered when fulfilling the following spatial and temporal criteria:

- When an eye movement shifts from one object to another it must finish in a position that is spatially correct relative to the participant's eye gaze pattern over the entire description or retelling.
- In the listening phase, the eye movement from one position to another must appear within 5 seconds after the object is mentioned in the spoken scene description.
- In the retelling phase, the eye movement from one position to another must appear within 5 seconds before or after the participant mentions the object.

However, as it is known that retrieved information about physical relationships among objects can undergo several changes (e.g. Kosslyn 1980; Finke 1989; Barsalou 1999), the global correspondence criteria might be too conservative. Several experiments have shown that participants can rotate, change size, change shape, change colour, reorganize, and reinterpret mental images (Finke 1989). Such transformations in which the image is changed in size and/or reorganized in structure may affect the results, in particular if they take place in the midst of the description or the retelling phase. Therefore, an alternative local correspondence measure was devised. Eye movements were considered correct in terms of local correspondence when fulfilling the following spatial criterion (temporal criteria were the same as in global correspondence coding):

- When an eye movement shifts from one object to another during the description or the retelling it must move in the correct direction.

The possible directions were up, down, left, or right, which gives four possible quadrants of 90° for the eyes to move in (Figure 2.3).

The key difference between global and local correspondence was that global correspondence required fixations to take place at the categorically *correct spatial position* relative to the whole individual eye-tracking pattern. Local

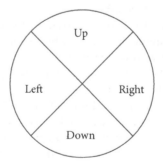

FIG. 2.3. The four possible directions for the eyes to move in

A.

B.

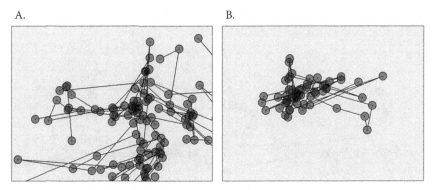

FIG. 2.4. (A) Example of one participant with mostly global correspondences. (B) Example of another participant with mostly local correspondences

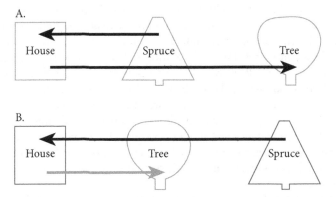

FIG. 2.5. Schematics of global (A) and local (B) correspondence. In global correspondence, the eye movement that corresponds with the tree is categorically correct relative to the house and the spruce, whereas for local correspondence only the direction is correct

correspondence only required that the eye move in the *correct direction* between two consecutive objects in the description. *Eye* movements were considered *incorrect* if neither the criterion for local correspondence nor that for global correspondence was fulfilled: typically, when the eyes moved with an amplitude below the threshold of 1.1° or moved in the wrong direction. Examples and schematics of local and global correspondence can be seen in Figures 2.4 and 2.5.

As a consequence of applying these spatial criteria, two binominal distributions were obtained from the data: eye movements either correspond to global or local correspondence criteria or they do not. The possibility that a participant would move his or her eyes to the correct position by chance was then defined. For global correspondence coding, both the direction and the distance of the

A.

B.

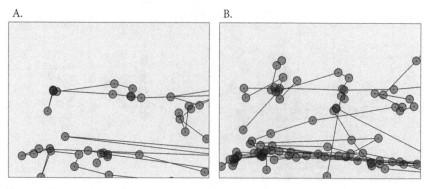

FIG. 2.6. Comparison of one person's eye movement patterns during listening phase (A) and retelling phase (B)

movement had to be correct. There were many possible movements. Conservative estimates were chosen, where the eyes could move in at least four directions (up, down, left, right). For each direction, they could move to at least two different locations (full and half distance). In addition to these possible movements, the eyes could also stand still (move with an amplitude below the threshold of $1.1°$). For global correspondence, the probability that the eyes moved to the correct position at the correct time was thus less than 1/9 (11 per cent). For local correspondence coding, only correct direction was required, and thus the local correspondence probability was 1/5 (20 per cent). A Wilcoxon Signed-Ranks test for significance between the number of correct eye movements and the expected number of correct movements by chance was devised to analyse the data (Wilcoxon 1945).

A few participants frequently re-centred their eye movements and shrank them into a smaller area on the whiteboard (thus yielding more local correspondence: see Figure 2.4B). However, the majority of eye movements kept the same proportions during the listening phase and the retelling phase. A comparison of one and the same person's eye movement patterns during the listening phase and retelling phase can be seen in Figure 2.6.

Results for correct eye movements were significant during the listening phase and retelling phase in both local and global correspondence coding. When listening to the pre-recorded scene description (and looking at a whiteboard), 54.8 per cent of the eye movements were correct in the global correspondence coding ($p = 0.003$) and 64.3 per cent of eye movements were correct in the local correspondence coding ($p = 0.003$). In the retelling phase, more than half of all mentioned referents to objects had correct eye movements, according to the conservative global correspondence criteria (55.2 per cent; $p = 0.004$). When allowed for re-centring and resizing of the image—as with the more liberal local correspondence—then almost three-quarters of all mentioned referents to objects had correct eye movements (74.8 per cent, p = 0.001). The subjects' spatial pattern of eye movements was highly consistent with the original spatial arrangement.

2.3.4 Picture viewing and picture description

In the second study, we asked another twelve participants—six female and six male students from Lund University—to inspect a complex picture and then describe it from memory. We chose Sven Nordqvist's (1990) picture as a complex visual stimulus (Figure 2.7). The study consisted of two main phases: a viewing phase in which the participants inspected the stimulus picture, and a description phase in which the participants described this picture from memory in their own words while looking at a white screen. Eye movements were recorded during both phases. At the beginning of the viewing phase, the participants were instructed to study the picture as thoroughly as possible and they were informed that they would describe it afterwards. The picture was shown for 30 seconds, and was then covered by a white screen. The following

Fig. 2.7. The stimulus picture. From Kackel i trädgårdslandet [Festus and Mercury: Ruckus in the Garden] by S. Nordqvist, 1990, Bromma, Sweden: Bokförlaget Opal. Copyright © 1990 by Bokförlaget Opal. Reprinted with permission

description phase (about 40 seconds after the picture viewing) was self-paced: the participants usually took 1–2 minutes to describe the picture.

The descriptions were transcribed in order to analyse *which* picture elements were mentioned and *when*. The eye movements were then analysed according to objects derived from the descriptions. For instance, see example (1) below:

(1)   01:20 – And ehhh to the left in the picture
       01:23 – there are large daffodils,
       01:26 – it looks like there were also some animals there perhaps,

This participant formulated a superfocus (a coherent utterance consisting of several foci that are connected by the same thematic aspect; see Holsanova 2008) from the referents 'left in the picture', 'daffodils', and 'animals there'. We would expect this person to move her eyes towards the left part of the white screen during the first focus. Then it would be plausible to inspect the referent of the second focus (the daffodils). Finally, we could expect the informant to dwell for some time within the daffodil area—on the white screen—searching for the animals (three birds, in fact) that were sitting there in the stimulus picture.

On average, the eye–voice latencies in this experiment were -0.75 seconds, and the maximum latency was 4 seconds. Therefore, the same spatial and temporal criteria for global and local correspondence were used as during the retelling of the spoken scene description (Sections 2.3.2–2.3.3).

Our results were significant both for local correspondence coding (74.8 per cent correct eye movements, p = 0,002) and for global correspondence coding (54.9 per cent correct eye movements, p = 0,005). The results suggest that the participants visualize the spatial configuration of the scene as a support for their descriptions from memory. The effect we measured is strong. More than half of all picture elements mentioned had correct eye movements, according to the conservative global correspondence criteria. Allowing for re-centring and resizing of the image—as with the more liberal local correspondence—makes almost three quarters of all picture elements have correct eye movements. Our data indicate that the mental record of the object position drives eye movements, and that spatial locations are to a high degree preserved when describing a complex picture from memory (Figure 2.8).

Additionally, the eye movement results from the picture description were almost identical to the results from the retelling of the spoken scene description, which suggests that the eye movement effect during imagery is non-specific to either verbal or visual elicitation per se.

2.3.5   Discussion

The results strongly suggest that participants make eye movements to appropriate spatial locations while listening to a spoken scene description (that was never seen

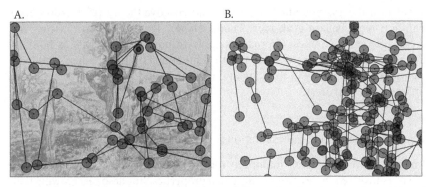

FIG. 2.8. One and the same participant's eye patterns after the viewing phase (A) and the description phase (B)

in the first place), while retelling it, and while describing a complex picture from memory. The data also indicate that the effect is equally strong irrespective of whether the original elicitation was spoken or visual. These data moreover, although strong, are in fact methodologically conservative. A more fine-grained method of analysis, capable of counting 'local' and 'global' correspondences between resizings and re-centrings, could make the results stronger still. Additionally, eye movements yielding no correspondence do not necessarily contradict the hypothesis that eye movements reflect an inner space. Since the saccadic amplitudes tend to be smaller during mental imagery (Brandt and Stark 1997), some of them could have been so small that they were not counted with our method of analysis. For example, Demarais and Cohen (1998) argue that certain individuals develop a tendency to suppress large eye movements while inspecting details of an image (much like learning to relax jaw tension in order to breathe more quietly when listening intently). Another possibility, as we suggested in Johansson et al. (2005), is that subjects shrink the picture, or parts of it, so much that they are able to 'scan' most of their mental image covertly: shifting their inner attention without eye movements (although this is hard to prove empirically with eye movement recordings).

2.4 Theoretical Implications

Mental imagery is a central component of our thought, and is specifically important for memory, planning, and visuospatial reasoning. In our studies (Johansson et al. 2005, 2006) we reported that people represent and re-enact previous experiences when they describe a scene from memory. These results can be interpreted as further support for internal image representations in the brain (e.g. Kosslyn et al. 2006). But they are also very much in line with simulation theory, embodied cognition, and enactive theory (cf. Hesslow 2002; Barsalou 1999; Ballard et al. 1997; Thomas 1999). This section will discuss how these different theoretical approaches apply to our results as well as how this methodology relates to the more practical questions of 'how', 'when', and 'why' we use mental imagery in thinking and reasoning, and how it can be applied to different research areas.

2.4.1   Internal image representations

Imagery seems to play on important role in recalling picture elements and for speakers involved in discourse with spatial properties. But despite a growing body of research on mental imagery, it is still unproven whether we really do have an 'inner space' with internal image representations. If internal images do exist, the most common claim is that they are constructed in a visual buffer of the working memory (e.g. Kosslyn 1994). Distance, location, and orientation of the internal image can be represented in this visual buffer and it is possible to shift attention to certain parts or aspects of it (Kosslyn 1994). Mast and Kosslyn (2002) propose, similarly to Hebb (1968), that eye movements are stored as spatial indexes that are used to arrange the parts of the image correctly. Neural findings that visual imagery and visual perception draw on most of the same neural machinery (e.g. Kosslyn et al. 2006), and the fact that areas of primary visual cortex are topographically organized and preserve spatiality from the retina (e.g. Kosslyn et al. 2006), have been interpreted as support for the existence of an inner space and a visual buffer. Eye movements during imagery could thus be connected either with 'generating' different parts of the image in the visual buffer, or with internal attention shifts when different parts of the image in the visual buffer are 'inspected'. Our results can be interpreted as further evidence that eye movements play a functional role in visual mental imagery. However, whether eye movements are connected to the generation of an image or the inspection of it is an open question.

A 'classic' objection to imagery experiments that support internal image representations is that the results only appear because when participants are asked to 'visualize X', they use their knowledge of what 'seeing X' would be like, and they simulate as many of these effects as they can (Pylyshyn 2002: 9). The eye movement effect would thus only be a by-product of these simulated behaviours. This objection is, however, very weak when it comes to our results, since participants were never explicitly told to visualize anything or to use mental imagery.

Additionally, it seems very unlikely that participants are able to mimic a behaviour so precisely in their eye movements. The number of points and the precision of the eye movements to each point are too high to be remembered without a support to tie them together in a context (such as an internal image).

2.4.2   Spatial pointers

The most common criticism to the function of eye movements during imagery is that they do not reflect an inner space, but merely indicate the way we use our environment as an external memory store. In this embodied view, the eyes 'leave behind' a deictic pointer or spatial index in the external world (Ballard et al. 1997). The 'scanning' of an image would in this sense be accomplished by binding the imagined objects onto the actual visual features in the world.

Pylyshyn (2002) calls the mechanism for binding imagined objects to perceived ones 'visual indexing'. The objects in the participants' memory would thus be associated with actual positions in the visual environment—the whiteboard—where slight visual features on the board and in the surrounding would serve as visual indexes. Thinking that something is at a certain location is then no more than thinking, 'this is where I imagine X to be located' (Pylyshyn 2002: 22). Such an association would assume no inner space with internal image representation, only the binding of active memory objects to real objects. Consequently, the eyes would just move to that position in the real world that was associated with the current propositional object. Visual indexes would make the existence of an inner space unnecessary as far as eye movements are concerned.

Nevertheless, we have also replicated these experiments in complete darkness (without any possible external visual features) where memory associations binding objects to positions in the external visual world would be impossible (Johansson et al. 2006). The results showed that the eye movement effect remains robust, and is significant for both experiments, even in complete darkness. On the basis of these results, visual indexes cannot be considered a plausible explanation for eye movement patterns during mental imagery.

Nevertheless, using the world as an external memory store by looking at blank spaces in it could be interpreted differently than according to Pylyshyn's visual indexes. According to Ballard et al. (1997), deictic pointers are more used as a memory support. Positions in the external world are in this view used as memory traces of an observed scene, and by looking at points in this external memory the cognitive demand upon working memory can be relieved. This view, however, does not rule out the possibility that internal representations of spatiality can be generated in the working memory. But in complete darkness there is nothing in the external world that could be used as memory traces and serve as a memory relief, which makes it hard for this view to explain the eye movement effect. The only possibility would be if the physical act of moving the eyes in different directions could serve as some support.

There has recently been a vivid debate about how 'looking at nothing' can facilitate memory retrieval of visual scenes and what role internal depictive image representations actually have in this process (see Ferreira et al. 2008; Richardson et al. 2009). Ferreira et al. (2008) argued that eye movements to blank spaces are driven by high fidelity visual internal representations, whereas Richardson et al. (2009) argued that these eye movements use both internal and external visuo-spatial information in an opportunistic and efficient way.

2.4.3   Perceptual activity theory and simulation theories

There are, however, alternative explanations from accounts where imagery experiences are not primarily considered to rely on the format of image representations. Instead, it is assumed that perception can be internally simulated by activating necessary regions in the brain (Hesslow 2002).

The 'perceptual activity theory' challenges the representational view and suggests that instead of storing images, we store a continually updated and refined set of procedures or schemas that specify how to direct our attention in different situations (Thomas 1999). In this view, a perceptual experience consists of an ongoing, schema-guided perceptual exploration of the environment. Imagery is then the re-enactment of the specific exploratory perceptual behaviour that would be appropriate for exploring the imagined object as if it were actually present. Eye movements would thus occur when these re-enactments happen during mental imagery experiences.

Barsalou (1999) suggests a similar approach to mental images in his 'perceptual symbol systems'. A perceptual symbol is in this sense *not* a mental image, but a record of the neural activation that arises during perception. Imagery is then the re-enactment or simulation of the neural activity. These simulations do not only contain sensory states, but motor and mental states as well. Still, they are never complete re-enactments of the original neural activity, and hence might contain distortions. Remembering something that occurred in a specific spatial location would thus make the eyes more likely to revisit that location than others during the re-enactment.

The perceptual activity theory (Thomas 1999) and simulation theories of this kind (e.g. Barsalou 1999; Hesslow 2002) can very convincingly explain eye movement effects during imagery without discussing the internal format of a representation. However, the problem for these theories is that there is no developed explanation, or exact model, of how these simulations or re-enactments are actually executed in the brain; they have a tendency to be able to explain almost everything without a model of 'how' it really happens.

2.5   Mental Imagery in Thinking, Reasoning, and Communication

The debate about whether we have image representations notwithstanding, there are also the important questions as to 'how', 'when', and 'why' we use mental imagery in thinking, reasoning, and communication. Knowledge of the tasks and situations in which we engage mental imagery, and what implications this has, are of great importance in many fields. Results can, for example, be directly applied to problem solving and education. The use of spatial-analogical representations, like charts, maps, layouts, and diagrams, is often recommended to solve certain problems (Engel et al. 2005). The ongoing mental processes can be traced with the help of eye movement patterns during problem solving (Kaller et al. 2009; Thomas and Lleras 2007).

A crucial issue in thinking, reasoning, and communication is the connection between mental imagery and language. According to Cognitive Linguistics, the meanings of words are grounded in our everyday perceptual experience of what we see, hear, and feel. Our concepts about the world are called mental models; that is, models that are built up from perception, imagination, knowledge, and prior experience, and that can be changed and updated (Johnson-Laird 1983; Gentner and Stevens 1983). Mental models are, in turn, largely based on image schemata: mental patterns that we learn through our experience and through our bodily interaction with the world and that help us to understand new experiences (Lakoff and Johnson 1980; Holmqvist 1993). Even metaphors are based on physical (embodied) experience of the world around us and are an important tool for us to express our thoughts. Metaphors map from a 'source' domain to a 'target' domain. For example, MORE is UP or FUTURE is AHEAD (at least in our culture). What types of concepts actually trigger mental models of spatiality? Will eye movements—as a reflection of our thoughts—be affected by these non-spatial metaphorical concepts?

From Johansson et al. (2006) we know that the eyes moved in a pattern that 'painted' the imagined scene on the whiteboard, and that engaging these 'imagery representations', supposedly, helped the participants to remember better and supported their descriptions and retellings. From the studies by de'Sperati (2003), Yoon and Narayanan (2004a), Huber and Krist (2004), and Matlock and Richardson (2004), we know that imagery eye movements can be found during mental rotation, mechanical reasoning, while mentally tracking a moving object and when exposed to sentences of fictive motion. In the area of problem solving, Freksa and Bertel (2007) have shown that eye movement patterns during imagery reveal different reasoning strategies when solving mathematical and spatial problems. From Polunin et al. (2008) we also know that eye movements correspond with time statements along an imaginary time line.

In sum, it seems that eye tracking can be used to study inner space in many situations: in memory retrieval, during descriptions and retellings, while solving problems, when engaged in metaphorical statements or fictive motion, and also during visualizations of dynamic scenes. Furthermore, by combining eye tracking and spoken discourse as in Johansson et al. (2005, 2006) we can directly measure the relationship between physical space and conceptual space. Therefore, we propose that eye tracking in combination with spoken discourse is not only a possible tool to answer questions about how and when mental models of spatiality are used, but should be considered as the most appropriate and potent method of today.

3

The Development of Semantic Space for Pointing and Verbal Communication

PETER GÄRDENFORS and
MASSIMO WARGLIEN*

3.1 Introduction

We present an analysis of the development of the semantic space of a child from gesture to verbal communication. As a driving example, we will analyse the different forms of pointing. Our aim is to show that the meaning processes involved in communication by pointing are essentially the same as those in spoken communication, and that the development of linguistic communication ability can be seen as a transition from pointing in physical space to pointing in mental spaces. The mental semantic space does not only contain a representation of the physical space (*where* an object is), but we also include *category space* that contains dimensional information properties (*what* an object is), *emotion space* (representing the value of an object), and *goal space* (representing the intention of the communication).

Our starting point is that the relevant semantic structures can be modelled with the aid of conceptual spaces with topological and geometric structure (Gärdenfors 2000). Using combinations of physical (visual) space with various mental spaces, we show that there is a semantic continuum in development, and that purely verbal communication may arise from a bootstrapping process grounded on gestural communication.

In Warglien and Gärdenfors (to appear), we propose a semantic framework based on a 'meeting of minds' that will form the background for our analysis.

* We want to thank Ingar Brinck, Susan Goldin-Meadow, the participants of the seminar in Cognitive Science at Lund University, and two anonymous referees for helpful comments. Peter Gärdenfors also gratefully acknowledges support from the Swedish Research Council for the Linnaeus project *Thinking in Time: Cognition, Communication and Learning* and from Ca' Foscari University for support during the writing of this chapter. Massimo Warglien gratefully acknowledges support from FIRB funding RBNE03A9A7.

According to this framework, the meanings of expressions do not reside in the world or solely in the mental schemes of individual users, but develop via communicative interactions (cf. Brinck 2001, 2004b). The fundamental role of human communication is indeed to affect the states of mind of others. A meeting of minds occurs in pointing when the interactors perceive that they align their attention in physical space and in verbal communication when the interactors perceive that they align their attention in mental spaces (Pickering and Garrod 2004).

The goal of this chapter is to develop this semantic framework to show that there is a continuity between gestural and verbal communication. Pointing is a special gesture that serves as an interface between the physical environment and the semantic spaces of the communicators (Brinck 2004a, 2008). It is often used in conjunction with words, and plays an important role in the acquisition of verbal language in children (McNeill 1992; Goldin-Meadow 2007). Not only do different types of pointing activities serve different purposes, but they also differ in terms of their cognitive representation, which we will model in terms of spatial structures.

A key idea of the chapter is that growing cognitive complexity is achieved by expanding the structure of the semantic space. The basic operation that is used to compose multiple domains can be modelled as a product of spaces.[1] The expansion by composition of spaces generates a continuum of communication situations. In this way, the spatial approach provides an underpinning for the developmental sequence of gestural and verbal communication.

We will use a classification of different kinds of pointing basically borrowed from Bates et al. (1975), but with some further refinements from Brinck (2004a), Tomasello et al. (2007), and Goldin-Meadow (2007). We call the individual doing the pointing the pointer and the onlooker the attendant. We will not be concerned with the exact timing of the different forms of pointing in child development. Our objective is rather to reconstruct the semantic developmental continuum. However, we will draw extensively from the existing empirical evidence.

The nature of the mental spaces that are introduced also affects the type of intersubjectivity that is involved. In this context, intersubjectivity means the sharing and representing of others' mentality. The term 'mentality' is taken here to involve not only beliefs, but all sorts of forms of mental states, including emotions, desires, attentional foci, and intentions (Gärdenfors 2007).

3.2   Imperative Pointing

During their first months children learn to coordinate their sensory input—vision, hearing, and touch—with motor activities (Thelen and Smith

---

[1] This can be seen as a special form of *compositionality* as it is treated in Warglien and Gärdenfors (to appear).

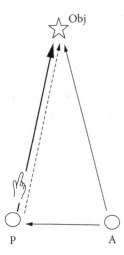

Fig. 3.1. Imperative pointing. P=pointer; A=attendant; Obj=object. The thick line is the direction of pointing. The thin lines are related to the attendant's gaze. The dashed line from the pointer to the object is the closure of the triangulation performed by the attendant

1994). This generates a narrow egocentric space that basically maps the visual field of the child.[2] The space is manifested, for example, by the fact that from six months the child can follow the gaze of their mother, if she looks at an object within the visual field of the child by turning her head (D'Entremont 2000). From twelve months the child can follow the gaze if she just turns her eyes towards the object (Butterworth and Jarret 1991). As we shall argue, the egocentric space forms the foundation for the development of semantic space.

Since Bates et al. (1975) made the distinction between imperative and declarative pointing, the imperative form has been recognized as the most elementary. It is performed in order to make the attendant do something for the pointer (for example, bring the toy they are pointing to). In this type of pointing the pointer treats the attendant as a causal agent that one can influence by pointing (Bates 1976; Brinck 2004a). In principle, imperative pointing is therefore not necessarily an act of communication—it could be like pushing a button triggering a chain of causal events. As a pointer, you can learn to point without considering other agents, for example as a mere result of reinforcement learning. However, in practice, imperative pointing in general has communicative intent. Infants who point imperatively often monitor the attention of their social partners.

---

[2] There is a potential ambiguity when we talk about visual or physical space: we may refer both to the actual physical space and to its representation in the mind of the child. In general, the context should resolve the ambiguity, but whenever necessary we will be explicit.

Cognitively, the only thing that needs to matter to the pointer is their own egocentric space in which the focal object is located. Thus from the pointer's view no intersubjectivity is necessarily involved. This conclusion is supported by Tomasello's (1999) observation that in this stage of development, children can master pointing without understanding the pointing of others. However, the attendant must understand the desire of the pointer. Nor does the attendant need to go beyond their egocentric space (Brinck 2004a). However, the attendant must identify the location of the object with the aid of the direction of the pointing and stopping at the first salient object in that direction (see Figure 3.1). What is salient is determined by the context of the situation. If no other clue is given, the first object found is chosen.

3.3   Emotive Declarative Pointing

Declarative pointing involves directing the attention of the attendant towards a focal object (Bates et al. 1975; Brinck 2004a; Tomasello et al. 2007). In contrast to imperative pointing, declarative pointing always involves intentional communication since the pointer wants to affect the state of the mind of the attendant. The crucial difference with respect to imperative pointing is that the child need not desire to obtain the object pointed at, but rather to achieve joint attention to the object with the attendant. The pointer thus takes the mental state of the attendant into account (Brinck 2004a).

Declarative pointing consists of one individual pointing to an object or spatial location and at the same time checking that the attendant focuses their attention on the same object or place (Bates 1976; Brinck 2004). The attendant in turn must check that the pointer notices that the attendant attends to the right entity. This attending to each other's attention is called 'joint attention' (Tomasello 1999; Tomasello et al. 2007) and it is a good, but fallible, mechanism for checking that the minds of the interactors meet in focusing on the same entity.

One should, however, distinguish two basic types of declarative pointing: emotive and goal-directed. (This corresponds to what Tomasello et al. (2007) call the expressive and the informative subtypes.) In emotive declarative pointing, the pointer wants the attendant to share emotions concerning the object. In contrast, in goal-directed declarative pointing, the joint attention to the object is instrumental to the attainment of a goal.

Some authors claim that the emotive form is the more fundamental (Brinck 2001). The evaluation of a shared object is mainly achieved by an exchange of emotive information about it. For example, the child points to an object that they find scary in order to obtain a reaction of fear or reassurance from the attendant. The main benefit for the child of this kind of exchange is that they can learn about objects vicariously. This primary function presupposes that the child can understand the emotions and the attention of the addressee, but it does not require the

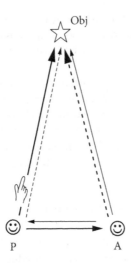

FIG. 3.2. Emotive declarative pointing. P=pointer; A=attendant; Obj=object. The thick lines relate to the pointer, the thin lines to the attendant. The dashed lines are the closures of the triangulations performed by both the pointer and the attendant

understanding of intentions or beliefs (Brinck 2008). It is well known that emotive intersubjectivity is practised in mother–infant attunement interactions (Stern 1985).

In addition to the visual space involved in imperative pointing, emotive declarative pointing builds on an emotion space. There have been many attempts to define such a space, but for our purpose it is enough to assume some generic (multi)dimensional space. A classical example would be a space with valence (positive–negative) and arousal dimensions (Osgood et al. 1957).

Minimally, emotive declarative pointing thus takes place in the product space that is the composition of visual and emotion spaces.[3] Emotive declarative pointing requires both spaces to be available for the participants. Adding the emotion in a pointing situation enriches the context. In turn, the visual space involved in pointing may enable the alignment of the emotions of the participants.

In emotive declarative pointing, both participants must check the attention of the other as well as the emotional state of the other (see Figure 3.2). If successful, it entails convergence of the participants in two domains: the egocentric space (gazes converge on the same object) and the emotion space (both express compatible emotions).

In an experiment by Liszkowski et al. (2007) an adult correctly identified what the child was pointing at, but, in different conditions, either expressed interest or

---

[3] This is in analogy with how Galilean motion takes place in the product of time and space.

disinterest in the object. In the disinterest case, which is a mismatch in emotion space, the child rapidly decreased pointing activities (as compared with the interest condition). The child seems to have learned that the object was not worth attention.

In emotive pointing, there is no need to have a separate representation of the spaces of the other. Just as an agent may assume that there is only one visual space (their egocentric space), it is sufficient that each participant assumes that there is only one emotion space and that the emotions of the other mirror their own. This makes the level of intersubjectivity minimal. However, children react if the attendant does not show an expected emotional response.

3.4   Goal-directed Declarative Pointing

Goal-directed declarative pointing can be introduced by an example from Liszkowski et al. (2007). A child observes an adult searching for an object that has been misplaced and shows him the object by pointing. More generally, this kind of pointing supports the fulfilment of the attendant's goal. The pointer understands the goal from the actions of the attendant and perceives the mismatch between the current state and the goal, and points in order to help the attendant achieve the goal. In this way the pointer gives the attendant sufficient information to solve the coordination. In the example, another solution would be that the child brings the object to the adult. It is important to note that the intersubjectivity of the pointer only requires understanding the goals of the attendant, not their beliefs (Brinck 2001, 2004a). In line with this, Gomez (2007: 730) proposes that 'behaviors are directly perceived as intentional, [...] without necessarily representing that they are driven by unobservable mental states'.

Recognizing the actions of somebody else seems to be a fundamental cognitive process. Going from understanding actions to understanding the goals behind them is not automatic. However, it develops during the first year in human children (Tomasello 1999). In other words, the intersubjectivity of goals is present when children begin to point in a goal-directed manner.

A natural representation of goals can be supplied by a goal space. In the case of pointing to an object, the problem is generated by a mismatch between the attendant location and the object location together with the attendant's lack of awareness concerning the location of the object. Pointing is triggered by the difference between the attendant's desired state and the current state. In this case, the goal space is derived from physical space: to reach a goal is to reach a location. The goal space is determined by the locations of entities in physical space. The perceived goal is that agent and object are at the same point. The difference is that in the goal space it is not the locations of the individual and objects that matter, but the distances between them.

Since the location of the attendant and the object are both points in physical space, the desired states can be represented as points in the goal state where the agent and the object have the same location.[4] Pointing solves the problem by helping the attendant to move to the object. Of course, an alternative (but more costly for the pointer) fulfilment of the goal is to bring the object to the attendant.

More generally, goal spaces can be more abstract than the physical space. In economics and AI, goal spaces are represented by abstract spaces.[5] However, we suggest that these spaces may be generated by metaphorical extensions from the original physical space. This is witnessed by the pervasiveness of spatial metaphors in relation to goals: 'reach a goal', 'an unattainable goal', 'the target was too high', etc.

In emotive declarative pointing, the physical (visual) space is composed with emotion space to help determine the meaning of the pointing gesture. In goal-directed declarative pointing, it is the composition of physical with goal space that determines the meaning of the pointing. More elaborate forms of declarative pointing can be derived from combinations of these primitive forms. In particular, pointing can be a form of inquiry to get *evaluative* information about objects related to the goals of the pointer (Brinck 2001, 2004a). In appropriate contexts, pointing can express questions such as 'Is this food good?' or 'Is that animal dangerous?'

3.5   How Joint Attention is Achieved

For declarative pointing (of both kinds), joint attention is necessary. To achieve this, the agents must ensure that they attend to the same thing, and that they both know that they are doing so. In imperative pointing, joint attention may not be achieved because the pointer may not check that the attendant attends to the desired thing.

Achieving joint attention in a scene where there is a pointer, an attendant, and a set of object involves the following steps (see Figure 3.3):

1. The pointer indicates the direction of the focal object (this can be done by pointing or by gaze directing).
2. The attendant looks at the angle of the pointer's indicated direction.
3. The attendant follows the direction until their own gaze locates the first salient object.
4. The pointer looks at the angle of the attendant's indicated direction.
5. The pointer follows this direction until their own gaze locates the first salient object and checks that it is the same object as they have indicated.

---

[4] Mathematically, these points form the diagonal of the product of the location spaces.
[5] The classical example is the General Problem Solver of Newell and Simon (1972).

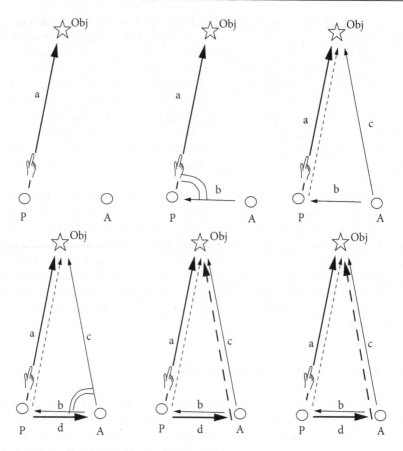

FIG. 3.3. Steps in achieving joint attention to an object

However, this is not enough for joint attention, but only guarantees shared attention, that is, that pointer and attendant look at the same object. To achieve joint attention, one more step is necessary:

The pointer signals in some way that he or she has located the same object (or signals a mismatch).

Figure 3.3 suggests a natural formal interpretation: each participant represents a visual space with location of participants and objects. When joint attention is achieved, each participant represents two overlapping triangles, cba and adc. Each triangle has to commute in the sense that the composition of a and b is equal to c and the composition of d and c is equal to a. This is a very concrete way to visually solve a system of equations.[6]

Normally, joint attention is achieved via a mutual gaze together with an emotive or evaluative expression. In the case of emotive declarative pointing, convergence in visual space has to be companioned with convergence in emotion space (cf. the example from Liszkowski et al. (2007) above). In the case of goal-directed declarative pointing, convergence in visual space has to be matched with convergence in goal space. For example, if the pointer indicates an object that does not fulfil the attendant's goals, the attendant should signal disappointment (there is no 'handshake').

Convergence in declarative pointing is both meeting of eyes and meeting of minds. In the emotive case, participants have to find resonating emotional states. Formally, this can be described as convergence in the product of the visual space and the emotion space. We have already seen that meeting of eyes, but misalignment of emotions is disappointing for the pointer. Conversely, an experiment by Liszkowski et al. (2004) with infant pointers shows that if the attendant responds with the correct emotion but simply does not look at the focal object, the infant expresses disappointment.

Similarly, in the goal-directed case, successful pointing implies convergence in the goal space. Pointing indicates attaining the goal by having the attendant move to the point where the object is. Again, if the pointer indicated an object that does not satisfy the attendant's goal, then a mismatch occurs (this time making the attendant disappointed).

Whether a pointing gesture is emotive or goal-directed may by itself be indeterminate—what type it is must be decided by context (Brinck 2004a). In our case, the context is generated by gazes, emotive expressions, or other cues. What kind of 'common ground' (Clark 1996; Pickering and Garrod 2004) is available to the pointer and attendant will depend on which product space is triggered.[7]

In step 3 above, the attendant was required to locate the first salient object along the pointed direction. A problem is that there may be several objects along that line, one of which must be chosen. In the absence of other contextual criteria, the most obvious is the first one encountered. But of course knowledge of the context may suggest the selection of another object. In an emotive context, for example when the pointer shows surprise, the selected object should be new to the pointer. In this case the pointing is emotive declarative. In goal-directed situations, the actions of the attendant generate a context including a goal that

---

[6] In topological terms this amounts to finding a fix-point (see Warglien and Gärdenfors, to appear).

[7] Just as in conversation, verbal cues allow speakers to quickly *align* the salient dimension in discourse (Pickering and Garrod 2004). In pointing, the alignment of product spaces is determined by visual and gestural cues.

determines which object is focal. This argument shows why it is necessary to multiply visual space with other spaces in order to resolve ambiguities.

In order to verify that the visual triangles constructed by the pointer and the attendant are the same, it must be assumed that the participants share the same visual space (Brinck 2004b). However, the representation of the participants need not be identical but just similar enough. For example, if the participants are in front of each other, they might perceive an opposite orientation of the space, but this will not disturb the possibility to triangulate with a third point in the space. In contrast, if direction were to matter, for example in the use of the words 'left' and 'right', they might easily miscoordinate. In general, checking that coordination is achieved may require a kind of visual 'handshake' between participants. This means that the attendant must expect a match–mismatch reaction from the pointer and vice versa.

Even if the participants correctly represent the perceptions of each other's visual space, the shape of the space itself may obstruct or create mismatches in the triangulation procedure. For example, obstacles can create non-convexities in the visual space: the salient object may be blocked from the view of the attendant. If all points between the participants and the focal object are visible to both participants, the problem can always be solved. This indicates the interactive importance of the convexity of the visual fields (Gärdenfors 2000; Warglien and Gärdenfors, to appear).[8]

The fact that a child can already from an early age follow the gaze of others, even if they look at points outside its immediate visual field, requires that the represented visual space is not just the current visual field but covers the entire physical space. This implies that the child can then understand pointing outside its visual field.

A much deeper transformation of the represented physical space comes from the ability to represent an allocentric space. This means being able to conceive of the space as seen from the point of view of another (Piaget 1954). The important fact to note is that this involves a shift of perspective. In general, this can be modelled via a coordinate transformation together with the unlimited extension of the space. What is involved is a combination of an allocentric representation of space with the egocentric one provided by the visual system. (This combination is indicated by the fact that we have double codes for referring to positions: egocentric 'left' and 'right' and allocentric 'west' and 'east'.)[9] A concrete example of the use of allocentric space is the ability to redirect somebody whose vision is blocked by an obstacle.

---

[8] An area is convex if for any two points in the area, all points *in between* are also in the area.

[9] Haviland (2000) provides several examples of languages that use 'cardinal' direction in the sense that they always refer to the allocentric space using 'north', 'south', etc. In these languages, storytellers 'assiduously orient pointing gestures in the "correct" compass directions' (13).

3.6   Declarative Pointing Composed with Words

As we have seen, when pointing does not select focal objects uniquely, composing visual space with further spaces (emotion space and goal space) is helpful. In addition to this, verbal language dramatically expands the possibilities of multiplying spaces.

As Goldin-Meadow (2007) and others have demonstrated, children combine pointing gestures with words long before they can rely on words alone.[10] In addition to the emotive and goal spaces, words trigger richer mental spaces. Objects are not only points in physical space, but are also represented in a 'category' space (Gärdenfors 2000) that has its own quality dimensions. (Physical space represents 'where' an object is and category space 'what' it is.) In Gärdenfors (2000) it is proposed that a noun corresponds to a multidimensional region in a category space. By using a noun in connection with pointing, the physical space is composed with such a category space. Mathematically, this is expressed by considering the product space of the physical and category spaces. Pointing and noun constrain each other: pointing indicates a linear region of physical space (where), while the noun indicates a region in category space (what) that determines a subset of the objects available on the scene. This makes it easier to identify the focal object. As an example from our personal experience, a child was pointing at two neighbouring objects, a toy and a saxophone, saying 'guitar', which was his noun for all music instruments. Actually a true guitar was located a few steps away, but pointing was discriminating between the two instruments, while the word was selecting between the two neighbouring objects.

However, sometimes a noun is not sufficient to select a unique focal object along the line of pointing, since there may be several objects of the same kind located in that direction. In these cases an adjective may do the job. According to Gärdenfors (2000), an adjective refers to a region of a subspace in a conceptual space. For example, 'red' denotes a (convex) region of colour space. Saying 'the red one' while pointing to similar objects close in space may define a unique solution that a combination of pointing and a noun could not solve.

Since the physical world is crowded with objects, pointing may often be indeterminate. We have now seen several examples that have a common pattern: by composing the physical space with different types of mental space (emotion space, goal space, category space), pointing becomes a multidimensional activity that facilitates the selection of a unique object. We do not only point in physical space, but learn to simultaneously point in our mental spaces. Facial expressions

---

[10] Leavens and Hopkins (1999) note that human infants seem to be more vocal while pointing than encultured apes. Across human studies, the mean percentage of gestures accompanied by vocalizations (linguistic or non-linguistic) is 82 per cent, while it is only 31 per cent for chimpanzees.

point into emotion space, actions point into goal space, and words point into category space.

3.7   Language without Pointing

When interactors are communicating about the external world, pointing is sufficient to make minds meet on a referent. However, when the interactors need to share referents in their mental spaces, a different tool is required. This is where language proves its mettle (Brinck and Gärdenfors 2003; Gärdenfors 2004; Gärdenfors and Osvath 2010). In a sense, language is a tool for reaching joint attention by 'pointing' to places in our inner worlds as shown above. This mechanism is bootstrapped by pointing, other forms of gestures and emotive expressions. As a matter of fact, Goldin-Meadow (2007: 741) goes beyond our metaphorical assertion and writes that in children, 'pointing gestures form the platform on which linguistic communication rests and thus lay the groundwork for later language learning'. For example, prelinguistic children about twelve months old can sometimes refer metonymically to an absent person by pointing to a place where that person has recently been or is normally located (Tomasello et al. 2007).

Goldin-Meadow (2007: 742) notes that 'mothers often "translate" their children's gestures into words, thus providing timely models for how one- and two-word ideas can be expressed in English'. Learning a word enables the child to make a projection (a dimensional reduction) from the product of physical space and category space to the category space alone. This projection reduces the redundancy created by mothers' translation of gestures into words. This suggests that mothers scaffold the developmental sequence in which children start communicating about physical space, then learn to use category spaces in combination with physical space to make more effective communication, and finally, by this dimensional reduction, make it possible to detach themselves from the physical space by projecting it onto category spaces. In the manner recommended by Wittgenstein, the child throws away the physical ladder when it is not needed anymore.

In this way, language becomes detached from the current environment (Hockett 1960). Language then opens up for new fields of communication: future cooperative plans, absent people (gossip), imaginary entities and situations (play language and storytelling). Once this level of representation is reached, the roles and function of communication change drastically. Words (rather than fingers) are mainly used to point to one's inner world, hoping that attendants can view a similar point in their inner world, from their perspective. Communication becomes a matter of 'meeting of minds' (Warglien and Gärdenfors, to appear). However, we view the processes of creating joint referents (and other meanings) as being essentially the same in pointing and in speaking (cf. Brinck 2001, 2004b, 2008). We do see traces of this mental pointing in the metaphors we ordinarily use to speak about communication: for example, 'Do you see what I mean?' and 'Do you follow me?'.

While reference in category space can lose connections to the physical space, as in narrative, it still resorts to pointing as the basic mechanism for achieving meeting of minds. In fact, pointing gestures are frequently reintroduced in storytelling and other detached uses of language. Their function now is to give a visual complement to what the words point to in mental space (Haviland 2000; McNeill 2005: 40). Bühler (1982) calls this 'deixis at phantasma'. Haviland (2000) provides several interesting examples of this phenomenon. One concerns a Zinacantec Tzotzil speaker who tells a story about returning to a place where he had left a dying horse. When he says 'it was getting late', he looks up at the place in the sky where the sun would have been at that time. This is a deictic gesture that metaphorically describes the time of the event in the story. Deixis at phantasma reinforces the claim that verbal language and pointing gestures are embedded in a unique semantic structure.

3.8 Summary

The evolution from simple imperative pointing to the sophisticated process of directing others' attention in inner conceptual spaces can be seen as a process that builds and combines physical space with mental spaces of growing complexity and dimensionality, generating multiple levels of mutual understanding. The mental spaces we have considered in this chapter are emotive space, goal space, and category space.

To sum up our analysis, the developmental sequence of pointing can be described as an expanding set of product spaces:

1. *Imperative pointing.* Only the mapping of physical space is implied. The pointer need not have any communicative intention (but in general has).
2. *Emotive declarative pointing.* The physical space is combined with emotion space. Communicative intent is present.
3. *Goal-directed declarative pointing.* The physical space is combined with goal space. The communicative intent here also implies a representation of the attendant's goals.
4. *Pointing together with words.* The physical space is combined with category space. In this case, the products of spaces have to be coordinated with a combination of communication modalities (visual plus auditory).
5. *Detached language.* In this case, communication is based on category space without combining it with physical space. Communication aims at pointing into the other's inner world.

We have shown how products of physical and mental spaces provide a basic framework to understand how these lie on a semantic continuum, and how purely verbal communication may arise from a bootstrapping process grounded on gestural communication. The theory represents in a single semantic framework gestural as well as verbal communication.

While our analysis has essentially aimed at establishing the semantic continuity of pointing gestures and verbal communication, we can also outline a pragmatic account. The numbering 1–5 below refers to the five stages above. However, from a pragmatic perspective it is natural to start with grasping (cf. Brinck 2004b):

0. *Grasping*. This is a direct action resulting in control of an object. The primary goal is to use the object (for sucking, for instance). Then this action can develop into a secondary goal of evaluating or learning about the object.

1. *Imperative pointing*. Instead of direct grasping, the pointing act, if successful, leads to somebody else performing the action and bringing the object to the pointer with the same result as for grasping.

2. *Emotive declarative pointing*. This does not result in any grasping of the object, but if joint attention is achieved, the pointer can achieve vicarious evaluation or learning about the object via the emotional, gestural, or linguistic reactions of the attendant. This form of declarative pointing still involves an imperative element on the part of the pointer: Help me evaluate the object!

3. *Goal-directed declarative pointing*. This form reverses the roles of the pointer and the attendant: here it is the attendant who wants to grasp (or interact with) the object (for using or for evaluating). The pointing helps the attendant to achieve this goal (which can also be achieved by bringing the object to the attendant). Of course the attendant may interact with the object at a distance (look at it, shoot at it), so grasping it is not necessary. This form has no imperative component, but is purely communicative.

4–5. *Transition to verbal language*. The use of words allows detachment of reference. Not only can one point to elements of the other's inner world, but to non-present or even non-existent entities. This provides ground for activities like counterfactual and strategic reasoning, prospective planning (Gärdenfors and Osvath 2010), play language, and narratives.

4

Drawing Motion That Isn't There: Psycholinguistic Evidence on the Spatial Basis of Metaphorical Motion Verbs

MARCUS PERLMAN and
RAYMOND W. GIBBS, JR.

4.1 Introduction

Motion verbs are pervasive in language and are commonly used to express both physical and metaphorical motion, such as in 1a and 2a, and 1b and 2b, respectively.

(1) a. John ran through the neighbourhood.
     b. John ran through the presentation.

(2) a. John tackled the quarterback.
     b. John tackled the problem.

In interpreting (1a), for instance, one might imagine John physically running through his neighbourhood or some similar scenario. But sentence (1b) does not express actual physical motion, because 'ran' here metaphorically expresses forward progress through John's presentation. Notice that the physical or metaphorical interpretation of 'ran' is not clear until the final noun is mentioned.

 How do people understand the contextually appropriate meanings of metaphorical motion verbs? There are several traditional answers to this question. One approach assumes that people understand the metaphorical meaning of 'ran' in sentence (1b), for example, by first analysing the literal meaning of the word, finding it inappropriate in context, and then drawing an inference, such as a conversational implicature, to get its contextually appropriate, metaphorical interpretation (Grice 1975; Searle 1979). This 'standard pragmatic view' does not predict anything about the exact meaning people infer when seeing 'ran' used metaphorically, such as whether people create a highly abstract or more detailed interpretation of this verb, perhaps based on their spatial, physical understanding of 'ran'. At the same time, this view would predict that metaphorical motion verbs increase the cognitive effort needed to understand their meanings compared to physical, literal uses of the same word. Psycholinguistic research on different aspects of indirect and figurative language processing, however, casts doubt on the plausibility of this view, and has especially noted that people can readily understand metaphorical words and phrases without necessarily going through a preliminary analysis of their so-called literal meanings (Gibbs 1994).

A different approach to understanding metaphorical motion verbs assumes that these word meanings are simply coded as alternative senses in their lexical representations. For instance, the metaphorical meaning of 'run' in (1b) is listed as one of its senses in contemporary speakers' mental lexicons. When hearing 'ran' in (1b), people automatically access all its stored meanings and then use context to infer which of these meanings is contextually appropriate (Swinney 1979). An alternative version of this approach posits that the different senses of a word like 'ran' are accessed in order of their frequency, such that in some cases, the metaphorical sense may possibly be interpreted first, and judged as context-ually appropriate, before physical senses of the word are ever examined (Tabossi and Zardon 1993).

The main difficulty with this second general approach to understanding metaphorical motion verbs is that the different senses of a particular word in the mental lexicon are all assumed to be synchronically independent. Thus, though possible connections between polysemous word meanings may have something to do with how these meanings come into the language historically, the motivated relations are presumed to be lost when the polysemous word is mentally coded in the minds of contemporary speakers. This position suggests, then, that people would not see much relevance between the meanings of 'ran' in sentences (1a) and (1b), and would, more specifically, not have any detailed understanding of the metaphorical meaning of 'ran' in (1b) on the basis of their experience with the physical idea of 'ran' in (1a). Contrary to this position, we will argue that people do, in fact, have detailed understandings of metaphorical motion verbs that are based on their spatial interpretations of the physical senses of these words.

Finally, one other related idea assumes that people's initial understanding of 'ran' in both sentences (1a) and (1b) are sufficiently abstract and/or underspeci-fied to cover any possible literal or metaphorical senses (Frisson and Pickering 1999; Jackendoff 1983). Although cognitive linguists and others have often com-plained about the impossibility of specifying highly abstract or underspecified meanings for polysemous words (Croft and Cruse 2004; Gibbs 1994), the basic claim of the abstractionist, under-specification view is that context does not disambiguate between literal and metaphorical senses, but hones an abstract meaning into a contextually appropriate specific one. Yet, like the other approaches above, this view does not predict that the interpretation of a metaphorical sense of a motion verb such as 'ran' in (1b) would use spatial information related to the physically grounded understanding of 'ran' in (1a).

Our preferred hypothesis for how metaphorical motion verbs are interpreted is motivated by an emerging body of psycholinguistic research showing that sentences such as (1a) and (2a) above, which express physical motion, are in significant part understood by means of mental simulations of the expressed action taking place (Barsalou 1999; Gibbs 2006a; Glenberg and Kaschak 2002; Richardson et al. 2003; Stanfield and Zwaan 2001). Thus, people understand the meanings of expressions like 'John ran through the neighbourhood' by engaging in a sensorimotor-based, embodied simulation of what 'ran' must be like in this specific context. This notion of embodied simulations is consistent with a theory of cognition grounded in perception, and opposes a traditional view of language understanding in which concepts are understood in terms of amodal or non-sensory features and linguistic meanings interpreted in terms of amodal or disembodied representations (Barsalou 1999; Gibbs 2006b).

Various psycholinguistic studies support the simulation view of understanding non-metaphorical, so-called literal language. Previous research demonstrates that appropriate bodily actions facilitate semantic judgments for action phrases such as 'aim a dart' (Klatzky et al. 1989) and 'close the drawer' (Glenberg and Kaschak 2002). For example, Glenberg and Kaschak (2002) demonstrate what they call the action-sentence compatibility effect (ACE). In one experiment, participants made speeded sensibility judgments for sentences that implied action either towards or away from the body (e.g. 'Close the drawer' implies the action of pushing something away from the body). Participants indicated their judgment by use of a button box, which contained a line of three buttons perpendicular to their body. Presentation of the sentence was initiated when the participant pressed the centre button, and yes or no responses (i.e. sensible or not sensible) were made with the two remaining buttons, requiring action either away from or towards the body. Glenberg and Kaschak found an interference effect, such that comprehension of a sentence implying action in one direction interfered with a sensibility response made in the opposing direction. This effect was interpreted as evidence that understanding language referring to action recruits the same cognitive resources needed to actually perform the action.

Another study investigated whether people mentally represent the orientation of a referent object when comprehending a sentence (Stanfield and Zwaan 2001). Participants were presented with sentences that implicitly referred to the orientation of various objects (e.g. the sentence 'Put the pencil in the cup' implies a vertical orientation of the pencil). After each sentence, a picture was presented, to which participants answered whether the pictured object had been in the previous sentence. For pictures that were contained in the previous sentence, the picture's orientation varied as to whether or not it matched the orientation implied by the sentence. Overall, participants responded faster to pictures that matched the implied orientation than to mismatched pictures and sentences. This empirical finding suggests that people form analogue representations of objects during ordinary sentence comprehension, which is consistent with the simulation view of linguistic processing.

These psycholinguistic studies have focused on people's analogue, spatial understanding of non-metaphorical language. However, many psychologists and philosophers raise doubts about the utility of the simulation view for understanding abstract concepts and language, including metaphor. For example, these scholars argue that people do not engage in embodied simulations of what some object or event must be like when hearing an abstract idea such as 'justice' or 'democracy'. Yet there is significant work in Cognitive Linguistics that strongly points to the possibility that people understand at least some abstract concepts in embodied metaphorical terms (Gibbs 2006a; Lakoff and Johnson 1999). More specifically, abstract ideas such as 'justice' are structured in terms of metaphorical mappings, where the source domains are deeply rooted in recurring aspects of embodied experiences (e.g. ACHIEVING JUSTICE IS ACHIEVING PHYSICAL BALANCE BETWEEN TWO ENTITIES). Many abstract concepts are presumably structured via embodied metaphors (e.g. time, causation, spatial orientation, political and mathematical ideas, emotions, the self, concepts about cognition, morality) across many spoken and signed languages (Gibbs 1994, 2006a; Kövecses 2002; Lakoff and Johnson 1999; Yu 1998). Systematic analysis of conventional expressions, novel extensions, patterns of polysemy, semantic change, and gesture all illustrate how abstract ideas are grounded in embodied source domains. To take our earlier example, the metaphorical expression 'John ran through the presentation' is motivated by the embodied metaphor of MENTAL ACHIEVEMENT IS PHYSICAL MOTION TOWARDS A GOAL (a submetaphor derived from CHANGE IS MOTION). Several Cognitive linguists have described how metaphorical motion in several languages is motivated by conceptual metaphors that have embodied source domains that provide metaphorical motion verbs with specific spatial meanings (Özçalişkan 2005, 2007; Radden 1996; Talmy 2006).

Psycholinguistic evidence reveals that embodied conceptual metaphors motivate people's use and understanding of different, but not necessarily all, metaphoric language (Boroditsky and Ramscar 2002; Gibbs 1994, 2006a, b; Gibbs et al. 2004; Wilson and Gibbs 2007). These experimental studies indicate that people's recurring embodied experiences often play a role in how they tacitly make sense of why many words and expressions have the specific meanings they do, as well as in people's production and processing of some verbal metaphors. In fact, some of these studies extend the work on simulative understanding of non-metaphorical language to processing of metaphorical speech. Thus, Wilson and Gibbs (2007) showed that people's speeded comprehension of metaphorical phrases like 'grasp the concept' are facilitated when they first make, or imagine making, a grasping movement. People may, for instance, be creating partial, but not necessarily complete, embodied simulations of speakers' metaphorical messages that involve moment-by-moment 'what must it be like' processes, such as grasping, that make use of ongoing tactile-kinaesthetic experiences (Gibbs 2006c). These simulation processes operate even when people encounter language that is abstract, or refers to actions that are physically impossible to perform, such as 'grasping a concept', because people can metaphorically conceive of a 'concept' as an object that can be grasped. One implication of this work is that people do not just access passively encoded conceptual metaphors from long-term memory during online metaphor understanding, but simulate what these actions may be like to create detailed understandings of speakers' metaphorical messages (Gibbs 2006b).

These recent psycholinguistic experiments on processing of both non-metaphorical and metaphorical meaning are consistent with our preferred hypothesis of how people interpret metaphorical motion verbs. Our specific aim, however, was to examine in more detail people's intuitions about the meanings of metaphorical, as well as physical, motion verbs to see if people may understand both types of expressions in similar ways. More traditional theories of word meaning, as reviewed earlier, do not predict that people should have anything more than highly abstract interpretations of metaphorical motion verbs such as 'ran' and 'tackled' as seen in the sentence pairs (1) and (2) above. People should, therefore, possess inconsistent understanding of any possible spatial meanings associated with metaphorical motions verbs, while having highly consistent intuitions about the spatial meanings of physical motion verbs.

On the other hand, the embodied simulation view suggests that people should interpret metaphorical motion verbs in consistent, specific ways, precisely because of their embodied understanding of these verbs' meanings. Again, people should interpret 'ran' in 'John ran through the presentation' based on their imaginative, embodied simulation of 'ran' in its physical sense. This simulation process, in other words, at least partially recreates the conceptual metaphorical mapping of MENTAL PROGRESS IS PHYSICAL MOTION TOWARDS A GOAL, but in a very specific sense of the type of physical motion involved (i.e. running).

We tested these alternative hypotheses by asking people to read physical and metaphorical motion sentences, and then draw a line within a circle to indicate their intuitions about the direction of the motion involved in each expression. Several studies have made use of drawing tasks to reflect people's conscious intuitions of how they understand different kinds of sentences, and we maintain that an off-line procedure such as the drawing task employed here offers details about the output of comprehension processes not easily obtained using traditional online methods. Tversky (1999) argues, for instance, that drawings reveal people's conceptions of things as opposed to their perceptions, while Matlock (2006) demonstrated that drawings can reveal insights into how people conceptualize objects, states, and events. In this vein, Richardson et al. (2003) used a forced-choice task and a computer-based drawing task to test people's intuitions about image schemas for both concrete and abstract verbs. In the forced-choice task, subjects selected the image schema that best fit verbs presented within a simple rebus sentence, with circles and squares representing agents and patients. Richardson and his colleagues found significant agreement among participants for both concrete (e.g. 'fled', 'pointed at') and abstract verbs (e.g. 'obeyed', 'warned'). They also found significant agreement among people in the computer-based drawing task, in which participants drew simple image schemas for the same set of concrete and abstract verbs. This pattern of consistency in people's drawings for abstract verbs is remarkable, because according to many recent theories of linguistic meaning, there is no obvious reason that abstract verb events such as 'respect' or 'obey' should be amenable to an image-schematic depiction. Yet, the fact that these verbs can be consistently depicted this way lends support to the view that even abstract events are understood by means of embodied concepts related to space and motion.

4.2   Study

The present study used a drawing task to investigate participants' intuitions about the directions of events expressed in various physical and metaphorical motion sentences. Participants read sentences, and in a designated space, drew an arrow to depict the direction of the expressed event. We generally predicted that participants would have consistent directional intuitions regarding the metaphorical motion sentences, and that these intuitions would be similar to their intuitions about the direction of the physical motion sentences.

4.2.1   Method

4.2.1.1   *Participants*

Sixty undergraduate students at the University of California, Santa Cruz participated in the study in order to satisfy a requirement of an introductory psychology course.

4.2.1.2   *Materials*

Forty-one pairs of sentences were created using forty-one different motion verbs (see Appendix for a full list of sentences). One sentence in each pair employed the verb in a physical motion sense, and the other sentence used the same verb metaphorically. The sentences were created to be as parallel in structure as possible (i.e. similar in grammatical form and length), and differed only in the use of different object noun phrases or complements. Additionally, the physical motion item of each pair was chosen specifically to express motion in one of four general directions: up, down, forward, and backward. In two dimensions, it was expected that forward motion would transfer to rightward-oriented depictions, and backward motion to leftward depictions. This expectation loosely

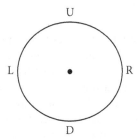

FIG. 4.1. Drawing space

corresponds to the English convention of writing left to right and previous research demonstrating the influence of this writing convention on how people conceive the spatial orientation of sequential events (Chan and Bergen 2005). In twelve of the sentence pairs, the verb was used in phrasal combination with a preposition, which was matched between conditions. Prepositions expressing absolute direction, such as 'up' and 'down', were not permitted.

The sentences were presented to participants in one of two versions of a packet. One version contained one sentence from each of the forty-one pairs, and the second version contained the other sentence from each pair. Thus, for each pair, a participant saw either the physical or the metaphorical item, but never both. Sentences were counterbalanced with respect to sentence condition, resulting in each packet containing twenty-one items from one condition and twenty from the other. In addition, there were two orderings for each packet version in which the second ordering was the reverse of the first. Sentences were presented in alternating order by sentence condition.

For each item, the sentence was presented on the left of the page and the drawing space on the right (see Figure 4.1). The drawing space consisted of a circle labelled at the top with 'U' for up, at the bottom with 'D' for down, and with 'L' and 'R' on the left and right. In the centre of the circle, a dot was drawn to represent John, the subject of each sentence. (The labelling was to ensure that participants depicted their spatial conceptualization of each sentence with consistent orientation with respect to the circle. Piloting without these labels showed that participants were often variable in their interpretation of the circle as having an up–down orientation as labelled or as a 'bird's eye view'.)

Each packet also contained a second section in which the sentences were presented again along with scales to rate each one for Ease of Understanding and Concreteness. In this section, each sentence was presented with two 7-point scales on which participants indicated 'How easy was the sentence to understand?' (1 to 7 = Easy to Difficult) and 'How abstract was the meaning expressed in the sentence?' (1 to 7 = Concrete to Abstract).

4.2.1.3   *Procedure*

Participants were seated at a table by an experimenter, given a packet, and told to follow the written instructions on the front page. The instructions advised participants to read each sentence carefully, and then to 'use the circle to the right as a space to draw a straight arrow that best depicts your sense of the direction of the event expressed by the sentence'. A description of the circle labels was also provided, although no information was given for how to translate these labels into an arrowed depiction of a sentence. Finally, participants were told that 'For some sentences, the direction of the event might not be completely clear, but you should make your best judgment'.

Participants first completed the drawing task, and then moved on to the second section where they rated the sentences for Ease of Understanding and Concreteness. The entire procedure typically took about 15 to 20 minutes to complete.

4.3   **Analysis and Results**

The data were analysed with two basic aims: 1) to compare people's directional intuitions between the physical and metaphorical motion sentences in each item pair, and 2) to compare the consistency of these intuitions between conditions across participants. Thus the first analysis determined whether participants had similar directional intuitions for both physical and metaphorical items for each sentence pair. Recall that a critical feature of the embodied simulation hypothesis is that people engage in similar processes when understanding physical and metaphorical motion sentences, and therefore, there should be a strong correlation between the directions of the arrowed lines drawn for each sentence within a pair.

Using a protractor, we measured the angle of each drawn arrow to the nearest 5 degrees. Next, we calculated the mean angle for each item. However, because of the periodic nature of this measure, it is not valid to simply calculate a straight mean. Instead, the mean angle was calculated by treating each arrow data point as a unit vector (i.e. with magnitude 1), and breaking it down into horizontal and vertical components using the cosine and sine functions, respectively (see Figure 4.2). The components were then added up, and based on these composites the mean angle was calculated using the inverse tangent function. (The ATAN2 function on Microsoft Excel was used, which automatically selects the appropriate angle of the two solutions to the equation $\tan^{-1} y/x = \theta$.)

Next, to determine the degree to which the mean angles between paired physical and metaphorical sentences were similar, we calculated the correlation between them, which showed the angles to be strongly correlated, $r(39) = 0.84$, $p < 0.001$. Another way to consider this result is in terms of the value $r^2 = 0.71$,

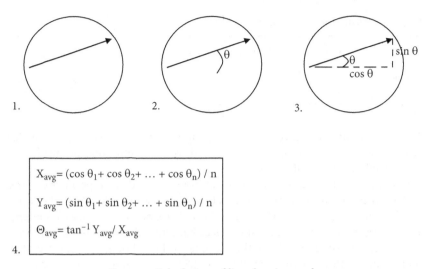

$$X_{avg}= (\cos\theta_1 + \cos\theta_2 + \ldots + \cos\theta_n) / n$$

$$Y_{avg}= (\sin\theta_1 + \sin\theta_2 + \ldots + \sin\theta_n) / n$$

$$\Theta_{avg}= \tan^{-1} Y_{avg} / X_{avg}$$

FIG. 4.2. Calculation of line drawing angle

indicating that 71 per cent of the variance in the metaphorical-sentence angles can be accounted for by the physical-sentence angles.

To get a more detailed sense of how the angles within each pair compared, we calculated the differences between the average angles of paired sentences. In total, across the forty-one sentence pairs, the average difference between paired sentences was 33.4 degrees. A more specific breakdown of these differences reveals that sixteen of forty-one items (39 per cent) had a difference of less than 10 degrees, twenty-seven (56 per cent) less than 20 degrees, and thirty-two (78 per cent) less than 45 degrees (see Table 4.1).

Our second major aim was to investigate whether people's directional intuitions for metaphorical motion sentences were relatively consistent in comparison to their physical motion counterparts. In other words, do people consistently depict the same direction for a particular metaphorical sentence, and how does this degree of consistency compare to the corresponding physical motion sentence? This question was addressed by considering the standard deviations for each item as a measurement of the consistency of people's directional intuitions. We reasoned that a small standard deviation reflects little variance in the angles participants drew for a particular sentence, and thus would imply that they had consistent intuitions about its direction. In contrast, a large standard deviation, indicating greater variance in the angles drawn, would imply more idiosyncratic intuitions.

Overall, the mean standard deviations by sentence condition were 62.3 for the physical motion sentences and 56.3 for metaphorical motion. An ANOVA with standard deviation as the dependent measure and sentence condition as a factor

TABLE 4.1. *Mean angle differences*

	0 to 10	10 to 20	20 to 30	30 to 45	45+	Total
Number	16	11	2	3	9	41
Per cent	39%	27%	5%	7%	22%	100%

showed that this difference was not significant ($F(1,80) < 1$), suggesting that people have roughly equivalently consistent directional intuitions for the physical and metaphorical uses of the verbs.

Since the physical/metaphorical sentence condition did not appear to be related to the consistency of people's directional intuitions, we wondered whether other variables such as the Ease of Understanding or the Concreteness of each sentence might be relevant instead. A t-test showed that sentences in the physical motion condition, compared to those in the metaphorical condition, were rated both as being significantly more concrete (means of 1.88 and 3.71, $t(80) = -13.2$, $p < 0.001$) and easy to understand (means of 1.52 and 2.18, $t(80) = -7.6$, $p < 0.001$). However, there was no significant correlation between these variables and standard deviations.

The findings described thus far indicate that people have strongly correlated directional intuitions for the physical and metaphorical uses of motion verbs, and furthermore, that these intuitions are roughly equivalent in consistency as measured by standard deviation. However, one potentially confounding possibility is that the significant correlations and similar standard deviations are an artefact resulting from participants drawing lines within a limited scope of the circle. For instance, the same effects could arise from a strong tendency to repeatedly draw arrows to the right, irrespective of the particular sentence.

For assurance that this was not the case and that participants were indeed using the whole circle to draw arrows, the results were broken down and analysed by quadrant. The 'right' quadrant included angles from 315 to 45 degrees, 'up' angles from 45 to 135 degrees, 'left' angles from 135 to 225 degrees, and 'down' angles from 225 to 315 degrees. The number of mean angles was compared between quadrants and sentence condition, as well as mean angle differences (based on the quadrant of the physical sentence) and standard deviations.

Table 4.2 shows that in both sentence conditions, participants frequently drew arrows in the up, down, and right quadrants, but less frequently in the left quadrant. Importantly, for all three commonly used quadrants, the angles showed roughly the same degree of similarity between physical and metaphorical sentences and the same magnitude of standard deviation. In contrast, lines drawn in the left quadrant were highly inconsistent between sentence conditions, as well as within particular items. In fact, if the left quadrant is expanded to include 120 degrees and the remaining three

Table 4.2. *Results by quadrant*

	Right (315–45)	Up (45–135)	Left (135–225)	Down (225–315)	Total
n (physical cond.)	14	9	6	12	41
SD (physical cond.)	64.9	47.6	88.2	57.4	62.3
N (metaphorical)	16	11	3	11	41
SD (metaphorical)	60.4	45.6	66.5	58.1	56.3
Mean angle difference	17.7	30.7	98.4	21.4	
Diff < 10	5 (of 14)	4 (of 9)	0 (of 6)	7 (of 12)	
Diff < 20	12 (of 14)	6 (of 9)	1 (of 6)	8 (of 12)	
Adjusted Quadrants	Quad 1 (320–40)	Quad 2 (40–120)	Quad 3 (120–240)	Quad 4 (240–320)	
Mean angle difference	17.2 (n=14)	21.8 (n=8)	99.9 (n=7)	21.4 (n=12)	
SD (physical)	63.8 (n=13)	45.9 (n=9)	89.1 (n=7)	57.4 (n=12)	
SD (metaphorical)	60.9 (n=14)	46.6 (n=12)	71.4 (n=4)	55.5 (n=11)	

quadrants collapsed to 80 degrees each, this trend is even stronger. In this case, for mean angles within the right, up, and down quadrants, the correlation between paired physical and metaphorical motion sentences increases to $r(32) = 0.914$, $p < 0.001$, while the correlation between paired items within the expanded left quadrant is not significant, $r(5) = -.317$ (although the power of this test is much smaller with $n = 7$, no correlation between sentences is apparent).

Thus, although participants were markedly less frequent and consistent in depicting sentences with a leftward orientation, they otherwise had thoroughly distributed consistent directional intuitions that were strongly correlated between physical and metaphorical uses of the motion verbs.

Finally, we sought to address the confounding possibility that the effects might be driven primarily by the presence of prepositions in some of the phrasal verb items (e.g. 'through' in 'John raced through the hallway'). Thus, according to this alternative, people are primarily making their line drawings based on the prepositions in some items and not the verbs. If this were true, then the mean angle differences should be smaller when people read sentences with prepositions. However, this was not the case. We separated the items into a phrasal verb group (i.e. those including prepositions) ($n = 12$) and a verb-only group ($n = 29$), and compared the mean angle differences and standard deviations. In all cases, the verb-only items had a smaller mean angle difference and standard deviation (for phrasal verbs, mean angle difference = 43.9, mean SD for the physical condition, mean SD = 63.8, and for the metaphorical condition, mean SD = 62.5; for verb-only items, mean angle difference = 29.1, mean SD across for the physical condition, mean SD = 61.7, and for the metaphorical condition, mean SD = 53.7). These results clearly show that the prepositions in some of our items were not the reason for the consistency in people's line drawing between the metaphorical and physical statement.

4.4   Discussion

The analysis sought to accomplish two basic aims. First, mean angles were used to compare people's directional intuitions between the physical and metaphorical motion sentences in each pair. It was found that the angles drawn for metaphorical motion items were strongly correlated with the angles drawn for their physical motion counterparts, and notably, that in 39 per cent of cases, the difference between the angles was less than 10 degrees. Second, standard deviations were used as a measure of the consistency of people's directional intuitions for physical and metaphorical motion sentences. Overall, the standard deviations were actually smaller for metaphorical sentences than for physical sentences, although this difference was not significant. Standard deviations were not found to correlate with participants' sentence ratings for Ease of Understanding or Concreteness. And finally, we eliminated two potentially confounding explanations for the results. It was confirmed that people were frequently using the majority of the circle space to depict the sentences (with the interesting exclusion of the left quadrant), and thus the correlation between paired-sentence angles and the similar standard deviations between conditions were determined to be valid effects. Furthermore, it was shown that the prepositions associated with the phrasal verb items were not responsible for driving these effects.

At this point, it is also necessary to address a potential criticism of the drawing task itself, which is that it may not reflect people's normal online processing of metaphorical motion sentences. Instead, it may be argued, participants could have deliberately translated the metaphorical sentences into physical motion, and based their drawing on this physical interpretation. Although we cannot be certain some participants did not apply this strategy, we offer a couple of observations to mitigate this concern. First, the low Ease of Understanding ratings for the metaphorical sentences, although a little higher than the ratings for physical motion sentences, nevertheless indicate that participants probably achieved a fair understanding of the metaphorical meaning for many of the verbs. Consequently, we can be confident that the metaphorical meanings were at least activated as participants drew in the circles.

The second basis to allay this possible criticism comes from the finding that the standard deviations were roughly similar between physical and metaphorical motion sentences. If participants were relying heavily on a translation strategy, this extra layer of process should contribute some variance to the angles participants drew for metaphorical sentences. Since this was not the case, it remains likely that participants displayed similarly consistent directional intuitions for metaphorical motion, because such sentences are naturally understood by simulations activating the same essential embodied schemas.

We also bring attention to an advantage of the drawing task as an analogue, detailed measure of people's intuitions and conceptualizations. More traditional online measures—for example, the use of reaction time to measure spatial interference in a visual discrimination task—are limited to gross, categorical reflection of how participants understand the spatial orientation of events, such as those described in the sentences used in this study. However, because of the analogue nature of the drawing task measure, we are able to tap into the detailed spatial meanings people create as they understand various sentences.

Taken together, the data collected in this study are inconsistent with traditional accounts of how metaphorical motion verbs are represented within the mental lexicon and understood in context. For example, accounts positing that polysemous senses are organized as separate lexical entries should predict that the physical and metaphorical meanings of the verbs are represented and understood independently of one another (Swinney 1979; Tabossi and Zardon 1993). If this were the case, there is no clear reason to explain why people have such consistent directional intuitions for metaphorical motion verbs, since the verbs' meaning should be independent of any notion of physical motion. Similarly, the hypothesis that people's understanding of motion verbs is sufficiently abstract to account for both physical and metaphorical uses also cannot explain people's consistent directional intuitions for the metaphorical sentences. However, this set of results is congruent with our claim that people engage in a simulation of the physical actions alluded to by each verb, and use the products of that simulation as a basis for inferring specific metaphorical verb meanings in context.

4.4.1   Implications for Cognitive Linguistics

Our empirical data support research from Cognitive Linguistics demonstrating how motion can be conceived in metaphorical terms, primarily through the source to target domain mappings in widely shared conceptual metaphors. At the same time, the present studies employ experimental methods that allow us, as metaphor scholars, to remove ourselves from the task of inferring something about conceptual structures underlying the meanings of, in this case, metaphorical motion verbs. As we have argued earlier (Gibbs and Perlman 2006), Cognitive Linguistic analyses alone are often met with scepticism within the fields of psycholinguistics and cognitive science because of the use of trained linguistic intuitions which may be theoretically biased. Cognitive Linguistic analyses, in some instances, are difficult to falsify and sometimes are not compared to explicit alternative hypotheses aiming to account for the same linguistic phenomenon.

But our studies both examined the intuitions of ordinary university students and explicitly contrasted the predictions of our preferred embodied simulation hypothesis against other views that are unable to account for the findings we have reported. Moreover, the experimental task employed in our study asked people to share their intuitions in a simple, non-linguistic manner which, in many psychologists' view anyway, is a better reflection of the possible influence of embodied, conceptual structure on language understanding than are methods that ask people to verbally explain or describe their intuitions about matters of meaning (see Murphy 1996). We see this work, then, as offering an important, and at least here, supporting complement to Cognitive Linguistic conclusions on the embodied, specifically spatial, understanding of metaphor.

4.4.2   Future directions

There are several future directions for psycholinguistic work on the understanding of metaphorical motion. As noted by both Cognitive Linguistic and developmental psychological studies, languages differ in the way that they express ideas about motion. For example, English and Turkish both metaphorically conceive of time as TIME IS MOTION ALONG A PATH, but English encodes the manner of motion while Turkish does not (Özçalişkan 2005), a difference that children in the two languages pick up at an early age (Özçalişkan 2007). One possibility is to examine adult speakers' intuitions about the direction and manner of motion using some version of our drawing task to see if metaphorical motion verbs are interpreted differently in typologically distinct languages. The drawing task, in particular, provides an easy way to assess cross-linguistic intuitions about metaphorical motion.

  Another issue for future study is suggested by psycholinguistic work showing that the level of abstraction for a metaphorically used verb serves as an important cue to whether that verb is used with metaphorical meaning (Torreano et al. 2005). Thus, verbs that are understood at a higher level of abstraction are rated as more metaphorical than the same verbs when they could be interpreted at the physical level. This finding is consistent with the idea that people may create more or less detailed, specific interpretations of metaphorical verbs depending on their level of abstraction. Under our view, people's simulations of the actions referred to by verbs, even when used metaphorically, may give rise to differently detailed interpretations, again depending on how abstract the verb typically is in its most physical sense.

4.5   Conclusion

A fairly substantial amount of psycholinguistic research has demonstrated the importance of embodied simulations in the understanding of literal language about space and movement, and several recent projects have shown how embodied simulations are also relevant to understanding certain forms of metaphorical language. The present study extends this work to show that people have definite, generally consistent intuitions about the spatial meanings of metaphorical motion verbs. Our findings may best be interpreted as supporting the claim that people engage in embodied simulations during ordinary language processing, which in the case of metaphorical motion verbs demands that people imagine the physical action implied by a verb and use this information to create a specific metaphorical interpretation of the verb in context. These results are not congruent with earlier hypotheses that metaphorical verb meanings are highly abstract, and perhaps unstructured, compared to the meanings of concrete, physical motion verbs. Instead, metaphorically used motion verbs are interpreted in specific, embodied ways that make it possible for people to draw motion that really does not exist. Most generally, the psycholinguistic study of metaphorical motion words offers a window into the way people construe conceptual space, and experience metaphorical meaning in an embodied manner.

Appendix

Sentence	predicted	angle	diff	SD	Conc.	Ease
John bombed the city.	270	283.7	14.8	77.8	2.8	1.7
John bombed the exam.	270	268.9	14.8	36.0	3.6	1.7
John bowed to the audience.	270	283.3	1.4	62.3	1.6	1.4
John bowed to the pressure.	270	284.7	1.4	36.5	4.8	2.4
John built a little confidence.	90	80.3	3.8	26.2	3.8	2.3
John built a little house.	90	76.5	3.8	63.5	2.1	1.7
John climbed the corporate ranks.	90	83.3	7.8	15.2	4.4	2.3
John climbed the stepladder.	90	75.5	7.8	24.0	1.3	1.2
John closed the deal.	180	254.8	46.4	86.3	3.8	2.0
John closed the door.	180	208.4	46.4	96.1	1.5	1.2
John crushed Mike's delicate ego.	270	275.3	4.3	56.0	4.2	2.4
John crushed Mike's soda can.	270	271.0	4.3	60.8	1.5	1.3
John delivered the message.	0/360	16.4	9.1	48.5	2.2	1.6
John delivered the pizza.	0/360	7.3	9.1	75.0	1.6	1.4
John donated some clothes.	0/360	16.4	22.8	70.6	1.7	1.3
John donated his time.	0/360	39.2	22.8	64.0	3.3	2.1
John dived into the pool.	270	300.3	42.3	49.3	2.0	1.5
John dived into the project.	270	342.6	42.3	68.2	3.9	2.2
John dropped the class.	270	267.7	2.0	31.1	2.6	1.4
John dropped the glass.	270	269.7	2.0	46.7	1.4	1.2
John elevated his broken leg.	90	63.8	21.4	31.5	1.7	1.4

(continued)

Sentence	predicted	angle	diff	SD	Conc.	Ease
John elevated his social status.	90	85.2	21.4	17.3	4.0	2.3
John fled a bear.	180	130.1	108.8	94.1	2.6	2.3
John fled a responsibility.	180	238.9	108.8	86.3	4.0	2.4
John followed the car.	0/360	17.2	8.0	47.9	1.7	1.5
John followed the rule.	0/360	25.2	8.0	59.9	3.2	2.0
John gave Mike his pencil.	0/360	16.2	0.6	66.4	1.3	1.4
John gave Mike his word.	0/360	15.6	0.6	59.2	4.2	2.1
John grew proud.	90	79.5	11.0	25.3	4.1	2.3
John grew tall.	90	90.5	11.0	4.7	2.1	1.4
John hit the town.	0/360	356.0	16.9	67.3	4.9	2.6
John hit the wall.	0/360	12.9	16.9	89.9	3.6	2.1
John ignited a bar brawl.	90	63.7	4.9	62.2	3.5	2.4
John ignited a bonfire.	90	58.8	4.9	53.0	2.2	1.7
John jumped onto the bandwagon.	90	22.9	18.0	69.8	4.0	2.0
John jumped onto the truck bed.	90	40.9	18.0	79.1	1.7	1.5
John lifted Mike's spirits.	90	85.4	3.1	46.3	4.2	2.3
John lifted Mike's suitcase.	90	82.3	3.1	48.9	1.6	1.4
John lowered his arm.	270	284.0	7.5	52.7	1.7	1.4
John lowered his prices.	270	276.5	7.5	56.0	2.6	2.2
John mounted a bicycle.	90	33.6	7.1	79.3	2.3	1.8
John mounted an investigation.	90	40.7	7.1	56.8	4.9	3.2
John opened his drawer.	180	185.8	108.9	106.6	1.5	1.4
John opened his mind.	180	76.9	108.9	46.1	5.0	2.3
John pulled a garden hose.	180	203.9	143.2	97.4	2.2	1.8
John pulled an all-nighter.	90	60.7	143.2	70.1	3.7	1.8
John pushed his luck.	0/360	8.7	6.8	60.1	4.4	2.1
John pushed his stroller.	0/360	1.9	6.8	61.0	2.0	1.7
John raced through the hallway.	0/360	2.4	15.1	41.2	2.2	1.8
John raced through the test.	0/360	17.5	15.1	48.0	2.9	1.7
John raised his hand.	90	87.8	11.3	10.2	1.2	1.2
John raised his voice.	90	76.5	11.3	18.4	2.5	1.6
John ran from a bully.	180	249.4	87.3	96.9	1.5	1.3
John ran from a relationship.	180	336.7	87.3	107.7	4.1	2.3
John ran through the neighbourhood.	0/360	16.4	10.1	35.5	2.3	1.7
John ran through the presentation.	0/360	6.3	10.1	47.7	4.1	2.2
John received a discount.	180	50.2	132.1	94.1	2.3	1.7
John received a punch.	180	182.3	132.1	77.5	2.4	1.8
John removed the gas cap from the car.	180	85.7	104.5	98.3	1.4	1.4
John removed the name from the list.	180	190.2	104.5	70.2	2.6	2.0
John returned to his mobile home.	180	265.9	41.9	79.1	2.2	1.8
John returned to his normal self.	180	224.0	41.9	67.2	4.6	2.4
John sank Mike's toy boat.	270	276.4	8.2	19.8	1.5	1.3

(continued)

Sentence	predicted	angle	diff	SD	Conc.	Ease
John sank Mike's only hope.	270	268.2	8.2	43.4	4.1	2.5
John sat on the committee.	270	286.8	14.8	69.7	3.6	2.3
John sat on the couch.	270	272.0	14.8	40.7	1.4	1.4
John settled into a bed.	270	274.1	43.4	58.9	2.1	1.5
John settled into a routine.	270	317.5	43.4	57.3	3.9	2.4
John shot a bullet.	0/360	18.6	10.2	57.1	2.2	1.5
John shot a glance.	0/360	8.4	10.2	64.9	3.4	1.9
John sped through the intersection.	0/360	23.2	17.3	52.4	1.9	1.3
John sped through the reading.	0/360	5.9	17.3	26.6	2.9	1.8
John swallowed his food.	270	261.8	1.6	43.5	1.4	1.2
John swallowed his words.	270	260.2	1.6	61.6	4.3	4.4
John tackled the problem.	270	325.4	12.9	60.7	3.8	2.2
John tackled the quarterback.	270	338.3	12.9	66.6	1.4	1.2
John took a break.	180	282.5	92.3	76.1	3.0	1.7
John took a napkin.	180	14.8	92.3	86.9	1.5	1.2
John was struck by a bat.	180	220.6	143.8	72.2	2.2	1.6
John was struck by an idea.	180	76.8	143.8	80.6	3.8	1.9
John withdrew his bet.	180	215.5	15.9	62.0	3.2	1.8
John withdrew his hand.	180	199.6	15.9	79.5	2.7	2.1

5

Differential Use of Dominant and Non-Dominant Hands: A Window on Referential and Non-Referential Functions

NICLA ROSSINI*

5.1 Introduction

The question of whether language and gestures are separate entities is of great importance as far as the relationship between IMAGERY, SPACE, EMBODIED COGNITION, and communication is concerned. The study presented here concerns the analysis of planning gestures (Kendon 2004) versus referential gestures in map-task activities with blocked visibility, in order to assess whether there is a link between language, self-orientation in space, planning as self-orientation, and gesture.

This topic has already been addressed in a number of studies, with a variety of different interpretations of the communicativeness of gesture with communicative acts (see Wei 2006 for a review) and, on a more general level, on the self-orientational function of language.

The question of the role of gesture in dialogue and communicative acts has already been addressed through experiments that vary the visibility of the speaker to the listener. Mahl (1961) was one of the first scholars to suggest a key role and influence of visibility on the production of gestural and behavioural cues. However, Rimé (1982) proved that blocked visibility does not completely prevent the production of gestures, and consequently argued that the role of gestures is not strictly 'linguistic' or communicative. Other scholars following the same experimental line, such as Krauss et al. (1995), have come to the same conclusions. An

* I am grateful to my students at the University of Luxembourg, BSE, for their willingness to informally repeat the map-task experiment with me and act as control sample. A special acknowledgement goes to David McNeill and Sotaro Kita for discussing with me some points of an early version of this chapter, and to Jean Hudson, Ulf Magnusson, Carita Paradis, and Karl-Erik McCullough for their comments to the final version of it.

alternative hypothesis is suggested by Cohen and Harrison (1973), and more recently de Ruiter (2000): their suggestion is that the resilience of gestures when the partner is not visible is due to the adoption of behavioural patterns typical of default conditions, that is, face-to-face interaction. Alibali et al. (2001) focus their investigation on the quality of gestures (representational or descriptive gestures, or those gestures illustrating the mental content, versus beat gestures, that follow the rhythm of the concurrent speech) during cartoon retellings under conditions both of visibility and blocked visibility. Their research underlines the fact that, because representational gestures are per- formed at a considerably higher rate during conditions of visibility, these gestures are more likely to serve communicative functions, while the function of gestures in general is both communicative and self-orientational. Janet Bavelas and colleagues (Bavelas et al. 2008) further claim that dialogic condi- tions influence the production of gestures in interactions, and that, because gestures are ultimately demonstrations, dialogical and visibility conditions profoundly influence them. These studies for the most part focus on the communicativeness of gestures, but neglect a key role of language, that is, the self-orientational or planning function. The field of linguistics tends to disregard this important facet of language use: with the exception of Leonard Bloomfield (1933), who defines thought as a means to talk to ourselves, the communicative—or 'external' in Lurija's definition—side of language is usu- ally considered to be the only valid subject of inquiry. Nevertheless, this key function of language has been central for psychologists such as Vygotskij, Lurija, and Piaget. Piaget (1954) coined the expression 'egocentric speech' for a particular use of spoken language oriented to the self that he observed in three to Five-year-old children. Piaget described egocentric speech as being triggered by the impossibility of assuming the point of view of others during communication. Vygotskij and Lurija (1930) identify three stages of ontological development for language: these are external speech, egocentric speech, and inner speech. External speech is the communicative, and ultim- ately social manifestation of language, and is firstly acquired by imitation. Egocentric speech is a further evolution of external speech, and helps the child organize his behaviour and has thus a self-oriented function. When egocentric speech is internalized, it evolves into inner speech, which is silent and medi- ates meaningful behaviour and voluntary acts. Vygotskij (1962) and Lurija (1961) do not share Piaget's idea that egocentric speech (private speech, in their terminology) is intended by the child to be communicative, but rather interpret it as spoken thought (Vygotskij 1962). The self-oriented function of language described by these authors is a component of the analysis of speech and gesture production in interaction presented here.

5.2   Nonverbal Phenomena during a Map-task with Blocked Visibility

Given the usually disregarded dual function of gestures and language (see e.g. Lurija 1969 for the role of gestures), a new phenomenon has been observed under conditions of blocked visibility during a route description task, namely, the differential use of hands for several purposes, such as

a) conveying information—the aspect of gesture that is most closely related to the referential function of language, and
b) planning and self-orientational functions such as the shift of NEW to GIVEN (for the psycholinguistics concepts of GIVEN and NEW see Halliday 1985).

Participants show a tendency to use their dominant hand for referential aspects, while their weak hand tends to express self-orientational and other psycho-pragmatic functions.

The original purpose of the data collection presented here was to provide data for speech analysis: the video-recordings were thus not explicitly designed to allow for the analysis of non-verbal cues. Nevertheless, given the potential importance of this finding, the data so far available will be discussed as a starting point for further research.

The analysis of the complex gestural strategy examined here is also intended to contribute to the investigation of the communicative function of gestures (see Rossini and Gibbon 2011; Rossini 2012). Because gestures—as well as language generally—incorporate multiple simultaneous functions, the usefulness of an entirely listener-oriented theoretical approach is limited, due to the neglect of self-orientational function of language, and should thus be revised. The data were collected in 2003 within the 'map-task project' at the Università degli Studi del Piemonte Orientale. The map-task experiment is a method of data collection developed to study linguistic strategies for expressing path and motion.

During the experiment, two participants are asked to sit one opposite the other at a table with an artificial plastic wall that completely prevents them from seeing each other. One of them, the 'Giver', is provided with a map containing a path that needs to be described in detail to the 'Follower', so that they can draw the path on their map. Both maps have a clear start and end point. Participants are not previously warned about the fact that their maps are not exactly congruent with one another, in order to deliberately cause problems in synchronization. The corpus consists of 4 hours, 5 minutes, and 22 seconds of map-task conversations, with a total of forty-four Italian participants. The data collected were transcribed separately for speech by two coders. Non-verbal aspects of the conversations were transcribed by the same researcher twice under blind conditions. In particular, the rater was prevented from accessing subject information gathered during data collection. This information included, for instance, the level of education, personal details, and handedness of each participant. The measures adopted were aimed at ensuring the reliability of both the transcription and interpretation of the data. The inter-rater reliability for the speech transcript is +0.89, while the test-retest reliability coefficient for the non-verbal analysis is +0.99. The lower inter-rater reliability is largely due to a different sensibility to vowel prolongation in the two coders and as such has little bearing on the current investigation. The corpus has been enlarged since, with data from Mandarin Chinese speakers: at present, due to the intrinsic difficulty in recruiting and selecting Chinese speakers in Italy, the data available concern four Chinese participants. In this case, transcription for both speech and gesture has been done twice by the same transcriber. Because of the poor quality of the audio-source, unintelligible speech was decoded with the help of an external expert in non-verbal communication who is also fluent in Mandarin Chinese.

The analysis of co-verbal gestures in map-task activities under conditions of blocked visibility is particularly interesting because of the cognitive effort it places on the participants—it is designed to elicit the activation of different capabilities such as self-orientation in space and planning—and also because of the 'marked condition' of interaction give by this instance of blocked visibility (Rossini 2007): participants sit facing each other at the same table, but they are not able to see their partner.

The co-verbal gestures observable under these conditions are not elicited from imagistic short-term memory as with cartoon story retelling (McNeill 1992), but are generated through self-orientation in space and planning. Such gestures are simplified in form, being less complex in both handshape and trajectory (Rossini 2007). This allows the isolation of recurrent patterns that are more visible than in face-to-face interaction.

The fact that people tend to gesticulate even when aware that their gestures cannot be seen has already been noted by Rimé (1982). Our data support this evidence: participants gave non-verbal cues (gaze, posture shifts—i.e. shifts of the trunk, and gestures) even when under conditions of blocked visibility. While the number of gestures performed in blocked visibility is comparable to that occurring under normal conditions (Rossini 2007), posture shifts and gaze directed to the interlocutor are dramatically reduced. In particular, posture shifts occur in cases of arousal.

An instance of this phenomenon is recorded in one of the Givers, when the participant tries to describe a location on the map, but has problems retrieving a good term of comparison (Fig. 5.1). In uttering the word *come* ('like') followed by a long filled pause, the Giver looks towards the Follower.

Cases of posture-shifts probably related to planning are also recorded, as in the example shown in Fig. 5.2. Of course, co-verbal gestures are also indices of planning and self-orienting thought (Rossini 2007, 2012). As mentioned above, the gestures performed by the participants intent on the map-task are simplified.

FIG. 5.1. Case of gaze towards the interlocutor in concurrence with a hesitation

FIG. 5.2. A case of posture shift related to planning

This simplification has allowed the isolation of a particular gesture that has been named 'palm-down-flap' (Rossini 2007; see Fig. 5.8 for an instance). Because the gesture in question has no overt iconic relationship with the co-expressive speech. (for the notion of co-expressivity, see McNeill 2005), but displays a more abstract or metaphoric relationship with it, and because it has always been found in synchronization with specific passages during either route-direction (for the most part following the acquisition of common landmarks) or discourse organization coordinated with the confirmation of a successful communicative strategy, it is most likely attributable to planning activities. This type of metaphoric gesture has been recorded during face-to-face interactions for both Italian and American subjects (see Rossini 2007).

5.3   Instances of Differential Use of Dominant and Non-dominant Hand in Gesture

Many map-task participants show a differential use of the hands—that is, they prefer the use of one hand over the other—for the performance of gestures instantiating different linguistic functions. The dominant hand is typically used to perform gestures depicting shapes or trajectories or more abstract mental content; the non-dominant hand, meanwhile, is used for gestures related to

self-organization processes that are usually performed in concurrence with planning passages, such as the abandonment of an ineffective communicative strategy.
Due to the gestural representation observed during tasks with blocked visibility,
these planning gestures are recorded at least once per participant, with the non-
dominant hand (for a contrasting point of view on lateralization, see Hadar and
Butterworth 1997).

Gestures related to planning activities often emerge while carrying out complex tasks in interaction with others, particularly at frustrating moments. Frus-
tration and a marked condition of interaction are common contexts for these
gestures. Forty-three out of forty-four participants in the role of Giver showed a
differential gestural use for different linguistic functions. Curiously, each participant tends to show at least one case of differential use of the hand attributable to
planning activities during her/his task. This chapter presents and discusses some
instances of this pattern, which also constitute the most non-controversial
examples of differential use of the hands found in the corpus: these are instances
synchronized with yet another index of planning in speech or gesture.

Two types of differential use of the hands were observed. The first one is a
differential use of dominant and non-dominant hand associated with the previously mentioned 'palm-down-flap'[1] that has already been identified as an index
of planning (Rossini 2007). In such cases, the non-dominant hand performs the
'palm-down-flap' while the dominant one instantiates the referential function by
performing gestures linked to linguistic representation that are usually named
'illustrators' (see e.g. Ekman and Friesen 1969; Kendon 2004).

The second type of differential use of the hands occurs in cases of restatement
after a wrong-footing: in these cases, gestural production shifts from the dominant hand to the non-dominant one. A good example of the former type of
lateralization is observable in Fig. 5.3: here the participant, in the role of Giver,
is attempting a description of a path around a landmark on his map. After a filled
pause and a silent hesitation, he resumes his route-description, then interrupts it
again and restates the route described thus far by using a different orientation
strategy. The word *allora* (translated into English as 'let's see'), which is usually a
clear sign of planning (see Rossini 2007), is here an index of the shift in the Giver's
communicative strategy. Soon after the word *allora*, in concurrence with the
segment *vai avanti* ('go straight' on), he performs a gesture signalling the
abandonment of the old linguistic plan, that is, a horizontal cut performed
with palm down and away from body that cuts the air, starting from the body
and ending towards the frontal space of the speaker (see Kendon 2004 for the
meaning of this gesture). The gesture in question is performed with the Giver's
non-dominant hand, which was previously disengaged from gestural production

---

[1] Interestingly, a left-hand preference for metaphor in right-handed subjects with a Left-
hemisphere dominance for language functions has already been recorded (see Kita et al. 2007).

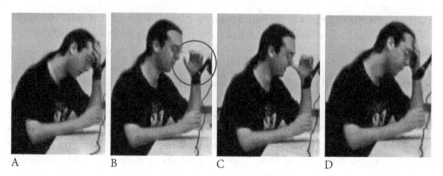

A   B   C   D

FIG. 5.3. Case of differential use of the non-dominant hand linked to planning activity for a participant in the role of 'Giver'

in a rest position. After the gesture is performed, the Giver's left hand goes back to the original rest position and is not engaged in any further gestural performance.

An instance of a 'planning' gesture observable in more than one participant is a horizontal trajectory with 'palm-down' handshape. Under normal conditions, this gesture is considered to be symbolic or emblematic: by depicting a clear line in the air, the gesture conveys the idea of something incontestable (Kendon 2004). The gesture described in Fig. 5.3 is a variant of the normal symbolic gesture described above. It uses the same handshape, but with a 'sloppy' hand (for the concept of 'sloppy hand' see Kita et al. forthcoming). It also has the same trajectory, although the path of the movement is not sideways but away from body.

Fig. 5.4 reports an interesting case of simultaneous differential use of the hands. The participant presented in the figure, who is left-handed, is in the role of the Giver: after receiving a negative response from her interlocutor, who is not able to find the previously specified landmark on her map, the Giver changes strategy and says *vabè, allora senti* ('OK, then listen'). After the abandonment of her original communicative plan, the Giver runs into some speech disfluencies: two single words preceded and followed by long hesitations. During this lexical-retrieval impasse, she performs a self-adaptor followed by a complex gestural representation with both hands that is synchronized with the word *girati* (literally, 'turn around').

The movement performed with the right hand is only marginally referential. Rather, the referential function is instantiated in the left hand, which performs a metaphoric representation of the Giver's attempt at lexical retrieval. The movement performed by the Giver with her right hand appears to be a way to focus attention on the map, although the interpretation in this particular case is questionable.

A   B

FIG. 5.4. Case of simultaneous differential use of dominant and non-dominant hand

A   B   C

FIG. 5.5. Case of simultaneous differential use of dominant and non-dominant hand

A clear example of differential use can be seen immediately afterwards (Fig. 5.5), when the participant retrieves an effective orientation strategy and the exact word to convey the instruction: she thus says *parallela* ('parallel'), and her right hand performs a rapid beat, while her dominant hand is held still, continuing to depict a route. This beat gesture, performed with the non-dominant hand, is an instance of a 'planning' gesture: as soon as she finds an effective way to convey her idea, the speaker beats to mark a new starting point while her dominant hand is engaged in the depiction of a path in concurrence with yet another lexical-retrieval impasse.

Other cases of the differential use of the dominant and non-dominant hand also concern gestural anchoring towards the same reference. The Giver already seen in Fig. 5.1, for instance, resolves a lexical-retrieval impasse signalled by a non-verbal sound by saying *hai un praticello affianco* ('you have a little meadow alongside'). Her gestural production starts in concurrence with the hesitation (Fig. 5.6). Both hands are engaged in gestural performance, although each hand is evidently conveying a different linguistic function. Her dominant hand is engaged in an iconic gesture with a superimposed beat pattern whose onset is synchronized with the non-verbal sound: this iconic gesture conflates the notions of 'lateral placement' and 'roundness', the latter deriring from the round shape of the picture representing the meadow on the Giver's map. Her non-dominant hand performs a 'palm-down-flap' gesture with a superimposed

Fig. 5.6. Instance of simultaneous and differential use of dominant and non-dominant hand

Fig. 5.7. Case of differential use of the hands with concurrent anchored referential function

beat instantiating a planning function: this gesture is synchronized with the word *praticello* and marks its significance in the Giver's communicative strategy.

The Giver performs the same kind of referential anchoring with her dominant hand 9 seconds later (Fig. 5.7), when she describes the path once again. While referring to the same landmark on her map, she describes its shape and calls it a *recipiente* ('container'): in synchrony with the word *recipiente* she performs two gestures: the first, performed with both hands rolling alternatively one over the other, is a metaphor frequently used when referring to common knowledge, or when discourse is not intended to be precise. The second is performed with the dominant hand, and has a strictly referential function: in this case the hand is cupped with palm away from body and roughly oriented towards the right. Referring twice to the same object on the map, the Giver in each case adopts a multiple strategy, employing both language and gest. Although the handshape is roughly similar for both gestures, which suggests a 'catchment' in the McNeillian sense (see e.g. McNeill 2005), the iconicity of the gestural production is more obvious in the second instance. This may be attributable to a focus-shift from the concept of meadow to the description of a round object.

Fig. 5.8. Differential use of the non-dominant hand associated with a *palm-down-flap*

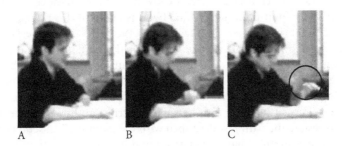

Fig. 5.9. Differential use of the non-dominant hand for the performance of a planning gesture

A similar instance is recorded for another participant, who performs a single planning gesture with her non-dominant hand at the beginning of the task: in this case, the participant performs a 'palm-down-flap' with her left hand while saying *allora* (roughly, 'let's see'), which is, once again, a clear index of planning (Fig. 5.8). The same behaviour is noted for another participant (Fig. 5.9) in the role of Giver, and also for a participant in the role of Follower.

The former performance (Fig. 5.8) is recorded at 00.01.17: after an unsuccessful first attempt to describe the path to his interlocutor, the Giver tries to synchronize with the Follower by going back to the beginning, and says *Allora. Praticamente la partenza è in basso a sinistra, no?* ('Let's see. In fact the departute point is down and to the left, no?'). As soon as his interlocutor confirms, the Giver performs a gesture with his non-dominant hand: the gesture in question is a horizontal cut, indicating definiteness (Kendon 2004). This gesture, which is performed with no concurrent speech, and follows a successful attempt to synchronize with the interlocutor, can be thought of as an index of planning: thus the subject is signalling alignment with his Follower as to the starting point. After this gesture, the Giver only uses his non-dominant hand for self-orientation in space, such as pointing left, or describing a path placed on the left side of the map. Interestingly, these four instances are the only uses of his non-dominant hand during his entire four-minute-long route description.

Another instance of the strong differential use of the hands for different linguistic functions was observed—as already noted—in a participant in the role of Follower. This time, the participants had already finished their task, and were checking over their route: the Follower expresses some doubts about the reliability of the path and tries to understand the appearance of the Giver's map. The first attempt to align with the Giver is accompanied by a beat gesture performed with the dominant hand. Since the alignment is unsuccessful, the Follower restates his question and simultaneously performs a 'palm-down-flap' with his non-dominant hand.

Other cases of differential gestural use involve the shift of movement from the dominant to the non-dominant hand. Two instances of this phenomenon are seen in another participant in the role of the Giver (the phenomenon is recorded at 00:01:10 and then at 00:01:19). In the first instance, the Giver is describing a path on the left-side of her map. During this attempt, she consistently uses her left hand to depict iconically the path to be conveyed, thus attempting to establish an orientation in space. Having described this segment, the Giver begins to proceed with her map description; however, she abruptly decides to restate the path just described with the parenthetical sentence *cioè, la giri e curvi verso destra* ('that is, you go around it and curve to the right'). With the second description of the round path, she now uses her right hand. This case is particularly interesting because of the objective location of the path and landmark to be described on the map, which is interpreted and then reinterpreted with opposite hands. The first description has a referential anchor, while the second is the result of both referential function and planning. The dominant hand takes on the referential function until the segment *fai un pezzo dritto* ('go straight on for a bit'), which is related to a new route segment, and immediately shifts to linguistic planning function. Soon after the speech string *cioè* ('that is'), which is an evident index of restatement, the non-dominant hand engages in movement. Moreover, the gestures that the Giver performs with her non-dominant hand during her restatement of the path description are not exact repetitions of those already performed with the dominant hand. These gestures are more iconic and space-anchored; during restatement, the Giver's gestures are more global, as if indexing a reinterpretation and appropriation of the space by the speaker.

This same differential use of the hands in gesture is recorded for another participant in the role of Giver, with a more emphatic transition from dominant to non-dominant hand and vice versa. When this subject first uses his non-dominant hand (00:01:17), the Giver and Follower have just realized that their maps do not match exactly. Nevertheless, the mismatch has not caused disorientation, and the Giver manages to guide his interlocutor to the second landmark. After this segment, the Giver needs to refer to the third landmark on his map, but prefers to synchronize with the Follower by directly asking if the landmark in question—a mine—is reported on his map. During this phase, and also during the Follower's answer, the Giver's dominant hand holds the stroke 'phase' of a pointing gesture. The Follower's response is confused at first, but the interactants eventually successfully synchronize.

As the Follower says *No. Si! Ce l'ho* ('No. Yes! I have it'), the Giver marks the successful alignment with his interlocutor with *ecco*[2] (roughly, 'there you go') and proceeds with the following segment. Interestingly, the non-dominant hand leaves the rest position in synchrony with the word *ecco*, performs an iconic gesture depicting the next segment of the path, and returns to the rest position. As soon as the Follower says *OK*, and signals alignment, the Giver's non-dominant hand leaves the rest position again and performs a beat with a loose precision grip. The gesture's onset is synchronized with a speech pause, and can be considered an index of linguistic planning. Subsequently, the Giver's non-dominant hand is engaged in an abstract reference to the next route segment when he is interrupted by his interlocutor with a request for clarification about a landmark. During the Follower's conversational turn, the Giver's hands are at rest. After the Follower's question, the referential function is activated in the Giver together with his dominant hand: the participant performs an iconic gesture of proximity while saying *più verso la miniera* ('[keep] closer to the mine'). After the participants have aligned on this point, the Giver almost exclusively uses his dominant hand with the referential function, thus showing the same differential use of dominant and non-dominant hands as the other participants.

Interestingly, this same planning phenomenon has been recorded in Mandarin Chinese speakers: as already stated, the same map-task experiment has in fact been repeated with Mandarin Chinese speakers, with a total four (two female and two male) participants recruited so far. These were given the same mismatched maps and obtained the same instructions as the Italian participants; recordings were conducted in Mandarin Chinese, with built-in microphone. All four participants showed a differential use of dominant and non-dominant hand for referential and planning purposes. Fig. 5.10 presents a relevant instance of lateralization of participant A in the role of Giver (the participant giving directions). After a long passage of negotiation of the task with both the experimenter and the other participant, A starts describing his route to his partner (00:02:00). The gestures recorded up to this point are representational iconic gestures performed with A's right hand. Having described the starting scenario with an attempt at negotiation of landmarks, A undergoes a speech disfluency problem (TOT), and says '有一个/*有一个' ('there's a/*there's a'. See Fig. 5.10).

---

[2] See Rossini (2007) for the word *ecco* as a clear index of planning.

1   2   3   4

Fig. 5.10. Instance of movement switching from the dominant to the non-dominant hand in the performance of a planning gesture by a Mandarin Chinese speaker

Here it is easy to see a passage from the dominant to the non-dominant hand: after having said '有一个' for the first time, A now repeats it with two synchronized gestures. The gestures in question are performed with the right hand: these are a representational and a para-discoursive gesture.

Soon after having received confirmation by his interlocutor, A says '好' ('Good/ OK') and thus signals a synchronization with his partner and a new step in his planning activity. The sentence in question is synchronized with a planning gesture, already described in Rossini (2007). It is interesting to note that in this case, as well as in the cases observed so far, the planning gesture is performed with the speaker's non-dominant hand.

Interestingly, the non-dominant hand is used in this case after a long hesitation pause and the word '好' (hao1), meaning 'good' or, as in the case discussed here, 'okay'.

5.4   Conclusions

Various hypotheses have been proposed regarding the role of gesture in communication. Some scholars, such as Butterworth and Hadar (1989), have suggested that gestures are not communicative, while others hold the view that gestures are intentionally communicative. Among these, Melinger and Levelt (2004) and de Ruiter (2000) hypothesize that gestures are intended by the speaker to be informative, regardless of whether their production is apprehended by the interlocutor. Others put forward the idea that gestures play a significant role in face-to-face interaction: Bavelas et al. (2008) have recently shown that gestures are mostly performed in dialogic as opposed to monologic situations, regardless of the face-to-face condition.

McNeill (1992, 2005) and Kendon (1983, 2004) highlight a single cognitive process underlying both speech and gesture. In particular, McNeill (1985 and subsequently) hypothesizes that not only do gestures share the same cognitive, psychological, and ontogenetic origin as speech, but they are also interlaced in the expression of language functions.

The data presented here are consistent with this hypothesis and with the findings discussed in Bavelas et al. (2008) to the extent that they show some interactive properties of face-to-face interactions with blocked visibility. The self-orientational function of the gestures recorded during the map-task is consistent with the speculation of psychologists such as Vygotskij (1962) and Lurija (1961) regarding the self-orientational function of language. Moreover, the results presented here confirm McNeill's (2005: 53–4) idea that gestures can be produced both to assist in the speaker's self-orientational task and to facilitate the receiver's decoding task. Gestures, as well as speech, may serve self-orientational and planning functions and thus be a means for self-orientation and self-organization (Alibali et al. 2001), even developmentally prior to becoming a means of communication and interaction. These results constitute strong evidence for embodiment and embodied cognition, in lending support to the hypothesis that there is no possible clear-cut separation between body and mind, space and cognition.

The observed phenomenon of the differential use of the hands in gestures instantiating different linguistic functions, such as the referential (in representational gestures), and the self-organizational function related to planning (Kendon 2004), may lead to further research on the differential involvement of brain hemispheres in language production (cf. e.g. Rossini 2012).

Further research should assess the replicability of these results. A task-oriented experiment involving step-by-step instructions to the interlocutor with no possibility of direct visual contact, for example, could serve this purpose. The experiment in question should be structured in two phases for each participant in order to allow the comparison of language production both during face-to-face interaction and under conditions of blocked visibility.

6

Embodied Interaction and Semiotic Categorization: Communicative Gestures of a Girl with Patau Syndrome

KRISTIINA JOKINEN, SILVI TENJES,
and INGRID RUMMO*

6.1 Introduction

Meaning is negotiated in the communicative situation, as part of the social activity the speakers are engaged in. However, meaning is a complex phenomenon, and an interesting research question is how interactive processes facilitate the construction and transfer of meaning among the participants. In order to understand the communicative meanings exchanged in the situation, it is essential to take into consideration the communicative situation as a whole (Schegloff 1984; Goodwin 1986, 2003c, 2007). The communicative situation includes, in addition to spoken language, bodily movements of the communicators—body posture, gaze, and hand movements (e.g. Kendon 1986, 1995, 2004; Streeck 1988; Streeck and Knapp 1992), and it is thus essential to take account of these aspects in studies as well.

In this chapter we will look at the relationship between hand gestures and meaning construction in communicative situations. We focus especially on the communication possibilities of a seventeen-year-old girl with the mosaic variant of Patau syndrome and her communication using hand gestures and contextual information. Patau syndrome, or Trisomy 13, is a chromosomal abnormality where the cells have three copies of the 13th chromosome. It may also be expressed as a mosaic variant, in which case some body cells have two copies of the 13th chromosome and some have three. The syndrome is relatively rare, and babies with Patau syndrome are often stillborn or die within a few days because of

* We would like to thank two anonymous reviewers for their helpful comments and suggestions concerning the earlier version of the chapter.

This research was partially supported by Estonian Science Foundation Grant 8008.

severe heart and brain defects which make their survival difficult. However, the prognosis is not necessarily bad: apparently the oldest survivor is twenty-seven years old, and the oldest with the mosaic variant thirty-six.

Our subject—we call her L—is a lively and happy girl, and she comprehends the speech addressed to her. She understands everyday topics and questions, and is also able to answer questions. However, her means to reply are incomplete. Her speech is disturbed due to motor dysphasia, a disturbance of speech caused by organic damage to the speech centres of the cerebral cortex. Most of her communication thus proceeds by hand and head movements accompanied by specific sounds.

We study L's communicative strategies, concentrating on the analysis of hand movements, spoken expressions, and general activity in bringing forth meaning. This allows us to understand the aspects of the concepts that she communicates, and how she generalizes certain gestures in communicative situations. Our main point of interest is the embodiment of semiotic categories in L's communication and the meaning constructed in space through her hand gestures. By studying the connection between gesture types and the underlying concepts, we explore how meaning is created through gesturing and what the defining features are for the concepts which get encoded into the gestures.

The results of the analysis of L's communicative behaviour can contribute to an understanding of the mechanisms of human cognitive abilities and perceptional processes in a broader sense. By observing L's use of sign language and hand gestures as well as the sounds she uses to construct and transmit meaning, and by observing the interpretations of her communication by those with whom she communicates, we seek to provide answers to the following questions:

1. How is meaning created in communication?
2. How is signification imparted when speech is missing?
3. How is meaning understood when it is transmitted with hand gestures?

Our theoretical framework follows contemporary approaches to linguistic and cognitive research. The analysis is based on theories of semiotic categorization (icon, index, and symbol) of signs, cooperative communication, and studies on hand gestures. The main claim of the chapter is that meaning is constructed in the framework of interactive situations. We present evidence for the claim that the meaning relation is based on the communicative situation rather than on the link between the sign and its referent—that is, that the roles and relationships of the participants, their shared knowledge, and contextual information are all crucial in creating meaning and may, in fact, have a more prominent role in the process than the type of connection between the sign and the referent. Our results also support the hypothesis that human communicative abilities may function separately from the speech abilities of the specific language. Speech is one mode of interaction and it allows sophisticated symbolic communication, but other modalities, like gestures and body posture, can also serve communicative functions. In other words, the human capability to form symbolic concepts and to understand meanings is not related only to spoken language, but rather cognition is based on the inherent human ability to observe and interact with the surrounding world in the first place.

The structure of the chapter is as follows. In Section 2, we first present the theoretical background to our work and discuss the semiotic interpretation of gestures from the point of view of Peirce's original sign classification and its modern developments. We then proceed to an examination of the relationship between gestures and meaning construal in Section 3, and summarize some earlier studies on gestures and their classification, especially the approaches of Kendon and McNeill. We then present our own data and discuss its analysis in Section 4. Finally, in Section 5, we draw some conclusions about how meaning is conveyed in conversation and how gestures help to clarify the meaning in space or convey the meaning altogether.

6.2   Theoretical Background

Many researchers have tried to describe how human cognition is related to embodiment. For instance, Varela et al. (1991: 172) present the argument in their attempt to study cognition not as the recovery of a pre-given and labelled external world (realism) or a pre-given inner world (idealism), but as embodied cognition. Using the term *embodied*, Varela et al. (1991: 173) draw attention to two important points:

(1) cognition depends on the kinds of experience that come from having a body with various sensory-motor capacities, and

(2) these individual sensory-motor capacities are themselves embedded in a more encompassing biological, psychological, and cultural context.

Embodiment is an important aspect of human cognition. However, in this chapter we also emphasize that meaning development does not occur in a void, but emerges via interaction with the environment. The second point above should thus be clarified further: the embodiment of cognition, which is grounded in the individual's experience of the world, is not only embedded in the context, but results from the interaction of the individual with the context. Individuals receive information through their sensory-motor capacities, but can also actively control and affect the world by their own physical and communicative acts. In fact, the important cognitive distinctions between objects and actions, the self and the others, spatial orientation, the foreground and the background, etc. are drawn by the individuals through experimenting with the environment and receiving feedback about the success of their acts.

Consequently, language and the meaning of words are jointly constructed in the individual's interaction with the world and with other communicative partners. However, the symbolic and conventional nature of language presupposes a sophisticated semiotic system which allows meaning to be transferred not only about the immediate environment, but also about the language itself and about situations which are not necessarily immediately present. Language is thus an abstraction of the individual's concrete experience of the world, but it is constructed in social interactions with the speaker's intention that the interlocutor should understand the meaning and react in an appropriate manner. The process of semiosis, or the communication of meaning, has thus two aspects: first, the establishment of a relationship between a sign and its referent, and second, the speaker's intention that the relationship is interpreted by the communicating partner.

We follow in our study C. S. Peirce's classification of signs and M. Lotman's interpretation of them in order to understand the relation between L's communicative means and meaning construction, and the semiosis of gestures in L's communication in general. Peirce realized that cognition has three basic semiotic dimensions: iconic, indexical, and symbolic. These dimensions of cognition are grounded in intuitions of similarity (iconicity), causality, contiguity in space-time, and part–whole relation (indexicality), as well as arbitrary conventional connections (symbolicity) between objects of attention. Peirce defines signs as follows: 'A sign, or representamen, is something which stands to somebody for something in some respect or capacity' (Peirce 1931–58, 2: 228). According to Peirce, a sign is elementary, and the smallest semiotic element. Single signs constitute complex signs: expressions which taken together form a language. Peirce's approach to signs has been called atomistic (Lotman 2002: 515), since it focuses on the (single) sign.

Peirce paid much attention to the exact description of the sign, and Lotman has in fact counted no less than eighty-eight definitions of it in Peirce's works (however, all are variations on essentially the same theme). Proceeding from his idea of the sign, Peirce created a rather complicated typology of signs, of which the most important part constitutes what Peirce himself called the second trichotomy of the sign: the iconic, indexical, and symbolic signs. When referring to an object (abstract or concrete), a sign can be an icon, index, or symbol, or some combination of these, depending on the connection between the object and the sign. Peirce considers this trichotomy the most important classification of signs. The basis of this classification is the nature of connections between signs and objects signified by them.

In modern semiotics, the sign–function relationship (or the sign–object relationship) has become a crucial issue. Interpretations differ between semiotic schools, although Peirce's systematization of the types of signs has remained. For instance, Lotman highlights the argumentation of several earlier researchers (e.g. Pelc 1986; Bally 1965; Benveniste 1966), and concludes that all Peircean sign types characterize only speech communication. He argues that the signs of language (means of communication in a wider sense) are based on a different logic: that is, they are grounded on the values of the sign rather than on the connections between the sign and the referent (Lotman 2002: 519). Lotman asks further if in this case the so-called position of signification in the concept can be handled as a sign value while the relation to the object would originate from interaction. Our studies support Lotman's conclusion and we believe there is an option to interpret the relation between the sign and its value through its use. We assume that signs cannot be defined solely on the basis of their connection to their referents, but via the sign values—a semantics which emerges in interactions (cf. the discussion on the classification of signs at the end of Section 3).

The iconic and indexical dimensions of signs are primarily non-verbal, while the symbolic dimension is primarily verbal (Hirsch 1995: 14). However, the primary vehicle for communication for the deaf is sign language: they use gestures in order to transmit signification rather than spoken language. The question is then how to apply Peirce's sign systematization to the gestural communication modality: the concept of sign should obviously be expanded in order to include sign language gesturing as well.

Gesturing is often related to the iconic dimension of the language. Iconicity is considered the basis for human communicative abilities (see for example Koch 2002; Itkonen 2005), but the communicative picture is more varied than this. For instance, Itkonen notes that 'There are four basic physical dimensions, namely vertical, horizontal, diagonal, and temporal. Speaking takes place in one basic physical dimension only, namely time' (Itkonen 2005: 114–15). He further presents five analogues between spoken and sign language, and among them is the claim that the iconic nature of the representation by gestures ceases to look unique (Itkonen 2005: 115–17). In sign languages, gestures work in a symbolic way in everyday usage, and can thus have all three semiotic interpretations from iconic representations via indexical signs to symbolic use. We will exemplify this con-clusion through the analysis of our material in Section 4, where signification is constructed via hand gestures.

One of the important aspects discussed in Peircian semiotics is the semiosis process itself. Among the many relations that exist between objects in the world, the semiotic relation occurs only when the relation enters the sign relation, that is it is recognized, and intended to be recognized by the other interlocutors, as a meaningful relation. For instance, there are many potential indexical relations in the world, but the indexical signs are only those that are used by interlocutors to carry meaning in communication. In a similar manner, iconicity does not exist until a comparison takes place, and symbols require acknowledgement of the conventional relation. The main question, therefore, concerns determining what kind of relation the semiotic relation is, and how it is learnt (Sonesson 1996: 129).

Some contemporary studies of language and cognition claim that pointing and translation are the most important faculties for the development of the power of linguistic symbolization in the course of evolution (Sinha 1999, 2005). Pointing or the referring act, and translation or the construal act, are the underlying functional components of the representational function of language, and the development of symbolization is essentially the process of elaborating this representational function. According to Sinha, we conceptualize *in* language (and not language), and we do it in order to *refer* to something, in the direction of something, or at somebody (Sinha 1999: 227). However, pointing as the primary ability for communication and linguistic development of human beings in general is rather controversial, since it presupposes joint and shared attention which requires elaborated cognitive skills to understand what the other person sees, and moreover, to infer exactly what the person is looking at. It is also difficult to explain how abstract concepts are formed (cf. discussion on pointing gestures in Section 3.).

We thus look for the explanation of semiosis in an interactive situation. It is important to clarify the notion of *origo* here. According to Bühler (1990 [1934]), reference is possible only with respect to a system of coordinates, the origin of which he calls the 'origo'. In their further discussion of the notion, Levy and Fowler (2000: 218) note that 'In the simplest case, when a speaker is making reference to entities that are perceptibly present so that they can, in one way or another, point to them ("ocular deixis" in a translation of Bühler's terminology), the origo is at the speaker and is the personal and spatio-temporal locus denoted by the expressions *I, here,* and *now'*. Every person has their own viewpoint, *origo*, and he or she communicates from this origo and assumes that the interlocutor does the same, i.e. communicates from the point of view of their own *origo*. Fillmore (1971) has proposed a psychological characterization of the same idea: he defines the egocentric perceptual space in terms of coordinates that are established by the vertical, unmistakably defined by gravity, and by reference to anatomical properties—front and back, bilateral symmetry—of the perceiver. Awareness of one's own front and back, left and right, is the basis for awareness of one's own orientation in space, relative to fixed objects, and also the basis for understanding other people's perception and point of view. We can thus say that semiosis is grounded in the perceptions of literally 'self-centred' speakers and the point of view from which they look at communicative situations. However, in order to get the meaning across, semiosis also assumes understanding the other person's viewpoint and realizing how it differs from one's own. The creation of meaning thus requires sophisticated coordination of language and action in order to construct shared understanding of the situation: that is, communication about the participants' goals and intentions. Communication is hence based on the interlocutors' cooperation towards the communicative goal: on their willingness to coordinate their actions and to code and decode meanings in communicative signs in order to achieve the common goal (cf. Allwood 1976; see also Jokinen 2009; Tenjes et al. 2009). Interaction also allows individuals to be rewarded for their (communicative) actions and language learning can take place. Through the development of advanced cognitive skills, such as non-egocentric representations and comprehension of shared attention, children learn the language as part of the cooperative interaction with their caretakers. In this the linguistic, emotional, and affective feedback from the environment guides the formation of semiotic signs that signify their intentions as well as physical and communicative acts.

6.3 Gestures and Language

6.3.1 Classification of gestures

The classification of gestures is as problematic as the classification of languages and dialects in linguistics. The question is: where can one draw the borderline? There are various competing classifications of gestures in the literature, although the terminology has often been somewhat confusing (see, for example, Feyereisen and de Lannoy 1991). For instance, McNeill divides hand gestures into icons, metaphoric, and deictic, gestures (McNeill 1985), but the distinction between iconic and metaphoric gestures is not always clear and of course, from the semiotic point of view, metaphoric gestures are as iconic as other similarity-motivated signs (Sonesson 2001). The first typology of gestures was presented by Efron (1941/1972), later clarified and extended by Ekman and Friesen (1969) and Kendon (1986). Efron distinguishes as 'physiographic' those speech-related gestures that present a sort of picture of some aspect of the content, and as 'ideographic' those speech-related gestures which, as he says, are 'logical' in their meaning and which portray not so much the content of the talk as the course of the ideational process itself. Efron also recognizes 'batons'—rhythmic repetitive gestures—and gestures which are standardized in form and which function as complete utterances in themselves, independently of speech. These are referred to as 'autonomous gestures', which include the forms that are quite often today referred to as 'emblems' following Kendon (1986: 32).

In general, typologies of gesture often involve two broad crosscutting dimensions: *representationality,* and *convention* or *autonomy* (Haviland 1996: 11). The first dimension has to do with whether and how the bodily movements that accompany speech depict or represent the referential content of what is being conveyed by an utterance, and the second describes the character of gestures as a more or less independent utterance. From the semiotic point of view, conventional gestures are symbolic by definition, while representational gestures can be iconic or indexical: some gestures seem tailored to the 'meaning' of speech, whereas others appear to be more closely aligned to the rhythm of talk. However, the semiotic interpretation of gestures is not straightforward, as is also noted by Haviland (2000); especially problematic is the line between symbolic (conventional) and indexical modes of signalling. Indexicality poses problems, since indexical signs represent a certain relation between two objects, the relation of which can vary itself from a typical indexical relation to a more conventionalized link. For instance, a relation between a gesture and its referent can be a deictic pointing, but the same pointing gesture can be used to signal important parts in the discourse. The interpretation of a gesture as an index or symbol thus depends on the situation, which guides the most salient or important relation in the situation to be taken as the defining basis (note also L's gestures which can refer to a location far away, to a specific location 'Pangodi', or to the next speaker as in the sample data example 2; see Section 6.4).

Kendon (1986, 1998, 2004) has studied gestures extensively, especially Neapolitan conversational strategies, while his work on Australian sign language, for instance, remains the authoritative description of the topic. He defines gestures as phrases of bodily action that have certain characteristics that permit them to be recognized as components of intentional communicative action. The word 'gesture' thus serves as a label for that domain of visible action which participants routinely distinguish and treat as governed by openly acknowledged communicative intent (Kendon 1986).

According to Kendon, when individuals organize the units of action for communication, they make use of whatever vehicles for meaning representation are available. These include spoken language, but also the possibility of representing meaning through visible action: in other words, by gestures. Gestures have a number of distinctive features that are related to hand movement in general, but still allow gestures to be recognized as special movements by the speaker. These characteristics include:

1. Gestures are 'excursions': phrases of action recognized as gesture move away from a 'rest position' and always return to a rest position.
2. 'Peak' structure: such excursions always have a centre, recognized by naive subjects as the 'business' of the movement, what the movement actually does, or what it was meant for. The peak has also been referred to as the 'stroke' of the gesture phrase.
3. Well-boundedness: the phrases of action identified as gesture tend to have clear onsets and offsets. These are called preparatory and recovery phases of the gesture action. Boundedness is in contrast to orientation changes or posture shifts which sometimes can be quite gradual and have no peak structure.
4. Symmetry: If you run a film of someone gesturing backwards it is remarkable how difficult it seems to be to see any difference from when you run the film forwards. This suggests that gesture phrases have symmetry of organization that practical actions, posture shifts (and of course spatial movements, etc.) do not have.

Kendon uses the term 'gesticulation' to refer to the gesture as a whole, comprising the preparatory phase in the beginning of the movement, the stroke or the peak structure, and the recovery phase at the end of the movement (Kendon 1998). Any movement that a speaker produces can share these features to a lesser or greater degree, but the more it does so, the more likely the movement is to be given a privileged status in the attention of the interlocutors, and the more likely it is to be seen as part of the individual's effort to convey meaning. According to Kendon, gesture is thus behaviour that is treated as intentionally communicative action, and it has certain immediately recognizable features which distinguish it from other kinds of activity such as practical actions, postural adjustments, orientation changes, self-manipulations, and so forth. Accordingly, gestures may function as utterances on their own, but they may also be employed as components of utterances in alternation with speech, or in conjunction with speech.

Considering our discussion of semiotic signs, we can immediately draw a conclusion that a communicative gesture is a sign that bears a certain recognizable relation between the communicative intent and the features of the gesture. In other words, communicative gestures are semiotic signs in a manner similar to any communicative spoken signs.

As a corollary, we can also conclude that classification of gestures may be difficult for exactly the same reasons as the classification of signs is difficult: although the signs in their purest form can be classified in general categories, their signification is built cooperatively in the interactive situation, and their exact interpretation usually depends on contextual understanding. For instance, the multimodal annotation scheme developed in the MUMIN network (Allwood et al. 2007) is unique because it uses semiotic functions in the analysis of spoken interactions, and the semiotic functions are extended to cover all gesturing: they are taken into consideration in the classification of hand gestures together with facial expressions and body posture. However, the interpretation of conversational gestures in terms of semiotic categories has proven to be difficult in practice. Although the annotation scheme, which has been used in annotating different languages, provides fairly satisfactory preliminary results in automatic gesture classification (see e.g. Jokinen et al. 2008), later developments of the scheme have considered more flexible categorizations. One alternative is to define overlapping semiotic categories for gestures that function simultaneously, for example as indexical and symbolic gestures. This, however, defeats the main attraction of Peirce's original trichotomy, as the distinctions between the three semiotic categories are blurred. An alternative is to consider semiotic categories as features that are assigned to gestures to characterize the relation between the gesture form and its most prominent semiotic function, and use another feature to characterize the intended meaning of the gesture in terms of general actions like pointing, offering information, stopping, structuring discourse, and so on (cf. gesture families with their own semantic theme, as suggested in Kendon 2004). The latter types of features are of course similar to semantic features used to categorize the semantics of words, and they can also be related to the sign values that Lotman (2002) introduces to define signs. The semantic themes, or the semiotic sign values of the gestures can also evolve in interactive situations in a manner similar to that in which the semantics of spoken words is created and developed in interactions. The signification of a sign, be it a gesture or a word, can emerge in the communicative situation as a result of a semiotic process whereby the meaning of the sign is determined as a joint effort by the interlocutors. Peirce's original classification of signs can thus be maintained with the help of Lotman's interpretation and the introduction of the interactive context.

6.3.2   Role of gestures presenting meanings

McNeill (1992, 1999) claims that gestures and speech interact in order to bring out a definite cognitive representation. In his view, the division of meaning between a gesture and an utterance is a justified one (McNeill 1985: 366), and he emphasizes that gesture and speech emerge together from the underlying propositional representation, which has both visual and linguistic aspects (Cassell et al. 1999). For McNeill, gestures proceed through imagistic representation into motor articulation and are in constant interaction with speech: 'Thus, in a traditional sense, gesture is not "nonverbal communication". The gesture is part of language, i.e. part of *verbal* communication' (McNeill 1999: 5).

Kendon (1972, 1980) has developed a similar view that gesture, like speech, serves as a vehicle for the representation of meaning. Through the analysis of gestures accompanying speech, he has also shown that gestures and speech are closed linked, and that there is consistency in how gesture phrases (defined in terms of the perceptually marked preparation, stroke, and recovery phases of the action—see above) are patterned in relation to speech phrases (viewed as intonation units, breath groups—specifically David Crystal's 'tone units': Crystal and Davy 1969). When one gesticulates during speaking, there is a corresponding gesture phrase for each semantically important sense group in speech, and the stroke of the gesture tends to coincide with the tone unit. In continuous discourse, speakers also group tone units into higher order groupings so that we can speak of a hierarchy of such units, and gesture phrases may be similarly organized. For example, over a series of tone units linked intonationally or by an absence of pauses into a coherent higher order grouping, the co-occurring gesture phrases are also linked. We can see this because they all use the same hand, there are no full recoveries between gesture phrases, and there is a thematic character to the handshapes used; and then over the next set of linked tone units the speaker organizes his gestural phrases in a contrasting way, using a different hand, different handshape themes, etc. (Kendon 1998). Furthermore, Kendon (1986) claims that gesture phrases are produced directly from the underlying semantic unit. Thus, gesture phrases often begin before the related tone unit and they are often ready before the completion of the tone unit. Moreover, if a gesture phrase expresses the content of the utterance, the characteristics reflecting this development will correspond to the most important informational point in the speech phrase. These characteristics occur either before the nuclear syllable of the sense group or synchronously with the nuclear syllable (Kendon 1991: 2).

In a similar discourse-pragmatic manner, gesture also appears to be related to syntax, picking out clause structure. For instance, Kendon (1998) presents an example of two people standing and looking at a mountain panorama and one of them explaining the names of the mountains to the other. By extending his arm full length, the speaker directs the recipient's attention to the various peaks with his index finger and simultaneously moves his hand in a way that sometimes suggests a curved contour, sometimes a jagged one: the speaker thus combines depictive movement with pointing.

Sotaro Kita (2004) has also studied how people express motion events with speech and gestures that accompany it, in an intercultural context. In his studies, spontaneous gestures were elicited by having adult participants narrate animated cartoons. The first study showed that speakers of Turkish, Japanese, and English expressed the same motion events differently, using different gestures and, furthermore, that the gestural differences mirrored lexical and syntactic differences between the languages. The second study demonstrated that the effect of the language on gestures was observable even within a single language. From these two studies, Kita concluded that speech-accompanying gestures are generated from an interface representation between spatial cognition and speaking. In other words, unlike McNeill and Kendon, Kita does not regard language and gesture as one and the same system, but as two separate systems which interact when a speaker expresses meanings.

Tenjes (2001a, 2001b, 2003) has also found that deictic gestures may perform, for example, two synchronous roles: 1) pointing out spatial relations and 2) denoting the most important concept in a sentence; meaning that if a gesture points to something in space, it will start to 'draw' the object in the air at the same time. If a gesture begins before the most important concept (i.e. the concept that the speech pointed to) in the sentence, then the deictic gesture must be related to language in a different manner because in different languages the object can occupy various positions in the sentence.

Much discussion has taken place concerning the difference between pointing and referring gestures. We do not go into the details of this discussion here since the conceptual difference between such gestures is unclear, and in semiotic terms they are all indexical signs. It may be worth mentioning, however, that many kinds of objects can be pointed at: actual objects in the world that surrounds the participants (actual object pointing) or objects that can have a physical location, but are not immediately present (removed and virtual object pointing). Moreover, things that cannot have any sort of object status at all, and can have no location, can also be pointed to (metaphorical object pointing). In studies of multimodal systems even the notion of *deictic pointing* gesture is also used (for example, Harper et al. 2000).

Many gestures which are not 'pure' pointing gestures also have a pointing component with the index finger extended. For instance, beats or baton gestures often have an index finger somewhat extended in order to give more emphasis to what is being expressed. Jokinen and Vanhasalo (2009) have argued in favour of a special type of pointing gesture, a 'stand-up' gesture, which appears somewhere in between pointing gestures and beats. The form of these gestures resembles that of a pointing gesture, but the movement and extension of the index finger are smaller. With the examples from various dialogue situations, especially narrative conversations and stand-up comedy (from which the gesture derives its name), they argue that stand-up gestures are not used for pointing, but rather to catch the interlocutor's attention in order to prepare them for an important point in the speaker's presentation. Stand-up gestures thus structure the discourse, and the manner in which they are used in communication is quite distinct from other gestures employing a pointing index finger. They can be said to have a pragmatic function (Kendon 1986). It is interesting that the same kind of gesture has also been identified by Rozik (1992), who talks about a particular kind of hand gesture, 'baton', which is crucial to understanding human dialogue in real life and in the theatre, and that the main function of these 'batons' is to indicate the nature of speech acts.

6.3.3   Gestures and communication situations

As already emphasized, meaning is created by the partners in communicative situations when interacting with each other. Many researchers have observed that conversation must be seen not as alternating monologues, but as a social system (e.g. Bavelas et al. 1992), where dialogue sets significant social or interpersonal as well as semantic and syntactic demands on the interlocutors. They need to organize their conversation, coordinate their contributions, and calibrate their meanings as they go along. The speakers must thus cooperate with their partners and be willing to give and receive feedback in order to monitor whether their utterances have been understood, whether they have understood the partner's message, and whether the partner is willing to continue in the first place. Non-verbal means of communication, such as gestures, body posture, and facial expressions are used especially to give and elicit non-intrusive feedback, although as already mentioned, gestures can also function independently in conveying meaning.

Following the discussion of Allwood (1976, 2001a, 2001b), we regard communication as rational activity by speakers, which requires that the basic enablements, Contact, Perception, and Understanding (CPU), are fulfilled. Speakers, in their deliberation of the shared goal as well as of the partner's intentions, are obliged to take their partner into consideration, monitor each other's communicative contributions and the communicative situation in general, and, if some of the enablements for communication are not fulfilled, react to the problems. For instance, if the speaker has lost contact, is not interested, or does not understand the partner's contribution, they are obliged to make these problems known to the partner, who, consequently, must adapt, their communication strategies to the level that is appropriate for the situation.

The feedback on the CPU enablements is important for smooth communication. It is often expressed non-verbally, and thus the speakers must be sensitive to the relevant non-verbal signals that are used, either intentionally or unintentionally, to indicate the state of communicative activity. Important questions in this context are thus, for example, to what extent non-verbal activity, especially gestures and facial expressions, co-occur with verbal expressions, and what exactly are the specific non-verbal expressions typically associated with specific communicative functions. To study these aspects in a more systematic way, the MUMIN network has developed an annotation tool which has been applied to Nordic languages such as Finnish, Danish, and Swedish (Allwood et al. 2007; Jokinen et al. 2008), and also to Estonian (Jokinen and Ragni 2007). The MUMIN annotation scheme has been developed especially for the analysis of gestures in interpersonal communication with particular regard to the role played by multimodal expressions for feedback, turn-taking, and sequencing.

In conversations, utterances are produced in social situations, under the guidance of communicative goals and principles of cooperation, and they function in order to convey certain content in the interactional setting. Gestures often highlight some aspects of the content, but they also support presentation of information, and coordination of different knowledge sources in the interaction. In our study of L's communicative strategies, we report on some of the characteristic uses of gestures abstracted over communicative situations where L interacts with other people. We show how communicative functions of L's gestures get understood in context and are translated into verbal utterances by partners, and how the relation between non-verbal gestures and symbolic meanings gets specified. The semiotic field (Goodwin 2003b) of her communicative signs is wide, but the exact meaning can be reached through the collaborative efforts by L and her interlocutors.

The results allow us to theorize about the basic laws of interaction as manifested through non-verbal signals. In particular, we can demonstrate how the signification of non-verbal gestures and spoken words is formed in a reciprocal joint activity, and how the mutual endeavour towards meaning is an essential part of the interaction where the participants have goals and intentions that they want to be understood by the partner. Concerning the cognitive representation of meaning and its relation to vehicles for the expression of meaning such as sound and gesture, we can also offer evidence that the two modalities function as two independent encoding systems. As Kendon (1986) has pointed out, meanings are not transformed into gestural form via spoken language format, but directly through the process where the speaker organizes the available units of action in order to express the intended meaning.

6.4   L: A Case Study of Gestures and Communication

For the present analysis the authors relied on their previous work with the video corpora materials as well as on notes taken while observing the girl L. in communicative situations. To research the video recordings of 'natural' activities (i.e. activities that would have taken place whether or not a camera was present), the authors employed microethnographical methodology. The material has been carefully and repeatedly looked through to identify patterns of interaction that provide empirical grounding for research claims. In the researchers' view, the final claims correspond to what can be seen and heard in the video-taped data. Of course, there are always some questions left open, and the possibility that another researcher would see the same material from a different perspective.

L, whose communication strategies will be presented below, utters complexes of multiple syllables and is able to produce combinations with vowels and labials to express colloquial words and names. She also makes spatial communicative gestures and, after a sign language course, also knows how to use the concepts of sign language. L has learned to pronounce colloquial words with a speech therapist, and as a result she enunciates and distinguishes independently the words 'yes' and 'no'. However, her pronunciation version for 'yes' is neither perfect nor precise; only a few sounds are present in her enunciation: [i:a]. Her language has an auditory–verbal as well as a visual side. The majority of her communication proceeds by hand and head movements accompanied by specific sounds, and she uses facial expressions intensively when communicating.

Our study of L's communicative strategies concentrates on the analysis of hand movements, expressions, and activity in conveying meaning, as well as other communication participants' understanding of the meaning presented by the girl. The transcription is based on the system by Sacks, Schegloff, and Jefferson (1974).

The conversational modalities of L are: 1) utterances, 2) facial expressions, 3) gestures, 4) 'loose' gestures of learned sign language, 5) presentation of learned words, using only some sounds, mainly vowels and labials. Her main question word is *öhö* [œhœ+rising intonation], which in combination with gestures can function as any (Estonian) interrogative word. The girl uses utterances, including shortened versions of words, containing mainly vowels and labials of the respective word, gestures and motions of sign language. Hand movements are generalized, languid, and not precise as to details. The meaning sphere of the gestures is broad and dependent on the concrete context.

The sample conversation took place at L's home and is about 1 minute and 15 seconds long. The participants were L, B (her elder brother), and their mother M. B was sitting in front of the computer, L was standing next to him, and M was some 1.5 metres away, recording with a video camera. Since M was holding the camera, she is not seen on the film but her voice can be heard.

In the situation, B has come over and his sister (L) and mother (M) would like to have a word with him. He, on the contrary, would like to work on the computer, but his sister has some important questions to ask. She wants to know where Anna, her four-year-old relative, is. The choice of this subject has an implication, as L knows that Anna is at the summer cottage of her grandparents in Pangodi (place name), at a nice little village where it is possible to swim. L wants to go there too; accordingly, she leads the conversation to the topic she is interested in.

The first fragment shows how L creates a conversational space in the communicative situation.

(1)   7 L: [öhö?]

Translation/explanation: *Where is Anna? I know Anna is not in Tartu, she is in Pangodi.*

(Holds her left hand on her brother's shoulder and waves to the distance with the right hand.)

8 M: [anna   või]
Anna   or
Translation/explanation: *Is it Anna about whom you are speaking?*

9 B: [pangodis   või]
in Pangodi   or?
Translation/explanation: *Do you want to know is she in Pangodi?*

10 L: a:
yes
Translation/explanation: 'a:' *is shortened from* 'jaa', 'jah', *Estonian affirmation* 'yes'.

11 B: jah   olime   pangodis
yes   we were   in Pangodi

As seen in Figure 6.1, taken from the beginning of the dialogue, L organizes the space around her to create a convenient, intimate room for a successful conversation. She puts her hand on her brother's shoulder and holds it there for one minute. From this act we can conclude that *touch* is clearly one component of L's language; it is a communicative modality for making meaning while communicating. At the same time she is ensuring that her brother will stay there and participate in the conversation. Physical contact assures greater closeness, so that it is impossible to ignore the one who is talking to you.

Universal interrogative of L is 'Öhö?' which, in combination with gestures and/or signs, may denote any Estonian question word. The conversation starts with the interrogative and in this case means 'Where is Anna?' or 'What is Anna

Fig. 6.1. Creating an intimate conversational space

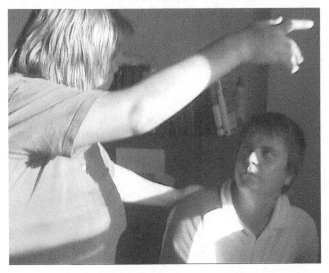

Fig. 6.2. Conceptualizing space, using the pointing gesture

doing?' L gets the answer that Anna is playing, but this was not the expected reply either. Figure 6.2 shows a gesture indicating how L holds her left hand on her brother's shoulder and waves to the distance with her right hand.

The semantic field of the gesture shown in Figure 6.2 is broad, and its most general sense is 'there' or 'far (away)'. The relation between an act and its meaning is usually complex and the precise sense depends on the communicative situation and concrete context. In the sample dialogue, the gesture is interpreted as 'Pangodi', an interpretation which is possible because of the shared knowledge of the interlocutors. Moreover, in this context it becomes apparent that the gesture as an indexical sign and the concrete hand movement can be defined as a referring gesture. By hand movement L refers to the place far away and to the people there; in other words, she conceptualizes the space and the object in space.

However, we can also notice that the signification is constructed in collaboration with the other communicative partners: L's referring gesture is followed by the situation where both M and B specify L's question, asking her assisting questions in order to clarify the exact meaning of the gesture (utterances 8 and 9).

It is usual that when having a conversation, L wants to ask different questions which she expresses through the interrogative *öhö* accompanied by an appropriate gesture. This is one of her communication strategies—by asking questions L can lead the conversation to the direction she has planned. Moreover, in this way she may get some help from her interlocutors who can assist her with formulating her thoughts (interpreting the ideas denoted by her signs/gestures verbally) and this is more precise than just sounds and movements. When her sounds, adapted words, and gestures are decoded into Estonian words, she can signal if the interpretation process was successful or not. This is L's mechanism to check if she has been understood.

The following fragment presents L's efforts to get her meaning understood further in the same communicative situation.

(2)   15 L: ia:?
                 to here?
                 Translation/explanation: *Is Anna coming here?*
                 (Indicates towards floor by using the pointing gesture.)
                 Translation/explanation: *Meaning of the pointing gesture is 'this place here'.*

        16 B: siia?
                 to here?

        17 L: a:
                 yes
                 Translation/explanation: *'a:' is shortened from 'jaa', 'jah', Estonian affirmation 'yes'.*
                 (Shows again the same pointing gesture.)

        18 B: ma   ei   tea   seda
                 I   don't   know   that

19 L: a:
        Translation/explanation: *Oh, now I remember that I had to go to Pangodi as well.*
        (Is knocking on her chest, then shakes her hand in the air and finally grasps with fingers the bridge of her nose.)
        (L is looking at her brother intensively.)
        Translation/explanation: *L is waiting for her brother's answer: she also wants to get to Pangodi, and her brother is the person who could take her there.*

24 L: ühaäe?
        Translation/explanation: *On which day are you driving to Pangodi?*
        'Ühaäe' is adapted from Estonian 'pühapäev' ('Sunday'), which for her marks whatever day of the week.
        (Points to her brother because this is a question to him.)

25 B: homme   võib-olla   lähen   jah
        tomorrow   maybe   going   yes

26 L: öhö?
        The interrogative.

27 B: aga   võib-olla   hoopis   tõlgin
        but   maybe   instead   I will translate
        B is working as a translator and a teacher.

28 L: aua?
        Translation/explanation: *What am I going to do?*
        'Aua' is shortened form of her name.
        (Points to herself.)

29 L: emme
        mummy
        Translation/explanation: *'emme' means 'mother' in Estonian child language.*
        (Shows the sign of the Estonian sign language BOAT (hands put together, interior sides touching each other, forming a shape of a bowl), moves the hands away from herself.)
        Translation/explanation: *Shall I go on a boat trip tomorrow?*

30 M: laevaga   sõitma   või
        boat   trip   or?

31 L: a:
        yes
        (Is nodding her head.)

32 M: nojah   memm   planeeris   seda   et
       well,   granny   was planning   this   that

33 B: he he

34 L: e: memmu
       ee-granny
       (Takes the receiver of the phone.)

35 M: et   kui   on   hea   ilm   siis
       that   if   it's good   weather   then

36 L: ee-memmu-memmu
       ee-granny-granny
       Translation/explanation: *Let's call to granny.*
       (Holds the receiver.)
       Translation/explanation: *L wants to call her grandmother.*

37 M: hakkad   memmele   helistama   või
       you start to grandmother   to call   or
       You start to call grandmother or?

38 L: a:
       yes
       Affirmation.

At the beginning of conversation, L had already tried to find out where Anna was, but she didn't get the expected response. In this fragment, she asks further questions to clarify whether Anna is at Pangodi. At the same time she is looking at B inquiringly as if checking whether her question was understood now; here we can notice self-rephrasing and indirect appeal for help with communication strategies (Dörnyei and Scott 2001; see also Goodwin 2003c). Her appeal for help has been understood—as we can see in utterances 16 and 18: B tries to help her by asking an adjusting question and then answering the original question. L replies to them using affirmation *a:* and a pointing gesture towards the floor; see Figure 6.3.

In the dialogue, two types of pointing gesture can also be observed. One of them (utterance 15) marks the space where L lives and has the referential meaning *here*. This is a typical indexical sign. The other (utterance 24) is a pointing towards her brother, as she wants him to respond to her. This gesture is shown in Figure 6.4 and it can also be interpreted as an indexical sign, but it is more than a mere pointing device: it is a turn-management signal (cf. Jokinen and Vanhasalo's stand-up gestures or Kendon's pragmatic gestures as discussed in Section 6.3.2.).

In other words, L knows how to assign turns to the interlocutors and is thus able to control the conversation so as to get the intended meaning across.

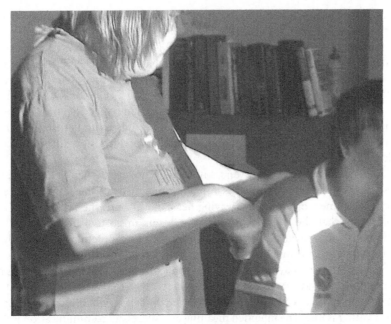

Fig. 6.3. Affirmation and pointing (towards the floor)

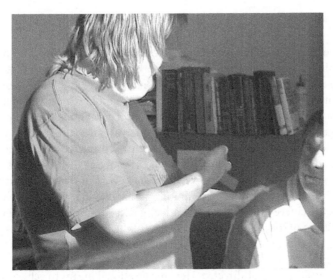

Fig. 6.4. Points to her brother because the question is to him (utterance 24)

Normally, such conversational fragments include two to three components: murmuring, L's own gesture, and/or a sign language sign.

L's utterance 19 is interesting from a psychological point of view. There L claims suddenly to recall that she is supposed to go on a visit to Pangodi too. The way she expresses this thought is very telling: her whole body, voice, and also physiognomy are involved. L knocks on her chest, which means *I*, after which she waves her hand in the air, the gesture meaning that she tries to recall something, and finally she grasps the bridge of her nose with her fingers. These actions are accompanied by the extended sound of *a:* which is modified on a large scale and expressively.

L understands B's verbal answers, but they do not satisfy her. She repeats her question *öhö?* (utterance 26), this time accompanied by the same gesture as described in line 7 of example 1, waving her hand towards the far direction, and also asking what she is going to do if she wants to go to Pangodi to see her grandmother and make a boat trip (utterances 28–9). Something seems to have been lost or is missing in the interpretation of L's intentions. However, as this is not the first time they are having a chat on this topic, the previous knowledge helps the interlocutors to understand each other. L wants to go to Pangodi for a boat trip, and the solution is to call the grandmother and ask if it is possible to visit Pangodi if the weather is fine. The intended meaning and successful communication is thus reached in context on the basis of the participants' common prior knowledge.

6.5   Discussion

The role of gestures in the communicative situation for creating and delivering the meaning is very important. Gestures may help the listeners to better distinguish the communicative functions of spoken utterances and 'noise' from meaningful words in speech. It is important to understand how non-verbal aspects of communication support the presentation of information and how the different knowledge sources are coordinated in interactions. In the case study of L we have reported some of the characteristic uses of gestures abstracted over the communicative situation. The results allow us to theorize about the basic laws of interaction as manifested through non-verbal signals. We can point out three aspects especially: the intentionality of communication and ability to use conversational strategies to achieve one's (communicative) goals; comprehension and cognitive representation of space and distances in spite of the minimal ability to express the concepts; and finally, the extension of semiosis into the social interaction with other interlocutors.

L's conversation is goal-directed. Her conversational means to achieve her goals is complex and requires quite remarkable cognitive processes. In fact, we can observe that in her communicative strategies she is able to construct and present abstract signification. For instance, she asks questions primarily in order to steer the conversation in the direction favourable to her. L also understands that people around her communicate in another way than that which is possible for her. She comprehends that they use more precise vocal concepts in their communication, and that it would be easier for the others to understand her if her gestures were translated into spoken words as well. She can signal in order to get her gestures translated into words by the surrounding people and also to give feedback as to whether the translation was successful or not. The feedback mechanism functions as a control mechanism for L, enabling her to surmise if the conversation partner has understood her intention. In other words, she is able to decide if the translator did the interpretation correctly, that is, to assesment whether the verbal symbolic presentation corresponds to her message.

The manifestations of space perception and means for eliciting the respective perceptual signification are less clear in L's case. She expresses spatial meaning with two different types of gesture: gesture moves and gestures of sign language. However, she produces considerably more languid and generalized sign language gestures than the deaf—observing her gives an impression of her being too lazy to move. Her most frequent gestures to indicate space can be described under the collective names *here* and *there*. She determines distances ('that there' or 'this here') with a gesture in the forward direction, but the precise meaning is created in the communicative situation and context. Although the semantic fields of these signs are broad, L is able to impart signification with hand gestures in communication situations, and it is possible to claim that she has gestures which carry spatial meaning ('this here', 'that there'); that they exist despite the severity of her disability and are used for constructing meaning. The same applies to her interrogative word, which is just a vocal fragment. L does not deliver speech beyond the vocalization of some concepts important to her, with or without labial sounds, but her feedback on the interlocutor's success in translating her intentions into words indicates that she understands the speech locution which is mainly arbitrary and symbolic. Without further studies it is difficult to hypothesize how language is actually presented in L's perceptions. However, we can say that her language comprehension area in the brain is obviously under control, although her ability to impart speech is missing (as is diagnosed in dysphasia).

At this point we need to consider the relation between human cognition and brain activity. Damasio (1994, 1999) discusses how human cognition is embedded in the body and created by experiencing the world through neural activity in the brain. This conforms to contemporary neuro-cognitive investigations into the neural infrastructure of cognitive processes (Rizzolatti and Arbib 1998), and it also supports linguistic views about how symbols that human beings construct emerge from forms of experience that have a crucial embodied component (Johnson 1987; Lakoff and Johnson 1999). For example, the universal experience of bodies situated within a gravitational field leads in all languages and cultures to a range of metaphors that contrast high and low, or up and down (e.g. the symbols used to describe social hierarchies). However, much of the analysis of embodiment focuses largely or entirely on the experience of an isolated individual, and as we have pointed out earlier, meaning is created and maintained in interaction with the environment and the other interlocutors: this plays a crucial role in the ways in which our brains shape cognition and consciousness.

In a similar manner, Goodwin (2003a, 2003b) has explained how meaning is built within situated human interaction. Human bodies, and the actions they are visibly performing, are situated within a consequential setting, and the positioning, actions, and orientation of the body in the environment are crucial elements for participants to understand what is happening, and to build meaning together. In his studies of the aphasic patient Chil, Goodwin notices how Chil's exercises to build meaning and action are not lodged within his body alone, but instead within a unit that includes his interlocutors, the sequential environment, and a semiotically structured material setting. According to Goodwin, the ability to constitute meaning must thus be examined in the context of other bodies and social processes rather than through examinations of linguistic output alone.

This seems an appropriate description of L's communication too. When it comes to her expressing meaning and intentions, it has already been mentioned how she uses the interlocutors' verbal ability to translate her own meanings into words. L's mother is her principal intermediary with the world, her 'language extension', in the same way as Chil's wife was the interpreter of his linguistic expressions. When characterizing the communicative landscapes of Chil, Goodwin (2003b) uses the concept of 'semiotic field', referring to the large meaning potential from which the participants build contextually relevant meaning and action in concert with each other.

6.6 Conclusion

At the beginning of our chapter we posed three questions that we focused on in our case study of L's communicative behaviour. We have shown that meaning is created in communicative situations via interaction, and it is built together with other interlocutors. Signification is imparted not only by spoken words, but by gestures and body movements, and it is understood as a result of an interactive process.

When thinking of Peirce's classification of signs and especially Lotman's interpretation of them (see Section 2), we can note that embodied cognition and interactive manipulation of symbolic structures are not so far apart as it would first seem. Peirce has described mental representations as a kind of mental translation in which the perception of something (an object or a sign) translates the perceived thing into a mental representation of the interpretant (see Osimo 2002: a convincing presentation of Peirce's standpoints on translation). Every following perception–translation–interpretation is thus a re-cognition, a new interpretation and clarification of the mental representation. If we consider this in the context of interaction and embodied cognition, we can express the same thought by saying that each communicative exchange between interlocutors affects the existing mental representations as a means of providing signification and, as regards neural activity, either reinforces or weakens the connections that encode the representation in the brain.

We postulate concepts as embodied signification, but as has been noted, meaning evolves dynamically: it is created in the communicative situation. The semiotic process is thus basically the construction of meaning in communicative contexts, and signification emerges from our relations and interactions with the environment and other people. The inclusion of the communicative situation in the analysis of semiosis allows us to study human language in a larger context: we do not focus only on how spoken language is constructed via mutual participation in interactions, but also on how participants bring forward intricate information through gestures and body postures. The expansion of collaboration and signification to this kind of reciprocal joint activity can be clearly seen in L's case.

To the best of our knowledge, our study is one of the first investigations concerning communicative behaviour of people with Patau syndrome (see too Rummo and Tenjes 2011). Hence, our research provides an important contribution to explaining the communicative capability of people with this diagnosis, and it also supports Goodwin's standpoint in creating a framework in which we can investigate 'the language and the meaning-making practices of speakers suffering from language impairment because of damage to the brain' (Goodwin 2003a: 17). Simultaneously, as a case study, it also expands our understanding of how meaning is constructed in human interaction and especially, how gestures are used as a communicative modality of language in general.

APPENDIX

Marks of semi-phonetic transcription

?	Rising intonation
[	Beginning of an overlap
]	End of an overlap
:	Stretched sounds (the colon is marked after the sound)
Capitalization	loud voice, e.g. AA
he he	laughter

7

Describing Adjacency Along the Lateral Axis: the Complementary Roles of Speech and Gesture

MARK TUTTON

7.1 Introduction

Lateral (left/right) adjacency and lateral direction are two spatial concerns which are complementary in nature. After all, if an object is *next to* another one, it follows that it is located in a certain direction away from it.[1] In situations where speakers communicate the adjacency of one object to another, the direction of the object being located (the 'Figure', following Talmy 2000) relative to the reference object (the 'Ground', ibid.) may also be salient: this is especially true if the speaker's addressee must subsequently locate the Figure. The present chapter is an analysis of how native speakers of (Australian) English encode lateral adjacency in spatial discourse, and whether such encoding is typically accompanied by the expression of left/right directional information. It understands utterances as a coalition of speech and gesture units (Kendon 2004), thereby inviting the possibility that gestures, as well as speech, express locative semantic information. Following this approach to locative utterances, it seems feasible that when speakers encode direction-neutral adjacency in a preposition such as *next to*, directional information may nevertheless be expressed by co-speech gesture. It needs to be emphasized that the spatial descriptions investigated here concern a medium-scale, internal space (a lounge room). Results cannot be generalized to apply to all spatial contexts, because the use of spatial language shifts depending on the scale of space under consideration (Lautenschütz et al. 2007). The aim of this chapter is to show that speakers express locative information multimodally and that co-speech gestures provide us with crucial insight into how speakers conceptualize spatial relationships. Such insight cannot be obtained through the analysis of speech alone: that is, co-speech gestures are key to unlocking the window into conceptual space.

---

[1] Direction is contingent upon the viewpoint and perspective adopted by a speaker. These two concerns will be addressed in what follows.

7.2   Why Study Locative Semantics and Gesture?

Before focusing on the reasons why gestures should be considered when studying oral spatial language, the term *gesture*, as it is used in this study, needs to be defined. The gestures investigated in this chapter are co-speech gestures—that is, they are produced concurrently with speech. These gestures lack the lexical qualities of so-called 'quotable gestures' (Kendon 1994)—for instance, the 'ok' sign—which can be used without speech. Co-speech gestures are tied to the speech which they accompany and are understood as 'symbolic movements related to the speaker's expressive intention' (Gullberg et al. 2008: 204). As far as the spatial domain is concerned, communicating the location of objects is a recurrent and important task in everyday life. Existing studies have shed light on this spatial sub-domain by identifying the semantic features of locative events which are selected for lexicalization (i.e. Figure, Path and Ground, according to Talmy 2000) as well as the grammatical categories used to encode locative semantics (see, for example, Lemmens 2005 for work on locative verbs cross-linguistically). While this type of lexical and grammatical approach has led to a better understanding of how languages encode static location, it is incomplete once language is considered within the context of face-to-face interaction: this is because speakers use co-speech gestures, in addition to language, to communicate information (Kendon 1988, 1994, 2004). The information expressed in co-speech gestures is semantically and pragmatically tied to that encoded in the co-occurring speech (Kendon 2004; McNeill 1992, 2005), thereby suggesting that utterances should be considered in terms of both speech and gesture units (Kendon 2004). In addition to operating on the communicative level, gestures also serve cognitive functions (McNeill 1992). As far as spatial discourse is concerned, it has been argued that gestures fulfil two roles: they can assist spatial cognition, while also providing a modality for communicating spatial information which may or may not be present in the co-occurring speech (Emmorey and Casey 2001). Previous studies have identified different ways in which speakers use gestures to express unlexicalized spatial information. Beattie and Shovelton (2006), for instance, have shown how gestures provide important information about object size, while McNeill (2000) has shown that gestures can express manner of motion in languages whose motion encoding strategies typically omit such detail. This suggests that gestures can be used to express spatial information which is different—yet complementary—to that encoded in speech. With these points in mind, the study of how speakers conceptualize and communicate locative relationships justifiably warrants the consideration of both speech and gesture.

7.3   Static Locative Relationships and the Lateral Axis

Static locative relationships concern the fixed location of an entity, or group of entities, at a point in space. The specification of location involves situating the object(s) being located (the 'Figure', following Talmy 2000) relative to one or more reference objects (the 'Ground', ibid.). The locative semantics of such relationships are typically encoded by spatial prepositions in English, with the Figure assuming the role of subject and the Ground that of object (Vandeloise 1986: 20). A basic locative expression which linguistically realizes both Figure and Ground is as follows:

(1)   The cat is *next to* the sofa

In this sentence the Figure is the *cat*, while the *sofa* fulfils the semantic role of Ground. The nature of the spatial relationship which holds between the two entities is encoded by the preposition *next to*. *Next to* encodes the adjacency of the Figure to the Ground, and in doing so relates to the topological concept of proximity. The locative relationship presented in this example may be conceptualized differently, with focus being placed on direction instead of adjacency. This leads to a linguistic expression like the following:

(2)   The cat is *to the left of* the sofa

To the left of encodes directional information and therefore belongs to the sub-category of *projective* prepositions (Herskovits 1986; Hörberg 2006). Hence, there are different ways in which the same locative relationship may be conceptualized for linguistic encoding: prepositional expressions such as *next to* and *beside* encode adjacency, whereas others, such as *to the left of*, encode direction. While *to the right of* and *to the left of* may be used when the Figure is adjacent to the Ground, any reading of adjacency is the result of pragmatic inference rather than lexical encoding. It is therefore possible to separate the direction encoded by these prepositions from the concept of adjacency, as in the example below:

(3)   Joanne is the fourth person *to the left of* the president.

In this example, *to the left of* is used to encode directional information without any suggestion of Figure/Ground adjacency. In fact, the Figure is located at some remove from the Ground—four people away.

The concepts of lateral adjacency and direction are conflated in the English prepositional expression *on the right/left of* (Herskovits 1986). This is shown in the following example:

(4)   Joanne is on the left of the president/on the president's left.

Yet the use of *on the right/left of* to encode Figure and Ground adjacency is restricted. An analysis of its use with different Figure and Ground objects reveals that as soon as the Ground can be conceptualized as a supporting surface for the Figure, a reading of support also becomes available. In terms of grammatical form, therefore, two combinations compete for expression: the adjacency reading encoded by *on the left* + *of*, and the reading of support encoded by *on* + *the left* + *of*.

(5)   The ball is on the right of the sofa.

(6)   The plant is on the right of the counter.

Without further contextual information, the interpretation of example 5 is that the ball is on the right-hand surface of the sofa, rather than being located adjacent to it. The same reading of Figure/Ground contiguity also emerges in example 6. However, once the Ground is no longer conceptualized as a supporting surface for the Figure, the reading of adjacency emerges:

(7)   The printer is on the right of the computer.

(8)   The driveway is on the right of the house.

In some cases both interpretations of adjacency and support are valid, leaving it up to context to direct the listener to the more appropriate reading. A sentence such as the following allows this double reading:

(9)   The lamp is on the right of the table.

The restrictions underpinning the use of *on the right/left* + *of* mean that the concepts of LATERAL ADJACENCY and DIRECTION are conflated with some difficulty in English. This problem of encoding can be avoided altogether by simply attending to each concept individually in locative utterances, as the following example shows:

(10)   The lamp is next to the table, to/on the right.

7.4   Direction and the Lateral Axis

While the prepositions *next to* and *beside* suggest that the concept of ADJACENCY can effectively be separated from that of DIRECTION, the two concepts are nevertheless natural partners. This is because if one object is adjacent to another, it follows that it is located in a certain direction away from it. The communication of directional information—whether this be in speech or gesture—entails referencing spatial axes or 'dimensions' (Lyons 1977). Three such axes exist: the vertical 'up/down' axis, the frontal 'forward/back' axis, and the lateral 'left/right' axis. Of these three axes, two are oriented horizontally (the 'lateral' and 'frontal' axes), while the other (the 'vertical' axis) is oriented vertically. Each axis extends out in two different directions while maintaining its horizontal or vertical orientation: therefore, the frontal axis runs forwards and backwards in a straight line, while the lateral axis runs both left and right. Herskovits (1986: 199) points out that it is more felicitous to parse each axis into these directionally different halves: this leads to the division of the lateral axis into the unidirectional *right* and *left* axes, the frontal axis into the *front* and *back* axes, and the vertical axis into the *up* and *down* axes. While such a fine-grained axial division certainly allows for directional precision, this type of breakdown is not critical as far as the present investigation is concerned. The objective of this chapter is to understand how lateral adjacency and direction—whether this be right or left—is expressed. As such, I will simply retain the use of the term 'lateral axis' in what follows.

The lateral axis is the only spatial axis for which *next to* is recurrently used,[2] thereby making it an ideal choice for understanding when and why speakers foreground adjacency (*next to*), as opposed to direction (*to the right/left of*). Nevertheless, even when *next to* is used to encode a locative relationship, it is feasible that directional information is present in gesture: this is because, as outlined earlier, speech and gesture can communicate different, complementary pieces of spatial information. Direction is also a principal way in which location is expressed (Landau and Jackendoff 1993, and Vorwerg, in Ashley and Carlson 2007). In line with this, work by Ashley and Carlson (2007) shows that speakers attend to directional information when processing spatial terms such as *near* and *far*. In their experiment, participants were asked to respond 'yes' or 'no' to whether spatial expressions of the type 'X is near Y' accurately described the spatial relationship between two letters X and Y, which were visually represented on a screen in front of them. Reaction times were faster when the direction of the letters relative to each other was maintained from the first ('prime') trial to the second ('probe') trial, than they were when this direction changed. The authors concluded that speakers must have mentally encoded direction in addition to distance, otherwise reaction times would not have differed significantly between conditions. With this conclusion in mind, it seems feasible that when speakers use *next to*—a preposition which also requires an appreciation of the distance between Figure and Ground objects[3]—they may also attend to directional information. One way of exploring this possibility is by examining the locative utterances produced by speakers describing relationships of adjacency along the lateral axis. Taking into account both speech and gesture, there are several ways in which speakers may express both adjacency and direction. Firstly, both concepts may be lexically encoded, resulting in locative predicates of the type '*next to* the door, *to the right*'. Another possibility is that direction will not be lexically encoded, but will be revealed in gesture instead. The range of ways in which

---

[2] In the task from which data in this chapter are drawn, only one use of *next to* occurs with a gesture communicating direction along the frontal axis. This suggests that *next to* is almost exclusively reserved for establishing location along the lateral axis—at least as far as the locative relationships described for this study are concerned.

[3] For example, under normal observational conditions a fork cannot be said to be *next to* a plate if the two objects are a metre apart on a table: this is because distance plays a role in the acceptable use of the preposition. This acceptability is also contingent on the nature of the objects assuming the Figure and Ground roles. Therefore, while a metre may be too great a distance to describe a fork as being *next to* a plate, it would be a perfectly acceptable distance if I was talking about two boats docked beside each other in a mooring.

speakers may express lateral adjacency and lateral direction in speech and in gesture is as follows:

1) Lexically encoding both adjacency and direction. There are two ways in which this may occur:
   - through the use of a prepositional form which simultaneously encodes both adjacency and direction; i.e. *on the right/left of* or the variants *on his/her/its left*;
   - through the combination of a direction-neutral preposition of adjacency with a directional expression, i.e. *next to* the table, *to the right*.
2) Lexically encoding adjacency and expressing lateral direction in gesture, i.e. 'the dog is *next to* the table' (with a co-speech gesture indicating direction to the left).
3) Lexically encoding lateral adjacency and direction, while also expressing direction in gesture, i.e. 'the dog is *next to* the table, *to the left*' (with a co-speech gesture indicating direction to the left).

The further possibility of expressing adjacency in gesture has not been noted above. This is because it is difficult to accurately determine whether a gesture expresses adjacency or not. In certain examples the gestural expression of adjacency may be inferred, such as when the gesture trajectory is a minimal movement to the right or to the left of the location associated with a Ground object. Such a movement amounts to an indication of proximity, and the reading of adjacency is pragmatically inferable. However, in many cases there is room for ambiguity, and there can be no reliable measure to judge whether the distance covered by the gesture reflects an expression of adjacency or not. This is in contrast to left/right direction, which can be clearly depicted by a speaker gesturing to their left or to their right. The upshot of this is that gestures can more easily be assessed for the expression of lateral direction than they can for adjacency. In the interest of avoiding an inevitably weak set of criteria by which a gesture may be judged to express adjacency, the analysis which follows will concentrate on the gestural expression of direction.

In order to examine whether speakers express lateral direction in speech or gesture when describing lateral adjacency, a set of data was obtained. These data are drawn from a larger study which examines how speakers of (Australian) English describe static, locative relationships in everyday spatial scenes. As far as the present chapter is concerned, the data sought were utterances in which prepositional encoders of adjacency, such as *next to*, were used. In addition, all other utterances which recruited spatial prepositions to describe lateral adjacency were extracted: this was to identify syntactic conditions in which speakers could have used *next to* and its synonym *beside*, but chose not to. By doing this, insight into whether, and how, speakers use other spatial prepositions to describe lateral adjacency may be obtained.

7.5 **Method**

7.5.1 Subjects

Data are drawn from ten speakers—six female and four male—all of whom are native speakers of (Australian) English. Participants were all students at the University of New South Wales, Sydney, at the time of the experiment (December 2006). They were not informed that gestures were a subject of investigation prior to the experiment, and all received a small payment for their participation.

7.5.2 Stimulus

The visual stimulus for the data presented here is a picture of a living room (see Figure 7.1). This was one of two pictures described by participants for this research project, with half the participants describing this picture first, and the other half beginning with their description of the second picture (a street scene). The pictures were drawn by an Honours (4th) year university student in fine arts,[4] following specifications by the researcher as to the objects depicted in the scene as well as to their placement. The idea of the living room scene was to understand how speakers

FIG. 7.1. Stimulus picture

---

[4] Drawings by Peta Dzubiel.

describe the location of familiar objects in an everyday, lived-in space. The laminated picture was placed on a music stand slightly in front and to the left of the speaker (who was seated), and a list of fourteen items was attached next to the picture on the music stand.

7.5.3   Procedure

Participants were placed into male–female pairs, with one person being assigned the role of 'Describer' and the other the role of 'Receiver'. The two participants, who did not know each other prior to the experiment, were seated opposite each other. A brief warm-up exercise followed in which participants were given two questions to ask each other. These questions were used to relax participants and the information sought was inconsequential to the locative description task. The researcher then issued the Describer and the Receiver with their respective copies of the instructions, before reading both aloud. The Describers was told that they had five minutes to describe the picture to the Receiver, and had to focus on the location of the fourteen objects on the list next to the picture. The order of the objects on the list was determined randomly in Excel and was different for every Describer so as to cancel out any order effects. The Receiver was also given a copy of the list to hold and was not allowed to interrupt the Describer during their description. Describers were told to provide enough detail about the picture for Receivers to be able to identify it from four alternate versions which would be presented to them: the three incorrect versions would each have just one of the fourteen items in the wrong place. This meant that location had to be clearly specified.

Following the description, the Receiver was allowed five minutes to ask the Describer any questions they had about the picture. Data from this second, interactive half of the experiment have not been used in the present study for the following two reasons:

1) The questions asked by the Receiver largely determine the information provided by the Describer. This means that the Describers' utterances are more geared to responding to the Receivers' needs than they are to showing how the former actually conceptualize lateral locative relationships.
2) One of the aims of this study is to understand whether and to what extent, speakers partner the concept of lateral adjacency with that of lateral direction. This partnership cannot be explored in the second half of the experiment because Receivers can ask Describers to focus on one of these concerns and not the other (e.g. 'so the dog is to the left of the table?'). This means that an accurate assessment of whether Describers habitually partner the two concepts cannot be made.

The experiment was filmed in a studio at the University of New South Wales. Two cameras were used, one filming the Describer, the other the Receiver. The experimental set-up is represented diagrammatically as follows:

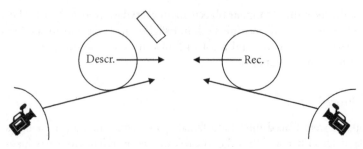

FIG. 7.2. Experimental set-up

7.5.4   Coding of speech and gesture

All descriptions were transcribed in video-annotation software (Elan). Speech was transcribed verbatim and gestures were identified in terms of the stroke phase.[5] Only locative utterances in which one of the fourteen objects appeared as either Figure or Ground were coded. A locative utterance was defined as any utterance which communicates the location of an object or group of objects, with no restrictions as to obligatory constituents (for example, verbs or spatial prepositions). This was to access as broad a range of locative utterances as possible, while also recognizing that the expression of location can be achieved with a minimum of lexical expenditure: for example, pointing to a location in gesture space associated with an object and naming it.

The following brief transcription code will be observed in the presentation of forthcoming examples:

underline	an underlined word or part thereof indicates co-occurrence with a gesture stroke
..	two dots represent pauses of up to three seconds
next to	italic is used to highlight salient spatial units

The data were searched for any use of adjacency-encoding prepositions, such as *next to* and *beside*. The utterances in which these prepositions were used were then examined for any further lateral locative information: this entailed attending to both speech and gesture. An example of an utterance which lexicalizes a locative relationship with *next to* before providing further lexical locative specification is the following:

(11)   *next to* the mirror *to the left* is a portrait of a boy it looks like   (EngDesc1)

---

[5] A stroke is 'the meaningful part of the gestural movement where the spatial excursion of the limb reaches its apex' (Gullberg et al. 2008: 213).

TABLE 7.1. *Types of utterances expressing adjacency along a lateral axis with a preposition, and frequency*

Utterance type	Frequency
a. *next to*[1]	10
b. *next to* + directional gesture	23
c. *next to* + lexicalized left/right direction[2]	7
d. *next to* + lexicalized left/right direction[3] + directional gesture	8
e. *beside* + directional gesture	1
SUBTOTAL *next to/beside*	49
f. *to the right/left of*	2
g. *to the right/left of*[4] + directional gesture	8
h. *to his/her right* + directional gesture	1
i. *on his/her right* + directional gesture	1
SUBTOTAL *left/right*	12
TOTAL	61

[1] This total includes two utterances which contained a gesture which was ambiguous as to whether directional information was expressed or not. Given this ambiguity, and for the sake of conservatism, these two gestures were not considered to express directional information.
[2] Lexicalized as *to the right/left* and *on the right/left*.
[3] Directional units included *to your left, to the right/left of, left of [...] on its left, on the right*. Also two statements of directional motion, i.e. *moving left*.
[4] Includes one example of *to your left of*.

The data were also searched for any other prepositional expressions used to describe relationships of lateral adjacency. A complete list of these is detailed in Table 7.1.

As far as gestures were concerned, locative utterances as a whole needed to be examined: this is because direction-expressing gestures (hereafter *directional gestures*) need not align with the spatial linguistic unit. Gestures were considered to express left or right direction when there was a clear, voluntary movement of the speaker's hand or arm to the right or left. Such right/left movement may be executed in either the preparation phase or the stroke phase of a gesture, meaning that an examination of both gesture phases was required.

7.5.5 Viewpoint and perspective

The gestural depiction of direction necessitates speakers adopting both a viewpoint and a perspective. There are two types of viewpoint: speaker viewpoint and addressee viewpoint (Perniss 2007). A speaker viewpoint is when a speaker's gestural representation reflects a spatial layout as the speaker sees it. In contrast, an addressee viewpoint is when a speaker's gestural representation reflects a spatial layout as the addressee would see it: this entails a 180-degree rotation from the speaker's viewpoint. Adopting an addressee viewpoint is difficult as far as left/right direction is concerned, because it means that the speaker has to express direction according to the addressee's right and left—which is the opposite to their own. Given such complexity, it is not surprising that all of the examples which emerged from the data use a speaker viewpoint.

Perspective is a separate concern from viewpoint. McNeill (1992) describes two types of perspective: observer perspective and character perspective. Observer perspective involves the speaker remaining external to the visually depicted scene and using their hands to represent visually depicted objects or manipulations on these objects. In contrast, character perspective involves the speaker assuming the role of an entity in the visual stimulus. In this case, the speaker's body becomes the character's body, meaning that the speaker's hands are used as though they are the character's hands. As far as the present experiment is concerned, all examples extracted from the data used observer perspective.

The common use of speaker viewpoint and observer perspective across the utterances results in a homogeneity which allows for easier conclusions to be drawn from the analysis.

7.6   Results

Table 7.1 reveals the nine different ways in which speakers use prepositional forms to describe relationships of lateral adjacency.

To his/her right and *on his/her right* (utterance types 'h' and 'i' in Table 7.1) were included in the analysis, even though they are complete prepositional phrases rather than individual prepositional units. This is because speakers could have feasibly used *next to* and *beside* in their place—for example, *next to* (him) as opposed to *on his right*. The crucial factor was thus identifying prepositions or prepositional expressions which could have been replaced by a direction-neutral preposition of adjacency.

Directional information which did not pertain to the Figure/Ground objects of the relationship encoded by *next to/beside* was not included. Therefore, directional expressions such as *on the left* in the following utterance were not considered:

(12)   so next to the door *on your left* it starts with a photo   (EngDesc10)

This sentence was classified simply as a use of *next to*, because *on your left* does not refine the relationship of adjacency encoded by *next to*. Rather, *on your left* serves to establish a starting point for the speaker's analysis.

Utterances were only counted in one category. Therefore, an utterance like the following, which begins with *left of* but finishes as an expression which lexically encodes both *next to* and left/right direction (again), was just counted in the category '*next to* + lexicalized left/right direction':

(13) *left of* the fireplace.. there's a cat.. sitting next to the fireplace *just on its left*
(EngDesc10)

7.6.1 Direction-neutral prepositions: the use of *next to* and *beside*

There are ten examples of speakers simply using *next to* to encode locative relationships without directional specification being provided in speech or in gesture (utterance type 'a', Table 7.1). Overwhelmingly however, when speakers did use *next to*, they also provided directional information in either speech, gesture, or in both modalities. The most frequent way in which this occurred was by recruiting *next to* and expressing direction in gesture alone (utterance type 'b', Table 7.1): this '*next to* + directional gesture' combination accounted for twenty-three of the sixty-one examples found, and is more than twice as frequent as the second most common way of encoding lateral adjacency. An example of this *next to* + directional gesture combination is illustrated in Figure 7.3.

(14) 'and next to the ball is a bone'   (EngDesc9)

Fig. 7.3 is a drawing depicting the beginning, middle, and end points of the gesture stroke phase associated with example (14). The lexical units which co-occur with

Fɪɢ. 7.3. Expressing lateral direction in gesture alone

the stroke are underlined in the locative expression. The speaker executes this directional gesture with the left hand, which is extended flat with the palm facing forward and slightly down. The right hand is in a post-stroke hold and bears a very similar form to the left hand: it represents the Ground object, *bone*. This example shows how gesture can be used to express directional information which is not co-present in the linguistic utterance. It also indicates how gestures can target directional information independently of adjacency. This gesture's trajectory results in a considerable distance between the two hands, as evidenced by their respective locations at the end of the gesture stroke (see Figure 7.3): the distance communicated in gesture here is not commensurate with the distance between the ball and the bone in the stimulus picture (cf. Figure 7.1). It therefore follows that the motivation of this gesture is not to express adjacency. Rather, the speaker uses the preposition *next to* to encode this information, while foregrounding the unlexicalized directional information in gesture. Gestures can thus reveal that speakers attend to directional information when lexically encoding adjacency. The gestural presentation of this information complements the lexical expression of adjacency, thereby enabling a semantically rich, yet economical, locative predicate.

Overall, *next to* was used in forty-eight of the sixty-one examples encoding adjacency along the lateral axis. In stark contrast to this, only one example of *beside* was noted and no examples of *by* were found. Therefore, *next to* and *beside* were used in a total of forty-nine locative utterances, meaning that speech and gesture could each have been used on forty-nine occasions to express directional information which was complementary to these adjacency-encoding prepositions. Gestures expressed such information on thirty-two of these forty-nine occasions: this includes instances when gesture alone was used, and instances in which direction was expressed in both speech and gesture. Speech, on the other hand, was used on fifteen occasions: this is again inclusive of instances when speech alone encoded direction, as well as instances in which both speech and gesture were used. These results are reflected in Table 7.2 below. The columns 'utt. type' in this table refer to utterance types (cf. Table 7.1) included in the calculation of frequencies.

Overall, when speakers recruit *next to* and *beside*, directional information is habitually present in the utterance—be this in speech, gesture, or in both modalities. Of the forty-nine utterances which encoded lateral adjacency with *next to* and *beside* (utterance types 'a'–'e'), thirty-nine of these also included

TABLE 7.2. *The use of speech and gesture to express directional information with* next to *and* beside

next to/beside: condition	Gesture	utt. type	Speech	utt. type
direction expressed	32	b, e, f	15	d, e
direction not expressed	17	a, d	34	a, b, f
Total	49	a, b, d, e, f	49	a, b, d, e, f

speech and/or gesture units which expressed left or right direction: this is represented in Figure 7.4. This indicates that speakers concurrently attend to adjacency and direction when encoding relationships of lateral adjacency. Moreover, it builds on the results obtained by Ashley and Carlson (2007) by showing an important correlation between the distance-related concern of adjacency and the processing of directional information. A limitation of the present work is the relatively small number of speakers (ten) and hence the amount of data available: the current findings might therefore be further exploited in work which deals with a larger sample size.

Of the thirty-nine utterances which expressed direction in addition to using *next to* and *beside*, twenty-four of these detailed this directional information in gesture alone. This compares to seven which did so in speech alone, and eight which recruited both speech and gesture units (see Figure 7.5). Therefore, when

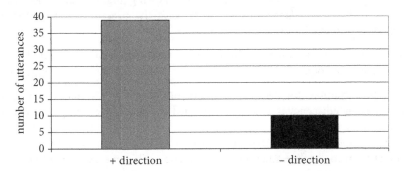

FIG. 7.4. The use of *next to* and *beside* with and without directional information in the locative utterance

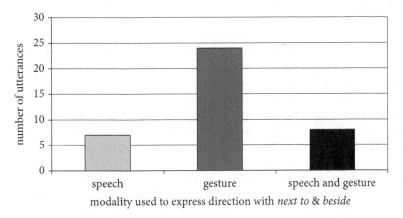

FIG. 7.5. The expression of directional information across speech and gesture when using *next to* and *beside*

speakers recruit just one modality to express directional information alongside *next to* and *beside*, gesture (twenty-four examples) is favoured over speech (seven examples). Naturally, given the small quantity of data, a certain caution needs to be applied to this finding.

7.6.2   The use of direction-encoding prepositional forms

In addition to using direction-neutral prepositions to describe relationships of locative adjacency, speakers also employed direction-encoding prepositional expressions. These expressions, which mostly included examples of *to the right/left of*, were nevertheless much less frequent in the data. Although *to the right/left of* encodes direction as opposed to adjacency, its occurrence in the data shows that speakers sometimes allow the relationship of adjacency to be pragmatically inferred. An example of this is the following linguistic utterance (which begins with *on the floor* and ends with *book*; the preceding speech segment provides contextual backdrop).

(15)   [there's a sofa.. someone sitting on it..] on the floor *to the right of* the sofa.. there's a book   (EngDesc10)

In this example the Describer singles out direction as the salient spatial information; adjacency is lexically unencoded but nevertheless open to pragmatic inference by the Receiver.

Only one example occurred in the data of a Describer using a single prepositional form to conflate adjacency and direction. This one example of *on his/her left* suggests that speakers do not habitually conflate the two types of information in a single spatial unit. This is a little surprising, considering the economy such a form allows. Nevertheless, there are restrictions on the use of *on the right/left of* (and hence on its variants, such as *on his/her left*) when used to concurrently encode adjacency and direction (see Section 7.3). Such restrictions very likely impede the productive use of such forms. Speakers therefore recurrently express adjacency and direction in separate expressive units, and this is realized by the simultaneous recruitment of speech and gesture units: speech encodes adjacency, while gesture expresses direction.

Of the sixty-one utterances describing relationships of lateral adjacency, fifty-one express directional information (utterance types 'b'–'i' in Table 7.1). This shows that speakers recurrently attend to directional information when describing the location of one object adjacent to another on a lateral axis. As far as the experiment itself is concerned, it suggests that the provision of directional information, even when encoding adjacency, was a strategy used by Describers in the communication of location. Crucially, this information is expressed most often in gesture. The graph in Figure 7.6 shows how speech, gesture, and both speech and gesture were employed to express direction in these fifty-one utterances.

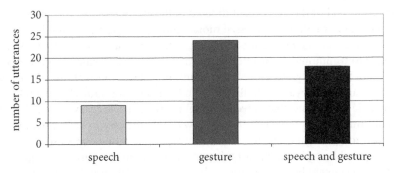

FIG. 7.6. Frequency of directional information in speech and gesture across all utterances expressing directional information

Directional information was two-and-a-half times more likely to be expressed in gesture alone than it was in speech alone: there are twenty-four examples of the former expressive condition as opposed to just nine of the latter. There were eighteen examples in which both modalities were used to express directional information. This means that the use of gesture alone was the most frequently observed way of expressing directional information, followed by the combined use of speech and gesture. Altogether, gesture is recruited to express lateral direction in forty-two of these fifty-one utterances, as opposed to speech, which encodes such information in twenty-seven utterances.

7.7   Discussion

7.7.1   The use of gesture to express unlexicalized lateral direction

The results show a clear tendency for participants to attend to directional information when lexically encoding adjacency. Of the forty-nine utterances which encode location with the direction-neutral prepositions *next to* and *beside*, thirty-nine of these also include left/right directional information—be this in speech, in gesture, or in both modalities. Another critical finding of the current study is that the most common way in which speakers describe relationships of lateral adjacency is by recruiting a prepositional encoder of adjacency and executing a directional gesture. Crucially, the directional information expressed by these gestures is not lexically encoded in the locative utterance. This result points to a communicative economy in the use of speech and gesture, such that speech encodes adjacency through *next to* or *beside*, while gesture concurrently expresses the unlexicalized left/right direction. It is important to remember that the communication of directional information was pivotal to this experimental task: both Describer and Receiver were aware that the four pictures which the Receiver would have to choose from at the end of the experiment differed in the location of just one object. Since directional information is expressed more frequently in gesture than it is in speech when *next to* and *beside* are used, the implication is that speakers intended their gestures to communicate directional information to their partner. If speakers were not aware that their gestures were communicating such information, and if—as it has been argued above—such directional information was crucial to the task, it is reasonable to assume that direction might have been lexically encoded in the locative utterance as well. This, however, was only the case in eight utterances, as opposed to the twenty-four utterances in which gesture alone was used.

One possible argument against this purportedly communicative use of gesture is that speakers might be using gesture to highlight the relationship of adjacency, with the expression of direction being a corollary of this. But if this were the case, it should not matter if speakers gesture to the right or the left: however, in all examples, speakers gesture the correct directional information (from speaker viewpoint, observer perspective). This result aligns with research by McCullough (2005), in which speakers' gestures were shown to correctly reproduce lateral information pertaining to object location as well as to motion event paths. McCullough reports that lateral directional information was correctly reproduced in 90 per cent of cases: this shows that speakers not only attended to left/right directional information, but also that such information was important enough to be faithfully reported. In another cartoon-based study, Kita and Özyürek (2003) also report that speakers regularly express the lateral direction of motion events in gesture alone—and do so correctly.

The results of the present study show that gestures allow us to better understand how speakers conceptualize certain types of static locative relationships. The strategy of recruiting *next to* and executing a directional gesture suggests the interconnectivity of ADJACENCY and DIRECTION in the conceptualization of static locative relationships. This finding builds on the results reported in Ashley and Carlson (2007), in which speakers were found to attend to both direction and distance information when processing the spatial terms *near* and *far*.

7.7.2   When speakers express left/right direction in both speech and gesture

There is one result from this study which is ostensibly puzzling. This is the finding that of the twelve instances in which speakers use either *to the right/left of*, *on his/her right*, and *to his/her right*—all of which lexicalize lateral direction—in ten of these instances they also use a directional gesture. There are two possible explanations for this. The first of these is that lateral directional information is highly salient at the time of utterance production, and therefore achieves expression in both speech and gesture. The second possibility is that gesture is used to express lateral directional information because the lateral axis is a problem area for spatial cognition and lexical encoding in English. Both of these possibilities are explored in greater depth below, beginning with the second of the two explanations.

From a developmental perspective, the lateral axis is the most difficult spatial axis for children to acquire (Piaget and Inhelder, in Levinson 2003a). The use of the terms *left* and *right* to designate spatial relationships within a relative frame of reference occurs late in childhood, around the ages of eleven and twelve (Levinson 2003a: 46). Even later in life, adults confuse the left/right distinction (ibid.: 207). Fillmore considers that recognizing left from right is difficult because there are no easier concepts which can explain these two notions (Fillmore, in Herskovits 1986: 158). This suggests that the left/right distinction is a problem area of spatial cognition, thereby opening up the possibility that gesture plays a role in helping us to demarcate our left from our right. If this is the case, then the gestural depiction of lateral direction concurrently with *to the right/left of* may be automatically triggered by our habitual use of gesture to differentiate the two halves of lateral direction.

Aside from possible cognitive difficulties in grasping the differences between left and right, there is a second, linguistically based reason for the intervention of gesture in the communication of lateral directional information. There is a notable deficiency in the number of lexical items available in English to encode direction along the lateral axis, as opposed to along the frontal or vertical axes. The clearest example of this is that there is no lexical verb in English which encodes left or right direction.[6] This starkly contrasts to the frontal and vertical axes, for which numerous lexical verbs encode directional information. A table with a sample list of direction-encoding verbs and other spatial linguistic units (adverbs and prepositions) for each of the three spatial axes is provided (Table 7.3).

TABLE 7.3. *Lexical units encoding a precise direction (i.e. up, down, forwards) for each spatial axis*

Axis	Lexical verbs	Spatial linguistic units
vertical	ascend, rise, arise, raise, escalate, sprout, mount, scale, (up)lift, increase, boost, skyrocket, soar, raise, descend, fall, lower, sink, dive, drop, decline, slump	high, up, above, over, low, down, below, beneath, under(neath)
frontal	advance, forward, further, progress, regress, reverse	in front (of), forward(s), ahead, onward(s), back, backwards, behind
lateral	NIL	all are combinations with right/left, i.e.to/on the left (of)to/on the right (of)

[6] This was an observation made by Daniele van de Vèlde during a paper given by the author at the SILEXA workshop, Université Lille 3, France, January 2008. I thank her for this most productive remark.

Whereas the basic list provided here includes twenty direction-encoding verbs for the vertical axis and six for the frontal axis, not a single one exists for the lateral axis. Moreover, the range of direction-encoding adverbs and prepositions for the lateral axis is severely restricted: the only ones which exist necessarily include the lexemes *left* or *right*, as no other word in English encodes either left or right direction. In contrast to this, the vertical axis has a rich range of lexical items which cover both directional extremities, while the frontal axis possesses a range which is smaller, yet far more substantial than that for the lateral axis. Given the lack of any lexical verb which encodes left/right direction, and taking into account that the only ways in which such information may be lexicalized requires the recruitment of the lexemes *left* and *right*, it is possible that English speakers have learned to use gesture as a means of overcoming this gap in the English lexicon. The habitual use of gesture for this purpose may therefore lead to a greater reliance on gesture as far as expressing LEFT and RIGHT are concerned—a reliance which reveals itself even when these concepts are lexically encoded.

There are two ways of determining the validity of this explanation. The first of these is to look at other languages which also have a poor range of lexical items encoding location along the lateral axis, and to see how speakers gesture when encoding the concepts LEFT and RIGHT. The second way is to assess how speakers in the current study use gesture when encoding location along the frontal and vertical axes. That is, do speakers use gesture to express the forward/back, up/down directional information which they concurrently encode in speech? Ongoing analysis of the data upon which the current study is based suggests that this is indeed the case. Consequently, the dual expression of left/right directional information in both speech and gesture does not appear to be a phenomenon which is restricted to the lateral axis. Therefore, the cross-modal expression of lateral directional information seems to be triggered by the salience of this information at the time of utterance production, as opposed to a gap in the English lexicon or cognitive difficulties associated with this axis. Nevertheless, a full investigation into how speakers gesture when lexically encoding direction along the frontal and vertical axes is required to substantiate this claim.

7.8 Conclusion

The present study has shown that the concepts of LATERAL ADJACENCY and LATERAL DIRECTION are far from being mutually exclusive. The results indicate that speakers recurrently attend to lateral directional information when lexically encoding adjacency: this provides insight not only into how speakers conceptualize lateral locative relationships, but also into how these relationships are communicated. Speakers most frequently express left and right directional information in gesture when using *next to*, and this directional information is not lexically encoded elsewhere in the utterance. Since the provision of directional information was pivotal to successfully describing the locations of objects in the stimulus picture, it is very likely that these gestures were intended to communicate directional information to addressees. These results show that speakers recurrently express different, complementary pieces of locative semantic information in speech and gesture: adjacency is encoded by the prepositional unit *next to*, while lexically unencoded directional information emerges in gesture. This coalition of speech and gesture reinforces Kendon's observation that the two modalities can together realize an 'economy of expression' (1988: 133).

Nevertheless, lateral directional information may emerge concurrently in both modalities. The cognitively difficult nature of the left/right distinction, along with the deficiency of lexical items encoding lateral direction in English, were both suggested as possible explanations for this phenomenon. A more likely reason, however, is that directional information is highly salient at the time of utterance production: this thereby triggers its expression in both speech and gesture.

The results presented in this chapter derive from descriptions of a particular type of space containing particular types of adjacency relationships. The proposed interconnectivity of lateral adjacency and direction reported here might be further explored in future experiments which examine lateral adjacency at different scales of space: for example, at small-scale space (such as expressing the locations of chess pieces on a chess board), and at large-scale space (such as directing a listener around a city centre).

8

Towards a Cognitive–Semiotic Typology of Motion Verbs

PER DURST-ANDERSEN, VIKTOR SMITH, and
OLE NEDERGAARD THOMSEN

8.1 Introduction

8.1.1 The cognitive semiotics of motion in reality, mind, and language

The present chapter argues that the lexico-grammar of spatial situations—not only dynamic movement, but also static location (cf. Talmy 1985, 2000)—cannot be understood except as an integral part of the semiotic triad of reality, mind (perception and conception), and language: language structures the mind's construal of motion in reality, and thus motion in language should be explained on the basis of the (Gestaltist) psychology of motion in *mind*. Accordingly, the tentative typology of motion verbs to be proposed in this chapter is based on an experientially founded typology of motional situations represented in the mind. A mental motional situation is basically *perceptual*: human beings perceive motional situations in reality by forming concrete mental *sensomotoric* representations ('pictures') of them with diverse figure–ground constellations and identify them as belonging to different categories according to correspondingly stored abstract percepts ('images'). There are two kinds of picture: static ('stable') and dynamic ('unstable'). We shall argue that we are able to form only one situational picture at a time. A single situational picture is thus a *simple situation*—a stable picture is a *state*, an unstable picture an *activity*, and with respect to spatial situations, we shall use the term *perceptual* location and motion, respectively (cf. Blaser and Sperling 2008; Smith 2009).

Our mental processing of situations goes beyond identifying simple situations in perception: situations may be *conceived* of as possibly integrated with one another into *complex situations*. Thus a 'snapshot' of what at first sight seems to be only a state or an activity may actually turn out to be the end point or the starting point 'focus' on an integrated, complex situation involving a causal activity followed by a resultant state, that is, an *action*. In the first case, the state in focus is preceded by a *causal* activity; in the second case, the activity in focus is succeeded by a *resultant* state, in the normal course of events. The state-focused action will be termed a *past event*, whereas an activity-focused action will be termed an *ongoing process*. With respect to complex spatial situations (actions), we shall use the term *conceptual* motion, owing to the fact that the causal connection cannot be perceived, only conceived (cf. Blaser and Sperling 2008; Smith 2009). Accordingly, cognition is biplanal, involving the perceptual imaginal plane and the interpretive conceptual ('idea') plane. On the concrete, token level we speak of pictures and 'thoughts', while on the abstract, type level we use the terms image and idea, respectively.

When now turning to language proper and the typology of motion verbs in the mental lexicon, we must, of course, add the sign vehicle—the verbal expression—to the above concepts. According to the present model, a motional verb sign is an 'omnipotent' symbol, that is, a type applicable to any situational token covered by its semantic contents (Durst-Andersen 2008b). The semantic contents of the sign dovetail the biplanal cognition, that is, the prelinguistic perceptual and conceptual mental structures: the linguistic sign object construes cognitive-semantically the image, and the sign interpretant construes cognitive-semantically the idea, respectively. The relation between reality and mind and language is one of intentionality—inherent intentionality between reality and mind, *derived* intentionality between reality and language, language 'reaching' reality *via* mind. Therefore, we imprecisely speak of the sign object as the (derived) image, and of the sign interpretant as the (derived) idea. (Our bipartitioning of the cognitive-semantic domain into an abstract, perception-based image level and an abstract, conception-based idea level is found elsewhere in theoretical linguistics: spatial vs conceptual structure in Jackendoff 2002; cf. the experiential vs the logical sub-function within the ideational metafunction in Halliday and Matthiessen 1999.) Perhaps we should clarify what we mean by this: whereas there is only one single reality 'out there' (the Peircean dynamical object), there are two cognitive-semantic contents to grasp it. In the first place, the perception-based semantic image (cf. Peirce's immediate object) 'mirrors' reality. Additionally, however, it is *interpreted* by the conception-based semantic idea (cf. Peirce's immediate interpretant). To put it in another way: the imaginal–situational level is the interpretive basis for the ideational–propositional level, where the imaginal content is interpreted propositionally (see Figure 8.1). The propositional structure is the scope for grammatical (indexical) tense–aspect–mood operators (Durst-Andersen 2008a, b, 2011). The most obvious case is actions: corresponding to the potentially causal activity situation we have an activity (ground-) proposition p, and to the potentially resultant state situation a state (ground-) proposition q, connected by the logical relation of implication. This is the verb model of an action (cf. Durst-Andersen 1992); see Figure 8.1.

An ongoing process focuses on the causal activity, this triggering the assertion of the activity description p, whereby the state description q may or may not be true as well; whereas a past event focuses on the resultant state, this triggering the assertion of the state description q, whereby the truth of the activity description p is presupposed.

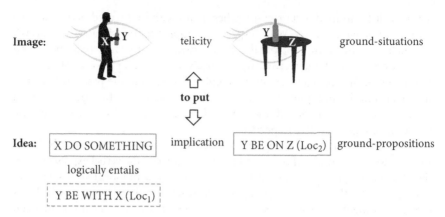

FIG. 8.1. The cognitive-semiotic representation of the English lexeme *to put*, as in *he put the bottle on the table*

The findings of the chapter are primarily based on empirical studies undertaken by its authors and their affiliates (see the references), some of these within the *SugarTexts* protocol (Smith 2003, 2005, 2006, 2009; Smith and Nedergaard Thomsen 2009). The theoretical framework is that of cognitive semiotics (mental grammar and supertypology), as developed by Durst-Andersen (esp. 1992, 2011) and illustrated by Smith (2005), and functional discourse pragmatics, developed by Nedergaard Thomsen (e.g. 2008).

8.1.2   Reflecting on *The construal of spatial meaning: Windows into conceptual space*

Reflecting on the title of the present volume—*The construal of spatial meaning: Windows into conceptual space*, we could say that there are two levels of mental ('conceptual') space to cope with reality, namely the *perceptual* level of experience based on input from the senses, and the *conceptual* level based on second-order cognition, in other words thinking. That is, one domain of the mental space is visuo-spatial, the other its interpretive conceptual counterpart. Together they are construed cognitive-semantically, *in casu* by different clausal configurations involving linguistic motion verbs. A typology of these configurations and their defining motion verbs is a vital window into the human mind. We study the mental spaces through the linguistic cognitive-semantic spaces, but the only way to do this is to investigate how people communicate about motion in reality. Outside the scope of the title, we will maintain that just as semantics is the window into mind, it is also—derivatively—the window into reality: we live in a *universe of discourse*, so to speak.

8.2 Background, Aims, and Scope

8.2.1 Lexicalization typology

Motion event research has grown into a well-established and highly productive field. Its theoretical cornerstone is the classic studies by Talmy (1975, 1985, 2000), supplemented by works primarily by Slobin (1996a, b, 2004, 2005), but also by others (for an overview, see Mora Gutiérrez 2001). Despite the overwhelming number of specific works within motion event research and despite the seemingly growing awareness of the need for a more fine-grained, less schematic approach than the Talmy–Slobin framework (see e.g. Berthele 2004; Beavers et al. 2009), the core assumptions and variables of the framework are still upheld.

Talmy's basic hypothesis is that even though people's conceptualization of a directed motion situation appears to be universal—involving the same fundamental components to be lexicalized (besides figure and ground: *motion* itself, *manner* of motion, or *cause*, and *path*, i.e. trajectory)—the ways of lexicalizing it in different languages are not the same because not all the components are able to be co-lexicalized in the same verbal morpheme in a *major* lexicalization system (Talmy 1985: 76).

Apart from cases where only motion is lexicalized in the verb, as in English *move*, either the *manner* component co-lexicalizes with the verb's motion component, leaving the path behind to be lexicalized in what Talmy terms a *satellite*, as in so-called satellite-framed, or manner languages, or it is the *path* that is lexically 'incorporated' into the *verb*, in so-called verb-framed, or path languages, whereby the manner component becomes secondary, left for optional expression in some sort of adverbial phrase (e.g. a gerund of a manner of motion verb).

Thus, we have a neat, binary typology of major lexicalization patterns, and derivatively of languages, in that it is assumed that at least most languages fit into one of these types, manner and path languages. We do not say that this typology is wrong, but we question the homogeneity within each type and some of its basic notions: manner itself and figure–ground.

8.2.2 Prerequisites for a typology of motion verbs

A proper understanding of the linguistics of motion, we shall argue, requires the following cross-classifications:

- *Situation types* and *verb classes*: motion event semantics is fundamentally based on *space*, so a *typology of situations* is required that is primarily founded on visuo-spatial experiential structures (for some examples of time-based theories, see Vendler 1967; Lyons 1977; Langacker 1991a, b). As stated above, the typology to be proposed here is founded on visual perception, differentiating simple situations (one picture) from complex ones (two pictures). Within the former, simple situations, it distinguishes between states (stable pictures) and activities (unstable pictures), and within the latter it distinguishes what could be termed 'moving' (e.g. waving one's hand) from simple locomotion, i.a. moving in a certain direction (e.g. walking), or in various directions within the limits of one location (e.g. walking around). Complex motion—what is often referred to as 'motion event', 'translocation', 'directed motion', or 'translational motion'—is i.a. going (activity) from one location (source state) to another (destination state), e.g. via a trajectory. Basically, it is a motional *action* in the sense of a motional activity followed by a resultant locational state; and this action is either an ongoing process or a past event. Accordingly, there are four types of situations:

o Simple situations (one picture)
  ▪ States (a stable picture)
  ▪ Activities (an unstable picture)
o Complex situations (two pictures)
  ▪ Processes (an activity (in)tending to 'cause' a state)
  ▪ Events (a state 'caused' by an activity)

The two types of complex situations have hitherto been mixed up, both having been called 'events'—presumably due to the assumption that 'x is walking to L_2' involves a lot of changes (up to the final one), and that 'x walked to L_2' involves a final change. In our terminology an ongoing process (with a present–future perspective) involves an *intention*, not necessarily personal, within an activity to change a state—a directedness towards a resultant state, while a past event (with a present–past perspective) involves a state that has changed *because of* an activity. Since ongoing processes and past events focus on only one situation of their underlying bi-situational complex (action), they can be pointed to per se by indexical–grammatical means, whereas the underlying actions, by being bi-situational (involving two pictures), cannot be so indexed—they can only be symbolized: an action is a *collective concept* of processes and events, and only in that capacity may it be symbolized by an aspect-neutral English infinitive, like *leave*, or by what is common to the perfective and imperfective aspect of Russian aspect-specific infinitives, like the perfective *uijti* 'to have left by walking' and the imperfective *uxodit* 'to be leaving by walking'. On the other hand, while all languages may refer by *grammatical* (indexical) means to states, activities, ongoing processes, and past events because they have a mono-situational focus, they are not capable of naming by *lexical* means—lexicalizing—all four types of situations: they may only name states (the *state verbs*), activities (the *activity verbs*), and actions: that is, the complex situations that are the common denominator of events and processes (the *action verbs*). We shall call these lexical classes of verbs *verb classes*:

• Simplex verbs (one situation)
  o State verbs
  o Activity verbs

- Complex verbs / Action verbs (two situations)
  - o Imperfective form (an activity (in)tending to cause a state)
  - o Perfective form (a state caused by an activity)

- *Ontological domain* concerns the semantics of verbs and verbal expressions in terms of the *mental representation of domains of reality*—what is known as 'process types' in Systemic-Functional Linguistics (see Martin and Matthiessen 1990). Verbal situations, before they are classified into simple vs complex situations, are cross-classified into four different domains of reality, namely primarily space or location—which is especially relevant for this chapter—but also possession, mental experience, and quality/property. It is obvious, for instance, that the English verbs *have* (state), *administer* (activity), and *give* (action), over and above representing different verb classes, involve the ontological domain of possession. In the same way, Russian *stojat'* 'stand' (state), *idti/xodit'* '[+/–determinate] walk' (activity), and *ujti/uxodit'* 'leave by walking' ('leaving by walking' [process, imperfective]'/'having left by walking [event, perfective]') all involve space, more narrowly 'spatial position' [+vertical].

- The *experiential–imaginal* and the *ideational mode*: verbal expressions mediate two distinct levels of content, namely the experiential, image level with *ground-situations* and, paired to it, the proposition-based idea level with *ground-propositions*. From a lexico-grammatical point of view, a verb, then, is an *image–idea pair*. On its experiential, image level it is classified into verb classes, namely state (stable image), activity (unstable image), and action (unstable + stable image). Furthermore, on this level, the verb configures a *participation frame* where perception-based functions such as figure, ground, manner, and path are configurational participants (see Figure 8.1). On the propositional–ideational level the verb is represented as a propositional structure that interprets its type of experiential image in terms of implied propositions (cf. Figure 8.1). On this level the verb configures a *propositional frame*. Recognizing these two semantic levels allows us to detect and describe differences between corresponding verbs and verbal expressions in different languages that, even though they refer to the same situation in reality, interpret it differently. Thus, a complex motion situation—a motional action—may be construed by a manner verb in one language, by a path verb in another, and by a manner–path verb series in yet another language: Eng. *walk into*; Fr. *entrer dans*; Chin. *zǒu* (=walk)*jìn* (=enter). In the satellite-framing case of English, the path (change-of-state) coding satellite—the lexical preposition *into*—is required for the clausal nucleus to denote a motional action, since the verb itself solely denotes an *activity*. In the verb-framing case of French, an external path specification is redundant, path being inherent in the path-coding *action* verb. In Slobin's terms, the 'thinking for speaking' of a manner language like English requires manner (except for motion verbs of French origin, like *arrive*), whereas that of a path language like French does not. In the case of Chinese verb serialization, the manner verb is an *activity* verb, whereas the path verb is an *action* verb. Grammatical operators of tense–aspect–mood must in principle be left out of consideration when cross-classifying the verbal lexemes since they only have the verbal lexemes in their scope. This means that *walking into the room* and *walked into the room* both symbolize a motional action, i.e. relocation from being outside the room (L_1) to being inside the room (L_2).

As a basis for further analysis, we will make the following assumptions, where at least (a) and (b) are also an integral part of Talmy's general approach: it is assumed that, (a) the semantic modelling required must incorporate insights gained on pre-linguistic visual cognition, (b) figure/ground segmentation is a key variable in the perception and conceptualization of real-world situations, and (c) all motion detection relies on some form of 'delay-and-compare' processing, where contradictive visual information is compared over time (see e.g. Rasche 2005; Borst 2000; Zacks and Tversky 2001). Much seems to suggest that the delay-and-compare processing can be performed on two distinct cognitive levels and that 'motion' is hence two very different things from a cognitive point of view. In a study by Blaser and Sperling (2008), the term *perceptual motion* is suggested for motion detected through first-order processing of immediate visual stimuli partly based on 'build in' neural wetware, whereas the term *conceptual motion* is suggested for motion detected through higher-order processing (relying on general-purpose cognitive systems) that does not necessarily involve any immediate visual stimuli at all (a simulation, if you will, of first-order visual motion). Further arguments for identifying two distinct levels of processing are offered by Dodge and Lakoff (2005). These two levels correspond to our simple situations (activities) and complex situations (actions) as well as to our simplex verbs and complex verbs (see above).

In the following we shall delve into our main concern, namely the cross-classification of motional verbs as informed by a typology of motion situations. Thus, we shall start out with the situation typology. Then we shall turn to the verb classification proper. For illustration, we shall, more or less, stick to the three satellite-framing, manner languages, English, Russian, and Danish. The example material primarily relates to well-known observations on the respective languages already familiar from the existing literature, including our own previous work. Rather than making new empirical observations, focus is thus on explaining existing ones, drawing on our integrated framework and further clarifying the cross-linguistic interconnections between them. The examples will be examined from a holistic point of view, starting with state verbs since the structure of state verbs is simple and is transparent with respect to perception strategy. We concentrate mainly on these three manner languages because there are so many differences between them and these differences are so systematic that we have to recognize at least two, possibly three subtypes of manner languages. This owes to the fact that Talmy's notions of manner and figure–ground are ambiguous and thus may be interpreted differently, as seems to be the case for Russian and English/Danish.

8.3   Situation Typology

8.3.1   Simple and complex situations

As sketched in the introduction (Section 8.1), the basis of our situation and verb typologies is the perceptual notion of an image, that is, an abstract mental picture. Vision is fundamental to human cognition and language, but, in principle, all senses perform the same function of acting as a mediating link between reality and mind. Situations in reality are grasped by human beings in the shape of some kind of picture and are interpreted by conceptual structures. Vision plays a crucial role in perception by putting a structured 'form' (images) upon the outside 'substance' (as represented in the mind by pictures), framing reality into different wholes and foregrounding and backgrounding different elements within them.

Situations are classified into simple and complex situations. Simple situations are states and activities—both are identified and distinguished by means of perception: states provoke stable pictures (e.g. someone is sitting on a chair) while activities provoke unstable pictures (e.g. someone is jumping up and down) on our perceptual screen. Complex situations (i.e. the so-called actions) are fundamentally different, although they consist of an activity and a state: whereas states and activities are perceivable, real-world situations, actions are merely *conceivable*—they are partly a mental construct. They are never grasped in their totality at once, in one single macro-picture containing at the same time both a causal activity and a resultant state. Rather, they are grasped *either* as an activity, whereby the ensuing state must be inferred, *or* as a resultant state, whereby the causal activity must be inferred, or backtracked.

8.3.2   Stable and unstable pictures

Although the structure of a concrete picture is itself determined by physiological facts about vision—distinguishing between focus of attention and periphery— recent research from eye-tracking studies suggests that different experimental subjects start forming the same stable picture *at different places* and do so in a systematic way (see Nisbett et al. 2001; Nisbett 2003). American English-speaking students start with the figure, whereas Chinese-speaking students start with the ground. Corresponding to these different *strategies of perception* one may surmise that speakers of American English and speakers of Chinese may describe what they see in different ways—they may have different *naming strategies*. It has been shown that these cultural differences in perception strategies between American English and Chinese may have dramatic, but foreseen effects on performing non-linguistic tasks (see Hedden et al. 2008). In addition to the different perception and naming strategies, we hypothesize that there are also different lexicalization patterns and even different gestural patterns for dealing with motion events (for experimental data, see Zheng and Goldin-Meadow 2002).

In the following we shall go into more detail with a Gestaltist analysis of mental situations. In an unstable picture portraying an activity where someone, X, is carrying something, Y, there are two figures and two grounds: from one perspective, we see the carrying person, X, as figure against a location L as ground; from a complementary perspective we see the carried thing, Y, as figure and the carrier, X, as the immediate ground. In other words, there is a stable element in the unstable picture: Y does not change place *in relation to X* while X is carrying it. Accordingly, we shall call the carrying X the *primary figure* and the carried Y the *secondary figure*, and similarly L the *primary ground* and X (the carrier) the *secondary ground*—Y's ground. With respect to naming strategy and lexicalization, there is a typologically important choice concerning *perspective* here, since it is impossible to have two different starting points at the same time (cf. Nedergaard Thomsen 1994; Durst-Andersen 2002, 2006): either the starting point is the primary figure (the carrier X) or the secondary figure (the carried Y). In this way different languages may 'view' the same situation in different ways. Later we shall illustrate this point by the typological behaviour of English, French, and Russian.

8.3.3 Situational distinctions relevant for verbal classification and grammaticalization

Languages may relate differently to the three distinctions within the proposed typology of situations:

- *Simple vs complex situation* corresponding to a distinction between one picture, i.e. one situation (non-action), and two pictures, i.e. two situations (an action)
  - o *Activity vs state* within simple situations (non-actions) corresponding to a distinction between unstable and stable pictures
  - o *Event vs process* within complex situations (actions) corresponding to a distinction between a mental model of past events involving 'causation' (a state caused by an activity) and a mental model of ongoing processes involving 'finality' (an activity (in)tending to cause a state)

These three distinctions are important typological determinants: the activity vs state as well as the event vs process distinctions are responsible for different *semantico-syntactic types*: active-stative languages are founded on the activity vs state distinction, whereas ergative languages are built on the event vs process distinction, the ergative construction denoting an event, the antipassive a process (for further details, see Nedergaard Thomsen 1994; Durst-Andersen 1992, 2002). These distinctions are also responsible for different *aspectual systems*: the English progressive vs non-progressive aspectual distinction is based on the activity vs state distinction, as evidenced very clearly by results from research on first language acquisition (Durst-Andersen 2000); the Russian perfective vs imperfective aspectual distinction is based on the event vs process distinction (Durst-Andersen 1992). However, the simple vs complex distinction is even more important: primarily, at the semantico-syntactic level, it is the basis for the distinction between intransitive and transitive verbs—a simplex, intransitive verb like Danish *arbejde* 'work' automatically turns into a complex, transitive verb, if a prefix is added, e.g. *udarbejde* 'develop, create'. Secondly, what is called purely aspectual pairs in Russian and other Slavic languages are restricted to complex situation verbs, whereas so-called procedurals are solely found in simplex situation verbs (Durst-Andersen 1992). Thirdly, this distinction is also responsible for the meaning split in the French *passé simple* between 'an action viewed in its totality' (i.e. two situations viewed as one) and what is called inchoative meaning (i.e. a situation coming into existence) (see Durst-Andersen 2008a).

8.4   Towards a Typology of Motion Verbs: the Case of Russian, Danish, and English

Now we are prepared for the main part of the chapter, namely the taxonomies of motion verbs of Russian, Danish, and English. Some languages, like Russian, have verbs for all four situation types: for example, the state verb *stojat'* 'stand'; the activity verb *idti/xodit'* 'walk'; the imperfective process verb *uxodit'* 'to be leaving by walking'; and the perfective event verb *ujti* 'to have left by walking'—the two latter comprising, of course, an aspectual pair. Other languages, such as English and Danish, distinguish sharply between states (*stand, stå*) and activities (*walk, gå*) within simple situations, but use activity verbs, for example *walk* and *gå*, in the composition of (phrasal) complex verbs that name complex situations, such as English *walk to the station* and Danish *gå til stationen*. In so far as *uxodit'* 'to be leaving by walking' (process) and *ujti* 'to have left by walking' (event) are two grammatical forms of the same lexeme, and thus constitute a pair that cannot be separated lexically as different lexemes, we should not treat them as belonging to different verb classes in the mental lexicon: they both name an action—a complex situation—but present it as either a past event (the perfective aspect) or as an ongoing process (the imperfective aspect), respectively. In short, the verbal lexicon of a language seems to reduce the four situation types of states, activities, events, and processes to the three verb classes of state verbs, activity verbs, and action verbs. This leaves the event vs process distinction to grammar, that is, to the category of diathesis (ergative vs antipassive, as in Dyirbal), aspect (as in Russian, Chinese, English, Hindi, Turkish, etc.), or to various semantico-syntactic structures having the same effect. This is crucial, because when a verbal lexeme is to name an action—an activity related to a state by telicity—which is the collective concept of processes and events, there are divergent possible starting points, namely the state with its figure–ground constellation (as in ergative languages), or the activity with its two different figure–ground constellations (as in accusative languages). Chinese and similar, so-called verb serializing languages are based on quite a different solution to the problem of only focusing on one image (situation) at a time: they name first the activity situation and then the state (event) situation *in sequence*. This constitutes an iconic (diagrammatic) treatment of complex situations—but, evidently, not all languages are this transparent in their semiotic treatment (see Durst-Andersen 2011).

8.4.1   State verbs

8.4.1.1   *Definition*

State verbs (*be, have, sit, lie, hang, stand, relate, correspond*, etc.) denote a single situation in reality which involves no activity: a state situation corresponding to a stable picture in perception. States are classified into different kinds of state relations in terms of the domain of reality denoted, namely spatial location, possession, experience, and quality ascription. The verb *lie* is thus a location-based state verb, more narrowly classified as a horizontal position verb. A verb like *stand* is also a position verb, namely a vertical position verb. This may be modelled as in Figure 8.2a.

In the domain of possession, there are verbs like *have*; in the experience domain, sensing verbs like *see*; and in the domain of qualities there are expressions like *be red*. Location verbs are important for our subject matter, in that their semantics is inherent in actional motion verbs (actions whose resultant state is a location).

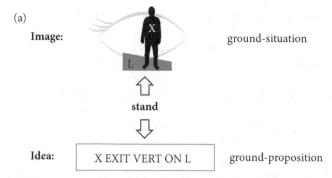

Fig. 8.2a. State: Stable image. The verb model of 'stand'

8.4.1.2   *The verb model of states and its three semantic components*

It appears that many languages, among the state verbs they have at their disposal, include the same posture verbs, as do for instance, Russian, Danish, and English. This may be an indication that they are based on the same underlying verb model. There is a problem, though, for the very same state situation in spatial reality may be conceived and verbalized differently, as for instance the location of a house: where Russian has vertical position *dom stoit na uglu* '(lit.) the house *stands* at the corner', Danish uses horizontal position *huset ligger på hjørnet* '(lit.) the house *lies* at the corner', and English is neutral as to spatial orientation: *the house is at the corner.* Even though the posture verbs of the three languages are defined in the same way, they are nevertheless used quite differently (for statistical evidence, see Durst-Andersen 2006). Our hypothesis is that Russian, Danish, and English code different *perception strategies*; in other words, the 'same' picture of reality provokes three different linguistic images in terms of mental focus. This difference in perception strategy is correlated with different *naming strategies*: the three different verbaliza-tions of the same external situation can be explained by claiming that the three languages relate differently to the same three components hypothesized to define the verbal model of states. Superordinately, a concrete spatial location verb denotes the existence—permanent or temporary—of some spatial figure in relation to a spatial ground, the location. Like in motion verbs, the denoted mode of action, *in casu* the state, has a specific what might be called *mode of existence*, that is spatial orientation, for example vertical or horizontal position. In all three languages—Russian, Danish, and English—an X, being in a certain mode of existence, is located on a certain location. The above difference between Russian, Danish, and English may be due to a specific 'focus' in the ideational–propositional structure, whereby a specific part of it is profiled, leaving the rest outside as presupposed material. English might thus be said to focus on the very *fact* of existence, whereas Russian and Danish have focus on the *mode* of existence: the kind of position occupied by the figure, for example horizontal or vertical. English accordingly prefers a general, *abstract* (copular) existence verb *be* to a specific, concrete position verb, whereas in Russian and Danish, a *concrete* spatial position verb is the preferred choice. Russian has 'stand' where Danish has 'lie', in the unmarked cases. This specific choice is due to different naming strategies: Russian takes its point of departure in the figure, which is 'built vertically up from the ground' (it has a height dimension), and thus chooses the image–idea pair of 'stand'. Danish, on the other hand, takes its vantage point in the ground, the earth here, which is 'lying horizontally under' the figure (the ground has a latitude–longitude dimension) and therefore chooses the image–idea pair 'lie'. English is quite different in that it is based on the neutral, existential interrelationship between the figure and the ground. If this explanation is true, the parameter 'mode of existence' is threefold ambiguous: either (a) we are talking about the *figure*'s mode of existence (Russian: the building has a height dimension), or (b) we are dealing with the *ground*'s mode of existence (Danish: the location 'at the corner' is horizontal), or (c) the very *fact* of existence, as in the English case (for further examples and discussion, see Durst-Andersen 2006).

Why there should be this kind of difference between Russian, Danish, and English has never been explained before. However, one thing is clear: children acquiring Russian, Danish, and English all learn the 'same' position verbs in their respective languages, but when learning to speak their mother tongue *idiomatically*, they have to adapt to the specific norms of *usage* of their speech community—if there is a mismatch between the child's and his models' wording, the child naturally has to accommodate. To do so, he has to first realize that he adopted a wrong perception strategy and next he must adopt the one accepted in his speech community.

8.4.1.3   *Location vs position verbs*

Two subgroups of state verbs are distinguished according to spatial location, namely general *location verbs*, which involve an entity's *mere existence* on a ground, and specific *position verbs*, involving an entity's *specific* spatial orientation in relation to a ground (what we call 'position'), be it vertical, horizontal, or other. These two subgroups are typologically important because any given language has to choose which one of them should prevail in that language: either it has focus on spatial existence per se (English, French, Spanish, Italian, etc.) or on specific position (Russian, Swedish, Danish, Dutch, etc.). (For descriptions of a variety of languages, see Newman 2002.) This choice is not only restricted to state verbs, it also determines how a language deals with activities and actions, since a state forms an essential part of an activity description (as a necessary condition) as well as of an action description (as a necessary condition of the causal activity and additionally as a resultant state). We shall come back to this in a moment.

8.4.2   Activity verbs

8.4.2.1   *Definition*

Activity verbs (*carry, drive, walk, swim, beat, creep, crawl, cry, play, work, sing*, etc.) denote a single situation in reality which involves activity and provokes an unstable picture in perception. Their semantics is accordingly the unstable *image* of an activity (Peircean immediate object) coupled with its propositional description (Peircean interpretant). Their coupling of image and idea comprises a verb model of activities. Whereas state verbs only denote states, activity verbs *entail* an underlying state description: for instance, in the case of *creep*, a description to the effect that the figure is in a lying or flat, horizontal position while moving. We shall hypothesize that all activity verbs *entail* a specific state description, be it a description of a domain of reality of spatial location, of possession, of

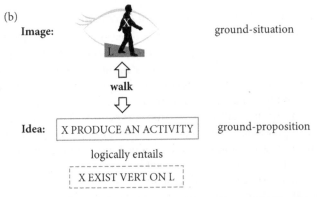

FIG. 8.2b. Activity: Unstable image. The verb model of 'walk'

experience, or of qualification. This entailment of a simultaneous state of the figure represents the fact that the figure could not be walking without also being in an upright, vertical position, which accordingly constitutes a necessary, although not a sufficient condition for using the verb *walk*. The state description entailed by the activity description itself will accordingly be termed its *entailment structure*. An entailment structure is also found with action verbs because they, too, involve an activity description, in addition to the autonomous resultant state description. Summing up, the activity verb *walk* designates a single, unstable situation. Being a verbal predicate (Peircean rheme), it 'telescopes' an underlying proposition that describes the unstable element: that a figure is performing an activity on a certain location (trajectory), while being at the same time in a vertical position (i.e. the entailed state). The verb *walk* is thus a position-based activity verb, the equivalent within activities of the position verb *stand* (cf. Figure 8.2a on p. 128). The verb model of *walk* is illustrated in Figure 8.2b.

The motional activity of 'walking' may be converted into a motional action by attaching a satellite path preposition or particle to the simplex manner verb (e.g. *walk (in)to, walk out (of)*). The resulting complex predicate automatically sym-bolizes a motional action, where the path satellite designates an autonomous (i.e. not entailed) resultant state. Mandarin Chinese is a language that fleshes out our model rather iconically, cf. (1) from Beavers et al. (2009: 35):

(1) . . . héng   fēi   dà-xī-yáng   dào   Měiguó
     horizontal   fly   Atlantic.Ocean   arrive/to   America
     [horizontal]   Motion+Manner   Trajectory   Motion+Path   Ground
     '. . . fly across the Atlantic to America'

It is obvious that the manner–activity verb 'fly', specified as occurring 'horizon-tally', is combined with the figure's trajectory 'the Atlantic Ocean'.

8.4.2.2   *Two types of figure–ground—two types of manner*

The distinction between what we call the situational, or image level of a verbal lexeme and its ideational, propositional level allows us to be quite specific in our characterization of verbal lexemes. It gives us the possibility to detect hitherto unnoticed, but crucial, differences between languages that are usually described as belonging to the same type, as for instance English and Russian. Let us take a concrete example: the English expression *X is carrying Y* denotes an activity and therefore comprises not only an activity description, but also an entailed state description. The expression should be understood: (1) *experientially* as a simple situational structure of one single, unstable image involving two different types of *figure*, namely *primary*, X, and *secondary*, Y; and (2) *ideationally* as a complex propositional structure with an activity description 'X be performing an activity while being at a certain location', as well as a state description 'Y be in a sitting or hanging position with respect to X'. Both descriptions are necessary since Y's position on X is a necessary condition for X's performing the activity of 'carrying'. If this state description is not true, the activity description cannot be true either. In short, the activity description entails the state description of Y's position on X.

Now some languages, such as English, may take their point of departure in the *primary figure, X's activity*, while others, such as Russian, start with the *secondary figure, Y's position*. In other words, what we saw above when examining state verbs repeats itself here: whereas English focuses on the activity performed by the primary figure (X), Russian focuses on the secondary (entailment, Y) figure's position relative to the primary figure (X), which now functions as its immediate ground (for evidence, see below). Thus, from this perspective, even though English and Russian are both manner languages in the Talmy–Slobin typology, they belong to two altogether different subtypes.

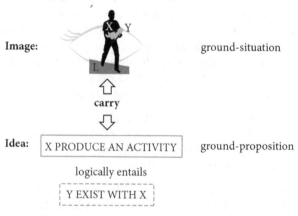

FIG. 8.3. Activity. The verb model of 'carry'

The notion of *manner* likewise refers to two different kinds: either (a), the 'manner' of the secondary (entailment, Y) figure's position with respect to the secondary ground (X), that is, to *Y's mode of existence*, or (b) to the *primary (X) figure's specific way of performing an activity.* Evidently, what at the image level is quite alike ([X carrying Y]) is at the idea level quite different: (a) *mode of existence* is static (i.e. the position of the secondary figure remains the same during the activity); (b) *manner of activity* (including the required means) is dynamic and changes throughout the primary figure's performing its activity.

We thus conclude that the splitting up of Talmy's notion of manner into two distinct subtypes corresponding to the two different types of figure, the primary, asserted, and the secondary, entailed, implies that the so-called *manner languages* cover two distinct subtypes. (For a treatment of the different kinds of manner in English and Spanish, see Cifuentes Férez 2007.)

8.4.2.3   *Automotives and locomotives*

The primary distinction within motional activity verbs is that between location-based ones, such as *work, iron, wave, clap, hop*, and position-based ones, such as *carry, drive, walk, swim, creep, crawl, fly, roll, pull*. In the latter group, it is the position of the figure that determines the semantics, whereas in the former it is other variables in the situation (and hence on the location) where the activity is performed—for example the presence of an iron. The former we shall term *movement verbs*, the latter *simple motion verbs*. Only the latter subgroup of activity verbs is of special interest to motion event research. Simple motion verbs may be further classified into *automotives* and *locomotives*, according as the primary, activity figure is identical (cf. *auto*-motives) or not to the secondary, entailed state figure. Automotives—*walk, run, swim, fly, creep, crawl, climb*—denote a motion where the primary figure is identical to the secondary, entailment figure that occupies a certain position in relation to the ground, be it vertical, horizontal, or other. Locomotives, on the other hand—*lead, chase, carry, bring, roll, push, pull, drag*—denote a motion where the primary figure is *not identical* to the secondary, entailment figure that occupies a certain position relative to the ground, vertical, horizontal, or otherwise. The semantic distinction drawn here between auto- and locomotives tends cross-linguistically to be correlated semantico-syntactically with mono- vs divalent, and intransitive and transitive verbs, respectively. This pertains to Dyirbal, for instance, where the verb meaning 'lead' (where the primary figure is ahead of the secondary figure/ secondary figure is behind primary figure) is divalent and transitive, and where the secondary figure (the undergoer) is the primary topic, the language being ergative (Nedergaard Thomsen 1994). This also applies to Russian where simple motion verbs (i.e. position-based activity verbs) form a closed group of thirteen imperfective verb roots (cf. Durst-Andersen 1997; also Nesset 2007) that occur in stem pairs with a sub-aspectual distinction between *experiential* situation description and *ideational* characterization, similar to the progressive vs non-progressive aspect in English. This amounts to a total of twenty-six verbs:

Intransitive motion verbs—automotives
- 'while secondary figure (X) be in a [vertical] position, primary figure (X) perform an [±intense] activity': *idti/xodit'* [–intense] 'walk, go'; *bežat'/begat'* [+intense] 'run'.
- 'while secondary figure (X) be in a [horizontal] position, primary figure (X) perform an [±intense] activity': *polzti/polzat'* [–intense] 'creep, crawl' (ground: earth); *plyt'/plavat'* [–intense] 'swim' (ground: water); *letet'/letat'* [+intense] 'fly' (ground: air).
- 'while secondary figure (X) be [hanging/sitting], primary figure (X) perform an [±intense] activity': *lezt'/lazit'* [–intense] 'climb, crawl'; *exat'/ezdit'* [+intense] 'go, drive'.

Transitive motion verbs—locomotives
- 'while secondary figure (Y) be [standing/walking/running], primary figure (X) perform an [±intense] activity': *vesti/vodit'* [–intense] 'lead, take'; *gnat'/gonjat'* [+intense] 'chase, hunt (forward)'.
- 'while secondary figure (Y) be [lying], primary figure (X) perform an [±intense] activity': *katit'/katat'* [–intense] 'roll, wheel'; *taščit'/taskat'* [+intense] 'pull, drag'.
- 'while secondary figure (Y) be [hanging/sitting], primary figure (X) perform an [±intense] activity': *nesti/nosit'* [–intense] 'carry'; *vezti/vozit'* [+intense] 'cart, convey, take'.

As with the state verbs, the vertical position is once again the natural choice for Russian. *Idti/xodit'* 'walk, go' is by far the most frequent of all automotives and is the default choice: *avtobus idet* 'the bus is coming [going]', *xorošo idet* 'it is selling [going] well', *dožd' idet* 'it is raining [rain is going]', *segodnja idet 'Revizor'* '"The Government Inspector" is [goes] on tonight'. The same applies to locomotives. Here *vesti/vodit'* 'lead, take' is the default choice (and can substitute for the others if one does not know the exact position of the secondary figure)—for example *vesti ogon'* 'fire on', *vesti peregovory* 'carry on [lead] negotiations', *vesti vojnu* 'wage [lead] a war', *vesti samolet* 'pilot [lead] an aircraft', *vesti delo* 'run [lead] a business', etc. The grammatical distinction between what is normally called the 'determinate' and 'indeterminate' verbs of motion in Russian (and 'uni-directional' vs 'non-(uni-) directional' in Nesset 2007) amounts to a distinction between a concrete, scenic *situation description* (determinate *on idet v školu* 'he is walking to the school') and an abstract *characterization* (indeterminate *on xodit v školu* 'he goes to school, i.e. is a pupil'), corresponding roughly to the aforementioned distinction between the progressive and the non-progressive in English; however—as already indicated—in Russian limited to thirteen verbs that are all imperfective. Notice that in English, 'characterization' means *personal* characterization, whereas in Russian, it also covers what might be called *situational* characterization. (For instance, a person is indeed walking at the moment of speech, but this specific activity is not referred to, only his *role* activity performed within the limits of a park or a forest. This extra element is responsible for the fact that indeterminate verbs in Russian sometimes are translated into progressive forms in English.)

8.4.3   Action verbs

8.4.3.1   *Definition*

Action verbs comprise both accomplishments and achievements in Vendlerian terms (cf. Vendler 1967; Dowty 1979; Foley and Van Valin 1984): *kill, give, send, sell, buy, lose, win, die, redden, leave, stop, find, sit down, stand up, lay, put, set, hang up, carry out, bring to, drive to, walk to, beat up, bring up.* They are situationally complex on the experiential, *image* level, in other words they all denote two situations: an (unstable) activity followed by a (stable) state. Accomplishments are lexicalized using a *prospective* viewpoint, that is from the activity to the state (cf. ongoing processes), while achievements are lexicalized using a *retrospective* viewpoint, that is from the state back to the activity (which then becomes irrelevant, i.e. punctual; cf. past events). Corresponding to this, the *ideational* semantics of action verbs is bi-propositional, one proposition p describing the unstable causing activity, the other q the stable resultant state. The *telicity* (causation or finality—depending on viewpoint, i.e. past event or ongoing process, respectively) obtaining between the activity and the state on the image level is paired with a *logical–propositional* relation of *implication* holding between the correlated propositions on the logico-ideational level. This can be illustrated as in Figure 8.1, and in Figure 8.4 (based on Durst-Andersen 1992).

Thus, the English verb *walk to* is a location-based action, or *relocation* verb—it describes a location-based state (q: 'X is located on L_2') as a result of a location-based activity (p: 'X performs a walking activity'). The mode of existence of the

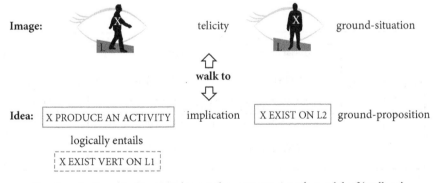

FIG. 8.4. Action: bi-situational mental construct. A verb model of 'walk to'

resultant state is indifferent. That is why the verb is a re*location* verb and not a re*position* verb. The verb entails a prior, *initial* state, where X is in a vertical position (r), because for the figure X to be able to 'walk' it has to be in an *upright* position (r: 'X be in [vertical] position while performing its walking activity'). The propositional semantics is then: 'while X exist vertically on L_1, X perform a walking activity [entailment structure + causal-activity description]; and X exist on L_2 [resultant-state description, which is true or false depending on the manifestation of the action as a past event or as an ongoing process, respectively]'. The total picture may be summarized as in Figure 8.5 based on the so-called action schema in Durst-Andersen (1992).

8.4.3.2   *From simple to complex motion—Russian vs English and Danish*

English and Danish, being mainly manner (satellite-framed) languages, have no autonomous, single lexical units to distinguish between location-based activity (2a and 3a) and location-based action (2b and 3b), but make the distinction by applying path satellites in a complex predicate construction (Nedergaard Thomsen 1991, 1992, 1995, 1998, 2002a, b, 2003; Harder et al. 1996) (the examples are borrowed from Durst-Andersen and Herslund 1996):

(2)   a. He ran quickly.
      b. He ran quickly to the station.

(3)   a. Han 'løb hurtigt.
      b. Han $_0$løb   hurtigt   hen til   stationen.
         he   ran   fast   [over] to   the station
         Figure   Motion+Manner   Path   Ground

On the face of it, there are two viable classifications for the Danish and English motion verbs, as in (2) and (3): either the verb is analysed as being *neutral* with respect to Aktionsart, as in Durst-Andersen and Herslund (1996), or it is seen as inherently denoting a motional activity—it is a 'simple motion' verb—as in Nedergaard Thomsen (2002b, 2003). This implies that in the former classification,

	PRECONDITIONS		
	Initial State [r]	Antecedent State [–q]	
Mover-Figure (x) defined States	x EXIST on L_1	x–EXIST on L_2	Moved-Figure (x) defined States
	POSTCONDITIONS		
	Final State [–r]	Consequent State [q]	
	x–EXIST on L_1	x EXIST on L_2	

FIG. 8.5. The Location-based Action Schema: Auto-motion

the English and Danish intransitive motion verb stems, by being neutral with respect to the distinction between denoting an activity (a simple motional situation), and an action (a complex motional situation), the same lexeme appears now as an activity verb (cf. 2a and 3a), now as an action verb (cf. 2b and 3b)—only the semantico-syntactic environment may determine the final reading (co-textual determination of mode of action). In the English case, it is solely the presence or absence of a path satellite that determines the reading, by being an index of the presence or absence of a resultant state. The progressive form does not change this: *he was running quickly* denotes an activity even though it presents it scenically, while *he ran quickly* could be a characterization of the person in question. Likewise, *he was running quickly to the station* denotes a complex, actional situation consisting of an activity as well as a state, but presents the action referred to as an ongoing process (like one unstable, 'moving' picture), while *he ran quickly to the station* is like a flashback where the figure's running-activity and his being at the station cannot be separated from one another—they are viewed in their totality. In the latter classification (cf. Nedergaard Thomsen 2002b, 2003), a manner verb always denotes an activity, but the *resultant* Aktionsart of the motional construction as a whole is determined compositionally by the Aktionsarts of the component situation-denoting elements: the host predicate (*løbe* 'run') and the co-predicate *hen til* ('[over] to')—as in the serialization construction in Mandarin Chinese, as shown in (1).

In Danish, the resulting Aktionsart of the motional construction can be read off directly by changing the simple past to the present perfect. (4):

(4) a. Han har 'løbet hurtigt (e.g. *hele sit liv* 'his whole life').
       he   has run   quickly

   b. Han er ₀løbet hurtigt hen   til stationen.
       he   is run   quickly [over] to   the station

(5) a. Han 'har 'løbet! (as a reply to e.g. 'It is Peter's turn.',
       he   has   run   said in a running competition)

   b. Han   'er 'løbet!   (as a reply to e.g. 'Peter, run to the
       he   is   run   grocer's!')
   '(he has left-by-running)' (path and ground contextually implied)

It appears from the above examples that the Danish perfect auxiliary *have* 'have' is used when a motion verb (construction) denotes an activity, whereas the perfect auxiliary *være* 'be' is used when it denotes a motional action. In other words, the change of auxiliary from *har* 'has' in (4a) and (5a) to *er* 'is' in (4b) and (5b) can be taken as a signal to the message recipient that the state is location-based. (The same is true in German: *er hat gefahren* 'he has been driving (e.g. the car)' vs *er ist gefahren* 'he has left (e.g. by car)'.)

If we include transitive motion verbs, the picture is the same as the above, cf. (6):

(6)   a. She carried the child (for nine months).
      b. She carried the child to the nearest neighbour (in 5 minutes).

(7)   a. Hun   bar   (på) barnet   (i ni måneder).
          she   carried   (on) the child   (for nine months)

      b. Hun   bar   barnet   hen til den nærmeste nabo   (på 5 min.).
          she   carried the child   [over] to the nearest neighbour   (in 5 min.).

All the (a) examples denote an activity at the lexico-grammatical level, whereas all (b) examples denote an action. At the propositional-semantic level, the (a) examples represent a characterization of the persons involved, whereas the (b) examples represent flashbacks of past actions successfully carried out. As indicated in the parentheses, the difference between (unbounded) activity and (bounded) action shows up in the optional time adverbials, which denote unbounded vs bounded time segment, as is, of course, well known.

Russian distinguishes location-based activity verbs that denote simple motion, (8a) and (9a), and location-based action verbs that denote complex motion, (8b) and (9b):

(8)   a. On   bistro   begal (ipf)   /   bežal (ipf).
          he   quickly   ran   was:running
          Figure   Motion+Manner   Motion+Manner
          'He ran/was running quickly.'

      b. On   bistro   dobežal (pf)   do   stancii.
          he   quickly   ran   to   station
          Figure   P+Motion+M   Path   Ground
          'He ran quickly to the station.'

(9)   a. Ona   nosila (ipf)   rebenka   (devjat' mesjacev).
          she   carried   child   (for nine months)
          F1   Motion+M   F2
          'She carried the child (for nine months).'

      b. Ona   otnesla (pf)   rebenka   k sosedke po domu   (za pjat' minut).
          she   carried   child   to nearest neighbor   (in five minutes)
          F1   P+Motion+M   F2   Path Ground
          'She carried the child to the nearest neighbour (in five minutes).'

The simple motion verbs in the (a) examples were examined above. The verbs in the (b) examples form a large group, which is traditionally called 'prefixed motion verbs', where the prefix is a Talmyan path satellite. They all constitute purely aspectual pairs of the type *dobežat'* (perfective) / *dobegat'* (imperfective) 'run to a certain place'. Accordingly, it can be argued that Russian marks the difference not only between an 'unergative' ('while on L, X do smth.' (9a)) and an 'unaccusative' propositional structure ('X do smth. and thereby X exist on L' (9b)), but also between a transitive and an intransitive variant of the distinction.

The upshot of the above analysis is that there is a clear-cut distinction between simple motion verbs—the (a) examples—and complex motion verbs—the (b) examples. The former group was classified above into auto- and locomotives. The latter group of complex motion verbs, denoting complex situations, are likewise cross-classified: corresponding to the subgroup of general state verbs termed location verbs, we have general *relocation* (phrasal) *verbs* (*carry to, bring to, take to, put, place,* etc.), and correspondingly, *reposition* (phrasal) *verbs* (*sit down, lie down, lay down,* etc.) as a dynamic counterpart to the specific static position verbs (or, 'placement verbs', cf. Tesnière 1976). Both may be further subclassified into automotives—*walk into, run into, swim into, fly into, creep into, crawl into,* etc. and *sit down, lie down,* etc., and locomotives—*carry to, bring to, take to, roll to, chase to, etc.* and *lay down, put,* etc. The two last-mentioned subgroups have important semantico–syntactic parallels, automotives being intransitive and locomotives being transitive.

8.4.3.3   *Reposition verbs in detail*

As we have defined an action verb, its content always includes that of a state verb. This pertains to action verbs in general, for example *move to* L (meaning 'change one's dwelling') which includes the content of *live in* L, and to reposition (placement) verbs specifically compare *lay down on* L which includes the content of *lie on* L. Although Russian, Danish, and English all have four quite specific position verbs (e.g. English *stand, lie, sit,* and *hang*) and corresponding (seldom used) reposition verbs (in English, *stand* (*a table in the corner*), *lay* (*a carpet on the floor*), *set* (*a hen on the eggs*), and *hang* (*a picture on the wall*)), the intimate relationship between these two groups of verbs has been more or less blurred in English and Danish. In Russian we observe an almost 100 per cent match, in the sense that if (as a subject, X) a noun requires *stojat'* 'X exist vertically on L', it requires (as a direct object, Y) *stavit'/postavit'* 'X do smth. and as a consequence Y exist vertically on L'.

The asymmetry in English is due to the introduction of abstract verbs for placing something in a position, namely *put* and *place* that, in fact, repeat the *general* existence focus (as dealt with above) from the location verbs. Instead, English has developed a group of action verbs where the activity itself, not the position, is specified (for instance, *install* and *bandage*) and a group where the ground location itself is included in the meaning (for instance, *cage* and *imprison*). The original placement verbs have undergone the same development as the original motion verbs, such as *carry* and *lead*: they all have corresponding phrasal verbs such as *set on, set back, set in, set up,* and *set out,* where the particles seem to specify either the direction of the activity, as in *set out,* or the position/the new quality of the direct object, as in *set up.* Thus, it turns out that *set,* which originally included a sitting-position in its state description, can be used to specify not only an upright position but also a certain quality, as in *he set up the machine*, though without losing its activity orientation (for further details, see Durst-Andersen 2006).

What has been said about English can to a certain extent be claimed to pertain to Danish as well. There are, however, some important differences. First of all, the post-verbal particle of a phrasal verb in English is normally placed immediately after the verb as in, for example, *set up a machine*, whereas in Danish it is always placed immediately after the direct object: *ₒsætte en maskine op*. The particle in Danish occupies the same position as the *predicative* co-predicate (Nedergaard Thomsen 2002a, 2003), for example *ₒskrive brevet rent* '(lit.) write the letter clean (free from imperfections), that is, make a fair copy of the letter'. This implies that both the satellite and the predicative have an attributive, *co-predicating* function, and this is signalled by the special word order position—the incorporating character of the verbal nucleus—the host predicate—is signalled by the stress reduction. Just as the clause *han ₒskrev brevet rent* should be read as 'he performed an activity of writing with respect to the letter and as a result of that the letter is in a state of being clean', the clause *han ₒsatte maskinen op* should be read as 'he performed an activity of setting-up with respect to the machine and as a result of that the machine is in an upright position'. Although Danish here applies the dynamic particles *op* 'up', *ned* 'down', *af* 'off', etc. (see Durst-Andersen and Herslund 1996; Harder et al. 1996; Nedergaard Thomsen 1998), it should be stressed that when posing questions concerning the state itself, in a situation where the activity is presupposed, the corresponding static particles occur (adding the static suffix -*e*), for instance, *er den oppe?* '(lit.) is it up?, that is, has it been set up?'; *er den nede?* '(lit.) is it down?, that is, has it been put down?'; *er du a'e* (underlyingly /af-e/)? '(lit.) are you off?, that is, have you been set down?', etc. Moreover, it should be taken into consideration that there exists a systematic alternation between the phrasal verb construction—the verb having a post-verbal particle—and the corresponding prefixed verb construction. (10) presents some illustrative examples of this quite general pattern, which is a characteristic feature of Danish (for further examples, see Durst-Andersen and Herslund 1996; Durst-Andersen 2006; cf. also Nedergaard Thomsen 1992, 2003; cf. also Hovmark, this vol.):

(10) a. Partiet   har   opstillet   kandidaterne.
         the party   has   up-put   the candidates
         'The party has nominated its candidates.'

      b. Han   'stillede   keglerne   op.
         He   put   the skittles   up
         'He set up (erected, put them in an upright position) the skittles.'

      c. *Han har opstillet keglerne.
         '*He has (nominated) the skittles.'

d. Han ₀stillede vasen op på bordet.
  'He put the vase (up) on the table.'

Example (10a) denotes *institution* (cf. Nedergaard Thomsen 1991, 1992): *opstille* can only take an agent that has the social authority or the permission to nominate candidates; while (10b) involves a concrete *locative* meaning:' *stille op* is concrete and denotes that the skittles are in an upright position. Notice that (10b) designates not a relocation, but a 'contained' movement (Talmy 1975; here from a horizontal to a vertical position within the same location)—and this is under-lined by the stress retainment, whereas (10d) denotes a relocation from a position not on the table to a position on the table—this being signalled by the stress reduction of the verb. The fact that Danish shows a systematic alternation between a subject-oriented, institutionalized construction (10a) and an object-oriented, concrete locative construction (10b/d) makes Danish and English look alike. However, the focus of the latter, locative construction (10b/d), is similar to the position focus within state verbs, thereby making Danish and English quite different. We concluded above, on the basis of the unmarked status in Danish of the horizontal position verb *ligge* 'lay', that Danish has a naming strategy that focuses on the ground location which is horizontal (cf. Durst-Andersen 2006). In the case of placement verbs as well as of all other verbs having a post-verbal particle, we observe manifestations of the same spatial focus: one cannot place a figure without having a ground in the shape of a concrete location, and it is only after having established this relationship between figure and a ground that it is possible to specify a direction.

8.5   Conclusion: Cognitive–Semiotic *Topology*—Mental and Semantic Spaces

8.5.1   The topological typology of Russian, Danish, and English

Prelinguistic, cognitive situations were shown to be grouped into four kinds reflecting our visual experiences of external (spatial) reality, namely two kinds of simple situations—states and activities—and two kinds of complex situations (actions)—state-focused events and activity-focused processes. We then hypothesized that (especially) verbal lexemes occur in lexical classes that directly reflect this situational typology: the prototypical function of the inherent cognitive–semantic modes of action (Aktionsarts) is to denote those kinds of mental situations. It turned out that languages do not *lexicalize* events and processes in themselves (these being situational variants), but leave their differ-entiation to *grammar*, for instance in the form of grammatical operators which index these variants. Instead, they go one step up the abstraction ladder and name (i.e. symbolize) their collective concept—the action—which in its totality has no counterpart in perceivable reality. This left us with three verb classes, namely state verbs, activity verbs, and action verbs. At the same time, and orthogonal to this, we developed a typology of verbs based on the concept of domain of reference that runs across the three verb classes based on situation types. The domains were: spatial location, possession, mental experience, and quality. The resultant cross-classification of verbs enabled us to paraphrase sentences with the aim of pinpointing the different factors that specific languages focus on. With respect to our topic, motion events and related issues, we ended up by proposing the following typology of verbs:

- State verbs
  - o Location verbs: e.g. Eng. *be*, i.e. 'X exist on L'
  - o Position verbs: e.g. Eng. *stand*, i.e. 'X exist [vertically] on L'
- Activity verbs
  - o Movement verbs: e.g. Eng. *wave*
  - o Simple motion verbs
    - Automotives—intransitives: e.g. Eng. *walk*, i.e. 'while [vertically] on L (trajectory), X perform activity'
    - Locomotives—transitives: e.g. Eng. *carry* (animate Y), i.e. 'while Y be [sitting/hanging] on X (on trajectory L), X perform a (supportive) activity'
- Action verbs
  - o Complex motion verbs
    - Relocation verbs
      - Automotives—intransitives: e.g. Eng. *walk to* L_2, i.e. 'while [vertically] on L_1 (trajectory), X perform activity and then as a result exist on L_2 (target)'
      - Locomotives—transitives: e.g. Eng. *carry to* L_2 (animate Y), i.e. 'while Y is [sitting/hanging] on X (on trajectory L_1), X perform a (supportive) activity and then as a result Y exist on L_2 (target)'
    - Reposition verbs
      - Automotives—intransitives: e.g. Eng. *lie down on* L, i.e. 'X perform activity and then as a result X exist [horizontally] on L'
      - Locomotives—transitives: e.g. Eng. *lay down on* L, i.e. 'While Y is accessible to X, X perform activity and then as a result Y exist [horizontally] on L'

We took Russian, English, and Danish as our primary sources of data since although these languages are normally typologized as prototypical manner languages, they are nevertheless typologically divergent. They differ in fundamental respects and in systematic ways, and we argued that the differences might be traced back to a difference of strategies, namely strategies of thinking-for-speaking applied when interpreting perceptual stimuli and strategies of naming the resulting mental constructs. Our analysis of prelinguistic, cognitive situations and of the semantics of the designating verbs suggested that a distinction should be drawn between primary and secondary figures, and correspondingly between primary and secondary grounds, linked to the important perceptual notions of stability and instability, respectively. Likewise, we demonstrated that Talmy's notion of manner should also be similarly subclassified, into static manner of existence and dynamic manner of activity. And last but not least, it was argued that the Talmyan telic path implies an autonomous resultant state situation. This state is not transparently coded in all languages, but in those that have aspect, like Russian and English, or have serial verb constructions, like Mandarin Chinese and Thai, it directly appears. We are convinced that if the cross-classification system above is systematically applied to path languages as well as to manner-path languages, we will face differences similar to those pointed out above. Admittedly, this requires a deep knowledge of the languages concerned—not only their verbal lexicons, but certainly also their grammars and the pragmatic uses of lexical items and constructions. That is why we concentrated on English, Danish, and Russian—only in passing mentioning other languages.

8.5.2 Theoretical afterword: the reality—mind—language topological homologies

To internal-semiotically cope with external reality, the mental capacity of man has evolved in the form of perceptual and conceptual mental spaces in mind as well as homologous imaginal and ideational semantic spaces in language. These same spaces have also, to be sure, evolved so as to be instrumental in his exo-semiotic communicative behaviour with his fellow man. The spaces are occupied by different 'items' arranged in taxonomies (networks) and projected as configurations in each homologous sphere. A crucial set of items is the situation typology in his mental space and the paradigmatic verb typology in his semantic space. The mental situation typology is used in his understanding, thinking, and communicating about the outer world, as is his semantic typology of spatial motion verbs. Investigating mental and semantic typology (and supertypology) is the *sine qua non* when trying to understand the workings of the human mind.

9

A Basic Level for the Encoding of Biological Motion

MILA VULCHANOVA and LILIANA
MARTINEZ*

9.1 Introduction

Language reflects the way we perceive the world and think about it. Humans pick out relevant features from reality, and use them as building blocks for constructing categories. We perceive, categorize, and describe what is going on around us in terms of situations and entities taking part in them. There is considerable literature on the principles of individuation and categorization of entities and events in the surrounding world (to name only some, Rosch et al. 1976 on the categorization of objects; Harnad 1987 on categorical perception; Zacks and Tversky 2001 on the segmentation and categorization of events; Mandler 2004 on the bases of conceptual thought). The conceptual domain of space has received special attention since it relies on perceptually accessible salient cues, which can be more easily compared to semantic models in the search for mapping principles between the domains of space and language. Although much work has addressed the linguistic encoding of spatial categories (the seminal work by Talmy 1985, 2000; but also Jackendoff 1983; Slobin 2001, 2004; Levinson 2003a; Levinson and Wilkins 2006; among others), the spatial domain has proved to be complex and interwoven with non-spatial factors (e.g. social or cultural) of human existence, which has hampered the construction of a unified and sufficiently detailed model for the description of spatial language. More specialized studies in separate semantic subdomains of space are necessary before a clearer picture can emerge.

This chapter discusses some results of an exploratory study of how motion situations are encoded in three so-called satellite-framed (Talmy 2000)

* Work reported in this chapter was conducted as part of *The Linguistic Encoding of Motion* project, Nordic Research Council NOS-H Grant # 10088. http://www.hf.ntnu.no/motionencodingfiles/index. html. We would like to thank Chris Wilder, two anonymous reviewers, and the editors of this volume for valuable comments and suggestions. We world like to thank Ole Edsberg for help with the cluster analysis.

languages—Bulgarian[1] (a Slavic Balkan Sprachbund language), English, and Norwegian (both of them Germanic languages)—and the implications of these results for a broader theory of motion categorization as reflected in language. Even though these languages belong in the same type, they are substantially different in their lexicons (Germanic vs Slavic), and, in addition Bulgarian displays an interesting deviation from the rest of Slavic in the domain of motion words (Smith 2006; Tasmowski 2010), most likely as the result of sustained contact with the other Balkan languages. Our purpose here is to map out the basic lexical inventory of the target languages in our study for basic biological motion situations, and to check for variation in naming preferences when the motion scenes vary on different parameters. Although dictionary definitions and corpus data may give some indication of how language relates to the surrounding world, they are not at all well suited for this type of study, since they contain no information on the actual spatial scenes referred to by the data. This is why experimental studies need to be devised to show the relation between linguistic expressions and spatial features. Our focus is on open-class forms, more specifically verbs, and on lexicalization patterns. The experimental set-up includes a free naming task for basic biological motion scenes featuring running, walking, crawling, and climbing. We propose some perceptually based parameters which capture the patterns we find in the grouping of biological motion scenes on the basis of the motion verbs used by the participants in our study to describe them. Some of the most salient parameters are *locomotion medium* (suspended vs supported motion), *speed, characteristic method of propulsion,* and *path vector orientation.* We hypothesize that these parameters are better equipped to capture the linguistic encoding of motion and meaning representation than, for example, approaches based on Talmy's (1985, 2000) typology. We show that the most experientially salient types of terrestrial biological motion correspond to semantic domains in which we can distinguish between a basic-level lexical item (or items) expressing the default case of the biological motion type, and more specific lexical items. The biological motion scenes which such more specific items are used to refer to may vary from the default scene on specific parameters, and yet they cluster together with the default case on major features, which distinguish the group as a whole from other major types of terrestrial biological motion.

9.2 Background

An important characteristic of language is that it imposes structure on the 'reality' it represents (e.g. Talmy 1985, 2000; Slobin 2001; Clark 2001) by selecting for expression only specific concepts and features. As a consequence, the

---

[1] Talmy (2000) suggests that Slavic languages are of the satellite-framed type. Bulgarian has attracted attention in this respect only recently; however, the general idea is that it deviates substantially from the satellite-framed prototype (Croft et al. 2010; Sinha and Kuteva 1995; Smith 2006; the current chapter).

linguistic expression of spatial situations, including motion, is constrained by a schema[2] consisting of a set of elements like the ones proposed by Talmy (1985, 2000): *motion, path, manner of motion, figure,* and *ground.* Motion-event typology focuses on how such elements are lexicalized or grammaticalized cross-linguistically. In terms of linguistic form, the verb is viewed as the main lexical item encoding the motion event, but languages differ as to what elements of the motion situation they choose to bundle into their most frequently occurring motion verbs. According to these preferences, Talmy (2000) divides languages into several types, the most common being languages in which *path* is expressed in the verb (verb-framed languages) and languages in which *path* is expressed in satellites (satellite-framed).

In recent years this typology has been criticized in that it does not adequately capture cross-linguistic variation or even the variety of expressions within a single language (e.g. Croft et al. 2010; Sinha and Kuteva 1995; Slobin 2004; Zlatev and Yangklang 2004; Pourcel and Kopecka 2005; Sampaio et al. 2008). Furthermore, recent research in cognitive interfaces and the cross-linguistic encoding of motion (Nikanne and van der Zee 2005, 2012; Dimitrova-Vulchanova 2004a, 2004b; Zlatev et al. 2010) has demonstrated that both *path* and *manner* are too crude to account for the linguistic evidence, and, as such, lead to controversial representations and accounts.

The notion of *manner* can be felicitously decomposed into a number of independent parameters pertaining to various aspects of the motion scene, including *path shape* (e.g. *zigzag, spiral*), terrain/medium (e.g. *walk* vs *fly* vs *swim*), instrument (e.g. *cycle, ski, sail*), figure orientation or curvature (*wriggle, shake*), speed (e.g. the contrast between *run* and *sprint*), or psychological state of the figure (e.g. *strut, saunter, trudge*). Talmy (2000) uses *manner,* however, to denote an accompanying event[3] (a co-event) conflated with the element of motion (e.g. rotation: *roll*), a particular type of contact with the substrate (*slither* vs *slide* vs *float*), the particular pattern of displacement of the centre of mass of the figure (*glide* vs *lurch*), or the characteristic cycle of body and limb motions (e.g. *run, crawl, waddle*), although he never defines the notion (see the criticism in Slobin 2006a). In view of this complexity, *manner* can hardly be viewed as a primitive in a semantic model (see Dimitrova-Vulchanova and Weisgerber 2007 for a proposal). At best, it is a useful 'short-hand' for a range of independent and well-defined features.

The notion of *path,* on Talmy's terms, is 'the path followed or site occupied by the Figure object with respect to the Ground object' (Talmy 2000: 25). Jackendoff (2002) defines *path* as the second argument of the function GO; it represents

---

[2] Here we use 'schema' descriptively. The notion of image schemas has been used differently in the cognitive linguistics literature and, as such, has become increasingly confusing. We agree in principle with the criticism and discussion in Zlatev (2005).

[3] Here we use 'event' following the accepted formal semantics tradition, as well as Talmy's wording, and refrain from a discussion of the aspectual implications of the term.

whatever is traversed in a traversing event of the type GO (X, Y). Importantly, *path* itself can be a function, and its starting and initial points can be specified (from–to). Alternatively, either its direction or curve/shape, or the configuration of an intermediate point, can be specified (route paths). This understanding of *path* is common in the language acquisition and conceptualization literature (Pulverman et al. 2006, 2008), as well as in work addressing the nature and development of human concepts (Mandler 2006). In this chapter we use *path* in this broader sense.

Despite his definition cited above, Talmy uses *path* only in the sense of directed motion to determine the strategies followed by languages in the linguistic expression of motion (e.g. satellite-framed vs verb-framed). Due to this restricted use of the term, the lexical encoding of *manner* and *path* has been considered complementary, and locomotion verbs that incorporate manner have been regarded as pure manner verbs, while the presence of a translational component has been neglected in semantic analyses. However, cross-linguistically we find 'manner' verbs (e.g. Bulgarian *katerja se*, Norwegian *klatre*—'climb/clamber', German *klettern*, Bulgarian *tŭrkaljam se*, Italian *rotolare*—'roll') which uncontroversially include both a *manner* and a *path* element: the *figure* in motion occupies distinct points in space at different points in time (cf. the spatio-temporal sequencing and the ordered set of spatio-temporal pairs of Verkuyl 1993, 1999), and the notion of *path* can also be used to describe such verbs (see Weisgerber 2008 for a similar proposal).

Particularly interesting with respect to the encoding of *manner* and *path* features are what we here label 'verbs of biological motion'. The term 'biological motion' denotes the patterns of body and limb motion which animate creatures employ to achieve translational motion defined as progression along a path. Biological motion is a well-established term in the locomotion literature (Alexander 1996) and differs from non-biological motion in several ways (however, see Bejan and Marden 2006 for a unified perspective on all motion). Its recognition and expression in language is of paramount cognitive and social importance to human beings (Mandler 1996; Troje 2002). It is by definition self-agentive and involves the cyclic iteration of events of greater complexity (the cycles/patterns of internal motion of the body and limbs), the function of which is to cause translational motion (Dimitrova-Vulchanova 1996/99). A viable hypothesis concerning the factors that play a role in biological motion categorization can draw on evidence from research in visual perception. As it turns out, the human mechanisms for biological motion recognition are extremely robust, are present from early on and may even be innate (Simion et al. 2008). Biological motion can be recognized from strongly impoverished stimuli, for example when the moving figure is reduced to a point-light display (the classical experiment in Johansson 1973; also Giese 2004). Based on the literature on the importance of perceptual cues for biological motion recognition, we want to propose a set of parameters which play an important role in the linguistic encoding of biological motion.

9.3   Research Questions and Proposal for a Finer-grained Analysis of *Motion*

It has become clear that *manner* and *path* are pre-theoretical terms which may overlap, if not defined properly (e.g. *path shape* in verbs traditionally defined as manner verbs: *zigzag, spiral, curve*), and are useful only in the description of major lexicalization strategies (e.g. the *path/manner* contrast). Detailed typological investigation and research in conceptual structure, however, requires a more refined system, taking into account the different parameters of these notions. We propose a finer-grained feature analysis for the representation of biological motion based on parameters independently argued to apply in the identification and categorization of motion scenes both in visual perception (Thornton and Vuong 2004, among others) and in linguistic semantics (Dimitrova-Vulchanova 2004a, b; Weisgerber and Geuder 2007; Weisgerber, 2008; Vulchanova et al. 2012). The main features we suggest are given in the list in (1) below.

(1)   a. *Locomotion medium* (e.g. terrestrial vs aquatic vs air)
          – *Interaction between figure and medium* (e.g. suspended vs supported)
       b. *Species* (human vs non-human)
       c. *Characteristic method of propulsion*—the use of body and limbs (no limbs/ body undulation vs bipedal vs quadrupedal)
       d. *Characteristic speed* (fast vs normal vs slow)
       e. *Figure orientation* (front-forwards vs front-backwards vs head-up vs head-down)
       f. *Figure posture* (erect vs supine/lower than usual)
       g. *Path* (presence vs absence of translational motion)
          –*Vector orientation* (horizontal: towards vs away from vs left-to-right vs right-to-left; vertical: up vs down)
          –*Path shape* (circular, zigzag)

Evidence of the relevance of these parameters comes from different sources. For instance, *figure orientation* and *vector orientation* have been shown to influence the visual perception of motion and motion type identification in point-light displays (Shipley 2003). The notion of *path*, which is here defined as the presence vs absence of translation (progression in space), offers a rich inventory of potential further specifications (such as e.g. *start point, end point, path length*), which have been studied extensively in the linguistic literature (see Jackendoff 2002 for a recent discussion of types of *path*). Speed has been recently addressed in work by Gries (2006), Stefanowitsch (2008), and Malt et al. (2008) in connection with the characterization of *run* verbs. However, to the best of our knowledge, up to this point, no approach presents an exhaustive characterization of the parameters and features listed in (1).

All of the parameters in (1) can in theory combine on all of their values, potentially yielding a host of possible motion scenes. Thus, an instance of [terrestrial/human/bi-pedal/supine/slow/translational/underspecified-path-shape] motion would be *crawl*. In many cases, specific parameter values will tend to co-occur in nature. For instance, human terrestrial motion is by default bi-pedal, head-up, a fact reflected among other things in that inverted point-light displays are processed more slowly, if at all (Shipley 2003; Reed et al. 2003; Loucks and Baldwin 2009). Likewise, not all features are relevant for categorization in all cases. For example, for the verb *swim*, the manner in which the swimmer uses her limbs or body does not play any role whatsoever. Rather, the aquatic medium and whether motion is self-propelled or not are important, as in *swim* vs *float* (Geuder and Weisgerber 2006; Lander et al. 2012). Our current work suggests that languages encode in their lexical items certain (proto-)typical combinations of features that correspond to higher perceptual salience and experiential frequency of motion scenes. We refer to this as the *default setting of parameters*. This is in line with the theory of Rosch et al. (1976) who proposed that humans use features that naturally co-occur in experience to assign objects to categories, and to determine how good an example an object is of a category.

Our featural approach is justified by findings in recent research addressing motion identification and visual cues involved in the processing of motion scenes. Most of this research employs the classical point-light display paradigm of Johansson (1973), demonstrating that the identification of locomotion relies on both top–down and bottom–up processing, and that local low-level feature information is highly relevant and more robust, in that it is not affected by dividing attention (Thornton et al. 2002). Furthermore, this research in the visual perception of motion has shown that manipulating features of the display (i.e. our parameters) such as figure orientation, inversion, or vector orientation may influence recognition strongly (Shipley 2003). In a recent learning experiment, Jastorff et al. (2006) demonstrate that learning speed and accuracy for human movements are quite similar to those obtained for completely artificial articulated patterns generated using individual features otherwise present in human locomotion. This study shows that familiarity or biological relevance of the underlying kinematics or skeleton does not (as would be the case if processing was exclusively top–down/gestaltic) seem to be critical for the visual learning process.

With respect to terrestrial biological motion, at least four basic types of biological motion can be distinguished: walking, running, crawling, and climbing. Walking covers supported gaits (i.e. at least one foot is on the ground at all times), usually involving 'normal' to slow speed. Running applies to quick suspended motion (i.e. there are intervals in which none of the feet touches the ground). Crawling is slow supported motion, with the body near and/or parallel to the ground. Climbing covers motion in both directions along a vertical axis. Languages tend to have at least one lexical item encoding each basic type, but this is not necessarily so. Thus, Ewe has only one verb *dzò*, for jump, hop, and fly, while Asante does not have verbs corresponding to *run* and *fly* (Dimitrova-Vulchanova and Martinez, in preparation). A similar situation obtains in Mandarin Chinese (Dimitrova-Vulchanova and Dąbrowska, in preparation). In the lexicons of our target languages, English, Bulgarian, and Norwegian, there are verbs of biological motion corresponding to all four basic types. In addition, all three languages have more specific verbs (e.g. English *strut, pace*; Norwegian *sprade* 'strut', *spasere* 'take a walk'; Bulgarian *pripkam* 'scurry', *razxoždam se* 'take a walk') and general motion verbs (English *move*, Norwegian *bevege seg*, Bulgarian *dviža se*). In line with the findings in Rosch et al. (1976), it is expected that the lexical items expressing the default settings of each biological motion category will be the most widely used ones when describing scenes belonging to that category. This is why we dub them *basic-level* lexical items for that category.

With this in mind, our study has two main goals. Our first goal is to find whether there are basic categories from the point of view of granularity[4] within the semantic field of biological motion. The intention is to check whether in the description of scenes of biological motion, participants would resort to the motion verbs we define as basic-level in these languages (e.g. *walk, run, crawl, climb*), to the superordinate general motion verbs (e.g. *go, come, move*), or to more specific manner verbs (e.g. *gallop, scurry, jog, pace, saunter*, and the like). Our second objective is to zoom in on the features comprising 'manner' and to establish whether there is variation in naming preferences when the scenes vary across the different parameters: *speed, interaction with substrate, method of propulsion, path vector orientation, presence vs absence of translation, species*.

9.4   The Verbs

In this study, we will concentrate on the following verbs in the domain of biological terrestrial motion:[5]

(2)   a. For the running type: English *run*, Norwegian *løpe*, and Bulgarian *tičam/ bjagam*

       b. For the walking type: English *walk*, Norwegian *gå*, and Bulgarian *xodja/ vŭrvja*

---

[4] On the notion of granularity see Dimitrova-Vulchahnova and van der Zee (eds) (2012).

[5] For English, the main definition source is Cambridge Advanced Learner's Dictionary, but Merriam-Webster Online, Oxford English Dictionary online, and MSN Encarta Dictionary for English were also consulted for a counter-check. For Bulgarian, the dictionary used was Andreichin (2004), and for Norwegian, the online versions of Bokmålsordboka and Nynorskordboka.

c. For the crawling type: English *crawl*, Norwegian *krabbe/krype*, and Bulgarian *pŭlzja/lazja*

d. For the climbing type: English *climb*, Norwegian *klatre*, and Bulgarian *katerja se/slizam*

These verbs are good candidates for *basic-level* status in the sense of Rosch et al. (1976), in representing a level of organization of knowledge that supports the identification of human locomotion and the ways humans talk about it. Additional criteria that can be used to determine basic-level status are frequency, age of acquisition[6] (Lakusta and Landau 2005), dictionary definitions, and results from free recall tasks. Free recall tasks were conducted with ten to twelve native speakers of the target languages who were asked to write down as many motion words as they could recall. 90 per cent of the verbs elicited from all participants were members of the class listed in (2) above. It deserves mention that in the case of Bulgarian, specific verbs were absent in the sample, except for *razxoždam se* (stroll), *krača* (pace), and *podskačam* (jump around), all mentioned only once. Both Norwegian and English responses included specific verbs, fifteen in English and twenty-eight for Norwegian; however, each verb occurred once or twice at most. We therefore expect the target verbs to be selected more readily than the more abstract or more specific verbs in the description of events in that domain.

Verbs of running. The main verbs denoting running are English *run*, Bulgarian *tičam*, *bjagam*, and Norwegian *løpe*, *springe*. These all encode roughly the same meaning, described by dictionary definitions in all three languages as 'move fast by propelling oneself with quick and abrupt motions of the legs from the ground'. The two run-verbs in Bulgarian have more or less the same status with respect to register; however they display a [+/-directed motion] distinction, as revealed in constraints on their context of usage and combinability with lexical or semi-lexical prefixes (Vulchanova et al. 2012). In Norwegian, on the other hand, there is a distinction of register. The verb *løpe* belongs to the formal Bokmål variety, while *springe* is more informal, being typical of particular dialects where it is employed consistently instead of *løpe*. Some examples are given in (3) below. Observe that the Bulgarian distinction cannot be straightforwardly demonstrated in simple illustrations due to the rich aspectual and semi-lexical prefixal inventory of the language which interacts with syntactic complementation in a complex way (for analyses and discussion, see Lindstedt 1985; Verkuyl 1999, 2008; Dimitrova-Vulchanova 1996/99; among others).

---

[6] For English, it has been established that the verbs we label basic-level are present earlier than more specific verbs, such as *stroll*, *jog*, etc. (Lakusta and Landau 2005). However, Mandler and McDonough (2000) argue that the basic level is also subject to development, at least in the domain of object categorization/nouns.

(3) a. We had to run to catch up with him   (English)
     b. Bjaga za zdrave   (Bulgarian)
        '(He) runs for health/ recreation'
     c. Detsata tičat po poljanata.   (Bulgarian)
        'The children (are) run(ning) on the meadow'
     d. Jeg løp og løp   (Norwegian)
        'I ran and ran'
     e. Han selv ønsket ikke å springe omkring i skogen...   (Norwegian)
        'He himself did not want to run around in the forest'

In addition to their biological motion meaning, the verbs *run, løpe, springe,* and *bjagam* (run2), but not *tičam* (run1), have the meaning of 'flee, move away (by running) when in danger or being chased'. English *run*, and Norwegian *løpe* also have extended meanings along the lines of 'move quickly', 'function', 'develop in time', which are far more widely used than the biological motion meanings.[7] Gries (2006) notes that only 25 per cent of *run* occurrences have the sense of what he labels 'fast pedestrian motion'. Due to limitations of space, we do not address metaphorical uses in this chapter.

Verbs of walking. The most central verbs encoding walking are English *walk,* Norwegian *gå,* and Bulgarian *xodja* (walk1), *vŭrvja (walk2),* as illustrated in (4) below. These all have the meaning of 'move forward by putting one foot in front of the other usually at a moderate pace'.[8]

(4) a. Peter is walking along the road.   (English)
     b. Petŭr vŭrvi/xodi po pŭtja.   (Bulgarian)
     c. Petter går langs veien.   (Norwegian)

Observe that the dictionary definition of the 'walk' verbs already captures the [+traversal] feature we assume to be present in verbs of biological motion, in contrast to traditional views which regard them as (pure) manner verbs. This means that cases like walking on a treadmill are non-default instances of walking which would require explicit reference to the absence of traversal, as confirmed by our experiment. The Norwegian verb *gå* is ambiguous between the more specific meaning (= 'walk') and a meaning of general motion along a path, in which it is predominantly used.[9] *Gå* is also used to express a variety of abstract meanings of the type 'happen', 'develop in time'.

---

[7] For English, a search in the ICAME corpora collection (The Brown Corpus) revealed that *run* was used in its biological motion sense in 21.95 per cent of the hits.

[8] As defined in Longman and Encarta Dictionary.

[9] A search in the Oslo Corpus of Tagged Norwegian Texts (http://www.tekstlab.uio.no/norsk/bokmaal) showed that for 1,000 randomly chosen hits, 10.8 per cent of instances of the verb *gå* could be interpreted in the biological motion sense.

Verbs of crawling. For the description of crawling scenes, English mainly uses the verb *crawl*, Bulgarian uses the verbs *pŭlzja* (crawl1) and *lazja* (crawl2), and Norwegian uses the verbs *krabbe* 'crawl' and *krype* 'creep, crawl'. Illustrations are given in (5) below.

(5) a. There's an ant crawling up your leg.   (English)
     b. For første gang så jeg henne krabbe   (Norwegian)
         fremover.
         'It was the first time I saw her crawling forwards'
     c. En bille krøp over gulvet.   (Norwegian)
         'A beetle was crawling across the floor'
     d. Zmijata/bebeto/gŭsenitsata pŭlzi.   (Bulgarian)
         'The snake/baby/caterpillar is crawling'
     e. Mravkata/deteto lazi.
         'The ant/baby is crawling'

All verbs in this category mean 'move slowly in a prone position, with the body along, close to or touching the surface'.[10] For *pŭlzja* (Bg) and *krype* (N), the use of limbs is not required. *Lazja* (Bg) and *krabbe* (N), however, apply only to scenes where limbs are used, in addition to the specification of 'prone' body position, and this appears to be the case for non-metaphorical uses of *crawl* in English.[11] Thus, in Norwegian, *krabbe* applies only to humans (due to the specific locomotion pattern it denotes), while *krype* is used for crawling by non-human species (e.g. insects), as well as metaphorically.

Verbs of climbing. For the description of biological motion along the vertical axis, and adhering to an inclined surface, English uses the verb *climb*, and Norwegian the verb *klatre*. Both verbs can be used to denote motion either up (6a, b) or down (6d, e). Bulgarian splits the domain of vertical biological motion into two, using the verb *katerja se* for upward motion (6c), and *slizam* for downward motion (6f).

(6) a. The koala is climbing the tree   (English)
     b. Koalaen klatrer opp treet.   (Norwegian)
         'The koala climbs up the tree'
     c. Koalata se kateri (*nadolu) po durvoto   (Bulgarian)
         'The koala climbs (downwards) on the tree'
     d. The sloth is climbing down the tree.   (English)
     e. Dovendyret klatrer ned/nedover treet.   (Norwegian)
         'The sloth climbs down1/down2 the tree'
     f. Lenivetsŭt sliza po dŭrvoto.   (Bulgarian)
         'The sloth climbs down the tree'

[10] Cambridge Advanced Learner's Dictionary.
[11] We owe this observation to Chris Wilder.

An interesting difference between English and Norwegian is that while English *climb* encodes the upward direction by default, as demonstrated in (6a, d), in Norwegian both upward and downward motion have to be overtly specified, as shown in (6b, e). In Bulgarian, on the other hand, the upward direction is lexically encoded in *katerja se*—'climb' (note that the PP in (6c) realizes a location, not a direction). While *klatre*, *katerja se*, and *slizam* are usually restricted to biological motion and require a characteristic use of limbs and clinging to a vertical or steep surface, *climb* can be used with the more general meaning of 'go up, move upwards', very similar to German *steigen* (Weisgerber 2008). This use of *climb* is not considered here, as none of the scenes in the experiment show non-biological notion.

The Bulgarian verb pairs. The paired Bulgarian verbs for walking, running, and crawling deserve special attention. A quick check of standard monolingual Bulgarian dictionaries reveals very similar, or even overlapping, definitions. Quite often, one of the verbs is used to explain the meaning of the other. There is indeed some overlap in the use of the verbs in each pair, *xodja/vǔrvja* (walk1/walk2), *tičam/bjagam* (run1/run2), and *pǔlzja/lazja* (crawl1/crawl2), and native speakers may experience problems in explaining the potential difference between the two verbs in the pair, as revealed by elicitation queries conducted during the preparation of the experiment and in interviews with participants right after the experiment.[12] Furthermore, there has been no experimental research to determine to what extent speakers agree on how to use those verbs. As is widely assumed, language does not tolerate redundancy in the lexicon. True synonyms are rarely attested cross-linguistically (Lyons 1977). One way to approach this issue is to look for differences on the level of language as a system, as revealed in patterns of occurrence and collocational restrictions and in restrictions on the mapping of conceptual and semantic information to syntax. Another approach, experimental in nature, can simply test how native speakers use the items in question in the naming of visual stimuli representing instances of the locomotion patterns involved. In this study we follow the latter approach and look at native speaker naming preferences.

9.5 Hypotheses

On the basis of the general motion encoding properties of the target verbs in the three target languages, our hypothesis is that the speakers of these languages will use the basic-level verbs of biological motion, rather than general motion verbs,

---

[12] In Bulgarian, the use of two verbs is generally motivated diachronically, as Old Bulgarian had the so-called aspectual verb pairs, with one verb denoting the general scene (e.g. the specific motion pattern), and the other denoting the goal-oriented, bounded (telic) event. Such pairs are still found in Modern Russian (Foote 1967), e.g. *xodit'* (roughly corresponding to *walk*) vs *idti* (*go*), and to a limited extent in Modern Bulgarian, e.g. *xodja* (*walk*, imperf.) vs *otivam* (*go*, perf.). There are also differences in the constraints on use of verb1 and verb2 in certain idiomatic set expressions in Modern Bulgarian.

or more specific (subordinate) verbs. We expect basic-level verbs to be preferred over superordinate ones (e.g. *move, go*) because the former are informationally richer, as they encode not only translational motion but also other specifications (e.g. medium, velocity, cycle, posture, species, figure orientation, etc.), which are highly salient in the biological motion domain. Furthermore, we expect the target verbs to be preferred to more specific/concrete verbs (e.g. *strut, gallop, lope*), because they encode the most commonly occurring settings of experientially established locomotion categories. We also predict that non-default scenes of biological motion will elicit a less uniform response across verb types, since such scenes are more difficult to categorize, and thus more difficult to name than scenes with default setting of the parameters (e.g. Pavlova et al. 2001; Thornton and Vuong 2004). With regard to the distribution of the target verbs across answers, we predict that the responses for Bulgarian will display the two-way split found in the lexicon. Since Norwegian *gå* has two senses, a basic-level one equivalent to English *walk*, and a general motion sense equivalent to English *go*, it is expected to be used more frequently across scenes (i.e. also for scenes which do not depict walking), compared to the walking verbs in English and Bulgarian.

9.6   The Experiment

Method: materials, participants, and procedure. The participants were adult native speakers of the respective languages: sixteen for Bulgarian, sixteen for Norwegian, and twelve for English.[13] Each of them watched a sequence of video clips on a computer screen and was asked to provide a free description in their native language of the action in each clip. The clips were viewed in a single session, preceded by detailed instructions on the screen. Participants were advised to provide the first word/description that came to mind and were allowed to work at their own pace. Each clip was shown only once and could not be played back for reference. Participants were then prompted to type their responses in a text box that appeared under the image and proceed to the next clip.

The stimuli were selected from documentaries or created by the experimenters with the aim of providing a range of biological motion scenes performed in natural settings by animate beings (humans, non-human primates, other animals). The clips showed five full cycles of the action, or, for slower actions, a time interval of approximately 5 seconds. The scenes were shown in a pseudo-randomized order, to ensure that similar scenes were not presented close to each other. The scenes we used covered variations with respect to cycle structure and/or body configuration (e.g. crawl on all fours, crawl on one's stomach, bipedal

---

[13] The difference in the number of participants for the three languages should not influence the results for the purpose of the present study.

walk, quadrupedal walk, bipedal run, quadrupedal run, quadrupedal trot), species (e.g. human, ape, bird, cat, dog, etc.), age differences among the actors (baby vs adult), speed (slow vs normal vs fast), translation vs non-translation (regular running vs running on the spot or running on a treadmill), vector orientation (horizontal: towards vs away from camera, vertical: up vs down), figure orientation (front-forwards vs front-backwards; head-up vs head-down), path shape (straight, circular), substrate (ground vs branch vs leaf, smooth vs grassy surface). Since we wanted to elicit preliminary responses to a variety of instances, the scenes presented in the experiment were not matched with respect to parameters such as physical setting, physiological characteristics of the agents, viewing angle, etc. Our purpose was not to control for all such factors, but to find general indications of their role and potential significance in motion categorization and naming, and thus help to direct attention to specific features for further research. We are aware that the results should be interpreted accordingly.

9.7   Results and Discussion

It is clear from the verb counts (Table 9.1) that in each language, a few motion verbs occur much more often in the descriptions of the twenty-nine target scenes than any other verbs. In English, these are the verbs referring to four motion domains: *run* (22 per cent of all verbs used in the answers), *walk* (21 per cent), *crawl* (17.5 per cent) and *climb* (8.3 per cent). The overall lower occurrence of *climb* can be explained by the smaller number of scenes encoding motion along the vertical axis (see discussion below). In Bulgarian, these are the verbs *hodja* 'walk1' (15.9 per cent), *pŭlzja* 'crawl1' (14.9 per cent), *tičam* 'run1'(11.6 per cent), *bjagam* 'run2' (9.5 per cent), *lazja* 'crawl2' (5.6 per cent), *katerja se* 'climb up' (5.2 per cent) and *vŭrvja* 'walk2' (4.5 per cent). As expected, the counts for the individual verbs are lower than in English due to the two-verb split in Bulgarian, but if we sum the verbs of highest frequency for each of the domains running (21.1 per cent), walking (20.4 per cent), and crawling (20.5 per cent), the counts are comparable to those in the English descriptions, and none of the more specific biological motion verbs surpasses the target verbs in frequency. In the domain of climbing, the Bulgarian verb *katerja se* is the most frequently occurring one (5.2 per cent), but it is still not as frequent as English *climb*. On the one hand, this is due to the split in Bulgarian between the description of climbing upwards (*katerja se*) and downwards (*slizam*, 1.5 per cent). On the other hand, Bulgarian participants sometimes use verbs of directed motion—*kačvam se* 'go up' (1.7 per cent) and *spuskam se* 'go down/ descend' (0.9 per cent)—instead of biological motion verbs. Put together, these four verbs of climbing up or climbing down amount to a proportion (9.3 per cent) comparable to that of the other two target languages. In Norwegian, the most commonly occurring verbs cover the domains of walking (*gå*, 24.8 per cent), running (*løpe*, 23.9 per cent), and climbing (*klatre*, 9.9 per cent). The domain of crawling is represented by three verbs: *krabbe* (9.3 per cent), *åle seg* 'crawl/ wriggle' (6 per cent), and *krype* 'creep' (5.6 per cent). Together, these verbs give a proportion of 20.9 per cent, comparable to those for English and Bulgarian target verbs that refer to crawling.

TABLE 9.1. *Overall frequencies of verbs (in %) for the three target languages across the 29 target scenes*

Bulgarian	English	Norwegian
tičam 'run' - 11.6 *bjagam* 'run' - 9.5	*run* - 22.1	*løpe* 'run' - 23.9
hodja 'walk' - 16.0 *vurvja* 'walk' - 4.5	*walk* – 21.0	*gå* 'walk' - 24.8
pulzja 'crawl' - 14.9 *lazja* 'crawl' - 5.6	*crawl* - 17.5	*krabbe* 'crawl' - 9.3 *åle seg* 'crawl, wiggle' - 6.0 *krype* 'creep, crawl' - 5.6
katerja se 'climb up' - 5.2 *slizam* 'climb down' - 1.5	*climb* - 8.3	*klatre* 'climb, clamber'-9.9
general motion - 4.1	general motion - 2.9	general motion - 0.4
more spec. biol. motion - 8.8	more spec. biol. motion - 17.2	more spec. biol. motion - 14.2
	other manner of motion - 4.3	other manner of motion - 0.4
intrinsic motion - 1.1	intrinsic motion - 0.6	intrinsic motion - 2.2
rotation - 2.8	rotation -1.4	
directed motion - 4.3	directed motion - 1.2	directed motion - 0.2
tandem motion -1.3	tandem motion - 0.9	tandem motion - 0.2
non-motion - 8.8	non-motion - 2.6	non - motion - 2.8

Due to the lack of space, the less commonly occurring verbs have been grouped into the following categories: (1) More specific biological motion: biological motion verbs which can be defined 'a kind of running/ walking/ crawling/ climbing'; (2) Directed motion: verbs like *arrive, reach, pass, leave*, etc. which encode direction of motion as defined by Jackendoff (2002); (3) General motion: verbs like *move*, which can refer to any kind of motion; (4) Rotation—verbs like *turn* and *circle*; (5) Tandem motion: verbs encoding that one entity moves in tandem with another, e.g. *follow* and *chase*; (6) Intrinsic motion: verbs encoding a dynamic relation between parts of the same entity, rather than its displacement with respect to a reference object, e.g. *ripple, bulge*, etc.; (7) Other manner of motion: verbs indicating translational motion + manner, which is not necessarily biological, e.g. *slide, slither, float*, etc.; (8) Non-motion: various kinds of verbs not expressing motion e.g. *look around, search, hunt, attack, ambush*, etc.

There are interesting differences in the proportion of non-target motion verbs between the three languages (these are the categories 'general motion', 'more specific motion', 'tandem motion', 'directed motion', 'other manner of motion', 'rotation', and 'intrinsic motion' in Table 9.1). Norwegian resorts to such verbs less often than English and Bulgarian (Norwegian 16.4 per cent vs English 25.6 per cent/Bulgarian 22.4 per cent). English and Norwegian moreo display a pattern different from Bulgarian. Bulgarian has a higher proportion of non-motion verbs (8.8 per cent vs 2.6 per cent in English and 2.8 per cent in Norwegian), general motion verbs (4.1 per cent vs 2.9 per cent in English and 0.4 per cent in Norwegian) and directed motion verbs (4.3 per cent vs 1.2 per cent in English and 0.2 per cent in Norwegian). English and Norwegian resort more often to more specific verbs of biological motion (English 17.2 per cent/Norwegian 14.2 per cent vs 8.8 per cent in Bulgarian), most likely due to their having a much richer inventory of such verbs in their lexicons (Öztürk et al. 2011). Considering these results from the perspective of Slobin (2004), we can see a connection between the size of the manner-of-motion verb vocabulary in a language and the frequency of attending to manner in language use: Bulgarian is clearly a less manner-salient language than English and Norwegian. However, in all three target languages, the domains of running, walking, crawling, and climbing are represented by similar (within each language) proportions of basic-level biological motion verbs, which so far supports our hypothesis that these verbs are more central in naming these motion domains. We need to examine the distribution of the target verbs for the separate scenes to establish whether the target verbs have been used consistently across scenes. In order to support our hypothesis about the importance of certain spatial features in the categorization and naming of motion scenes, we will also look into what common underlying spatial features characterize scenes described by the same verb.

Being able to apply a verb to a scene means that the scene belongs to the motion type encoded by the verb, but since not all participants for the same language use the same verb, belonging to a given motion category is a matter of degree, rather than absolute. We take higher verb counts as an indication that some scenes are better examples of a certain motion type than others. Cases where the description of a given scene fails to yield a high count for a target verb may be explained by two factors. On the one hand, there may be other salient features in the scene, pertaining either to space/motion (e.g. direction of motion or path shape) or to non-motion (e.g. intentions, social factors)[14], which encourage the use of other types of verbs (cf. the categories in Table 9.1). On the other hand, a scene may be characterized by a combination of spatial features that allows it to

---

[14] This finding is highly coherent with ideas put forward in Tomasello (2001) and Zacks and Tversky (2001) that human categorization is highly susceptible to the teleology of events, and that humans attend from very early on to agents' intentions and goals. Furthermore, recent research in infant cognition based in eye-tracking has demonstrated that infants as young as 12 months can predict other people's action goals (Falck-Ytter et al. 2006).

be viewed as belonging to two or more biological motion categories (or the 'grey zone' between them), in which case more than one of the target verbs applies, thus reducing the score for each.

In the descriptions of many scenes, there is a preference for a particular target verb (or pair of verbs in Bulgarian), but there are too few observations within an individual scene to ascertain whether this is statistically significant. For this reason, we use a cut-off point one third[15] to categorize the scenes into running, walking, crawling, climbing, and grey zone scenes (scenes which elicit more than one verb type within a single language or across languages). Then we analyse the occurrence of each of the target verbs (or pairs of target verbs) across all scene types, to see whether the use of this verb is restricted to a particular scene type (Table 9.2a), which would suggest a strong correlation between scene type and target verb. In addition, the descriptions of each scene type are examined to see whether it is described consistently by one target verb (Table 9.2b), which, if it is the case, would establish the verb as the common denominator for the scene type. Both types of analysis will provide evidence for a connection between the features which are common to all scenes in a group (and thus considered as default settings), and the basic-level verb.

Grouping of the target scenes according to naming preferences. The grouping of scenes according to naming preferences is given in Table 9.2. Eight scenes (woman, hunt dog, dog on a treadmill, dog running in a circle, chimpanzee, koala, lizard moving on four legs, lizard moving on hind legs) are unanimously classified as running scenes by all languages, while one scene, man running on the spot, is described in Norwegian predominantly by the more specific motion verb *jogge* 'jog', and therefore fails to reach the one third cut-off point for the basic-level verb *løpe*. For all running scenes, the default settings are suspended motion on the horizontal axis, and the presence of effort.

Six scenes (woman moving forwards, woman moving backwards, chimpanzee, koala, tiger, bird) are unanimously categorized as walking, and four other scenes fall into the walking category according to at least one of the languages. The scene with a crocodile walking falls into the grey zone in English, because of the predominant use of more specific verbs describing the sideways swaying of the body during motion. The scene of two monkeys moving around a tree does not reach the one third cut-off point in English and Bulgarian, because of the predominant use of verbs referring to the circular path or of non-motion verbs. The scene of a chameleon moving slowly on a twig does not reach the cut-off point in Norwegian because of the predominant use of non-motion verbs (*ballansere* 'balance'). There is also a scene for which both walking and crawling verbs reach the cut-off point in Norwegian—a beetle moving slowly on a twig—

---

[15] For instance, if more than one third of the descriptions of a scene contain basic-level running verbs in a particular language, the scene is classified as a running scene for that language.

while for Bulgarian and English this scene is classified as crawling. On the whole, however, the default setting for all scenes classified as walking is supported motion on the horizontal axis, at normal-to-slow speed.

Five scenes are uniformly classified as crawling (woman moving on all fours, baby moving on all fours, man crawling on his stomach in a military fashion, a caterpillar, and a tortoise). The beetle scene mentioned above is classified as crawling in English and Bulgarian only, although in these two languages it also elicited a few occurrences of walking verbs. Two snake scenes, which are classified as crawling in Bulgarian and Norwegian, fail to reach the cut-off point in English because of the predominant use of the verb *slither*. On the whole, crawling scenes are characterized by slow supported motion and 'prone' posture, either with contact between the body and the surface, or, at least, with a posture lower than the usual for the species and more body and limb contact with the surface than is usual. On the further subdivision of the crawling domain, see the section on cluster analysis.

Three scenes are classified as climbing scenes (two scenes of koalas climbing trees, and a sloth moving down a tree). In all three scenes, the common setting is

TABLE 9.2. *Mutual distribution of basic-level verbs and scene types.*
TABLE 9.2A. % **within verb** *(e.g., what proportion of all running verbs were used to describe running scenes/ walking scenes/ crawling scenes/ climbing scenes/ grey zone scenes)*

| | | | \multicolumn{6}{c}{scene type} | | | | | |
			Cl	Cr	G	R	W	WCr
verb	bg	other verbs	3.8	18.0	12.0	34.6	31.6	
		climbing	93.0	7.0				
		crawling	2.1	94.7			3.2	
		running				100.0		
		walking	1.1	11.6			87.4	
	eng	other verbs	5.6	11.1	37.0	27.8	18.5	
		climbing	96.6	3.4				
		crawling	1.6	91.8	4.9		1.6	
		running				100.0		
		walking	1.4	4.1	6.8	1.4	86.3	
	no	other verbs	3.2	18.9	21.1	24.2	31.6	1.1
		climbing	95.7		2.2			2.2
		crawling		92.8	1.0			6.2
		running			4.5	93.7	1.8	
		walking	.9	3.5	4.3	.9	83.5	7.0

TABLE 9.2B. % **within scene type** (e.g. to what extent running scenes in general are described by running verbs/ walking verbs/ crawling verbs/ climbing verbs/ other verbs)

			scene type					
			Cl	Cr	G	R	W	WCr
verb	bg	other verbs	10.4	18.8	100.0	31.9	32.8	
		climbing	83.3	2.3				
		crawling	4.2	70.3			2.3	
		running				68.1		
		walking	2.1	8.6			64.8	
	eng	other verbs	16.7	16.7	83.3	27.8	23.8	
		climbing	77.8	1.4				
		crawling	2.8	77.8	6.3		1.2	
		running				71.3		
		walking	2.8	4.2	10.4	.9	75.0	
	no	other verbs	6.3	16.1	62.5	18.0	23.4	6.3
		climbing	91.7		3.1			6.3
		crawling		80.4	3.1			37.5
		running			15.6	81.3	1.6	
		walking	2.1	3.6	15.6	.8	75.0	50.0

motion along the vertical axis, and adhering to a vertical surface. For further analysis of the domain of climbing, see the cluster analysis section.

Distribution of the target verbs across scene types. For all four domains of biological motion, the results show that the target verbs are used in 80–100 per cent of cases to describe the respective scene type (Table 9.2a). Furthermore, each scene type is predominantly described by the respective target verbs (65–90 per cent in Table 9.2b). The domain of running shows an especially high degree of autonomy, with almost no overlap with other biological motion domains, both with respect to the scenes described by running verbs, and the types of verbs by which running scenes are described. This is not so for the walking, crawling, and climbing domains, where there is partial overlap, especially between walking and crawling. This suggests that there is a clear divide along the line between supported and suspended terrestrial biological motion, and a less clear distinction in the domain of supported motion between normal vs 'prone' posture, and normal vs slow speed. It appears that walking and crawling are on one end of the velocity criterion, and as such enter an opposition with running terms, rather than with each other (see also Malt et al. 2008, 2010). The walking domain seems to be the most diffusely defined, with walking verbs extending even to the descriptions of lower-speed running scenes. The high proportion of climbing verbs used in climbing scenes (Table 9.2a) shows the climbing domain's independence from the other three domains (despite that fact that some climbing verbs were used in crawling scenes—see Table 9.2a; and some crawling and walking verbs were used for climbing scenes—see Table 9.2b), suggesting a relatively robust divide with respect to horizontal vs vertical motion. In order to seek an independent confirmation of this rough division between the domains, and to find more fine-grained distinctions based on naming preferences, we conducted a cluster analysis, which is discussed in the next section.

Cluster analysis. Cluster analysis has proved useful in revealing patterns of grouping in collections of objects, and thus potential similarity (cf. the seminal work by Tversky 1977), and is specifically appropriate in the field of matching perceptual stimuli to lexical items to reveal patterns of lexical preference, as shown in Malt et al. (2008). Therefore, in addition to the distribution analysis of verbs across scene types, we conducted a cluster analysis and calculated Simpson's diversity index (D). Our aim was to show finer distinctions within the conceptual fields of the target verbs. For this reason, the clustering criterion included all motion verbs occurring in the descriptions. The distance of branching in the cluster tree is intended to show the degree of similarity between scenes, and to give an idea as to whether a scene is central or peripheral within its cluster.

The method we used in our analysis was *hierarchical agglomerative clustering with average linkage.* We employed a *multiset* distance measure which takes into account the frequency of occurrence of verbs in the description of each scene.[16] For all three languages, the cluster analysis (Figure 1 a–c) revealed a clear structure of the locomotion field with four distinct groups, based on type of locomotion (running, walking, crawling, and climbing). The field of running displays greater similarity with a tighter clustering structure, while crawling displays the greatest diversity. Overall, for all three languages, the more similar the stimuli are in terms of the basic features adopted in our analysis, the closer the clustering in terms of verbs used. Some features, however, turn out to be more predictive of the clustering and linguistic categorization than others. For example, species appear to have significance primarily in the domain of crawling (humans vs other mammals vs reptiles), while speed and supported vs non-supported gait are generally significant. Among the languages studied, English displays the tightest grouping of the field as reflected in the linguistic items used and greatest degree of similarity within each basic type of locomotion, while Bulgarian is the most diverse (Bulgarian displayed a much lower average Simpson's index (D) than English or Norwegian: 0.39 vs 0.56 and 0.62, respectively). Furthermore, variation in the situations on more than one parameter results in greater distance in the

---

[16] For more details on the cluster analysis and a formal definition of the *multiset* measure, see Vulchanova et al. (2012).

cluster plot. This is best demonstrated in Norwegian, where all scenes showing high velocity running (a lizard running very fast, a dog running fast around a tree, a chimp running fast and a dog galloping across a field) display a high degree of similarity, forming a very tight cluster, and are separated by several branches from the scene of a dog running on a treadmill (i.e. running on the spot).

The clustering patterns show that the most distinctive feature for motion along the horizontal axis (running, walking, and crawling) is *characteristic speed*. The cluster analysis revealed a basic split between lexical items naming high-speed scenes (e.g. *run*) and all others (e.g. *walk* and *crawl*), the latter both performed at a normal-to-low speed. This basic split is most evident in the cluster plot for Bulgarian, where walking and crawling situations form one big cluster and are joined on the same branch in the hierarchy. The significance of speed as a salient parameter in the linguistic categorization of motion was also identified in a recent study by Malt et al. (2008) for English, Spanish, and Japanese. Our results independently confirm the salience of velocity in the identification and naming of basic-level biological motion, with a clear split in the lexicon between items for fast motion and items for slow or normal motion, clearly making motion at high velocity the non-default feature in the pair. Velocity is a major factor distinguishing walking from running, with even greater variation across gait-types in quadrupeds (e.g. *walk* vs *amble*, *trot* vs *pace*, *canter* vs *gallop*). Our experiment was not explicitly designed to check for the role of velocity, as we used scenes shot in natural surroundings which were not subject to any manipulation.[17] There are some indications, however, that each of the three main gait types—walking, running, and crawling—has its 'default' velocity: high for running, low for crawling, and normal-to-low for walking.

Two factors directly related to the *speed* of biological motion are the interaction of the *figure* with the terrestrial *substrate* (*suspended* vs *supported* gaits), and *cycle*—the way the agent moves its limbs and body, in order to achieve translational motion. This categorization distinction corresponds to established facts from biomechanics (Alexander 1989, 1996), where the importance of velocity (alongside gravity and limb length) for the transition between gait patterns is captured in the so-called Froude number.[18] It has been discovered that the transition from supported to suspended gaits happens across species at particular Froude numbers, where supported locomotion corresponds to lower velocity, and suspended motion corresponds to higher velocity. Here, two factors in our stimuli appeared significant: suspended vs supported motion (i.e. running vs walking/ crawling), and erect posture vs 'supine'/'lower than usual' posture (i.e. walking vs crawling). Our expectation that the naming of the target scenes would consistently reflect the value of the parameter *supported* vs *suspended* was borne

---

[17] Except for one clip which was generated by running a sequence backwards.

[18] $F = \frac{V}{\sqrt{g \cdot L}}$ Where V = velocity, g = force of gravity, and L = limb length.

out. The cluster analysis revealed a major split between the clustering of suspended motion scenes (running) and supported motion scenes (walking,
crawling, and climbing). All scenes with suspended motion were overwhelmingly
identified with verbs of running in all three languages. Furthermore, the clusters
reveal a split within the walking and crawling domain due to the difference in the
type of supported gait, with crawling being characterized by supine posture (e.g.
having more points of contact with the ground) compared to walking. To the
extent that velocity and suspended vs supported gait are interrelated, their
respective weighting ought to be checked further in an experiment which teases
the two apart (Dimitrova-Vulchanova and van der Zee, in preparation).

As shown both in the distribution analysis (Table 9.2) and the cluster analysis
(Figure 9.1), there was much less uniformity across the target languages with
respect to walking and crawling scenes. Our data clearly show how different
factors may supersede others across languages in the categorization of motion.
Posture may prove to be a further dividing factor. While the default value for
walking is *erect posture*, or at least erect limbs and some distance between the
torso and the ground, the default for crawling is *supine posture*, non-erect limbs,
and nearness or contact with the ground. These features clearly influence the
naming of walking vs crawling for humans. In other cases, however, it is not so
clear what the difference between 'erect' and 'supine' is, as the species in question
have only one posture available. This was demonstrated in the naming of the
scenes of a beetle, and a tortoise, responses to which varied on the walking–
crawling continuum. Since categorization is a learning-based process (Giese and
Poggio 2003; Giese 2004), it will be natural for a particular type of biological
motion category (and therefore biological motion verb) to be most commonly
associated with the feature configuration in which it most often occurs in our
experience (Rosch et al. 1976). Therefore, verbs usually associated with human
postures may be extended to scenes which lack a dedicated lexical item due to
their restricted relevance in our experience.

Another factor which proves to be important is *species*, though it does not have
equal weight in all cases. In our data, the domain of walking shows itself to be
'anthropocentric', with the clips of human locomotion scoring highest in the use
of target verbs, and a great deal of variation in the naming choices for motion by
non-human species, such as insects and reptiles. This is most evident in the
Norwegian cluster plot (Figure 9.1c), where the scenes showing non-mammal
normal-to-slow motion appear on a separate branch. The clips showing humans
crawling on all fours also elicited the most systematic crawl verb responses in
English and Bulgarian. The species factor was most visible in the naming of
crawling scenes in all three languages, but most clearly in Norwegian, where the
verb *krabbe* was exclusively reserved for human locomotion, with a non-signific-
ant use for some other legged creatures (a tortoise), but not for insects. This is
clearly visible in the cluster plot where the human crawling scenes form their own
cluster. The scenes showing non-human agents produced much less uniformity

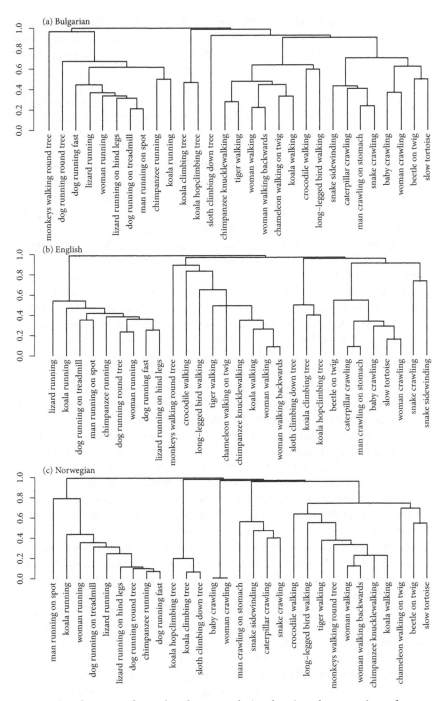

FIG. 9.1. Dendrograms from the cluster analysis, showing the grouping of scenes according to the naming patterns for each of the three target languages

in the answers. These findings might point in the direction of the presence of an anthropocentric (human) gestalt-like prototype (Thornton and Vuong 2004; Pavlova et al. 2005 for adult categorization; Shipley 2003). However, recent research in biological motion categorization provides evidence also of the role of experience and factors that influence visual perception, such as point of view. For instance, Pavlova et al. (2001) show that four-to-five year olds more readily identify point-light displays of dogs walking than humans, most likely due to experience of a specific view of dogs, which are comparable/closer in height to young children than adult walkers.

Another important factor in the categorization of scenes of 'supine' terrestrial locomotion is the manner used to propel the body: *use of limbs* vs *undulations of the body* vs *friction with the substrate surface*. In Norwegian, the verb *krype* 'creep' was used for locomotion scenes of legged creatures. In Bulgarian, both *pŭlzja* (crawl1) and *lazja* (crawl2) were used in the naming of the scenes of humans crawling; however, across all scenes the verb *pŭlzja* (crawl1) has a much higher frequency. *Pŭlzja* was the only verb used to name scenes of 'limbless' locomotion (snakes), and the one predominantly used where the body of the agent has contact with the surface. The two snake scenes showed the greatest variation and differences across the three languages in terms of the choice of verb. Only in Bulgarian were these scenes characterized overwhelmingly by target verbs. In English, the verb predominantly used for the snake moving in a 'default' way (technically called 'lateral undulation') was *slither*, with clear emphasis on the friction between the body and the substrate. In Norwegian, the snake scene and the scene of a man crawling on his belly (soldier-fashion) were predominantly characterized by verbs referring to the winding body, and, consequently, to the path-shape (*åle seg* 'crawl, wriggle', lit. 'move like an eel').

Verbs of climbing clearly instantiate a group of biological motion verbs, where *manner* cannot be dissociated from *path*. In Norwegian *klatre*, and Bulgarian *katerja se/slizam*, both the contact of the limbs with the vertical surface and the translation in space are necessary features, without which no scene can be felicitously described as an instance of climbing. It is a language-specific matter, however, to what degree these verbs specify a vertical path. Both in English and in Norwegian, the relevant verbs encode motion along a vertical *axis*, but the direction is not specified: it can be either up or down (cf. the analysis for German *steigen/klettern* in Weisgerber 2008). Still, there is some evidence that motion upwards is the default (it is the direction implicitly understood when the verbs appear unmodified), while motion downwards is usually specified through modification by satellites or adverbial phrases. This was clearly demonstrated in responses to the climbing down scene in the experiment. In Bulgarian, each of the two orientation vectors along the *vertical axis* is lexicalized in a separate climbing verb, revealed in the cluster plot by two separate groups.

Although the target verbs of walking, running, and crawling appear to be under-specified for axis of motion, motion along the *horizontal axis* seems to be the default. Thus, some of the scenes where the surface was slightly inclined (the scene of a caterpillar, a snake, and a beetle moving along an upward 15–20° angle path) elicited satellites overtly expressing this non-default path orientation (English *up*, Norwegian *opp*, *oppover*), and in a few cases triggered the use of climbing verbs.

The presence of a translational component could not be checked across all types of motion in our set-up. There were only two scenes explicitly targeting this parameter, a man running on the spot and a dog running on a treadmill, where the translational motion parameter was removed. Prior to the experiment, we hypothesized that the concept of running is a kind of *dot object* concept (Pustejovsky 1995; Jackendoff 2002), deriving its conceptual structure as inherited from two main types: biological motion (*manner*) and translational motion (*path*). Our expectations regarding the two scenes where the path-traversal component in *run* was factored out were that participants could still felicitously apply a run-verb in the naming task. This expectation was borne out. Further evidence that the *path* parameter/translation is lexically encoded in run-verbs is the fact that participants in our study commonly used adverbial phrases explicitly spelling out the absence of translation in those particular scenes, thus signalling that the latter deviated from the default. At the same time, it is worth noting that the translational interpretation is the default one when the target run-verbs are used in their basic-level biological motion sense.

9.7 Conclusion

The present study had the following objectives: (a) to check to what extent naming preferences reflect the presence of perceptually salient features in biological motion scenes, and the relative importance of these features; (b) to investigate how motion verbs encode such features and whether our target languages display different levels of granularity in the encoding of biological motion (i.e. a neutral/superordinate level vs a basic level vs a specific/subordinate level). Our experiment has demonstrated that participants show a preference for the basic-level biological motion verbs to both more general (superordinate) and more concrete (subordinate) verbs. The participants' naming patterns provide evidence that perceptually salient features are important in the categorization and linguistic encoding of biological motion. The most salient features that have emerged in our study are *speed, characteristic method of propulsion, vector of motion, species*, and the presence of *translational motion*. Our categories reflect the way the values of these parameters naturally co-occur in our experience. Most scenes featuring a variation from the default on one or more of these conditions produce uncertainty in the naming, shown in an increase in the range of lexical items used across participants, or trigger what we here label the *non-default explication* function—the use of modifying phrases to explicate how the motion occurring in the scene differs from the default. Special patterns of locomotion tend to elicit more specific gait verbs, and there are certain differences across the three target languages in the focus on features encoded in the respective verbs used. Our results also revealed a basic split in the locomotion lexicon between terms used for high-velocity situations and normal-to-slow locomotion (all other basic locomotion types).

Our general results have shed some light on the issue of universality of conceptual features and their encoding in language. The data support the view that many conceptual primitives are indeed based on universal perceptual characteristics (also Malt et al. 2010), and that the conceptual domain of biological motion has a similar basic structure in the languages we have studied, as revealed in the groupings in the cluster analysis. The main difference across languages resides in how these features/primitives are encoded (or 'bundle' to use Jackendoff's term) in lexical items and underdetermine their felicitous use. Apparently, there are robust features that underlie the linguistic categorization of motion (which are also semantically relevant) confirmed in our study by the overall high confidence level for canonical (default) scenes across all three languages. Our data also indicate that in naming processes there appears to be a prototypical packaging of the features that characterize biological motion, while marginal members of the category are difficult to name.

Our study has also provided evidence of interesting differences among languages supposed to belong in the same group in the popular typology proposed by Talmy (1985, 2000), though not concerning the basic-level target verbs. This diversity is primarily displayed in how these languages partition the superordinate and the subordinate domains, a property which can be broadly subsumed under the notion of granularity (Zacks and Tversky 2012; van Staden and Narasimhan 2012).

An interesting question in this connection is what is more salient in motion identification, the motion pattern (cycle) or the body-shape/form, or rather the combination of both (see Smith 2005 for a developmental study). The present study provides a good starting point for further research in the area, generating concrete direct experimental developments (Coventry et al., in preparation; Dimitrova-Vulchanova and van der Zee, in preparation), as well as work on setting up a cross-linguistic typology of expressions of biological motion (Dimitrova-Vulchanova and Dąbrowska, in preparation). Further research is needed to establish the status and factors that mandate the use of subordinate terms, and the semantic structure of that domain (Öztürk et al. 2011).

10

Danish Directional Adverbs: Ways of Profiling a Motion Event

HENRIK HOVMARK*

10.1 Introduction

Danish directional adverbs (DDA) (for instance *op* 'up', *ned* 'down', *ud* 'out', and *ind* 'in'; See Table 10.1) contribute substantially to the well-known coding of path in a motion event, that is, the construal relation between figure and ground (Talmy 2000). Syntactically they enter into the matrix 'verb + directional adverb + prepositional phrase' (*han kørte / ud / til lufthavnen* 'he went by car / out / to the airport'), and can be categorized as satellites within Talmy's terminology, coding salient specifics of direction (especially so-called 'conformation', i.e. geometric information about the path; cf. Talmy 2000, II: 53–7).

TABLE 10.1. *DDA, overview. Words in parenthesis indicate (weak) or ((very weak)) representation in actual language use (cf. Table 10.2)*

	-Ø (dynamic)	*-e* (static)	*-ad* (procedural)
'up'	*op*	*oppe*	*opad*
'down'	*ned*	*nede*	*nedad*
'out'	*ud*	*ude*	*udad*
'in'	*ind*	*inde*	*indad*
'in horizontal dir.'	*hen*	*henne*	*(henad)*
'over'/'across'	*over*	*ovre*	*((overad))*
'around'	*om*	*omme*	*((omad))*
'home'	*hjem*	*hjemme*	*hjemad*
'forward'/'ahead'	*frem*	*fremme*	*fremad*
'back'	*tilbage*	*tilbage*	*((tilbagead))*
'away'	*bort*	*borte*	—

* I should like to thank the editors and two anonymous referees for valuable comments on this chapter. I am also indebted to Kasper Boye for discussions and comments on earlier versions of this work, and to Gillian Fellows-Jensen for proofreading the text. Of course, I am alone responsible for any remaining errors or inaccuracies in the final version.

An analysis of DDAs using Talmy's classification is in general relatively straightforward, Danish being in its terms a typical satellite-framed language. However, Danish directional adverbs are characterized by an important special feature as satellites—they have different forms: a zero-form (*ud-Ø*), a form with a derivative *-e*-suffix (*ud-e*), and a third form with a prepositional *-ad*-suffix (*ud-ad* '-wards').[1] Furthermore, the forms are distinguished prosodically: all forms receive primary stress; the zero-form obviously only receives primary stress, whereas the *-e*-suffix receives no stress and the prepositional *-ad*-suffix ('-wards') receives secondary stress.[2] I refer to the three forms as the dynamic DDA (-DYN), the static DDA (-STAT), and the procedural DDA (-PROC) respectively:

(1) han   kørte   ud   til lufthavnen
     he   drove   out-DYN   to the airport
     'he went by car out to the airport'

(2) katten   er   ude   i gården
     the cat is   out-STAT   in the yard
     'the cat is (outside) in the yard'

(3) vandet   flød   udad   mod gaden
     the water flowed out-PROC   towards the street
     'the water was flowing outwards towards the street'

This leaves us with an interesting question: what are these different forms used for? As satellites, DDAs are in general used to code direction in the expression of motion events in Danish, but an analysis would also have to account for the semantics of the forms. What do they conceptualize? How do they contribute to the coding of the motion event of which they intrinsically form part?

The semantics of the three different forms of DDAs have previously been described rather vaguely as 'analogous' to three different 'aktionsarten' ('action', 'state', and 'activity') (Harder et al. 1996: 160). This analysis provides a fruitful framework for the description of the semantics of DDAs (their so-called

---

[1] In some cases a prepositional *-efter*-suffix ('-after') is also used (*udefter* 'out-after'), but the *-ad*-form is by far the most frequent and normally the productive one (see Table 10.2), and I will for the sake of convenience use only this form. Similar inflection is found in the other Scandinavian languages and it would be a plausible hypothesis that the results presented in this study apply to the use of the directional adverbs in these languages as well (for Swedish, see for instance Teleman et al. 1999, vol. II). However, I should like to make it absolutely clear that I have only looked at data from Danish in the present study.

[2] One of the DDAs, *tilbage* (see Table 10.1), deviates from the formal pattern in several respects: it is an adverbial compound (*til-* 'to-' + *-bage* '-back'; *-bage* is etymologically a genitive plural form of the noun *bag* 'back(side)'); and the dynamic and the static forms are identical. However, the formal distinction between a zero-form (*tilbage-Ø*) and a derivative *-e*-suffix-form (*tilbage-e*) is neutralized by the fact that schwa + schwa becomes simple schwa in Danish (cf. Hansen 1980: 198; Harder et al. 1996: 194). See also Section 10.5 on other peripheral members of the paradigm.

'content-syntactic job' within functional grammar: see Harder et al. 1996: 159f.), but it is not clear whether DDAs, seen in isolation, actually encode the three different 'aktionsarten' or not (note the use of the expressions 'analogous' and 'correspond to'). The framework of Cognitive Linguistics, including the description of DDAs as satellites with reference to Talmy, is also mentioned, but it is not developed any further (Harder et al. 1996: 160). In this study, I propose another analysis, which integrates the semantics of the three forms of DDA into the overall conceptual space of the motion event. More specifically I argue that the core semantics of the forms can be described as different ways of profiling a dynamic goal-oriented motion from p to q in a path event frame (Talmy 2000, I: 265) (Section 10.3). I argue that the dynamic DDA (*ud-Ø*) can be accounted for as profiling the entire path event frame (Section 10.4); that the static DDA (*ud-e*) can be accounted for as profiling the locational end point in the path event frame, the source and the preceding path of motion being unprofiled and the path of motion being presupposed or fictive (Section 10.5); and that the procedural DDA (*ud-ad*) can be accounted for as profiling, first,) the procedural aspect of the path of motion in the path event frame (thus leaving the source and goal of the path of motion unprofiled within the overall scope), and second, the specific kind of direction involved in the path of motion (Section 10.6). The analysis is supported by several strong, linguistically coded conceptual constraints in the use of DDAs in the construction of motion events in Danish.

Referring to the title of this volume, the analysis can be described as a window into the mental space of speakers of Danish: the ways of profiling a motion event encoded by the different forms of Danish directional adverbs reveal how speakers of Danish point to different parts or aspects of the motion event and make dynamic use of this pointing out when communicating (Gärdenfors and War-glien, this volume). As will be demonstrated in the following, the specific conceptualizations encoded by each form seem inconspicuous, and yet, at the same time, they relate to basic notions at stake in a motion event, such as process and transition (Durst-Andersen et al., this volume), and fictive (or metaphorical) motion (Perlman and Gibbs, this volume).

The present study is just one of several which have explored, refined, or even challenged Talmy's general description of motion events (Strömquist and Verhoeven, 2004). The typological distinction between verb-framed and satel-lite-framed languages has been challenged for instance by Zlatev and Yangklang (2004) and Slobin (2004), proposing an additional third type: so-called 'equipol-lently framed languages', or languages where path and manner are expressed by equivalent grammatical forms (Slobin 2004: 249). Likewise, the distinction between verb-framed and satellite-framed argument structure is discussed by Pedersen (this volume). Also, a language can be characterized by the presence of both verb-framed and satellite-framed elements, for instance French (Kopecka 2006). Berthele (2004) has explored the variation in the construal of motion events, not just between separate languages, but also between dialects within the same language. The notion of manner has been subject to further considerations based on experimental data (Vulchanova and Martinez, this volume); and an attempt to redefine the very notion of a motion event, including the types of manner involved, is offered by Durst-Andersen et al. (this volume). Finally, the relation between language and gesture in the expression of motion events cross-linguistically has become a growing field of interest (see for instance Brown and Gullberg 2008). The studies testify to a growing interest in the variation in the carving out of motion events inter- and intra-linguistically. To a certain degree, the studies point to the need to revise Talmy's general typological framework in some respects, but, on the other hand, the framework still seems to be a fruitful point of departure, yielding interesting results which can easily be compared.[3]

In the present study, I follow Talmy's classification and terminology in the definition of *motion, motion events, path event frames*, and *event types*. *Motion event* will for instance be defined as the linguistic conceptualization of a situation containing either 'motion' (MOVE) or 'continuation of a stationary location' (BE_{LOC}) by a figure in relation to a ground, the movement, or location of the figure being expressed by a path (Talmy 2000, II: 25); and *path event frame* will be defined as the 'entirety of a path of motion' (Talmy 2000, I: 265; see foo below, Section 10.3). In addition, I refer to the three 'aktionsarten': 'action', 'state', and 'activity' (Durst-Andersen and Herslund 1996: 65–70). Finally, I employ a few concepts from Langacker, first of all the base-profile distinction (Langacker 1987; Croft and Cruse 2004: 14ff).

The present study concentrates on the analysis of the basic meaning and function of the three different forms of DDAs, but an additional point will also be made. Cognitive Linguistics is a usage-based paradigm which emphasizes the fundamental importance of dynamic construal operations and conceptualization processes in specific communicative contexts (Langacker 1997: 248; Chafe 1994). However, what is often presented is the reflex of these operations in the static 'system' of language (for instance the description of the core semantics of the three different DDAs in Sections 10.3–6). One way of integrating the procedural, context-sensible aspect of language into the analysis is to describe the semantics of a linguistic item as instructional (cf. Harder 2007). According to this view, linguistic analysis should take into account the 'interactive flow' of language: input, process, and product properties. The linguistic sign is

---

[3] It should be noted that considerable work has been done in recent years on event types as semantic domains, also in Germanic languages (for instance Berthele 2004 for German, Newman and Rice 2004 for English, van Oosten 1984 for Dutch, and Viberg 2006 for Swedish). The present study can be seen as a step towards, or a part of, a similar investigation of event types in Danish. The results of the important work done on complex predicates (for instance Harder et al. 1996) should also be taken into account in such an investigation.

carrying along a systematic, usage-based structure, but the structuring effect of this structure will always be dependent on the mental and communicative processes in contextual interaction.[4] Since language is expected to be relatively stable as a symbolic system so as to be able to serve as an efficient means of communication, it is equally expected that linguistically coded conceptual constraints in a linguistic item (for instance DDA) should be used consistently with possible instructional constraints in other linguistic items in the utterance (regarding DDAs, for instance the verb and/or the preposition), preventing the linguistic output from being illogical or nonsensical—and this is actually what is found in the present analysis (see Sections 10.4–6). On the other hand, it is also expected that linguistic items and their instructions can be used dynamically by language users to shape the output according to, for instance, different attentional construal operations or saliency judgments. In line with this argument, I also take a brief look at some of the variations in the use of the three forms of DDA (see Section 10.7). The important result is that the variations, as expected, are not completely random but, on the contrary, restricted. Furthermore, the variation possibilities do not seem to be equally distributed between the DDAs. In fact, the data suggest that the construal operations involved in the use of the static DDA are highly restricted conceptually, restrictions which are reflected in linguistic coding; whereas the procedural DDA to a much higher degree is used actively by the speaker to attentionally highlight or point to a specific conceptualization of a situation.

10.2   Data

The data used in this study were first of all collected from KorpusDK, originally two corpora of about 28 million words each (Korpus 90 and Korpus 2000), now assembled into one corpus. Korpus 90 covers the period 1983–92, and Korpus 2000 the period 1998–2002. Korpus 90 is a subset of the corpus of The Danish Dictionary (*Den Danske Ordbog*, 2003–5).

KorpusDK is generally considered to be a very well-balanced corpus. The sources were collected explicitly to cover a wide range of text types and language use, including spoken language and informal genres, and the corpus gives a fairly precise impression of modern Danish. KorpusDK is, however, rather small by modern standards. I have also used Google, as well as special collections of spoken language housed at the Dictionary of Danish Insular Dialects at the University of Copenhagen.

KorpusDK is accessible on the web (http://ordnet.dk/korpusdk) and a range of search possibilities is available—for instance search on specifically composed

---

[4] The more general motivation for the interest in an instructional semantics in this study is the view of language as an intrinsic and dynamic part of human practice, cf. for instance Bourdieu (1980) or Hanks (1996); see also outline and further references in Hovmark (2007: 21–5).

TABLE 10.2. *Instances of DDAs in KorpusDK (excluding the most frequent fixed expressions without any clear spatial meaning). Numbers in parenthesis indicate instances of the form* -efter

	-Ø (dynamic)	-e (static)	-ad (-efter) (procedural)
'up'	*op* 78280	*oppe* 6243	*opad* 1155 (264)
'down'	*ned* 44124	*nede* 5811	*nedad* 1065 (116)
'out'	*ud* 82351	*ude* 15081	*udad* 238 (31)
'in'	*ind* 38261	*inde* 12070	*indad* 311 (22)
'in horizontal'	*hen* 18547	*henne* 1865	*henad* 4 (0)
'over'/'across'	*over* 4102	*ovre* 1207	*overad* 0 (0)
'around'	*om* 1184	*omme* 413	*omad* 0 (0)
'home'	*hjem* 17731	*hjemme* 8872	*hjemad* 263 (10)
'forward'/'ahead'	*frem* 27544	*fremme* 2378	*fremad* 1552 (95)
'back'		*tilbage* 39461	*tilbagead* 0 (0)
'away'	*bort* 3937	*borte* 1638	–

collocations, morphological variants, and inflected forms. Statistical analysis based on either the mutual information method or t-score (statistical measures of significant, non-random co-occurrences) is also possible. It should be pointed out that the semi-automatic tagging of word classes is not entirely reliable, and in the present study it was necessary to adjust some of the search results. This is especially the case for the search on the form *om*, which can be used as conjunction and preposition as well as adverb, and for the search on the form *over*, which can be used as noun and preposition as well as adverb. In these two cases a partly manual analysis and sorting of the concordances was carried out. Manual analysis of the concordance for *henad* was also necessary due to *hen ad* being erroneously interpreted as *henad* in the corpus. Table 10.2 shows the number of instances of DDAs in KorpusDK (excluding the most frequent fixed expressions without any clear spatial meaning).

To make the argument as clear as possible, especially in the first sections describing the systematic differences between the three DDAs, a number of the examples have been simplified. However, most of the examples in Sections 10.6 and 10.7, discussing the interplay between system and variation, are authentic.[5]

10.3   Basic Paradigmatic Meaning of DDAs

The fact that DDAs have different forms, and thus constitute a small paradigm, leaves us with a twofold analytical task: defining not just the semantics of the

---

[5] For more examples and data, see Hovmark (2007).

forms, but also the common semantic feature that the forms systematically modify (see Heltoft 1998: 86). This is of course a classic analytical problem, well known within the structuralist tradition as the interplay between substance and forms within a paradigm. In the present, Cognitive Linguistic analysis I use the concepts of *base* and *profile*. As already mentioned, I suggest that the common base of the DDAs is the conceptualization of a path event frame, and that the three forms of DDA profile this base in three different ways: as mentioned above (Section 10.1), I argue that the dynamic DDA (*ud-Ø*) can be accounted for as profiling the entire path event frame; that the static DDA (*ud-e*) can be accounted for as profiling the locational end point in the path event frame, the source and the preceding path of motion being unprofiled and the path of motion being presupposed or fictive; and that the procedural DDA (*ud-ad*) can be accounted for as profiling, first, the procedural aspect of the path of motion in the path event frame (thus leaving the source and goal of the path of motion unprofiled within the overall scope), and second, the specific kind of direction involved in the path of motion (see Table 10.3).

TABLE 10.3. *DDA: conceptual base and profiling*

	path event frame	
-Ø (dynamic)	-e (static)	-ad/-efter (procedural)
full profiling	final profiling	medial profiling

A path event frame is defined by Talmy as 'the so-conceived entirety of a path of motion' (Talmy 2000, I: 265; cf. Talmy 2000, I: 257–62), and can be visualized as in Figure 10.1.

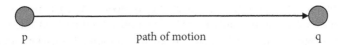

p   path of motion   q

FIG. 10.1. Path event frame: 'beginning point' (source) (p), path of motion, 'ending point' (goal) (q)

More precisely, the basic paradigmatic meaning of DDAs can be defined as 'a dynamic goal-oriented motion from p to q'. Accordingly, the semantics of the three DDAs can be visualized as in Figures 10.2–4 (details in the argument for each form, including linguistic data, follow in Sections 10.4–10.6):

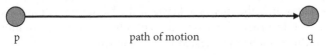

p   path of motion   q

FIG. 10.2. Dynamic DDA: full profiling

(4) pigen   kravlede   op   i træet
     the girl   climbed   up-DYN   in the tree
     'the girl climbed the tree'

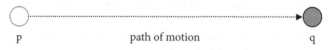

p   path of motion   q

Fig. 10.3. Static DDA: final profiling

(5) fiskerne   er   ude   på havet
     the fishermen   are   out-STAT   on the sea
     'the fishermen are out at sea'

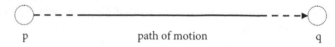

p   path of motion   q

Fig. 10.4. Procedural DDA: medial profiling

(6) børnene   løb   nedad   mod stationen
     the children   ran   down-PROC   towards the station
     'the children ran down towards the station'

I understand the base of the paradigm, that is the path event frame, as a 'set of conceptual elements and interrelationships that [...] are evoked together or co-evoke each other' (Talmy 2000, I: 259). And likewise I understand the profiling as a linguistically coded cognitive process in which specific parts of the frame are attentionally foregrounded and backgrounded respectively; the frame is presupposed, and the backgrounded parts could be reconstructed if necessary, given sufficient context (Talmy 2000, I: 266). This understanding is in line with basic tenets in Cognitive Linguistics, developed by Fillmore, Langacker, and Talmy, using slightly different terminologies (cf. Croft and Cruse 2004: 7ff). It should also be stated that I understand a path event frame as dynamic, not static: this will be important to bear in mind, especially when looking at the so-called static DDA (see below, Section 10.5). In the present analysis, the paradigmatic base-profile semantics of DDAs are defined as the profiling of a basic path event frame in different ways, no more, no less; furthermore, it is understood that these different ways of profiling a path event frame are brought into use in the conceptualization and linguistic coding of motion events in Danish (dynamic as well as static motion events). It is the interplay between the basic instructional semantics of the DDAs and the instructional semantics of other constituents of motion events in Danish which will be investigated in the following.

Defining the basic paradigmatic meaning of DDAs as a path event frame is of course motivated by the fact that DDAs intrinsically form part of the linguistic coding of motion events in Danish, in which the DDAs formally play a role as satellites (or as free locatives) and more specifically are used as co-predicates, receiving primary stress, in the complex predicate construction (cf. Harder et al. 1996). It seems natural that the frame and profiling possibilities of DDAs should be compatible with the motion event frame. However, the use of the path event frame also has the more specific analytical advantage of integrating the coding of motion and space, since DDAs contribute to the coding of specifics of direction (in the stem: *ud-/ind-/..*) as well as motion (in the different forms: *-o/-e/-ad*) within a motion event. One of the very interesting features of DDAs is how the construal of spatial meaning is conceptualized within a frame which also conceptualizes motion. DDAs can be said to specify the spatio-temporal frame for the process expressed by the verb in the motion verb (cf. Hovmark 2007; and a similar analysis by Kopecka 2006: 86–8 of French verbal prefixes as path satellites).

The presence of the basic, common concept of a linear trajectory in the different DDAs can be distinguished directly in linguistic coding. It is an interesting fact that all three DDAs can be modified by quantifiers, but also by exact specifications of distance. In both cases, the linguistic coding presupposes the conceptualization of a linear trajectory and motion along such a line (cf. Talmy 2000, II: 138).

(7) han   kravlede   længere/2 m   ned   i brønden
     he   crawled   further/2 m   down-DYN   in the well
     'he crawled further/2 m down the well'

(8) han   kravlede   længere/2 m   nedad   i brønden
     he   crawled   further/2 m   down-PROC   in the well
     'he was crawling further/2 m downwards in the well'

(9) butikken   ligger   længere/halvvejs/2 km   nede   ad gaden
     the shop   lies   further/halfway/2 km   down-STAT   by the road
     'the shop lies further/halfway/2 km down the road'

In examples (7)–(9) the modifications are used to specify more exactly how far the figure has come, or is to be found, along a linear trajectory leading to the goal. What is being modified here is not the verb, but the DDA, and the modification presupposes the conceptualization of a line to which the specifying modification can be applied.[6]

Two ways of conceptualizing reality in language lie behind the classification of the three different DDAs in this study. First, the path event frame can be said to involve two different concepts, 'one involving the concept of a discrete translocation and the other involving the concept of progression along a linear extent' (Talmy 2000, II: 138). This inherent distinction in the frame is crucial to understanding the use of the procedural DDA as opposed to the dynamic DDA (and the

---

[6] Hellberg (2007: 26) has independently made observations similar to the one suggested in Hovmark (2007) and here, on Swedish *långt/längre/längst fram*, referring to the SCALE schema.

static DDA). And second, the distinction between fictive and factive motion (Talmy 2000, I: 269) is crucial to the understanding of the use of the static DDA as opposed to the dynamic DDA (and the procedural DDA). In Sections 10.4–6, I show how the proposed analysis of the different DDAs is compatible with a number of strong constraints in the use of each of the DDAs in the linguistically coded conceptualization of motion events in Danish, taking these two basic ways of conceptualizing reality as the point of departure.

10.4   The Dynamic DDA: Full Profiling

I argue that the dynamic DDA (*ud-Ø*) can be accounted for as profiling the entire frame, that is the change of position or state from p to q along a path of motion. This is compatible with the fact that the dynamic DDA is used in complex predicates to express the aktionsart 'action' (transition) in Danish. The common or standard way of expressing that a figure is accomplishing a full trajectory and changing position from p to q, for instance moving from a point outside a room, transgressing the boundary to the room, and finally reaching a point inside the room, is to combine a dynamic DDA as a 'co-predicate' receiving 'unit accentuation' with the motion verb, forming a complex predicate (cf. Harder et al. 1996: 161 and 168–9).

(10) han   løb   ind   i værelset
      he   ran   in-DYN   in the room
      'he ran into the room'

Leaving out the DDA, as in (11), would not only make the verb express non-transition (i.e. the aktionsart 'activity'), but it would also change the attentional focus in the utterance, highlighting the type of activity. The motion verb would be fully accentuated, and an opposition to other kinds of activities like walking, sleeping, working, etc. could be presupposed pragmatically.

(11) han   'løb   i værelset
      he   ran   in the room
      'he was running in the room' (i.e. as part of a continuous non-transitional process)

The role of DDAs is very important, since (non-)transition is not necessarily coded in the verb stem in Danish, but is dependent on additional linguistic coding.[7] Naturally inherent in the use of the dynamic DDA in complex predicates

---

[7] It should be noted, however, that transition could also be coded in other ways. In Danish, a verb like *komme* 'come' codes transition in the root, but its deictic counterpart *gå* 'go' does not. In both the present and the preterite, the finite inflection of a non-transitional root can also imply the conceptualization of one, singular event, and preterite *han gik* ('he walked') could mean both 'he was walking'

is an attentional focus on the result or the goal, but it should be remembered that what is coded specifically when the dynamic DDA is added to a motion event is the concept of transition and completion. In the present analysis, focusing on the relational semantics of the forms within a paradigm, it can be argued that the dynamic DDA profiles the full and actual (or 'factive') change of position from p to q inherent in the basic path event frame (as opposed to for instance the 'fictive' change of position encoded in the static DDA; see section 10.5).

I now turn to the static and the procedural DDA in more detail and describe a number of salient constraints which can support the proposed base-profile analysis.

10.5   The Static DDA: Final Profiling

I argue that the static DDA can be described as profiling the end point of the path event frame, and that the preceding path of motion can be described as a case of 'fictive motion' (Talmy 2000, I: 99–175). The concept of fictive motion has received a lot of attention in Cognitive Linguistics (cf. Croft and Cruse 2004: 54–5; also Perlman and Gibbs, this volume). It is defined by Talmy as 'sentences that depict motion with no physical occurrence', as in sentences like *this fence goes from the plateau to the valley* or *the cliff wall faces away from the island* (Talmy 2000, I: 99). The general point is that static scenes—or situations—are subject to construal, and this construal can involve dynamic terms (Croft and Cruse 2004: 54). The fence in the first sentence above does not move of course, but the form and the location of the fence are conceptualized and linguistically coded using dynamic terms (*goes*) involving a sequential scanning of the fence, from its point of departure to where it ends, following its trajectory in the landscape. It is this very general phenomenon in linguistically coded construal processes which can be used to explain the semantics of the static DDA. The term static refers to the fact that the static DDA is only used to describe a static scene or situation on the 'factive level' (Talmy 2000, I: 100), or to locate one, and only one, specific point (i.e. not a sequence of points). But at the same time, it can be argued that the location of this scene or point is being conceptualized as the end point of a presupposed, sequentialized path of motion in a path event frame, as in (12):

(12)   butikken   ligger   længere/halvvejs/2 km   nede   ad gaden
       the shop   lies   further/halfway/2 km   down-STAT   by the road
       'the shop lies further/halfway/2 km down the road'

(perhaps opposed to running, etc.) and 'he left' (he carried through one specific motion event away from the place, i.e. he didn't stay). Further on the semantics of *come* and *go*, see for instance Viberg (2006: 114–16), or Wilkins and Hill (1995).

The static location of the shop is specified by pointing out a singular point which can be found further (or halfway or 2 km) down a linear trajectory seen from a viewpoint which by default would be the deictic centre established by the speaker and hearer in communicative interaction (cf. Langacker 1991b: 328).

This analysis of the static DDA as a case of fictive motion is in line with an analysis of English *across* as an example of 'subjectification' and 'abstract motion' (Langacker 1998). Langacker is comparing the sentences *a giant chicken strode angrily across the street* and *there was a KFC outlet right across the street*, and relating the two instances of *across*. Langacker argues that in the first sentence *across* conceptualizes a full dynamic movement by the figure (the chicken), involving all the points along the path, from p to q. But in the second sentence, the use of *across* presupposes the conceptualization of a static end point of a preceding path of motion: 'Although the trajector is static, the conceptualizer traces a *mental* path [..] in order to specify the trajector's location in relation to the landmark' (Langacker 1998: 74; cf. also Langacker 2006). Langacker's terms are different, but the analysis is basically the same as the one proposed here.[8]

One point is noteworthy in Langacker's analysis: the shift in senses in the two uses of *across* is compared to the construal process involved in deriving a stative-adjectival participle from a verb (*break—broken*), and Langacker exactly terms this a 'restriction in *profiling*': 'the derived sense profiles a single-configuration relationship equivalent to the last in an ordered series of relational configurations profiled in the original meaning' (Langacker 1998: 76). The same kind of construal process can be said to apply to the static DDA and can be illustrated by the relationship between the sentences in examples (13)–(15).

(13)   børnene   er   inde   i huset   nu   (at 10 o'clock)
        the children   are   in-STAT   in the house now
        'the children are inside the house now' (at 10 o'clock)

(14)   børnene   gik   ind   i huset (at some point prior to 10 o'clock)
        the children   walked in-DYN   in the house
        'the children went into the house' (at some point prior to 10 o'clock)

(15)   børnene   er   ikke længere ude   i gården   nu (at 10 o'clock)
        the children   are   no longer   out-STAT   in the yard   now
        'the children are no longer outside in the yard now' (at 10 o'clock)

It can be presupposed that the children to be found inside the house at ten o'clock (*inde* 'in-STAT') eventually came there as the result of a previous event (*in* 'in-DYN'), and it is also implied that the children are no longer to be found outside

---

[8] The concept of fictive motion has recently also been used in an analysis of Swedish *fram* and *framme*, corresponding to Danish *frem* and *fremme* 'forward'/'ahead' (Hellberg 2007).

(*ude* 'out-STAT') at ten o'clock (cf. Hansen 1980: 192). The two situations in (13) and (14) mutually presuppose and exclude each other, and the relationship can be described as a logical one involving displacement and procedural progression in time (a 'before' and a 'now', a result and some process or action preceding this result). As a matter of fact, this distinction is actually coded linguistically in the case of DDAs—contrary to English *across*.

Being backgrounded, the notion of path might intuitively seem very weak to language users. However, the data show that language users pay very careful and systematic attention to the notion of translocation (which is implied by the path of motion in the path event frame) and to the restriction in profiling in actual discourse, that is in actual linguistic and cognitive processing. The suffix *-e* used to code translocation and completion is well established in Danish. The original DDAs in Old Norse, *op* 'up', *ned* 'down', *ind* 'in', *ud* 'out', *hjem* 'home', and *frem* 'forward', all had static forms (Falk and Torp 1900: 109f.), and in the course of time, a number of prepositions developed a static form too, and came to be used as directional adverbs. This goes for *over* 'over' and *om* 'around' (see Table 10.1), but other prepositions have also entered the paradigm in more restricted uses. This is first of all the case with *af* 'off', which has a static form in spoken language (Harder et al. 1996: 161), but data of spoken Danish, especially dialectal data, also display static forms for the prepositions *fra* 'from', *på* 'on', *forbi* 'past', and *i* 'in' (Pedersen 2001). Another question is how to determine the exact location of the starting point or source. This is a very complex question which involves an analysis of linguistic coding in combination with inferential cues, gesture, and common ground in actual discourse, and it cannot be dealt with here. Suffice it to say that the DDAs are often used in relation to the speaker's domain, or a deictic center (Harder et al. 1996: 162 f.; Hovmark 2007: 107–17).[9] This is actually very prominent when the static DDA is used as a free locative.

(16) fiskerbådene   lå   nede   i Assens (havn)
      the fishing boats lay   down-STAT   in (the harbour of) Assens
      'the fishing boats were anchored in (the harbour of) Assens'

In (16) the backgrounded starting point conceptualized in *nede* 'down-STAT' can hardly be the fishing boats: fishing boats do not go down (*ned* 'down-DYN') into a harbour in Danish, they go in. The use of *nede* 'down-STAT' must refer to the speaker's (and hearer's) relation to the harbour: the starting point of the path event frame evoked in *nede* must be the speaker's (and hearer's) viewpoint; and what is moving in the path event frame in *nede* is the speaker's focus of attention

---

[9] An analysis of the use of DDAs in actual discourse, based on empirical data, can be found in Hovmark (2007). In this study an investigation is made of how a group of dialect-speaking language users establish and maintain different deictic centres through the conventionalized use of DDAs, and the socio-cultural anchoring of this use is also touched upon. The deictic potential in the use of DDAs is also reflected in the adverbial compounds with deictic *her* 'here' and *der* 'there', as in *derned* 'there-down-DYN' and *heroppe* 'here-up-STAT', etc.

(cf. Talmy 2000, I: 269; Langacker 1991b: 320). The use of *nede* in this sentence reflects the speaker's construal of his or her relation to the harbour.

Let me now take a look at some of the constraints in the use of the static DDA which are in line with this analysis.

The analysis of the motion as being fictive is compatible with the fact that the static DDA can only be used with static verbs in complex predicates, not with verbs or constructions conceptualizing a future perspective. It can be argued that the profiling of the static DDA entails the conceptualization of the result of a preceding event, and consequently it can also be argued that this conceptualization should be incompatible with a predicate describing the opposite, that is the beginning of a coming event. This is also the case in the data. For instance, the static DDA is not found in constructions with modal verbs, which by definition are conceptualizing intentions about coming actions in the past or present ('force dynamics': Boye 2001).

(17)   han   vil/..   ud/*ude   til sin søster
        he   wants   out-DYN/*out-STAT   to his sister
        'he wants to go out to his sister' (i.e. he wants to see his sister)

Likewise, the static DDA cannot be used with verbs or constructions conceptualizing the beginning of a procedural progression or an intended action:

(18)   jeg tager over/*ovre   til min søster for at   se fjernsyn
        I   take over-DYN/*over-STAT to my sister in order to see TV
        'I'm going over to my sister to watch TV'

Perhaps the clearest example would be the impossibility of using the static DDA in an imperative construction with unit accentuation:

(19)   gå 'hjem/*hjemme nu!
        go home-DYN/*home-STAT now

A similar constraint is found when the verb codes transition in the root, for example *komme* 'come' or *blive* 'become': the static DDA cannot be part of a complex predicate receiving unit accentuation with this type of verb (Harder et al. 1996: 174–6).

As shown, the final profiling of the end point entails several constraints which could be explained by the conceptualization of the dynamic motion in the path event frame as fictive or not. Another important aspect of the final profiling of the static DDA is that only the one, single end point enters into the conceptualization of the motion event on a factive level, not the preceding series of points in the presupposed path of motion in the path event frame. This could be used to explain that the static DDA very often is not, or does not have to be, an integrated part of the complex predicate, receiving unit accentuation. On the contrary, the static DDA is frequently used as a free locative in motion events to specify the location of any kind of event; or to be more exact: the location of a figure performing an event of some kind. Indeed, it is interesting to see how the static DDA as a free locative can be used to locate all three types of events, or aktionsarten: actions, activities, and states (Harder et al. 1996: 187):

(20)   de   overfaldt   en dame   nede   på legepladsen
       they   attacked   a lady   down-STAT   at the playground
       'they attacked a lady down at the playground'

(21)   de   legede   nede   på legepladsen
       they   played   down-STAT   at the playground
       'they were playing down at the playground'

(22)   de   sad   nede   på legepladsen
       they   sat   down-STAT   at the playground
       'they were sitting down at the playground'

An important part of this argument is the singularity of the profiled entity (the end point). The configuration of the point in itself in specific conceptualizations is open to construal and could be any kind of bounded extent: an area, a circle, a container, etc. Like deictic *here/there* the profiled singular end point of the path event frame can be applied to any kind of spatial volume that the conceptualizer selects as suitable for the locus of an event. The sentences (20)–(22) are all conceptualizing more or less complex events. But they could also be described as answers to a 'where-question' (see Levinson 2003a: 65), answers explaining where—related to what ground—the figure and the event is or can be located. The construal of spatial meaning and the depiction of the location of the figure are in this case integrating a viewpoint (by default the viewpoint of the speaker: see above in this section).

10.6   The Procedural DDA: Medial Profiling

Describing the profiling pattern of the procedural DDA involves the inherent distinction between the concept of translocation and the concept of progression along a linear extent (see Section 10.3 above). I argue that the procedural DDA is profiling the path of motion from p to q in the path event frame, leaving the starting point (the source) and the end point (the goal) in the unprofiled background. This is in opposition to the dynamic DDA, which is normally used to conceptualize the aktionsart 'action' in complex predicates, but also to the static DDA. Even though the starting point is backgrounded in the static DDA, the concept of translocation is still present, since the conceptualization of a result of a preceding action, and the interplay with the profiling of the dynamic DDA in this respect, seems to be crucial to understanding the use of the static DDA (see Section 10.5 above). I argue that the profiling of the path of motion by the procedural DDA leads to two slightly different uses of the procedural DDA: one highlighting the non-translocational aspect of the motion event, and one highlighting the specific direction involved. I refer to these two uses as 'non-translocational use' and 'specific directional use'.

The overall analysis of the procedural DDA (profiling the path of motion) reveals that the procedural DDA, contrary to the dynamic and static ones, is very rarely used with adverbs of degree profiling the end point of the trajectory in a motion event (for instance *næsten* 'nearly, almost', *helt* 'all the way, fully'; cf. Paradis 2008a: 322–6). No examples were found in KorpusDK, and only very few through Google, whereas examples with the dynamic and static DDA are abundantly present. I return to a couple of the few exceptions in Section 10.7.

(23) det   var   helt   nede/?nedad   i hjørnet
      it   was   all the way   down-STAT/?down-PROC   in the corner
      'it was all the way down/?downwards in the corner'

(24) vi   nåede   næsten   ned/?nedad   til vandet
      we   reached   almost   down-DYN/?down-PROC   to the water
      'we almost got down/?downwards to the water' (i.e. we almost reached the water)

The backgrounding of the starting point and the end point, and the profiling of the path of motion, makes the use of the procedural DDA compatible with the coding of an event as non-transitional, that is the coding of the process of motion towards a goal which has not yet been reached (as in the English suffix -*wards*) (Harder et al. 1996: 162).

(25) han   kørte   indad   mod Lemvig
      he   drove   in-PROC   towards Lemvig
      'he drove (in) towards (the town of) Lemvig'

However, the profiling of the path of motion could also imply a focus on the possible quality or characteristics of the process: i.e. the 'internal structure' of the path of motion (Saeed 2003: 120). As a matter of fact, the procedural DDA seems to be most frequently used to express specific direction, profiling one of two oppositional pairs ('x (not y)'); see Figure 10.5:[10]

(26) døren   åbnede   udad   mod gården   [ikke indad]
      the door   opened   out-PROC   towards the courtyard   [not inwards]
      'the door opened outwards towards the courtyard [not inwards]'

---

[10] This might be the reason why the DDAs without an oppositional core semantic 'partner' within the paradigm (*hen, over, om, bort*, cf. Table 10.1) are rarely found and used in the procedural form (cf. Hovmark 2007: 74).

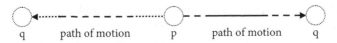

q   path of motion   p   path of motion   q

Fig. 10.5. Procedural DDA: specific directional use

Very often, the goal is not expressed:

(27) båden   flyder   langsomt udad   [ikke indad]
     the boat   floats   slowly   outwards   [not inwards]
     'the boat is floating slowly outwards [not inwards]'

The profiling of the specific direction by the procedural DDA is epitomized in a sentence like (28) where the procedural DDA is objectified as a form used to express direction (Danish: *retning*) (the example is authentic, as will be the remainder of the examples cited in this study):

(28) seksualiteten har to   retninger,   indad   og   udad
     sexuality   has two   directions, in-PROC   and   out-PROC
     'sexuality has two directions, inwards and outwards'

In (28), the directions are represented as alternatives, and a listing of the directional DDA as an alternative to another procedural DDA, or to other directional adverbials, is fairly common (for instance 58 times out of 311 instances in total for *indad* 'inwards' in KorpusDK). In (29), the y-element is also expressed as the non-chosen alternative:

(29) *vi*   bør   flytte   barrierer   udad   og   ikke   indad
     we   should   move   barriers   out-PROC   and   not   in-PROC
     'we should move barriers outwards and not inwards'

The frequent non-expression of the goal in the use of the procedural DDA is compatible with the profiling of the process and the backgrounding of the starting point and the end point. For instance, out of 311 instances of *indad* in KorpusDK, the goal is only expressed in 65 cases.

The attentional profiling of the directional specifications leaves the specific goal in the background: it seems to be irrelevant. It should be noted, however, that the goal is in fact sometimes expressed with a prepositional phrase in the specific directional use (30)—and that the expression of the goal can be left out in the non-translocational use (31):

(30) storetåen   bøjede   indad   mod de øvrige tæer
     the big toe   bent   in-PROC   towards the other toes
     'the big toe bent inwards towards the other toes'

(31) bjørnen   lunter   indad
     the bear   jog-trots   in-PROC
     'the bear jog-trots inwards'

The analysis of the specific directional use is compatible with the fact that the procedural DDA combines significantly with a verb that requires elaboration of a particular direction or position: *vende* 'turn (around)'. This verb occurs with a highly significant score in the statistics in Korpus 90 with the procedural DDA, and all the more so with the oppositional couples *opad/nedad* and *udad/indad*.[11] This could be taken even further. The fact that the procedural DDA highlights the specific direction might also make it a particularly suitable partner for verbs that one way or another conceptualize a salient change of direction or position (for instance *dreje* 'turn (around, into a new direction or position)', *svinge* 'swing', *bukke* 'bow', or *bøje* 'bend'), and verbs that directly code a deviation from a straight or normal line (*hælde* 'lean') or could imply or lead to such a deviation (*glide* 'glide'). Indeed, the data offer a number of examples of the procedural DDA combining with verbs of this kind. I give some examples, especially from constructions with *ind* and *indad* in KorpusDK.

The specific change in question can for instance be coded by the procedural DDA (32)—or by another adverbial (33):

(32) begge   dine øjne   er   begyndt at dreje udad   og   opad
     Both   your eyes   are begun   to turn out-PROC and   up-PROC
     'both of your eyes have begun turning outwards and upwards'

(33) så   drejede   hun til venstre ad   en   af de mange   sidegader
     then   turned   she to   left   by   one   of the many   sidestreets
     'then she turned to the left down one of the many sidestreets'

The verbs conceptualizing a deviation from a straight or normal line, or implying such a deviation, are also found with the procedural DDA:

(34) ryggen   krummer indad   for neden   og   udad   foroven
     the back   curves   in-PROC   at the bottom   and   out-PROC   at the top
     'the back (i.e. of the chair) curves inwards at the bottom and
     outwards at the top'

The data suggest a salient connection between the procedural DDA and verbs or expressions coding change of direction or position. However, the procedural DDA is also used with verbs that do not conceptualize any change of direction, as for instance *gå* 'go/walk', *svømme* 'swim', or *se/kigge* 'see/look'. It might be expected that these verbs would combine almost exclusively with the non-translocational use. But this is not the case. What is noteworthy and expected, on the other hand, is that when used with the procedural DDA to express specific

---

[11] Collocational statistics in KorpusDK can only be made separately in one of the two sub-corpora. Korpus 90 is considered to be the most well-balanced sub-corpus and is chosen by default.

direction, the typical pattern ('x (not y)' and 'non-expression of goal') applies to the motion event construction:

(35) jeg   vendte   om   og   svømmede indad
     I   turned around and   swam   in-PROC
     'I turned around and swam inwards'

Verbs like *pege* 'point', *søge* 'seek', *trække* 'drag', or *vandre* 'wander', which are also found with the procedural DDA, are interesting since they normally require some kind of specification. But the specification could be a specification of the goal as well as of the direction. In other words: they call for a choice between a profiling of either the goal or the path of motion towards the goal.

Likewise, it should be noted that the verbs that conceptualize some kind of change of direction or position are also found with the dynamic DDA. But in these cases it is normally no longer the specific direction which is being profiled—it is the full transition and the completion of the motion event, that is, the full movement from p to q.

(36) jeg   bøjede mig   ned   over ham
     I   bent   myself down-DYN over him
     'I bent down over him'

(37) de   drejede ind   på hovedgaden
     they   turned in-DYN   on the main street
     'they turned into the main street'

The use of the dynamic and procedural DDA with these verbs clearly exemplifies the choice between two different construals of spatial meaning in a motion event, each connected to typical linguistic patterns ('x (not y)', 'conceptual constraints coded in the verb', '(non-)expression of specific goal'). In rare cases the two construals actually combine in the same sentence, as in (38). First, profiling of the direction, and next, profiling of the goal:

(38) deres øjne ser   indad,   ind   i   mørket
     their eyes look in-PROC, in-DYN in-PREP the dark
     'their eyes are looking inwards, into the dark'

Allow me to summarize the findings in this section. The data show that the procedural DDA can be used to profile both non-translocation and specific direction. But the data also show that the procedural DDA is most frequently and also most saliently used to profile or foreground specific kinds of direction, a use which enters into a typical linguistic pattern ('x (not y)', 'non-expression of specific goal'). The combinatory patterns with different types of verbs also suggest that the use of the procedural DDA is not as narrowly bound up with specific linguistic constructions as the use of the static DDA is. The procedural DDA seems to be closely connected to a specific conceptualization and to a linguistic pattern. But the data also suggest that the use of the procedural DDA is to a great extent dependent upon and reflects the specific construal process and communicative choice by the language user in actual discourse, making the information about a specific direction prominent. I discuss this further in the following section.

10.7   Constraints and Variation: Possible Factors and Implications

I now return to the question of system versus variation. I draw upon the instructional approach as a possible means of integrating the procedural and dynamic aspects of language use into the description of the systemic patterns which for instance are at the basis of the proposed analysis of DDAs. In other words, I explore the possibility of giving a description of a system which is dynamic, not static.

As demonstrated, the suggested, static or systemic-paradigmatic difference between the three DDAs is compatible with a number of patterns and constraints in the data. Let us try to phrase this within the terms of an instructional semantics. The linguistic elements (in this case verbs, adverbials, and prepositions as constituents in the construction of a motion event in Danish), come with specific instructions. The claim is that the inherent instructions in the DDAs can be defined as three different ways of profiling a path event frame, and that these three instructions entail certain constraints on the possible combination with other linguistic items (as described in Sections 10.4–6). Looking at the corpus data, however, some of the constraints are stronger than others. It is clear that some constraints are absolute (for instance the coding of one, and only one, point in the static DDA), whereas other constraints should rather be understood as suggestions for suitable linguistic partners. The coding of dynamic, sequential motion in a verb is a strong constraint, ruling out the use of such a verb with a static DDA in complex predicates; the coding of some kind of change of direction or deviation is also an important signal, but looking at the data, it seems to be working more as a strong suggestion than as an absolute constraint. In fact, the verbs with a directional suggestion leave a certain number of construal options open for the language users.

The various constructions with DDAs highlight just how much an instructional semantics should be able to embrace: not only constraints, but also variation and possibilities. An analysis using the instructional approach is a twofold endeavour that will have to give precise descriptions of the interplay between constraints and possibilities for specific linguistic items, not just in linguistic context, but also in contextual interaction. Of course, this makes the description and analysis more complex. I give a few examples of this interplay in the following.

In KorpusDK we find the following text (39), including numerous examples of DDAs (I have underlined the examples and numbered them consecutively):

(39) Pas på ikke at (39a) <u>løfte skuldrene op</u> omkring ørerne, figur 3b. Gentag øvelsen så ofte som muligt i løbet af dagen. (39b) <u>Løft nu armene opad</u> skråt foran dig og (39c) <u>drej samtidig tommelfingrene opad</u>, figur 4b. Pas på ikke at løfte for højt, da dette kan provokere smerte. Fat håndvægtene. [..]. (39d) <u>Løft nu armene opad</u> (39e) <u>samtidig med at tommelfingrene drejes op imod loftet</u>, figur 6b. [..] (39f) <u>Stræk nu armene frem foran dig</u>, og sørg for at (39g) <u>skulderbladene kører med fremad</u>, figur 7b.

'Take care not to (39a) <u>lift the shoulders up-DYN</u> to the ears, figure 3b. Repeat the exercise as often as possible during the day. (39b) <u>Now lift the arms up-PROC</u> on the slant in front of you and (39c) <u>turn the thumbs up-PROC at the same time</u>, figure 4b. Take care not to lift too high, since this can cause pain. Grasp the dumbbells. [..] (39d) <u>Now lift the arms up-PROC</u> (39e) <u>and turn at the same time the thumbs up-DYN towards the ceiling</u>, figure 6b. [..] (39f) <u>Now stretch the arms forward-DYN</u> in front of you, and make sure that (39g) <u>the shoulder blades follow the movement forward-PROC</u>, figure 7b.'

In this text, which is a guide for the retraining of injured shoulders, all three DDAs are used extensively to indicate directions and positions in the different exercises. In the small section cited here, the dynamic and the procedural DDA are used in line with the proposed analysis and with the communicative intentions of the author. The dynamic DDA is used in examples (39a) and (39f), where the completion or the result of the motion is prominent, and the procedural DDA is used in examples (39b), (39c), (39d), and (39g), where the process of a motion and details of the process are prominent. In other words: the profiling possibilities are used actively in context within the general constraint (dynamic verb calling for a directional specification). But note example (39e), and compare with (39c). The two sentences have the same constituents and conceptualize the same situation, but the dynamic DDA is used in (39e). This can be explained by the presence of the preposition *(i)mod* 'towards' in (39e) (and numerous similar examples). The corpus data used in this study show that the procedural DDA only occurs with dynamic prepositions (*(i)mod* 'towards', *til* 'to'), or with prepositions that have the potential to be used dynamically (for instance *i* 'in(to)'), but the data also show that language users tend to economize with the procedural markers: the *-ad*-suffix is often removed and the preposition is retained. A Google-search on, for instance, *ned/nedad mod stationen* 'down-DYN/down-PROC towards the station' (September 2008) showed 147 hits for the dynamic and only 1 for the procedural DDA. This might be called a generalized instructional overruling by the preposition, which makes the use of the procedural DDA superfluous. A similar example can be seen when the preposition is *ad*—the preposition which is used as a suffix in the procedural DDA. In this case, only the preposition is used (*hun gik ud ad vejen* 'she walked out-DYN by the road' (i.e. 'she walked out the road') instead of ??*hun gik udad ad vejen* 'she walked out-PROC along the road').

It is clear that such examples theoretically form a challenge to the classic idea of a synchronic paradigm—form and meaning go together, and this would mean that both translocation (*ned* 'down-DYN') and non-translocation (*mod* 'towards') were conceptualized and coded in the same sentence ('she walked down-DYN to-PROC the station'). However, the use is systematic, and not the result of a random error. An obvious solution would be to describe the use of the dynamic DDA instead of the procedural as a neutral or default use of the dynamic DDA. Within the Cognitive Linguistic framework one could also argue that the dynamic DDA has in fact the potential for such a use, since the dynamic DDA in the present analysis profiles the whole path event frame, contrary to the static and the procedural ones; and that the dynamic DDA would therefore be able to represent the other two DDAs in a neutral or default use. However, such an explanation is difficult to prove, and concepts like neutralization should in general be used with extreme care and only if such a pattern can be reasonably motivated by other well-attested factors that are compatible with a Cognitive Linguistic approach. Such factors could for instance be a tendency towards reduction internally between linguistic items in the specific language—a kind of processing effect (*ad* + *ad* = *ad*)—or effects pertaining to the morphological form (the dynamic form is a zero-form and could be considered a primary or original form). The default explanation seems plausible, but further investigation into the semantics and use of the dynamic DDA is needed.

Neither the static nor the procedural DDA ever seems to be used in a neutral or default way—they are always used to make a specific coding in accordance with their respective ways of profiling the path event frame. As already mentioned, however, there is a difference between the static DDA and the procedural DDA. The use of the static DDA seems to be strictly governed by the basic conceptual features in the profiling—the one, singular point (versus a sequence), and the result of a preceding action (versus an ongoing or coming one). As shown in Section 10.6, the procedural DDA reflects to a much greater extent the language user's choice or preference in actual discourse as to how a specific spatial situation should be conceptualized. The procedural DDA is used to point to a specific direction, making this information prominent in discourse. The 'x (not y)'-matrix, which is characteristic of the use of the procedural DDA in discourse, is most certainly ideal for the pointing out of a feature because of its oppositional structure. Indeed, the procedural DDA seems to be so strongly associated with the communicative wish to emphasize a specific direction that language users sometimes use it in constructions where it does not normally appear. In Section 10.6 above, it was mentioned that the procedural DDA is normally not found with adverbs of degree profiling the end point (for instance *næsten* 'nearly, almost', *helt* 'all the way, fully'). Nevertheless, rare examples can be found, for instance in Google:

(40) træk   håndtaget   helt   fremad
      pull   the handle   fully   forward-PROC
      'pull the handle fully forwards'

(41) hun   læner   sig   helt   fremad
     she   leans   herself fully   forward-PROC
     'she is leaning fully forwards'

According to the 'rules', the dynamic DDA would have been expected, but the procedural DDA might have slipped into the utterance because of the language user's cognitive attentional focus on the specific direction of the motion described. These sentences are deviant and rare, but not absolutely unacceptable. In examples (40)–(41) the procedural DDA is replacing the dynamic DDA. Such exceptions are perhaps not totally unexpected considering the very common interplay between the procedural and the dynamic DDA. But in the following example (42), taken from a plate-smith's manual, it is the static DDA which is being replaced by the procedural, but probably for the same reason. Three consecutive positions of a stick are being indicated in the text, an upper, a middle, and a lower ('down'), within one and the same linguistic construction. First *med pinden helt oppe* 'with the stick all the way up-STAT', and next *med pinden i midten* 'with the stick in the middle'. But the third time the procedural DDA suddenly pops up:

(42) med   pinden   helt   nedad
     with   the stick   all the way   down-PROC
     'with the stick right downwards'

Again, this could be explained as a sudden shift in attentional focus by the language user, making the conceptualization of the specific direction prominent. The data suggest that the instruction about specific direction might be so strongly associated with the procedural DDA that it can trigger the use of this DDA, even in linguistic patterns that would normally rule it out. This suggestion calls for further investigation, for instance with respect to the acceptability of the use of the three DDAs in various more or less prototypical or deviant linguistic patterns.

In a strictly rule-based analysis, examples (39)–(42) might be discarded as 'faults', 'exceptions', or 'irregularities'. In Nedergaard Thomsen (1998: 70), it is for instance claimed that the procedural DDA will always agree with a procedural preposition. Confronted with the huge number of 'exceptions' in the data in these constructions, such an approach seems untenable, at least in a simple version. On the other hand it would be just as naïve to claim that the use of DDAs were always 'emergent' or 'constructional' and governed by the communicative intentions of the speaker in actual discourse.[12] The use of DDAs is clearly characterized by numerous constraints and some of these constraints are also very strong and coded in linguistic patterns. What the study really indicates is that cognitive constraints can be of different kinds and work at different levels of language. The very strong conceptual constraints at work in the use of the static DDA would

---

[12] Cf. the discussion of usage and linguistic structure by Boye and Harder (2007).

seem to reflect very basic kinds of ordering of the world by speakers of Danish, conceptualized in language and grounded in very general cognitive operations. The constraint in the use of the procedural DDA seems to reflect a conceptualization which is subject to a much more flexible coding in language. The constraint in the use of the procedural DDA, the matrix 'x (not y)', however, is strong in another sense, since it has a great potential for attentionally highlighting a specific conceptualization in actual discourse.

10.8   Conclusion

In this study I have proposed an analysis of the semantics pertaining to the three different forms of DDAs. It is a fact that DDAs are used to construe spatial meaning by coding information about the geometric properties of the path in a motion event. Having different forms, however, DDAs also serve as important linguistic items, being used to specify details in the motion event (for instance (non-)translocation, or action versus activity), or being used as free locatives to specify the place where an event takes place. It is clear that DDAs code specifics of both space and motion and that an analysis would have to be able to account for both functions. Thus, I have suggested that the basic, paradigmatic meaning of DDAs could be described as the conceptualization of a path event frame, and that the core meaning of the three DDAs respectively could be described as different ways of profiling this frame (Talmy 2000; Langacker 1998). This analysis is based on the observation of numerous constraints in the use of DDAs in different corpora of Danish.

It has already been shown that DDAs play an important role in the conceptualization of motion events in Danish, especially how they are used to code different aktionsarten in complex predicates (Harder et al. 1996). This study offers an explanation of this use within the coherent framework of Cognitive Linguistics. It is argued that the respective profiling by each form within the minimal basic frame, the path event frame, makes it possible to specify or highlight different aspects of a motion event: (non-)translocation, the process of motion, or the specific kind of direction. More generally, DDAs can be said to provide a path event frame for verbs that do not code this frame in the root (cf. Kopecka 2006). They also code linguistically what is only presupposed in other languages (for instance the possible fictive motion and default deictic point of view in the use of English *across*). The use of the static DDA has proved to be very frequent and systematic in the data. The study also sheds new light on the use of the procedural DDA, which is subject to considerable variation. The data show that the use of the latter is influenced by several factors, cognitive as well as contextual—attentional focus in actual discourse, triggering instructions in other linguistic items, and an oppositional matrix structure—which could be explored in more detail in future studies. The study points to the considerable variation to be found in the linguistically coded conceptualization of motion events within the general, typological frame defined by Talmy (cf. Berthele 2004).

However, the study has also attempted to approach a more general, analytical problem. The general theoretical claim within Cognitive Linguistics is that language and language use are systematic, but that the system is also dynamic. This means that an analysis should also be able to reflect and integrate the dynamic aspect into the description of the systemic patterns. Some of the constraints observed in this study are for instance very strong, and linguistic coding is very strict, but there is also quite some variation to be found in the data. A simple rule-based description would meet a nicely congruent reality in the data for the static DDA, but not for the procedural DDA. On the other hand, the data clearly show that the use of the procedural DDA conforms to regularities, cognitive as well as linguistic. I have drawn upon an instructional semantics in this study in order to be able to account for this variation and to be able to provide a description which is not just internally coherent, but which is also as exhaustive as possible: that is, able to explain all acceptable instances in the data (excluding only instances of technical processing errors, deficient language faculties, possible misprints, etc.). A combination of a cognitive and an instructional approach could be a way of integrating the dynamic into the static, and this study should be seen as an attempt to grasp the differential use of all three DDAs within one and the same framework.

Finally, the analysis suggests that the basic, Cognitive Linguistic instruction in DDAs seen in isolation should be kept at a very basic level, in order to be able to account for the more or less different and variant outcome of these instructions in linguistic context and in actual discourse. The study also confirms that an analytical approach having at its core a concept of construal should take great pains to specify the relationship between different construals in actual discourse and more general, persistent patterns in language and cognition. The variation between the dynamic and the procedural DDA would at first sight appear to be a free constructional choice by the language user. It should, however, rather be understood as the outcome of restricted possibilities, influenced by the conceptualizations in the verb and the preposition, within the overall pattern of motion event expression in Danish.

11

How German and French Children Express Voluntary Motion

ANNE-KATHARINA HARR
and MAYA HICKMANN

11.1 Introduction

Much recent research in developmental psycholinguistics has revived debates around the question of the relative impact of universal vs language-specific determinants in first language acquisition. In this context, children's acquisition of spatial language has been a recurrent illustration of the need to address this question in a cross-linguistic perspective. Space is indeed a most basic domain of human cognition that occupies much of our daily lives. It is therefore not surprising that all languages should provide complex systems to express spatial information. Past research in this domain has typically aimed at showing the existence of universal spatial distinctions across languages and assumed that children acquire the corresponding spatial devices along a universal sequence based on the development of their general cognitive capacities. However, linguistic spatial systems also present considerable variations, for example in the types of distinctions they highlight and in the types of devices they provide to express them. Furthermore, recent psycholinguistic research indicates that such language properties may influence the course of children's language acquisition and may even have an impact on their cognitive organization by bringing them to select particular types of spatial information.

The present chapter addresses these questions in a study of how children express motion events in German and in French. These two languages present divergent typological properties that result in different prototypical patterns in the expression of motion. Particular attention is placed on the implications of Talmy's (2000) distinction between *satellite-framed* and *verb-framed* languages (e.g. Germanic vs Romance, respectively) for how children learn the devices available in their language to describe voluntary motion during first language acquisition. Such analyses of how children and adults verbalize motion events gives us deeper insights into the conceptualization of spatial semantics in two different speaker communities, showing how language-typological factors and general developmental factors interact during language acquisition. Thus, our results in the field of language acquisition constitute another window onto conceptual space, especially in the developing mind.

11.2 Space across Languages

Human languages provide complex systems for the expression of spatial information. These systems encode a number of universal distinctions, such as the distinction between static and dynamic situations or between motion events that take place within a general location or imply a change of location. However, they also show considerable variations (Levinson 1996, 1997): for example they provide different lexical and grammatical devices to express spatial relations (e.g. prepositions/postpositions, cases, predicates), focus on different dimensions (a given spatial distinction may be fundamental in one language and not marked in another), and bring speakers to rely on different reference systems (e.g. absolute, relative, intrinsic).

Talmy (1985, 2000) proposes a dichotomy between *satellite-* and *verb-framed* languages based on their lexicalization patterns. As illustrated in (1) and (2), satellite-framed languages (e.g. Germanic) encode MANNER in the verb stem (English/German *climb/klettern, run/rennen*) and PATH in verbal satellites such as particles (*down/runter, away/weg*). In contrast, as shown in (3), verb-framed languages (e.g. Romance) encode PATH in the verb stem (*descendre* 'to descend', *partir* 'to leave') and MANNER by peripheral constructions such as prepositional phrases (*à quatre pattes* 'on all fours') or gerunds (*en glissant* 'by sliding').

(1) The bear   climbs   down   the tree.

(2) Der Bär   klettert   den Baum   runter.
     'The bear   climbs   the tree   down.'

(3) L'ours   descend   l'arbre   en glissant.
     'The bear   descends   the tree   by sliding.'

When verbalizing motion events, speakers preferentially choose those constructions that are most typical of their language. Recent research (Bowerman 1996, 2007; Levinson 1996, 1997; Slobin 1996, 2006) suggests that some of these language-specific properties affect human spatial conceptualization. One implication of this view is that speakers are thereby invited to direct their attention to different aspects of reality, so that they foreground and background different types of information across languages.

Although German stands among other satellite-framed languages, few studies have examined how motion is expressed in this language. In a detailed classification of German motion verbs, Weber (1983) shows that the vast majority encode MANNER, since twenty of the thirty-five semantic components that characterize these verbs actually correspond to some aspect of MANNER. With respect to German satellites, Haggblade (1994) finds a great number of different (separable and insep-arable) particles and adverbs that express PATH, for example *durch-* ('across'), *rauf-* ('up'), or *hinter* ('behind').[1] Moreover, some of these satellites contain up to three different semantic aspects of PATH, for instance the particle *drüber-* ('there + across + in the direction of the speaker'). Given the very complex morphology of these devices, Altmann (2011: 37ff) calls them 'double-particles'.

As for French, several recent studies (Hickmann 2003, 2006, 2010; Hickmann et al. 2009) have shown its predominant verb-framed properties. French speakers typically encode PATH in the main verb (*monter* 'to ascend', *traverser* 'to cross', *partir* 'to leave') and MANNER in peripheral constructions such as gerunds (*en nageant* 'by swimming') or prepositional phrases (*en vélo* 'on his/her bike'). Since the expression of MANNER requires quite complex constructions, French speakers (even adults) rarely encode both semantic components simultaneously, prefer-ring to encode PATH only, unless they want to strongly highlight MANNER for discourse purposes. Exceptions also occur, such as the verbs *grimper* ('to climb upwards') or *s'envoler* ('to fly off'), which lexicalize MANNER and PATH simultan-eously.[2] Linguistic analyses (Kopecka 2006) have also shown that some French motion verbs contain a prefix that can express various kinds of information including PATH in some cases, for instance the verb *traverser* ('to cross') which emerged form the Latin verb *transvehere* (*trans-* 'across, through'; *vehere* '/go travel'). However, in contrast to similar devices in satellite-framed languages, this phenomenon is not productive and quite marginal, constituting a minor sub-component of a predominantly verb-framed language.

11.3   Space in Language Acquisition

11.3.1   General cognitive determinants

Despite diverging claims concerning language acquisition across available theoreti-cal models, there is a general consensus that general cognitive and perceptual factors partly determine the acquisition process. With respect to the acquisition of spatial language, it has long been assumed (Piaget and Inhelder 1947; E. Clark 1972, 1980; H. Clark 1973) that general cognitive factors underlie children's linguistic development in this domain independently of the target language. On the basis of a review of several studies concerning the acquisition of

---

[1] Haggblade's (1994) analysis includes a variety of devices (prefixes, particles, prepositional phrases, and adverbs) that may not be *satellites*, according to strict definitions (cf. Talmy 2000).

[2] Although French provides verbs that lexicalize PATH and MANNER in literary and/or higher registers, common verbs rarely combine both information components, with the exception of *grimper* ('to climb up'). In particular, no such verbs were ever used for other event types (downward motion and boundary crossing).

prepositions across languages, Johnston (1988) concludes that all children follow a similar developmental sequence: they first learn prepositions that encode containment (*in*), support (*on*), and occlusion (*under*), then those that encode proximity (*next to*), and at last those that refer to distinctions on the sagittal axis (*behind, in front of*). This recurrent order seems to reflect the relative complexity of spatial markers and suggests that universal cognitive constraints influence acquisition.

Furthermore, from a few months of age on and throughout the prelinguistic period, children already show a number of complex spatial capacities, for instance knowledge about object permanence, spatial and temporal relations, basic physical laws concerning motion, and causality (see review in Lécuyer et al. 1996). These results seem to support the nativist point of view, which claims the existence of some core knowledge that is innate and modular. According to Spelke (2003), human language later on provides the opportunity to combine knowledge from different modules, allowing humans to build representations that are more complex than those of other species.

In contrast, researchers who support the constructivist position argue that such early spatial knowledge is built by abstracting perceptual information and transforming it into mental representations. According to Mandler (1988, 1996), children perceive and analyse surrounding spatial information and reconstruct it in terms of *image-schemas*. Since this process requires the categorization of physical stimuli and the mapping of meanings onto these categories, Mandler assumes that *image-schemas* represent an important landmark during development from perception to language.

11.3.2   Langugage-specific factors

In addition to nativist and constructivist approaches, linguistic determinism (Whorf 1956; Bowerman 1996; Slobin 1996) proposes that our language influences 'how we think when we speak', getting us to focus our attention on particular aspects of reality. Thus, depending on the properties of their language, children learn to verbalize situations in certain ways, namely those that are most typical of their mother tongue, thereby paying more or less attention to different aspects in their surroundings. Several studies (Bowerman 1996; Choi and Bowerman 1991; Hickmann 2006; Hickmann et al. 2009) have shown that children talk about space more like adults who speak the same mother tongue than like children of the same age learning a typologically different mother tongue.

One study (Hickmann 2006; Hickmann et al. 2009) reports striking differences in how children (three to ten years) express motion in English as opposed to French. From a very early age, English-speaking children use the compact structures available in their language to express both MANNER and PATH of motion together in one single clause, specifically encoding MANNER in the main verb and PATH mainly in PATH-particles. In contrast, French children rarely express MANNER and PATH together, while French adults do not do so as frequently and as systematically as English adults. These results indicate that children learn very early to direct their attention to the types of information that are most salient to them as a function of the most prototypical and accessible linguistic means available in their native language. Indeed, expressing both MANNER and PATH in French requires more complex structures than in English because French typically encodes PATH rather than MANNER in the main verb (e.g. *monter* 'to ascend', *traverser* 'to cross'), so that MANNER has to be expressed by other linguistic means, including adverbial phrases (e.g. *à quatre pattes* 'on all fours') and especially subordinate constructions (e.g. gerunds as in *en courant* 'by running'). Given these typological properties, MANNER information is both less salient (not lexicalized in the main verb) and more difficult to combine with PATH information in French.

The study described below aimed at further examining this hypothesis in a controlled experimental situation that was identical to the one described above for English and French. Given its satellite-framed nature, and despite some particular properties, German lexicalization patterns for motion events are similar to those in English. In particular, most German motion verbs conflate MOTION and MANNER, while PATH is typically expressed in a wide range of satellites (especially particles). From a developmental point of view, German children should therefore talk about motion more like English-speaking children (frequent MANNER verbs and PATH satellites) than like French-speaking children (frequent PATH verbs, infrequent MANNER expressions). The following general predictions were therefore made: although children's MANNER+PATH responses were expected to increase with age in both languages, a language effect was expected at all ages such that German speakers should express both MANNER (in the verb stem) and PATH (in satellites), while French speakers should focus above all on PATH (in the verb stem).

11.4   Method

11.4.1   Subjects

The participants were monolingual German and French speakers of four age groups (twelve subjects per age). Three groups of children, boys and girls, were tested in kindergartens and schools of Augsburg and Paris. Their ages were approximately four years (mean 4;6, range 3;11 to 4;9), six years (mean 6;1, range 5;10 to 6;9), and ten years (mean 10;7, range 9;8 to 11;4). The control groups of adults involved students from the University of Munich and Paris.

11.4.2   Materials

Three different sets of animated cartoons served as stimuli to elicit productions (see Appendix). In all stimuli, characters entered the scene, carried out a displacement in a particular manner (e.g. walking, running, jumping), then left the scene. One set of *target* items (six *up-targets* and six *down-targets*) showed a background scenery with a vertical ground referent, along which displacements took place first upwards and then downwards (e.g. a bear walked onto the scene, climbed up/down a tree, and walked away). The second set of *target* items (six *across-targets*) involved a boundary crossing (e.g. a boy walked onto the scene, swam across a river, and walked away). In the third set of items (twelve *control items*) the characters appeared on one side of the scene against a blank screen, moved to the other side in a particular manner, and left. These displacements were carried out in the absence of any scenery that could provide relevant ground entities for the expression of PATH.

The rationale for these stimuli was two-fold. First, the particular events that were selected showed paths that were among the most familiar to children ('up', 'down', 'across').[3] Second, the contrast between target and control items allowed us to test participants in two different conditions. In target items MANNER and PATH were both salient, whereas control items highlighted MANNER information and minimized the salience of PATH. In addition, control items provided a way of determining whether children were able to produce MANNER information, particularly if they had not spontaneously mentioned this information when describing target items. The following main predictions were made. First, a language effect was expected with target items, but not with control items. When describing target items, German subjects were expected to combine MANNER+PATH and French speakers to focus on PATH. In contrast, irrespective of their language, speakers were expected to mainly focus on MANNER when describing control items. Second, an age effect was also expected in both languages: regardless of their language, children should become increasingly able to express both MANNER and PATH simultaneously, because of their growing cognitive capacities.

11.4.3 Procedure

Participants were seen individually in their school or university setting. They were presented with the cartoons on a computer screen and asked to narrate each cartoon as completely as possible. Primary school children and adults were told that a future addressee, who would not be able to see the cartoons, would have to reproduce the stories on the basis of their descriptions. Younger children were introduced to a doll and were asked to blindfold her as part of a game in which they would be telling her secrets. They were reminded throughout the session to tell her everything that had happened because she could not see and would also like to tell the story. This procedure ensured that subjects produced full

---

[3] Our concern for keeping sessions to a reasonable length and number of stimuli with young children led us to focus only on these three familiar paths. Research in progress presently uses stimuli showing two other types of path that are most familiar to children ('into' and 'out of ').

descriptions. Cartoons were presented in six different random orders in which target items always occurred before control items. A training item began the session. The entire session was audio-taped and transcribed.

11.5 Coding

The analyses focus on all utterances that described motion events. With respect to target items (*up, down, across*), participants gave rather complex descriptions, illustrated in (4) (10 year old) and (5) (adult): they typically provided information about the initial background and the general location of the figure (4a and 5a), then about the main target event (4b and c; 5b and c), and finally about the characters' departure from the scene (4d and 5d).

(4) a. Eine Maus kommt an einen Tisch, [...]
        'A mouse arrives at a table,'

     b. sie klettert an einem Tischbein hoch, [...]
        'she climbs up a leg of a table,'

     c. rutscht wieder runter [...]
        'slides down again'

     d. und verschwindet mit dem Käse.
        'and disappears with the cheese.'

(5) a. Donc petit ours est arrivé de la droite au pied de l'arbre, [...]
        'So, little bear arrived from the right at the foot of the stem,'

     b. il a grimpé jusqu'à la ruche, [...]
        'he climbed up to the beehive,'

     c. il est redescendu [...]
        'he descended again,'

     d. et il est reparti vers la gauche.
        'and he went away towards the left.'

For the quantitative analyses below, there was one answer per subject and per motion event. If subjects described a given motion event in several ways across utterances, only the richest response (i.e. the one that contained the most semantic information) was included in the analyses. Participants' descriptions were analysed with respect to all devices that expressed MANNER and/or PATH information. Among these devices a main distinction was made between main verbs (e.g. *klettern* 'to climb', *courir* 'to run') and all other devices that could express relevant information, including five different types of elements: a) German particles expressing PATH (e.g. *rauf* 'up', *weg* 'away'), b) prepositional phrases providing information about PATH or LOCATION (e.g. *auf den Baum* 'on the tree', *dans l'eau* 'in the water'), c) locative adverbs (e.g. *dort* 'there', *ici* 'here'), d) noun phrases denoting the moving figure and providing information about MANNER (e.g. *Fahrradfahrerin* 'cyclist', *nageur* 'swimmer'), and e) adverbial phrases expressing MANNER (e.g. *schnell* 'fast', *à quatre pattes* 'on all fours').

Responses can be divided into three main types, depending on the semantic content expressed: 1) only MANNER (hereafter MANNER-*only* responses), e.g. the responses in (6), 2) only PATH (PATH-*only* responses), e.g. examples in (7), or 3) both simultaneously (MANNER+PATH responses), e.g. examples in (8).[4] A fourth residual category included responses that expressed neither MANNER nor PATH (e.g. *gehen/aller* with no further specification), as well as occasional cases where participants did not give any response at all.

(6)   Die Frau fährt Fahrrad. 'The woman rides a bike.'
      Die Maus geht auf Zehenspitzen. 'The mouse goes on tiptoe.'
      Le garçon nage. 'The boy swims.'
      Un coureur va sur la route. 'A jogger goes on the street.'

(7)   Der Bär geht runter. 'The bear goes down.'
      Der Mann überquert die Strasse. 'The man crosses the street.'
      La fille traverse le lac. 'The girl crosses the lake.'
      Il part. 'He goes away.'

(8)   Der Affe klettert den Baum rauf. 'The monkey climbs up the tree.'
      Das Baby krabbelt über die Straße. 'The baby crawls across the street.'
      L'écureuil grimpe à l'arbre. 'The squirrel climbs up the tree.'
      Le garçon traverse la rivière en nageant. 'The boy crosses the river by swimming.'

11.6   Results

11.6.1   Upward motion

When describing upward motion, German speakers predominantly expressed MANNER+PATH simultaneously (80 per cent on the average), as illustrated in (9). As shown in Figure 11.1, this response type was predominant at all ages, despite the fact that it increased with age, particularly after age 6 (4 and 6 years 71 per cent, 10 years 86 per cent, and adults 93 per cent). As illustrated in (10), children

---

[4] Several verbs were considered to encode MANNER+PATH simultaneously as for example the French verb *grimper* ('to climb up'), which gives information about the manner of motion (using limbs) and its path (necessarily upward motion). Other verbs in this category were e.g. *escalader* ('to climb up'), *erklettern* ('to climb up'), *tauchen* ('to dive'), *plonger* ('to dive').

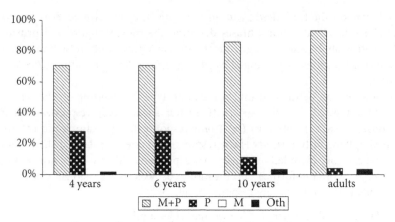

FIG 11.1. Responses for upward motion in German

also produced some PATH-only responses (4 and 6 years 28 per cent, 10 years 11 per cent), which practically disappeared at adult age (4 per cent). There were no MANNER-only responses. Responses in the residual 'Other' category (no response or responses that expressed neither MANNER nor PATH) were rare (4 and 6 years 1 per cent, 10 years 3 per cent, and adults 3 per cent).

(9) Die Maus ist da hoch geklettert. (4 years)
     'The mouse climbed up there.'

(10) Der Bär geht da rauf. (4 years)
      'The bear goes up on there.'

Figure 11.2 shows the corresponding response distribution in French, which shows two main response types, illustrated in (11) and (12). First, French adults also produced a number of MANNER+PATH responses (60 per cent), but they did so less frequently than German adults (93 per cent) and even less frequently than German four year olds (71 per cent). Second, French children and adults focused predominantly on PATH (on average 64 per cent), as illustrated in (12). However, these PATH-only responses decreased with age, while MANNER+PATH responses increased. As in German, MANNER-only (on average 1 per cent) and 'Other' responses were rare. Language comparisons within each age group showed that, although MANNER+PATH responses were generally more frequent in German than in French, this language difference was only significant at 10 years ($t(20)=-5.25$, $p < 0.01$). However, PATH-only responses were significantly more frequent in French than in German at 4 years ($t(15)=6.4$, $p < 0.01$), at 10 years ($t(16)=3.14$, $p < 0.01$), and at adult age ($t(8)=2.45$, $p < 0.04$). No significant differences were found at 6 years.

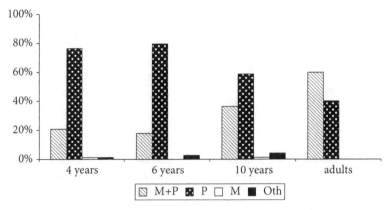

FIG. 11.2. Responses for upward motion in French

(11) L'ours grimpe à l'arbre. (10 years)
      'The bear climbs up the tree.'

(12) Un chat. Il monte. (4 years)
      'A cat. It's ascending.'

German speakers typically expressed the direction of vertical motion in verbal particles (*rauf* 'up', *hoch* 'up') or prepositional phrases with accusative case (*auf den Baum* 'on the tree'). In MANNER+PATH responses their main verbs encoded MANNER (e.g. *klettern* 'to climb', *kriechen* 'to crawl', *rennen* 'to run'). In PATH-only responses they mostly expressed sheer motion in the verb and PATH in other linguistic devices (e.g. *er geht runter* 'he goes down'). In contrast, French speakers encoded mostly PATH in the main verb (*monter* 'to ascend') and often did not provide any further information about MANNER, as shown in example (12) above. If they expressed MANNER+PATH simultaneously, they mostly used the verb *grimper* ('to climb up') that lexicalized both semantic components (cf. example 11). Remaining MANNER+PATH responses provided information about MANNER in gerunds, mostly among adults (*il monte en courant* 'he goes up by running'), or in other linguistic devices such as prepositional phrases (*monter avec ses quatre pattes* 'to go up with its four paws').

11.6.2 Downward motion

If we now compare these results to those concerning downward motion, the language-specific patterns of German and French are even clearer with this second event type. As shown in Figure 11.3, German speakers produced again frequent MANNER+PATH responses at all ages (on average 68 per cent), as illustrated in (13). However, PATH-only responses were frequent at 4 and 6 years (47 per cent

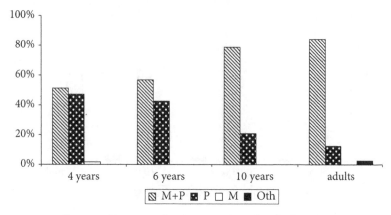

FIG. 11.3. Responses for downward motion in German

and 43 per cent respectively). In these cases children used either the motion verb *gehen* 'to go' or omitted the main verb and used only particles (above all *runter* 'down') to describe downward motion. An example is shown in (14). With increasing age, German speakers produced more MANNER+PATH responses and fewer PATH-only responses. MANNER-only and 'Other' responses were rare.

(13)   Dann springt die Katze wieder runter. (6 years)
       'Then, the cat jumps back down.'

(14)   Der Affe geht hoch und dann wieder runter. (4 years)
       'The monkey goes up and then back down.'

Figure 11.4 shows the corresponding results for French. PATH-only responses were predominant with this event type (on average 84 per cent) and this result holds for all ages (4 years 82 per cent, 6 years 88 per cent, 10 years 81 per cent, adults 88 per cent). Although occasional MANNER+PATH responses occurred and increased slightly with age (4 and 6 years 1 per cent, 10 years 14 per cent, adults 11 per cent), they remained far behind those elicited with upward motion (where speakers used the verb *grimper* 'to climb up'). Typical examples of these two types of response are shown in (15) and (16). Language comparisons within each age group showed that MANNER+PATH responses were significantly more frequent in German than in French at all ages: at 4 years (t(15)=−2.63, p < 0.02), at 6 years (t(57)=−3.43, p < 0.01), at 10 years (t(15)=−2.63, p < 0.02), and at adult age (t(16)=−5.16, p < 0.01). In addition, PATH-only responses were significantly more frequent in French than in German at all ages: at 4 years (t(16)=4.52, p < 0.01), at 6 years (t(68)=5.96, p < 0.01), at 10 years (t(16)=4.52, p < 0.01), and at adult age (t(18)=2.3, p < 0.04).

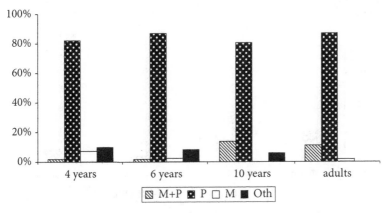

Fɪɢ. 11.4. Responses for downward motion in French

(15)   Le chat redescend en se laissant glisser. (adult)
       'The cat descends again by letting itself slide.'

(16)   Après il redescend. (4 years)
       'Then it descends again.'

As was the case for upward motion, German speakers encoded MANNER in the main verbs (e.g. *klettern* 'to climb', *rutschen* 'to slide') and PATH in other linguistic devices such as particles (*runter* 'down'). In contrast, French speakers encoded PATH in the verb (*descendre* 'to descend') and, if they expressed MANNER at all, they used gerunds to do so (*il descend en glissant* 'he descends by sliding') or in prepositional phrases (*il descend avec ses pieds* 'he descends with his feet').

11.6.3   Crossing events

We now turn to crossing events, in which a human character (e.g. a cyclist, a swimmer) crossed a boundary (e.g. a street, a river). As shown in Figure 11.5, MANNER+PATH responses were predominant at all ages in German (on average 76 per cent), despite the fact that this response type increased with age after 6 years (65 per cent, 10 years 89 per cent, adults 88 per cent). PATH-only responses were relatively infrequent and decreased with age, especially from 10 years on (4 years 21 per cent, 6 years 15 per cent, 10 years 4 per cent, and adults 10 per cent). In contrast to upward and downward motion, German responses to crossing events included occasional MANNER-only responses (on average 11 per cent), particularly among young children (4 years 13 per cent, 6 years 21 per cent, 10 years 7 per cent, and adults 3 per cent). Examples (17) to (19) show the three types of responses that were elicited with this event type.

(17)   Der Junge schwimmt durch den Fluss. (10 years)
       'The boy swims across the river.'

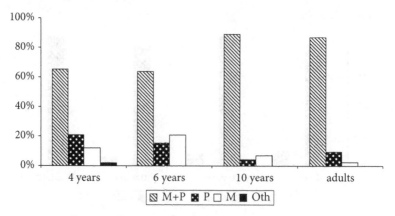

Fig. 11.5. Responses for crossing events in German

(18)   Der Mann geht über die Straße. (6 years)
       'The man goes across the street.'

(19)   Die fährt Schlittschuh. (4 years)
       'She is ice-skating.'

   As for French, Figure 11.6 shows that no typical pattern holds for all age groups. Adults produced many MANNER+PATH responses (57 per cent) but also many PATH-only responses (36 per cent) as illustrated in examples (20) and (21) respectively. However, children focused mainly on MANNER only (4 years 65 per cent, 6 years 46 per cent, 10 years 36 per cent), as illustrated in (22). At 10 years MANNER+PATH and PATH-only responses are equally high, but MANNER-only responses are still frequent. MANNER seems to be more salient with this event type than with the other two event types (up, down). Language comparisons within each age group showed that MANNER+PATH responses were significantly more frequent in German than in French at 6 years (t(16)=−3.16, p < 0.01), at 10 years (t(17)=−3.76, p < 0.01), and at adult age (t(22)=−4.54, p < 0.01). Although the frequency of these responses did not differ across languages at 4 years, MANNER-only responses were significantly more frequent in French than in German at this age (t(13)=2.35, p < 0.04).

(20)   C'est un homme qui traverse une route en courant. (adult)
       'It's a man that is crossing a road by running.'

(21)   J'ai vu un bébé, il a traversé une rue. (adult)
       'I saw a baby, it crossed a street.'

(22)   Il nage. (4 years)
       'He's swimming.'

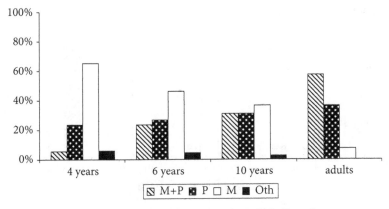

FIG. 11.6. Responses for crossing events in French

German speakers mostly encoded MANNER in the main verb (e.g. *rennen* 'to run', *schwimmen* 'to swim') and PATH in other linguistic devices such as particles (*rüber* 'across') or prepositional phrases (*durch den Fluss* 'through the river', *über die Straße* 'across the street'). However, they also sometimes encoded MANNER in subject nouns (e.g. *ein Jogger* 'a jogger', *ein Schwimmer* 'a swimmer') or in prepositional phrases (*auf ihrem Fahrrad* 'on her bike'). In comparison, when French speakers expressed MANNER and PATH simultaneously, they did so differently depending on age. Adults mostly used the French verb *traverser* ('to cross') and combined it either with a gerund (e.g. *en courant* 'by running', *en nageant* 'by swimming') or with a subject noun that contained MANNER information (e.g. *un nageur* 'a swimmer', *une patineuse* 'a skater'). Children's rare MANNER+PATH responses usually contained the more ambiguous PATH-verb *passer* ('to pass') and some subject nouns expressing MANNER, rather than the more complex gerund structures.

11.6.4   Control items

In control items, characters moved in a particular manner from one side of an empty screen to the other. Recall that these items were meant to focus subjects' attention on MANNER information. We therefore expected that speakers of both languages whould mostly produce MANNER-only responses. The results were rather surprising, particularly in German. As shown in Figure 11.7, although German children and adults expressed MANNER information, they also frequently combined this information with PATH in MANNER+PATH responses (4 years 28 per cent, adults 79 per cent). It is interesting that 6 and 10 year olds (14 per cent and 16 per cent respectively) focused mainly on MANNER only and did not mention PATH as often as 4 year olds. However, apart from adults, the typical pattern for control items was

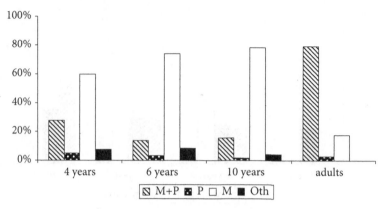

FIG. 11.7. Responses for control items in German

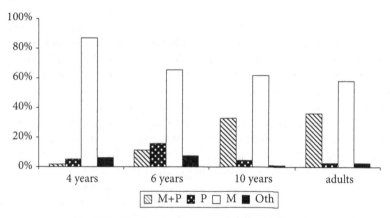

FIG. 11.8. Responses for control items in French

MANNER-only responses (4 years 60 per cent, 6 years 74 per cent, 10 years 78 per cent, adults 18 per cent).

Figure 11.8 shows that French MANNER-only responses were frequent in all age groups (4 years 88 per cent, 6 years 66 per cent, 10 years 62 per cent, adults 58 per cent). However, these responses decreased with age, while MANNER+PATH responses increasingly occurred among children (4 years 1 per cent, 6 years 11 per cent, 10 years 33 per cent), reaching a maximum of 36 per cent at adult age. In contrast to target events (*up*, *down*, *across*), PATH-only responses were infrequent, as expected since MANNER was foregrounded in these items. Language comparisons within each age group showed no significant differences at any age with respect to MANNER+PATH responses (as was expected with these items). However, adults produced more MANNER-only responses in French than in German (t(16)=3.16, p < 0.01). In addition, the French 4 year olds produced more MANNER-only responses (t(21)=2.2, p < 0.04) in comparison to German children of the same age.

11.7 Discussion

The aim of this experiment was to examine the expression of voluntary motion by children and adults of two typologically different languages, German and French. The results first confirm that these two languages differ strongly with respect to their lexicalization patterns (Talmy 1985). In addition, although they show developmental progressions in both languages, these progressions are not identical in German and in French. Taken together, these results indicate the impact of two different kinds of factors on children's verbalization of voluntary motion: language-specific determinants and general cognitive factors (Hickmann 2010; Hickmann et al. 2009; Harr 2012).

11.7.1 Language-specific determinants

The results first show clear differences in how children and adults described voluntary motion in German and French. As expected from the satellite-framed nature of German, speakers of this language mostly expressed MANNER and PATH simultaneously, despite some variations in their responses across ages and items. In particular, German children also produced some PATH-only responses, particularly with downward motion, but these responses decreased with age, while MANNER+PATH responses increased. In the majority of PATH-only responses, children combined a PATH-satellite with the semantically neutral verb *gehen* ('to go'), which did not encode any information about the manner of motion. Example (23) illustrates this kind of utterance:

(23) Die ist runtergegangen. (4 years)
      'She has gone down.'

Nevertheless, MANNER+PATH responses were the predominant pattern across all ages and items in German (Slobin 2006; Talmy 1985). Even the youngest German children (4 year) spontaneously packed these two semantic components into one single utterance. Like German adults, they mainly encoded MANNER in the main verb and PATH in particles or prepositional phrases. This type of construction, typical for a satellite-framed language, is indeed very frequent in German and typical in very young children's spontaneous productions. For example, PATH-particles are one of the first linguistic devices produced by German children and satellites are very varied in their narratives (Bamberg 1994: 220). In addition, our study showed that German children produced many varied and novel MANNER verbs reflecting much creativity in how they described the precise manner in which motion took place. For example, the four year olds produced interesting neologisms, such as *fahrraden* ('to bicycle'), *kraupen* (probably from the verb *krabbeln* 'to crawl', and the noun *Raupe* 'caterpillar'), or *tippseln* (roughly 'to trip in a clumsy way'). In utterances describing crossing events, speakers also used the German PATH-verb *überqueren* ('to cross') in combination with a subject noun like *der Radfahrer* ('the cyclist') or *der Schwimmer* ('the swimmer'). German adults even produced MANNER+PATH responses with control items, in which PATH was expressed in relation to the screen itself (e.g. *das Mädchen fährt Schlittschuh durchs Bild* 'the girl skates across the picture', *ein Jogger läuft von rechts nach links* 'a jogger runs from left to right'). However, with this type of event MANNER +PATH responses were less frequent among children, who mostly focused on MANNER (as had been expected at all ages with these items). One explanation for this verbal behaviour might be the typical satellite-framing pattern of German in which MANNER and PATH are expressed in one single utterance. It is likely that speakers of German have deeply internalized this pattern so that they are searching for some PATH information to express even if this type of information is not salient (Talmy 2000). In support of this point, it should be noted that very similar results were reported for English adults and children (Hendriks et al. 2008; Hickmann et al. 2009).

In French, both children and adults focused mainly on PATH (as expected for a verb-framed language), although adults also produced frequent MANNER+PATH responses (Hickmann 2006). French speakers encoded PATH in the main verb and this kind of verb was very frequent at all ages. If MANNER was expressed, speakers used mainly peripheral constructions or prepositional phrases (as illustrated in examples (24) and (25), respectively).

(24)   Voilà un garçon qui traverse en fait une rivière gelée en glissant. (adult)
       'Here is a boy who crosses in fact a frozen river by sliding.'

(25)   Il a traversé la rue à quatre pattes. (8 years)
       'He crossed the street on all fours.'

French responses were also much more varied as a function of event type as compared to German. In French, MANNER+PATH responses were most frequent with upward motion than with other event types in all age groups. This result can be explained by the frequent use of *grimper* ('to climb up'), which conflates MANNER and PATH within one lexical item (see footnote 2). Nevertheless, both German and French children also expressed more PATH-only utterances when describing downward motion as compared to upward motion. This result might be accounted for in two possible (and non-exclusive) ways. First, MANNER information is perhaps less important for downward motion than for upward motion, in the sense that gravity facilitates downward motion, so that the agent need not make as much effort to go down as to go up. Second, each of the stimuli that implied motion along a vertical axis presented upward motion just before downward motion. As a result, discourse factors could explain why speakers may have presupposed MANNER information when describing downward motion, once they had already mentioned this information for upward motion in the immediately preceding discourse. Such an explanation would particularly hold for events in which MANNER was held constant for upward and downward motion. Therefore, if children expressed only one semantic component, they could have focused either on PATH or on MANNER for upward motion, but more on PATH for downward motion.

With crossing events, French adults produced MANNER+PATH responses about one-third of the time (e.g. *un garçon glisse de droite à gauche* 'a boy slides from right to left'). In contrast, French children predominantly focused on MANNER alone and focused on PATH from ten years on. A similar but much weaker tendency could also be observed in German (in the present study) as well as in previous results concerning English (Hendriks et al. 2008; Hickmann et al. 2009). Note that such MANNER-only responses practically never occurred with up/down events. This pattern was not expected. One possible explanation may be that crossing events are conceptually more complex than upward and downward motion, partly because they involve a double boundary (at the initial and final phases of the trajectory), making it more difficult for children to construct complete representations, regardless of their language. However, this explanation would not account for the more frequent uses of MANNER verbs among French children. An additional possibility may be that the particularly low frequency of PATH verbs with crossing events among French children may be due to a lexical gap, according to which the relevant verb (*traverser* 'to cross') would be rare in young children's repertoire. Future research would be necessary to fully account for these results.

In summary, notwithstanding differences that were found among event types, speakers produced gradually more MANNER+PATH responses with increasing age, but they produced fewer such responses at all ages in French than in German. This result supports the view that French children have difficulties encoding both semantic components simultaneously or at least that they clearly choose not to do so.

11.7.2   General cognitive factors

Finally, despite crosslinguistic differences at all ages, children's productions also showed a similar developmental progression in both languages. In particular, regardless of their language, children's MANNER+PATH responses increased with age, and other responses (MANNER-only and PATH-only) decreased with age. Two types of cognitive factors may be responsible for these developmental progressions.

First, the results show that young children produced more utterances expressing only one piece of information in comparison to older children or adults, whose verbalizations were formally and semantically richer and more complex. This developmental progression presumably follows from children's increasing cognitive capacities that allow them to express multiple types of information simultaneously. Second, Talmy (2000) suggests that, apart from motion itself, which is the most basic property of any dynamic situation, PATH is more relevant than MANNER as a defining feature for motion events. Furthermore, this information is central for discourse representations, in order to allow the interlocutor to reconstruct location change, as well as in everyday life (for example, in navigation or way-finding situations). Our data indeed suggest that PATH was most salient in both languages (Talmy 2000). French speakers (verb-framed language) clearly preferred to encode PATH when they only expressed one piece of information. Similarly, in German (satellite-framed language), if children encoded only one component, they expressed PATH. More generally, although speakers expressed MANNER more often in German than in French, they expressed PATH equally frequently in both languages.

Both types of general cognitive factor can account for some of our results (Hickmann et al. 2009). However, neither of them can explain why developmental changes are more striking in French than in German. This difference in developmental rate is directly related to the striking cross-linguistic differences that were observed at all ages, as expected from the satellite-framed vs verb-framed properties of German and French. Thus, MANNER+PATH responses were generally more frequent in German at all ages, including among adults but particularly among children, who rarely expressed both semantic components at the same time in French, even at age six. Given the typological properties of these two languages and the fact that French frequently requires the use of complex syntactic constructions (e.g. gerunds) to express MANNER and PATH simultaneously (Slobin 2006), the acquisition of these structures constitutes a more difficult task in French than in German. As a result, French children take more time to acquire target-like structures than German children.

11.8   Conclusion

Our results show that speakers clearly express voluntary motion in very different ways depending on the particular typological properties of their language (Slobin 1996b, 2006; Talmy 1985). They further show that such differences affect children's productions from early on, suggesting that language-specific factors and general cognitive determinants should both be taken into account in our models of first language acquisition (Hickmann 2006; Hickmann et al. 2009). In particular, a language such as German (satellite-framed) leads speakers to pay more attention to the manner in which motion is carried out in comparison to a language such as French (verb-framed), at least insofar as they choose to express this information (cf. Harr 2012). This striking difference results from the fact that satellite-framed languages systematically rely on compact structures in which MANNER is lexicalized in the verb and PATH is expressed in satellites, whenever it is relevant. In contrast, depending on discourse needs, verb-framed languages provide two different types of structure: they either lexicalize PATH in the verb to express location changes, and in this case they leave MANNER to be encoded in more complex structures (if at all); or they lexicalize MANNER in the verb to express motion within a general location, but in this case PATH is not expressed at all. Further research is necessary to determine the extent to which such cross-linguistic differences in production might reflect deeper differences in speakers' underlying event representations that may influence children's cognitive organization during first language acquisition.

Appendix

Materials

Up- and down-target items
(T1)   A squirrel runs to a tree, up into and out of a hole in the tree, down, and away.
(T2)   A caterpillar crawls to a plant, up the stalk to eat a piece of leaf, down, and away.
(T3)   A bear walks to a tree, climbs up to a beehive to get some honey, climbs down to eat it, and walks away.
(T4)   A cat runs to a telephone pole, jumps up to a bird's nest, drops an egg, jumps down to lick the egg, and runs away.
(T5)   A mouse tiptoes to a table, climbs up to take a piece of cheese, slides down, and tiptoes away.
(T6)   A monkey walks to a banana tree, climbs up to take a banana, then slides down, and walks away.

Across-target items
(T7)   A man runs to a country road, runs across the road, and runs away.
(T8)   A girl rides to railway tracks on a bicycle, rides across the tracks, and rides away.
(T9)   A baby crawls to a street, crawls across the street, and crawls away.
(T10) A boy walks to a river, swims across the river, and walks away.
(T11) A boy walks to a frozen river, slides across the river on his boots, and walks away.
(T12) A girl walks to a frozen lake with skates on, skates across the lake, and walks away.

Control items

(C1) squirrel running; (C2) caterpillar crawling; (C3) bear walking; (C4) cat running; (C5) mouse tiptoeing; (C6) kitten running; (C7) man running; (C8) girl riding bicycle; (C9) baby crawling; (C10) boy swimming; (C11) boy sliding; (C12) girl skating.

12

Narrow Paths, Difficult Roads, and Long Ways: Travel through Space and Metaphorical Meaning

MARLENE JOHANSSON FALCK*

12.1 Introduction

Consider the metaphorical uses of *path*, *road*, and *way* in the following sentences:

(1) We have covered a lot of ground, and maybe the *path* through the undergrowth of arguments and data is not a very straight or a very clear one.

(2) Far from reaching the end of the *road*, we are only just beginning!

(3) A Steve Quirk hat-trick paved the *way* for Formby JSC's 9–1 win over Holborn Boys.

In all these sentences, there is an intimate connection between travel through space and making progress. We may infer that the further we travel along the metaphorical *path*, *road*, or *way* the more progress we make. However, despite the close connection between travel through space and progress in these sentences, there still seem to be important differences between the metaphorical uses of *path*, *road*, and *way*. A metaphorical path (1), and possibly a metaphorical way, can go through undergrowth and be described as neither clear nor straight. But can a metaphorical road be described in this way and can it go through similar terrain? The end of the metaphorical road in (2) may be reached by continued travel towards its end. Metaphorical paths and ways, however, do not typically take us to their ends (cf. e.g. *Far from reaching the end of the path/way, we are only just beginning!*). Finally, in (3) a metaphorical way has been *paved*. The phrases *pave the path/pave the road* seem much less apt in metaphorical contexts (cf. *paved the path/road for Formby JSC's 9–1 win*)?

* I am grateful to the Swedish Research Council (Vetenskapsrådet) for supporting this work. Many thanks also to Raymond W. Gibbs Jr., Marcus Perlman, two anonymous reviewers, and the editors of this volume for their very helpful comments on a previous draft of this chapter.

A comparison between metaphorical uses of *path*, *road*, and *way* inevitably suggests that these terms are far from completely interchangeable. At the same time, they are all similar in making use of travel through space to illustrate progress in other areas. So far, linguistic theories have tended to focus on either one of these issues, but not really addressed the relationship between differences connected with individual terms and systematicity at more general levels of abstraction.

On a traditional, Cognitive Linguistics analysis, the sentences above would all be analysed as linguistic realizations of the conventional conceptual motion metaphor A PURPOSEFUL ACTIVITY IS A JOURNEY. This fairly complex metaphor, in turn, arises from the more basic primary metaphors (Grady 2005; Lakoff and Johnson 1999) PURPOSES ARE DESTINATIONS and ACTIONS ARE MOTIONS. Analyses like these explain why there is systematicity among linguistic expressions such as (1–3) above, but they do not explain why there are also important differences between the expressions.

Another more recent linguistic approach to metaphor focuses on discourse metaphors and the link between analogical schemas and language use (Zinken 2007). On this view, lexical concepts are prompts for accessing a particular area of encyclopaedic knowledge and 'driving forces in the negotiation of habitual analogies' (p. 446). A 'discourse metaphor is a linguistic expression containing a construction that, in the appropriate context, prompts the speaker/hearer to construct an analogical meaning that has been negotiated in the discourse' (p. 450). Zinken's comparison between vehicle pairs such as *path–course* and *kettle–pot* in the discourse of German newspaper texts and political speeches convincingly shows that lexical items that belong to the same superordinate category are systematically associated with different figurative meanings. His view that lexical concepts are a factor in the development of figurative meaning is indeed plausible, and it partly explains why the metaphorical *path-*, *road-*, and *way*-instances discussed above differ. Zinken, however, does not explain why terms that belong to the same superordinate category tend to be structured in a coherent way at the levels of primary and complex metaphor. On Zinken's view, more general mappings such as these might well be 'post-hoc artifact[s] of sorting utterances on the part of the researcher' (p. 461). Zinken's theory, then, unlike the conceptual metaphor theory (above), does not explain why metaphorical *path-*, *road-*, and *way*-instances such as those in (1–3) above, are all based on the ideas that travel through space is progress and that the distance covered is an indication of how much progress has been made.

In this chapter, I focus on differences between metaphorical *path-*, *road-*, and *way*-instances and their relationship to our embodied experiences of paths, roads, and ways. My aim is to show how our experiences of these spatial concepts help us construe spatial meaning that is both based on 'stereotypical encyclopaedic knowledge' (Zinken 2007: 45) and coherent with metaphorical mappings at the levels of primary and conceptual metaphor.

The study is an extension of my previous analysis of metaphorical *road-* and *way*-expressions (Johansson Falck 2005), which showed that these are both structured by mappings that are coherent with the ACTION IS MOTION metaphor and one or more conventional conceptual motion metaphors (e.g. LIFE/A PURPOSE-FUL ACTIVITY/A RELATIONSHIP IS A JOURNEY, PURPOSES ARE DESTINATIONS, and TIME/CHANGE IS MOTION), and by people's embodied experiences of roads and ways. Both people's experiences of *road* and *way* in the sense of artefacts (e.g. *[T]hey drove up the road in a cloud of black smoke* and *The way now worked left across the slabby walls*) that take us from one place to another, and *way* in the extended non-metaphorical sense of a figure's literal motion through space (e.g. *I made my way through all the guard checkpoints*) are in line with how the sentences in my material (2005) are structured. The metaphorical *path*-sentences analysed here (e.g. (3) above) indicate that *path* functions in the same way. Most of these instances go back to *path* in the basic sense of an artefact, but there are also a few instances that are related to *path* in the extended sense of a figure's literal motion through space (e.g. *the path of the jeep/vehicle/hurricane* etc.; cf. *way*). No matter which sense of *path* is used, the instances are all structured in line with the motion metaphors above, and with travel along the path from one point to another, from A to B.

My present hypothesis, which is the focus of this chapter, is that the striking coherence between *path-*, *road-*, and *way*-expressions indicates that there is a close connection between the structure of the sentences and our experiences of travelling through space along paths, roads, and ways. Metaphorical language including *path*, *road*, or *way* is not only structured by conventional cross-domain mappings at the levels of primary and complex metaphor, it is also structured by people's embodied experiences of the real-world concepts that these terms refer to. Owing to their functional properties, the artefacts that *path*, *road*, and *way* refer to provide specific instantiations of the SOURCE–PATH–GOAL schema, and a specific embodiment of the primary metaphor ACTION IS MOTION. The spatial distances covered by these artefacts make the SOURCE–PATH–GOAL schema more concrete and easier to refer to. Similarly, the extended senses of *path* and *way* are useful scaffoldings for these structures. They too are connected with our experi-ences of travelling through space and are useful tools when we construe meta-phorical meaning in line with these structures.

My more specific claim, however, is that if metaphorical *path-*, *road-*, and *way*-instances are connected with conceptual mappings that include experiences of real-world paths, roads, and ways, then we would not only expect similarities related to their function (e.g. that they are all structured in line with the ACTION IS MOTION metaphor), but also important differences between the patterns of usage precisely because our experiences of paths, roads, and ways differ. Accordingly, we would expect similarities between the metaphorical and non-metaphorical instances of the same term. The terms *path* and *road*, which still primarily refer to artefacts, will in their metaphorical uses primarily be connected with our experiences of these artefacts. *Way*, however, which in its non-metaphorical uses is generally used to refer to someone's travel through space, is more likely to be connected with this kind of spatial experience also in its metaphorical uses.

Like the similarities at the structural level of *path-*, *road-*, and *way*-sentences (above), the differences and similarities at a more detailed level of abstraction would substantiate the view that people's uses of metaphorical *path-*, *road-*, and *way*-expressions ultimately go back to people's experiences of journeys through space along paths, roads, and ways.

To empirically study the usage patterns of these terms, I carried out a corpus analysis of how *path*, *road*, and *way* are used in non-metaphorical and metaphorical contexts. There are many ways of analysing travel through space on paths, roads, and ways, but for this chapter, I focus on two main facets: (a) phrases that modify the head nouns *path*, *road*, or *way* (modifying phrases include both *premodifiers*—e.g. attributive adjectives like *long [path]*—and *postmodifiers* (e.g. relative clauses like *[path] of the jeep*), but a distinction between these was not necessary for the purpose of this study); and (b) obstacles that hinder travel through space along, or near paths, roads, and ways.

These two facets, at the very least, provide important information about the situational context of the journeys and are excellent indicators of how the metaphorical uses of *path*, *road*, and *way* must be shaped by people's embodied experiences of these spatial concepts in non-metaphorical ways. That is, they are indicators of how spatial concepts are used to construe spatial meaning in metaphorical ways.

12.2 General Method and Material

My material consists of 1,000 random *path-*, *road-*, and *way*-instances from the *British National Corpus (BNC)*. First, the scope of each instance was extended to a context of several lines and the instances extracted from the corpus. Then the instances were divided into metaphorical and non-metaphorical uses (including both literal and metonymic instances) by means of a slightly modified version of the *Metaphor Identification Procedure (MIP)* (Pragglejaz Group 2007).

MIP involves contrasting contextual meanings with basic meanings. Data from the *Macmillan English Dictionary for Advanced Learners, Second Edition (MEDAL;* Rundell and Fox 2007) and the *Shorter Oxford English Dictionary on Historical Principles (SOEDHP;* Brown 1993) were used to determine the basic meanings of *path*, *road*, and *way*, and of phrases including these terms. These basic meanings were then compared with the contextual meanings of the *path-*, *road-*, or *way*-instances in my corpus. Each *path-*, *road-*, or *way*-instance that has a current contemporary meaning that is more basic than its contextual meaning, contrasts with this basic meaning, and can be understood in comparison with this meaning was marked as metaphorical (see Pragglejaz Group 2007). Instances that somehow involve a real spatial distance (i.e. those in the sense of an artefact, and those in the extended metonymic sense of a figure's travel through space, from A to B), were considered to be used in the basic sense of the term and analysed as non-metaphorical. The contexts of the instances were typically sufficient for a comparison between contextual and basic senses. The source text of a given instance was only consulted at times when this was necessary for a distinction between metaphorical and non-metaphorical meaning.

In this way, my material was divided into six main groups: non-metaphorical and metaphorical *path-, road-,* and *way-*instances. Section 12.3 below compares the usage patterns involving non-metaphorical and metaphorical instances of each term. Section 12.4 contrasts the usage patterns of metaphorical *path, road,* and *way.* The focus is on how these paths, roads, and ways are described, and what we learn about obstacles on, or near them.

12.3   What We Talk about When We Talk about Paths, Roads, and Ways

12.3.1   Path

The corpus analysis uncovered 659 non-metaphorical *path-*instances, and 284 metaphorical instances. The non-metaphorical instances are either in the basic sense of '[a] way from one place to another that people can walk along' (*MEDAL*), or in the extended sense of '[t]he direction that someone or something is moving in' (*MEDAL*). The metaphorical instances all contrast with these basic senses and can be understood by means of them. Instances that are ambiguous between non-metaphorical and metaphorical meaning and instances that are part of compound nouns (e.g. *path finders* and *path fibres*) were excluded from the study.

First, I analysed how non-metaphorical and metaphorical paths are described. This was mainly done by studying the modifiers of *path* (see Table 12.1 below).

The words and phrases that provide information about what non-metaphorical *paths* are like fall into seven main groups (see Table 12.1, A–F below). These modifiers say something about what kind of path it is, what the paths are made of (B), what properties the path has: those that make the path difficult (C1) or easy (D), who is on the path and/or what they do (E), and what paths do (F). Some modifiers have the function of referring to a figure whose motion through space constitutes the path (G).

Some of the modifiers of metaphorical *path* come from the source (S) domains. Others come from the target (T) domains. The source domain modifiers fall into four groups. They provide information about the properties of the path: if it is likely to be difficult (C1), or easy (D1) to travel along, and if it goes up or down (H1). One group of source domain modifiers distinguishes the path in question from other paths (e.g. *another, other,* or *the same [path]*) (I1).

TABLE 12.1. *Typical attributes of* path. *Frequencies of more than one instance are within brackets. (S = Source domain, T = Target domain)*

	Questions/ Statements used to categotize modifiers of path	Attributes of non-metaphorical *path*	S/T	Attributes of metaphorical *path*
A	What kind of path is it?	*coastal* (9), *coast* (5), *flight* (9), *garden* (8), *cliff* (5), *cliff-top* (2)		
B	What is the path made of?	*gravel* (4) *sandy* (2) *paved* (2)		
C1	Properties that are likely to make the path difficult (to travel along):	*narrow* (11), *steep* (7), *winding* (5), *curved* (4), *zigzag* (2), *twisting, difficult* (2), *rocky* (2)	S	*no[t] easy* (2), *not clear* (2), *narrow, not straight, risky, dangerous, crooked, rather tricky, longer than any other, unlikely to be smooth*
C2			T	*critical* (5), *punishment* (2), *more cautious, delicate, dead*
D	Properties that are likely to make the path easy (to travel along):	*clear* (6), *straight* (3) *good* (2), *pleasant* (2), *lovely, well trodden, well worn*	S	*well trodden, easy, clear, straight, fast, best*
E	Who is on the path and/or what do they do there?	... *that he and Lee had taken yesterday to get to the edge of the field.*		
F	What does the path do?	... *wound up the side of the mountain. ... rose with the gentle contours of the valley*		
G	The path is the direction in which something or someone is going	... *of the rays/the hurricane/oncoming English armies/the jeep/ lorry/the carriage/the train* etc.	T	... *of some earlier but recent decision, of full cultural control/of mind control/of meditation/of prayer*
H1	Vertical motion		S	*upward* (2), *downward, down, higher, lower*
H2			T	*downsizing, growth* (7), *upgrade* (2)
I1	Other		S	*another* (4), *other* (3), *same* (3)
I2			T	*career* (4)

Modifiers that come from the target domain also tell us that the path is likely to be hard to travel along (C2), and if the path goes up or down (H2). Another group of target domain modifiers describes actions, events, or processes that correspond to metaphorical motion along the path (e.g. *[the path] of full control*) (G). Four paths are described as career paths (I2). These too are indirectly related to vertical motion.

A comparison between the modifiers of non-metaphorical and metaphorical *path*-instances shows that there are both similarities and differences between them. C1, D, and G include modifiers that are found in both non-metaphorical and metaphorical *path*-instances. The rest of the modifiers are only used together with either one of these two kinds of *path*-instance. Interestingly enough, the similarities tend to be connected with real-world paths, and the differences with the context in which these instances are used.

The similarities in C1 and D, for instance, are all connected with properties that seem central to real world paths. Just like real world paths, non-metaphorical and metaphorical paths can be both hard (e.g. *narrow, winding,* and *difficult*) and easy (e.g. *clear* and *well trodden*) to travel along. The former type of path, however, is slightly more frequent. From Table 12.1 above, we thus see that some non-metaphorical paths are 'clear', 'good', 'straight', and 'paved' paths (see D), but the typical non-metaphorical *path* is 'narrow' or 'steep', not straight (e.g. *winding, curved, zigzag,* or *twisting*) or 'difficult' or 'rocky' (see C1). Similarly, metaphorical instances of *path* tend to be *critical path[s], punishment path[s]* (C2); or *dangerous, crooked,* or *risky [paths]* (C1), rather than *clear* or *fast [paths]* (D).

The modifiers of *path* in G, Table 12.1, are all connected with a spatial distance covered by a figure's travel through space. The modifiers of non-metaphorical *path* identify someone or something that literally moves from one place to another (e.g. *the path of the rain-bearing wind, the path of a Ford Sierra car*). Those in the metaphorical instances, refer to actions, events, or processes whose metaphorical motion through space constitutes the path (e.g. *[the path] of full cultural control, mind control, meditation, etc.*).

One of the main differences between the modifiers of non-metaphorical and metaphorical *path*-instances is that non-metaphorical paths, like the path in (4) below, are typically described in much more detailed and colourful ways than metaphorical paths.

(4)   [T]he path was barely wide enough, badly kept, branches low across it, dark after the bright sunlight on the heath.

While the descriptions of non-metaphorical paths can be fairly long, those which are metaphorical typically consist of a short phrase (e.g. *not easy, narrow, crooked*). Another important difference is that the modifiers of non-metaphorical *path*-instances are more varied. They fall into more categories, and include more terms from which we learn that the path is easy or pleasant (see D).

None of the differences between the ways in which non-metaphorical and metaphorical *path*-instances are described go back to a qualitative difference between real-world paths and metaphorical paths. As could be seen above, several of these differences instead appear to be related to the discourse in which they occur (e.g. non-metaphorical vs metaphorical).

Metaphorical *path*-instances, but naturally not non-metaphorical, include modifiers from various target domains. There are e.g. *cautious* or *delicate* (C2) metaphorical paths, paths *of some earlier but recent decisions* (G), and *career* paths (I2).

Moreover, from A and B above, we see that modifiers of non-metaphorical, but not of metaphorical, *path* say something about the type of path in question (i.e. that the path is referred to as a *coast, coastal, flight,* or *garden path*) and what the path is made of (there are e.g. *gravel* or *sand [paths]*). Given that non-metaphorical instances refer to real, and not imagined, journeys on paths, it does make sense to describe these by saying something about the landscape that they go through (e.g. the coast), or about what they are made of (e.g. sand or gravel). Metaphorical instances, on the other hand, focus on features connected with the travel from A to B, and the SOURCE–PATH–GOAL schema (see Johansson Falck 2010), and are less likely to include modifiers that are not relevant for this focus. Modifiers such as *coastal* and *cliff-top* less directly tell us what travel along the path must be like, than modifiers such as *narrow* and *crooked* do. From the latter two modifiers we may easily infer that the journey along the path may be somewhat difficult.

Another difference between the modifiers of non-metaphorical and metaphorical *path*-instances is that very many modifiers of non-metaphorical paths describe what the path does (e.g. *[it] wound up the side of the mountain*). The paucity of modifiers like these in the metaphorical instances is in line with the focus of these on a moving figure (see Johansson Falck 2010) and not the context of the motion.

As seems to be the result of a conventional use of *path* to discuss developments, more metaphorical instances than non-metaphorical discuss vertical movement (there are e.g. *growth path[s], upward,* and *downward path[s]*). These may go either up or down, but are more often upward (see H1 and H2 in Table 12.1).

To conclude, more differences than similarities were found between the modifiers of non-metaphorical and metaphorical *path*-instances. None of these, however, appear to be related to a qualitative difference between real-world paths and metaphorical paths. In that sense, they are not contradictory to the hypothesis that metaphorical paths, just like non-metaphorical, are closely connected with our experiences of physical paths. The largest groups of modifiers of metaphorical *path* are those that refer to the properties of the paths. These display many similarities to those of non-metaphorical *path*, and are all connected with our experiences of paths. The similarities between these modifiers of non-metaphorical and metaphorical *path*-instances substantiate my hypothesis. Just like real-world paths, metaphorical paths are closely connected with motion (cf. Gibson 1979). They may be anything from difficult to easy to move along, but are more often difficult than easy.

Next, the obstacles mentioned in the *path*-instances were compared. Twenty-four of the non-metaphorical *path*-instances include obstacles and twenty of the metaphorical ones. Table 12.2 below presents an analysis based on four specific questions: Where are the obstacles located? What obstacles are there (see 1)? What do we do with the obstacles (2)? How do the obstacles affect those who move along the path (3)?

As shown in 1 in the Table, typical obstacles on, or near, non-metaphorical paths are 'bushes', 'scrub', 'ruts and rubbish', or 'a thicket of hazel'. Obstacles on

TABLE 12.2. *What we learn about obstacles on non-metaphorical and metaphorical paths*

	Research questions	Non-metaphorical *path*	Metaphorical *path*
1	Where are the obstacles located (in bold)? What kinds of obstacles are there (the terms that refer to these are in italics)?	**On the path:** *bushes, scrub, ruts and rubbish, a hedge as big as a whale, rubble and hosepipes, grass and tangled weeds* **In the area through which the path goes, or will be made:** *wild roses, lupin and matagouri, giant cow parsley, a wall of vegetation, a thicket of hazel* **On the path and in the area through which the path goes;** the path *gets rougher, or narrower and the area of land a disturbed terrain of minor undulations full of potholes,* or *very rough as the gradient increases*	**On the path:** a) source domain concepts: *obstacles, stumbling-blocks,* and *pebbles, [littered with] pitfalls, [strewn with] trip wire,* and *[have] some slack [in them]*, b) target domain concepts: *grief [through which there is no easy path], disorder* or *ordeal* **In the area through which the path goes, or will be made:** *seek a path out of divisive ideological camps, set out a path* **On the path and in the area through which the path goes:** *they never [—] run smooth*
2	What do we do with the obstacles?	*slash, carve, scythe, fight,* or *weave a path,* [they have to] *fight, force,* or *bash* [themselves through them]	[the path is] *paved*
3	How do the obstacles affect those who move along the path?	*sufficiently arduous to justify a prolonged rest*	-

metaphorical paths may be typical real-world path obstacles (e.g. 'pebbles' or 'pitfalls'), concepts from the target domains such as 'grief' or 'disorder or ordeal', or they may simply be referred to as 'obstacles'.

The location of the obstacles in non-metaphorical and metaphorical *path*-instances is identical (see 1). In both non-metaphorical and metaphorical contexts they can be found on the path, in the area through which the path goes or is being made, or on both these locations. In the non-metaphorical (5) below, and in metaphorical (6), the obstacles—the bushes and the pebbles—are on the path. This is the most frequent location of the obstacles in both non-metaphorical and metaphorical *path*-instances. On the path, the obstacles inhibit the motion of those (people or things) that travel along the path. In this way, obstacles on metaphorical paths stop events, processes, and sometimes even feelings.

(5)   But at the time I took her, the bushes had grown across the path, and we got stuck, with her widow's weeds entangled in branches and thorns until she could move no more.

(6)   Perhaps she was being silly in thinking that her job was the stumbling-block between them; it was a pebble in the path certainly, but Maria Luisa was the actual stumbling-block.

The obstacles may also be located in the area of land in front of the path, or through which a path is being made (see 1, Table 12.2). The non-metaphorical instances describe how people 'fight', 'force', or 'bash' themselves through them, or 'slash', 'carve', or 'cut' a path. The metaphorical instances mention the 'no easy path' through 'grief', and 'disorder or ordeal' that are 'cast' into someone's path. The idea of literally getting through problematic terrain by somehow creating a path, or by finding a path (above) corresponds to metaphorical 'seek[ing] a path out of divisive ideological camps' or 'sett[ing] out' a path:

(7)   This is not a clear path to Maastricht that the Prime Minister has set out. It is a maze in which Tory Members wander blindly, from time to time colliding with each other.

The obstacles mentioned in both kinds of *path*-contexts may also be located both on the path and in the area of land through which the path goes, or will go (see 1). In (8) below, a very narrow non-metaphorical path is surrounded by 'marram [growing] everywhere around'.

(8)   The path was narrow—only the width of a boot—but it was clear of the marram that grew everywhere around.

Finally, obstacles on both non-metaphorical and metaphorical paths can be dealt with to facilitate motion/action (see 2, Table 12.2). Non-metaphorical paths can be cut, slashed, or carved, etc., and the metaphorical path in (9) below has been paved to facilitate green consumerism.

(9)   The path of green consumerism is paved with good intentions—but it is also littered with pitfalls.

The descriptions of the obstacles on metaphorical paths are somewhat less detailed than those on non-metaphorical paths (cf. the discussion of the modifiers of *path* above). They may indeed be referred to as *littered with pitfalls*, or *strewn with trip wire*, but as many as 65 per cent of these obstacles are not described at all. Apart from being referred to as *pitfalls, trip wire, slack, stumbling-blocks*, and *pebble[s]*, obstacles on the path are simply *obstacles*, or they are concepts from the target domain such as 'grief' through which there is 'no easy path' or 'disorder or ordeal' that are 'cast' into someone's path:

(10)   There was no man but one who could trouble her rest ever again, and whatever disorder or ordeal he cast into her path she knew she would go gladly, and gather like flowers.

Similarly, non-metaphorical *path*-instances, but not metaphorical ones, tell us how those who try to move along the difficult path are affected by their travel through space. For instance, the travel can be 'sufficiently arduous to justify a prolonged rest', and the path can be 'a real pain':

(11)   The path to the nest soon becomes a real pain with more and more obstacles to hinder progress.

In sum, obstacles found on both kinds of paths are very similar, and the locations of the obstacles are the same. This is consistent with the hypothesis that metaphorical uses of *path* go back to our embodied experiences of paths. Both the modifiers used to describe metaphorical *path*-instances and what we learn about the obstacles on, near, or along metaphorical paths show that these are not simply linguistic reflections of conventional conceptual motion metaphors at the levels of primary and complex metaphors. They are also intimately connected with the very specific contexts of travel through space that paths offer.

12.3.2   Road

The basic sense of *road* was determined to be 'a way that leads from one place to another, especially one with a hard surface that cars and other vehicles can use' (*MEDAL*). This basic sense was then distinguished from senses that contrast and can be understood by means of this sense. Of non-metaphorical instances, 751 were identified, and 49 metaphorical. Ambiguous sentences were excluded from the material, as were 147 instances of *road* that are part of a compound noun (e.g. *road users, road building proposals*, etc.), 29 instances of *road* in the metonymic sense of a place or building on the road, and 1 instance of *road* as part of an adjective phrase (e.g. *our road hungry Citroën*).

Table 12.3 presents a summary of the modifiers of *road*. The modifiers of non-metaphorical *road* fall into four main categories. The largest of these (see B) refers to different kinds of roads based on their sizes and functions (e.g. *main road* and *relief road*), and seems to be specific to roads. Real-world roads, but not paths, are typically part of big systems with roads of different sizes and roads that lead to other roads. The modifiers of non-metaphorical *road* may also say something about the area that the road goes through (e.g. *country road[s]*, or *forest road[s]*) (see A), or what the road is like (e.g. *narrow*, *busy*, or *tree-lined*) (see C and D). The latter group may be divided into modifiers that indicate that travelling along the road might be difficult (e.g. *narrow*, *busy*, or *sunken*) (C), and those that indicate that doing so is nice and/or easy (e.g. *good*, *improved*, or *scenic*) (D). These latter categories were also found in the non-metaphorical *path*-instances.

TABLE 12.3. *Typical modifiers of* road. *Frequencies of more than one instance are within brackets. (S = Source domain, T = Target domain)*

	Type of modifier	Modifiers of non-metaphorical *road*	S/T	Modifiers of metaphorical *road*
A	Kinds of roads based on the area they go through.	*country* (2), *village, forest, forestry, desert, lonely*		
B	Kinds of roads based on their size and function.	*main* (23), *side* (5), *trunk* (4), *high* (3), *higher, access* (3), *slip* (2) *distributor, relief* (5), *ring* (4)		
C	Properties that are likely to make the road difficult (to travel along):	*narrow* (5), *busy* (3), *roaring, sunken* (2), *poor, rough, long, winding*	S	*long* (2), *dangerous* (2), *rough*
D	Properties that are likely to make the road easy (to travel along):	*paved, surfaced, asphalt, improved, good, straight, new, empty, the most beautiful, tree-lined* (2), *attractive, scenic*	S	*straight*
E1	Other		S	*lonely, high, different*
E2			T	*alternative, electoral . . . of different regional governments having different tax rates*

The metaphorical *road*-instances include few modifiers. Some of these suggest that travel along the road is difficult (e.g. *long* and *rough*) (C). Others indicate that travelling along the road is easy (e.g. *straight*) (D). A few modifiers were also found that are connected with some kind of process (e.g. *[the road] of different regional governments having different tax rates*) (E1 and E2).

The specific terms used to describe non-metaphorical and metaphorical *road*-instances (see C and D) indicate that these two kinds of roads are quite similar. Just like real roads, they are *long, rough,* and *straight.* Not all kinds of roads, however, are mentioned in metaphorical contexts (e.g. *country, village,* or *forest road* (see A), or *main, side,* and *trunk road* (see B). Apparently, the most popular modifiers of metaphorical *road* say something about motion from A to B, and are in line with the SOURCE–PATH–GOAL schema (cf. *path* above). None of these metaphorical descriptions are very detailed descriptions of specific kinds of roads.

Another difference between non-metaphorical and metaphorical *road*-instances is that the latter may be described by modifiers that come from the target domain (e.g. *electoral road*), or by modifiers that emphasize that the specific road is different from some other road (e.g. *high*). The same sets of differences were also found between metaphorical and non-metaphorical *path*-instances (see *path* above). Once again, the differences seem connected with the different purposes that non-metaphorical and metaphorical instances serve. Given that non-metaphorical instances are not used to say something about target domains, it is not very surprising that these are not modified by target domain modifiers. Considering that metaphorical *road*-instances represent anything from actions, to events, to processes, and non-metaphorical instances nothing but an artefact that goes from one place to another, it is understandable that the need to distinguish metaphorical roads from one another is greater than the need to describe how one non-metaphorical road is different from some other road. Typically each road or path represents a different course of action, event, or process. By using one path or road to represent something, and another road or path to represent something else, it becomes easier for us to refer to and define these actions, events, or processes, and to compare them with one another. The properties of the artefact (e.g. that it is *lonely, high,* or *different*) simply become the properties of the action, process, or event that we wish to describe.

Very few non-metaphorical and metaphorical *road*-instances mention obstacles on or near the road (8 non-metaphorical and 4 metaphorical). Table 12.4 summarizes where these are located, what the obstacles are, and what people do to deal with the obstacles.

The few obstacles that are included in non-metaphorical *road*-instances are located on the road, or in problematic terrain, but not both in the area through which the road goes and on the road (cf. *path* above). Obstacles on the road may be either problematic areas in the surface of the roads (e.g. 'bumps', 'some deep ruts', and 'potholes'), or located on or above the surface (e.g. 'boulders or debris',

TABLE 12.4. *What we learn about obstacles on non-metaphorical and metaphorical roads*

Research questions	Non-metaphorical *road*	Metaphorical *road*
1 Where are the obstacles located (answers given in bold)? What kinds of obstacles are there (the terms that refer to these are in italics)?	**On the road:** *bumps, some deep ruts* and *potholes, boulders or debris, a particularly noisome pool, more visitors, a crash* **In the area through which the road goes, or will be made:** *In wild surroundings a natural amphitheatre containing two lochs is rounded and, just when the road seems to have lost direction and to be leading nowhere . . .* **On the road and in the area through which the road goes:** -	**On the road:** a) source domain concepts; *mere potholes on the road, a red light on the road, which later turns yellow and green.* b) target domain concepts; **-In the area through which the road goes, or will be made:** *break through the barriers of error, and to seek the road to truth* **On the road and in the area through which the road goes:** -
2 What do we do with the obstacles?	**obstacles will be** *cleared away,* there are *promise[s] to repair potholes that are considered dangerous*	
3 How do the obstacles affect those who move along the road?	-	-

'a particularly noisome pool', 'more visitors', or a 'crash'). As in (12) below, the obstacles tend to slow motion down rather than completely stop it.

(12)   Harris paused for a few seconds while he negotiated the cabriolet over some deep ruts in the high road.

Two out of the four metaphorical instances discuss obstacles located on the road. One of these is (13):

(13)   What we have had so far is a red light on the road. But red lights go yellow and then green. 'I think this is a temporary hold-up. I understand the Gulf Trust's anxiety, but I think they have not really focused on this case or heard the reasonableness of advanced payments.'

Obstacles in the form of problematic terrain in non-metaphorical *road*-instances may be for example 'wild surroundings'.

Metaphorical roads, as in (14) below, may go through 'the barriers of error'. The focus in metaphorical sentences is on taking people out of the problems and towards the goal at the end of the road.

(14)   [T]here exists in man's nature an undying capacity to break through the barriers of error, and to seek the road to truth.

In general, the modifiers that describe roads and the obstacles in metaphorical *road*-sentences, are consistent with the idea that people's metaphorical conceptualizations are based on what they know about real roads. Three out of four properties of metaphorical roads are also used to describe non-metaphorical *road*-instances. The locations of the obstacles in the non-metaphorical and metaphorical instances are the same. The small number of obstacles on these two kinds of roads, and the idea that metaphorical roads quickly take us to our goals once we get past the obstacles, are in line with what we know about roads. These are generally more efficient means of transportation than paths, and we more often travel along them than deal with obstacles on them. Unless it is part of our job to build roads, we typically do not deal with their surfaces; we simply travel, and we travel quite fast.

12.3.3   Way

The basic sense of *way* was identified as a '[a] particular road, path, or track that you use to go from one place to another' (e.g. *show me the way to the temple*), and an extended sense that is somehow connected with someone or something's motion through space (e.g. *the car was going the wrong way*) (*MEDAL*). My data show that today, *way* is seldom associated with a spatial artefact. Instead, the focus is on the action associated with *way*, that is, on travelling through space. In this sense, most non-metaphorical instances of *way* go back to experiences that are quite different from those associated with *path* and *road*. *Path* and *road* typically represent travel through space on something and *way* simply travel through space.

In my corpus, 201 non-metaphorical instances were found, and 777 metaphorical. One *way*-instance, which was part of the adverb *any way* (here spelled in two words), and cases that are ambiguous between non-metaphorical and metaphorical meaning, were excluded.

The analysis showed that phrases that modify *way* are slightly more frequent than *path*-modifiers, and much more frequent than *road*-modifiers. Modifiers were found in 49 per cent of *way*-instances, 47 per cent of *path*-instances, and 19 per cent of *road*-instances.

As shown in Table 12.5, the non-metaphorical instances in my material displayed very little variation. Four main groups were found. One of these groups includes modifiers that indicate that motion along the way might be hard (e.g. *long, longer, weary*) (see A1), and another one modifiers that suggest that motion along the way is easy (e.g. *short*) (B1). A third group of modifiers provides information about how far someone or something has travelled along the way (C). A fourth group includes modifiers that tell us that a given way is somehow different from some other way (E1). None of the instances refer to properties of *way* in the sense of an artefact, but to properties related to travel through space.

Three of these groups were also found in the context of metaphorical *way*-instances (see Table 12.5). The modifiers of both non-metaphorical and metaphorical *way* may be connected with difficult travel (the way is e.g. *long* or *uncertain*) (see A1 and A2), and with less problematic travel (the way is e.g. *short* or *safe*) (B1 and B2). Another similarity between the modifiers of non-metaphorical and metaphorical *way* is that both groups may provide information from which we

TABLE 12.5. *Typical attributes of* way. *Frequencies of more than one instance are within brackets. (S = Source domain, T = Target domain)*

	Type of modifier	Attributes of non-metaphorical *way*	S/T	Attributes of metaphorical *way*
A1	Properties that are likely to make the way difficult (to travel along):	*long* (4), *longer, weary*	S	*long* (9), *hard* (3), *uncertain, kind of rough, terrible, no easy*
A2			T	*a grave, withdrawn way/ a strange sort of… way, an odd way*
B1	Properties that are likely to make the way easy (to travel along):	*short*	S	*best* (12), *better, easy* (4), *lovely, safe*
B2			T	*great, sly, a typically sensible, attractive, an intriguing way, very obvious way, the politest way possible*
C	Distance	*all the* (2), *half* (2)		
D1	The way in which something is done		S	*the way… you walk/… things were going*
D2			T	*the way in which many keg beers are brewed and the ingredients used*
E1	Other	*other* (3), *another, wrong* (2), *south*	S	*same* (29), *only* (13), *different* (8), *every, certain, particular*
E2			T	*extended, a cheap, unique*

learn that one particular way is different from another (E1 and E2). Metaphorical *way*-instances are different from non-metaphorical ones, but similar to both metaphorical *path*- and *road*-instances, in saying something about an action on the way (D1, D2, E1, and E2). This use seems to be based on travel through space, and the purpose that metaphorical ways serve of further defining that other action (e.g. *the way in which many keg beers are brewed and the ingredients used*).

An analysis of obstacles identified fifteen non-metaphorical *way*-instances that discuss obstacles in a figure's way, and forty metaphorical. Table 12.6 presents a summary of these. It shows where the obstacles are located, and what the obstacles are.

Like the *path*- and *road*-instances discussed above, the non-metaphorical and metaphorical *way*-instances are remarkably similar with respect to where the obstacles are located. Motion along them is inhibited in very similar ways. In both non-metaphorical and metaphorical contexts, the obstacles may be in someone's or something's way. In (15), the 'Irish line' is literally in the

TABLE 12.6. *What we learn about obstacles in non-metaphorical and metaphorical ways*

	Research questions	Non-metaphorical *way*	Metaphorical *way*
1	Where are the obstacles located? What kinds of obstacles are there?	**In the way**: *all the guard checkpoints, the Irish line, a great, slithering, inchoate mass of effluence was crawling and creeping and smelling its way towards you* **In the area through which the way goes, or will be made:** *muddy waters, the swamp, the hole was even smaller* **In the way and in the area through which the way goes:** -	**In the way:** a) source domain concepts; *the crest of the wave* b) target domain concepts: *problems* (4) *difficulties* (2), *distress, strain, misgivings,* and *so-called idealists* **In the area through which the way goes, or will go:** *the concrete situation* **On the way and in the area through which the way goes:** -
2	What do we do with the obstacles?		**the way may be** e.g. *cleared* for the figure in motion (e.g. *other issues,* or *a supermarket*) by someone who is not part of that motion
3	How do the obstacles affect those who move along the way?	-	-

way of an English team, and in (16), the 'so-called idealists' are metaphorically in some people's way.

(15)   Four penalties from four attempts by the full-back gave Ireland a 12–7 lead at the interval, Kerr responding with one penalty from three attempts before Bracken got the touch as England forced their way over the Irish line.

(16)   Secretly we shall buy controlling interests in their strategic industries. This means we must control the governments of these states. By bribery—all men are corruptible—and by removing permanently any so-called idealists who stand in our way.

The obstacles may also come in somebody's or something's non-metaphorical or metaphorical way (as in e.g. *the crest of the wave is coming right his way* and *a great, slithering, inchoate mass of effluence was crawling and creeping and smelling its way towards you*); or they may constitute some difficult place that people or things have to find a way out of. In non-metaphorical (17) below, the shrinking of a hole that used to be the way out causes people to consider 'another way through', and in metaphorical (18) 'the concrete situation' is an obstacle that 'thought is freed from':

(17)   He had to pull himself up, the ceiling convulsed—and the hole was even smaller. 'It's no good, Belle,' Ace shouted. 'We can't fix it. Stay where you are. We'll find another way through'.

(18)   Once thought is freed from the concrete situation, the way is clear for symbolic manipulation.

There are numerous obstacles in both non-metaphorical and metaphorical ways and they are extremely varied. Obstacles in non-metaphorical ways may be anything from 'all the guard checkpoints' to 'muddy waters', and obstacles in metaphorical ways anything from 'misgivings' to 'so-called idealists'. The diversity seems related to the fact that *way*, unlike *path* and *road*, typically refers to someone's, or something's travel through space and not a physical artefact on which that someone or something moves. While all the *road*-instances and most of the *path*-instances in my material refer to a specific spatial artefact with certain prototypical properties, *way* typically represents a much less precise spatial concept. That being the case, *way* is not restricted to certain kinds of travel through space and certain kinds of obstacles, either in non-metaphorical or metaphorical uses.

To sum up, the kinds of obstacles on non-metaphorical and on metaphorical ways are similar with respect to how varied they are, and our perception of a way as the direction of motion from one place to another seems to be what allows this variation. Obstacles on both kinds of way are also similar when it comes to where they are located: in the way, or in an area of land that people have to find a way out of. The obstacles mentioned in these sentences support the hypothesis that there is a close connection between metaphorical uses of *way* and experiences associated with *way*, even though these are not primarily related to *way* in the sense of a physical artefact, but rather to a much less specified spatial concept.

12.4   Similarities and Differences between Metaphorical 'Path', 'Road', and 'Way'

All the metaphorical instances of *path*, *road*, and *way* in my material are coherent with the ACTION IS MOTION metaphor, and all the instances that involve goal-directed action are in line with the SOURCE–PATH–GOAL schema. To move forward is to do something on, or along all of these spatial concepts, and to slow someone's or something's motion down is to slow down whatever processes or events they are engaged in. If the action, process, or event is goal-oriented, the goal of that activity or event is located at the end of the path, road, or way. Obstacles to motion are thus not only obstacles to action, but also to progress, and to go far means to make a lot of progress.

When we see a path, road, or way we see a course or line from one place to another, from A to B, but the line is not just a line; it is strongly connected with the fact that paths, roads, and ways are meant for motion along that line (cf. Gibson 1979). The connection between paths, roads, and ways and travel through space from A to B is probably the most important reason why we use our experiences of paths, roads, and ways in the metaphorical ways that we do. It provides us with visible scaffoldings of the ACTION IS MOTION metaphor and the SOURCE–PATH–GOAL schema, and it makes paths, roads, and ways excellent scenes or contexts for our imaginary journeys through space.

However, just as there are differences between travel through space on real-world paths and roads, there are differences between the imaginary journeys that are set in *path-* and *road-*contexts. Similarly, differences between travel through space on a given artefact with certain prototypical properties and travel that is someone's or something's not very well-defined travel through space, are reflected by differences between imaginary journeys on paths, roads, and ways. Just like their non-metaphorical counterparts, metaphorical *path-*, *road-*, and *way-*sentences do not have the same usage patterns. First, they are not equally likely to be used in metaphorical ways. The word *road* is used in predominantly non-metaphorical ways (there are 751 non-metaphorical to 49 metaphorical instances), the metaphorical uses of *paths* constitutes almost one-third of the occurrences (659 non-metaphorical to 284 metaphorical instances), and *ways* are predominantly metaphorical (777 metaphorical to 201 non-metaphorical instances). The differences in frequency go hand in hand with the fact that *path* and *road* are associated with much better-defined concepts than *way*.

Their much more specific qualities are bound to make the metaphorical functions that they may serve much more restricted than those of the vague spatial concept 'way'. Inevitably, the meanings we may construe by means of our embodied experiences of paths and roads thus become more limited than those of ways. Second, the metaphorical scenes that are described by metaphorical *path-*, *road-*, and *way*-sentences differ.

Metaphorical *paths*, like non-metaphorical *paths*, and real-world paths, are usually trickier to move along than *roads* and *ways*. This is indicated by a large variety of words describing them as difficult (e.g. the path may be *narrow, risky, dangerous, crooked*, or *rather tricky*, etc.).

Metaphorical roads may also be problematic, but there is extremely little variation within this group; roads tend to be difficult primarily in the sense that they are long. Distance from our metaphorical goal further down the road is more important than the width of the road, which is taken to be wide rather than narrow.

Unlike metaphorical paths and roads, metaphorical ways are more often connected with easy, successful, or pleasant than with problematic motion. They are the direction in which people go when they do something, and are the way to go if there is something that we want to achieve. The abstract quality of non-metaphorical *way* is characteristic of metaphorical *way* too. Like problematic metaphorical roads, problematic metaphorical ways are usually *long*, but they may also be *hard, uncertain*, or *kind of rough*, etc. Unlike metaphorical paths, however, descriptions of metaphorical ways are not particularly detailed. The focus seems to be on distinguishing one way from another. We frequently talk about the *same, only, different, best*, or *easy* way, which presupposes that there are also other possible ways to go.

A comparison between the descriptions of metaphorical *path-*, *road-*, and *way*-instances shows that metaphorical *path*-modifiers are much more detailed than *way-* and *road*-modifiers. The observed difference reflects a similar difference between the non-metaphorical instances of the terms, and is possibly related to how fast and how concrete paths, roads, and ways are. Since paths and roads are concrete physical artefacts, they are likely to be easier to describe than ways which represent nothing but someone's or something's travel through space. The less detailed descriptions of *road* than of *path* seem related to the fact that motion along roads is usually faster than motion along paths, and so gives us less time to pay attention to the details of the road.

The general idea that journeys on roads are fast and efficient is also evident from the very small number of obstacles on the metaphorical road and the paucity of *road*-sentences that describe people who deal with obstacles. If we do indeed find obstacles on metaphorical roads, these are typically of the kind that slows us down on real-world roads too (e.g. 'red lights' and 'potholes'), and they are easily passed.

The metaphorical *path*-instances in my material are much more strongly connected with obstacles than the *road*-instances. Like the non-metaphorical instances, the metaphorical instances may either describe paths that are hard to travel along, or paths that go through and take someone or something out of difficulties. *Path*-instances that include obstacles describe aspects of motion that are also the focus of non-metaphorical *path*-sentences. As is often the case with non-metaphorical paths, the surface of metaphorical paths can be dealt with.

Metaphorical ways, like metaphorical paths, are often blocked by obstacles. The obstacles on these, however, are much more varied than those on metaphorical paths, and they usually come from the target domains. Our notion of what a way is allows that variation. The vagueness of the concept associated with *way* means that there is little to base the metaphoric imagery on. We do not really know what source domain obstacles would typically be in someone's way. Moreover, this means that we are not especially limited when imagining obstacles in someone or something's metaphorical way. Hence, a large number of target domain concepts may be obstacles in someone's or something's metaphorical way.

12.5 Conclusion

In a traditional Cognitive Linguistics analysis, the *path*-, *road*-, and *way*-instances discussed here would be analysed as linguistic reflections of motion metaphors such as ACTIONS ARE SELF-PROPELLED MOVEMENTS, PURPOSES ARE DESTINATIONS, DIFFICULTIES ARE IMPEDIMENTS TO MOVEMENT, and AMOUNT OF PROGRESS IS DISTANCE MOVED, etc. (see Lakoff and Johnson 1999: 190–2). No distinction, however, would be made between *path*-, *road*-, and *way*-sentences (cf. ibid.: 191), and little would be said about the relationship between motion metaphors and bodily experiences. Even though the 'language and logic of moving toward, reaching, or not reaching a destination are [considered to be] recruited from the source domain of movement through space' (ibid.: 190), these analyses do not reveal how, and in what different ways, artefacts and actions connected with different kinds of travel through space help us to structure the language and logic of that travel. Zinken's (2007) approach to discourse metaphors does provide one link between language and analogical schemas, but it does not consider how negotiations about the meaning of a given metaphor fit into the bigger picture. It falls short of providing an explanation for why we consistently use metaphor vehicles related to motion to structure action in the coherent ways that we do.

The present study opens a previously unexplored window into conceptual space. It suggests that human conceptualization processes operate on a much more specific level of abstraction than that of complex conventional cross-domain mappings. More specifically, it implies that metaphorical expressions including *path*, *road*, or *way* are shaped by people's embodied experiences associated with these terms. Without an intimate connection between ACTION and MOTION and between paths, roads, and ways and their function of taking us from one place to another, however, it seems hard, if not impossible, to explain why metaphorical *path-*, *road-*, and *way-*sentences are used in the metaphorical ways that they are. Detailed corpus studies are clearly necessary to learn more about this relationship. The application of corpus methods to Cognitive-linguistic metaphor studies is a growing field (see e.g. Deignan 2005, and Stefanowitsch and Gries 2007), but more corpus studies are needed to investigate how metaphors are used, and what their uses reveal about the relationship between people's embodied experiences and metaphorical language and thought.

13

The *Way*-construction and Cross-linguistic Variation in Syntax: Implications for Typological Theory

JOHAN PEDERSEN*

13.1 Introduction

In addition to being a lexeme that encodes a specific spatial concept, *way* plays a constructional role in the idiomatic English *way*-construction, which has its own spatial meaning. This construction has direct parallels only in some other languages. There is, for instance, no Spanish parallel to this construction type. The aim of this chapter is to present a cross-linguistic analysis of the *way*-construction and other English argument structure constructions, and assess the implications for typological theory. As exemplified in (1), the *way*-construction represents a characteristic expression of motion events in English:

(1)   I negotiated my way around her preposterous little father

(Banville 2005: 102)

The significance of a cross-linguistic analysis of the *way*-construction is not explicitly considered in the Talmian typology of motion events. Such an analysis, I believe, could be a valuable contribution to the ongoing discussion of Talmy's typology (e.g. Aske 1989; Berman and Slobin 1994; Gennari et al. 2002; Ibarretxe-Antuñano 2004a, b; Pedersen 2009a; Sinha and Kuteva 1995; Slobin and Hoiting 1994; Slobin 1996a, 1997, 2000, 2004; Talmy 1985, 1991, 2000; Zlatev and Yangklang 2004).

The *way*-construction, exemplified in (1), has often been used as evidence for the existence of schematic form-meaning pairs in grammar (e.g. Goldberg 1995). The *way*-construction is highly productive, and almost all of its individual words can be exchanged for others. Nevertheless, the number and order of constituents

* I am grateful to two anonymous referees for their comments on a previous version of this chapter.

are fixed, the word *way* and a possessive pronoun are obligatory constituents and only verbs that fulfil certain constraints can be used (e.g. Goldberg 1995, 1996; Israel 1996; Jackendoff 1990, 1992, 1997; Levin and Rappaport Hovav 1995).[1] Moreover, the core meaning of the construction involves directed motion, though typically it does not involve a motion verb (e.g. *negotiate* in (1)). These characteristics have led Jackendoff (1990) and Goldberg (1995), among others, to analyse the *way*-construction as a CONSTRUCTIONAL IDIOM, that is, a syntactic construction with a specific meaning contributed by the construction itself, in which only a subset of the terminal elements is fixed. Recent research has shown that parallel constructions exist in other Germanic languages as well (Toivonen et al. 2006), though these constructions may not necessarily involve a possessive pronoun and a fixed word equivalent to the English *way*.[2] In fact, the typical cross-linguistic counterpart to the *way*-construction is a reflexive construction, exemplified in (2), which is a characteristic Danish version:

(2) Han   kæmpede   sig   gennem   mængden   Danish
     he   fight-PST   REFL   through the crowd
     'He fought his way through the crowd'

In the literature on Talmian typology of motion events, the *way*-construction is only referred to very peripherally (see e.g. Callies and Szczesniak 2008; Mateu Fontanals 2000; Mateu Fontanals and Rigau 2002). This chapter aims to include the implications of a cross-linguistic analysis of the *way*-construction in this typology discussion.

In his seminal work on expressions of motion events, Talmy (1985, 1991, 2000) reports on characteristic typological differences of lexicalization between *satellite-framed* (e.g. Germanic) languages and *verb-framed* (e.g. Romance) languages. (3) and (4) are often cited examples from Talmy's work:

(3) The bottle   floated   into   the cave   (Talmy 1985)
     Flasken   flød   ind i   hulen   (Danish)
     La botella   entró   en   la cueva   flot-ando   (Spanish)
     the bottle   enter-PST.3SG in   the cave   float-GERUND

(4) I   kicked   the ball   into   the box   (Talmy 2000)
     Jeg   sparkede   bolden   ind i   kassen   (Danish)
     Met-í   la pelota en   la caja   de una patada   (Spanish)
     place-PST.1SG   the ball   in   the box   with a kick

---

[1] Nevertheless, as the *way*-construction becomes more productive, these constrains are becoming weaker.

[2] See Toivonen (2002a, 2002b) for Swedish; Seland (2001) for Norwegian; Verhagen (2003) and van Egmond (2006) for Dutch; and Ludwig (2005) for German.

Talmy claims that in expressions of motion events, some languages, for example Germanic languages, tend to lexicalize the path of motion (main event) in a satellite, and the manner of motion (co-event) by the verb.[3] Other languages, for example Romance languages, tend to lexicalize the main event by the verb, and may express the co-event outside the verb, typically by adding an adverbial.

Talmy's typology has been elaborated and criticized in an extensive literature. The main shortcoming of his typology is that some languages do not seem to fit in his binary typology (see e.g. Slobin and Hoiting 1994; Slobin 2004; Zlatev and Yangklang 2004) and that almost all languages show substantial amounts of data that do not fit the model (see e.g. Aske 1989; Berman and Slobin 1994; Gennari et al. 2002; Ibarretxe-Antuñano 2004a, b; Pedersen 2009a; Slobin and Hoiting 1994; Slobin 1996a, 1997, 2000, 2004; Zlatev and Yangklang 2004. See also Ibarretxe-Antuñano 2005, or Beavers et al. 2010 for an overview). In addition, the Talmian typology and later elaborated versions seem to ignore the insights provided by the CONSTRUCTIONAL VIEW, as represented particularly in Goldberg's and Jackendoff's work (see e.g. Goldberg 1995, 2006; Jackendoff 1990, 1997; Goldberg and Jackendoff 2004). They argue that the core meaning of clausal argument structure cannot be attributed to one single constituent, though they do not explicitly discuss the theoretical status of Talmy's typology. Pedersen (2009a) elaborates in detail a construction grammar account of Talmy's typology. He argues that the determination of whether lexical constituents, mostly the verb, are determinative of the argument structure relies on typological differences. In English, a Germanic language, a schematic argument structure construction plays a crucial role in the encoding of the basic meaning of complex events, such as the motion path of a motion event. In Spanish, a Romance language, the verb organizes the core meaning in a lexical construction. Talmy also proposes that the most fruitful research strategy is to develop a TYPOLOGY OF CONSTRUCTIONS, rather than a typology of languages. A similar point is made in Croft et al. (2010) and Beavers et al. (2010).

This constructional interpretation of Talmy's descriptive typology may concern more than expressions of the type of complex events, such as motion events, discussed in the literature on Talmian typology. Perhaps it is a manifestation of a GENERAL TYPOLOGY OF ORGANIZATIONAL PRINCIPLES in grammar. The contours of a general typology of clausal organization, formulated within the construction grammar framework, are outlined in Pedersen (2009b). According to a general typology of clausal organization, some languages, for example English, tend to organize the principal clausal information, the argument structure, by means of complex, schematic constructions, complementing this information by substantial, lexically encoded information; whereas other languages, for example Spanish, tend to organize the argument structure by lexical means around the verb, complementing this principal information by means of secondary, schematically

---

[3] His observations are generalized to concern MACRO-EVENTS in Talmy (1991, 2000).

organized, constructions. The principal aim of the present chapter is to provide evidence for this proposal, and to discuss the implications for the typology of motion events. The strategy is to analyse, cross-linguistically, English expressions whose argument structure, according to a construction grammar analysis, must be ascribed a schematic form-meaning construction—not predictable from lexical constituents. The cross-linguistic counterparts are then analysed, with focus on strategies for the encoding of argument structure. The *way*-construction is the case-study, though its analysis will be brought into perspective by discussing similar contrastive analyses of a number of comparable English expressions, such as ditransitive, resultative, and communicative expressions, and telic expressions of directed motion.

In the next section, I introduce some principles of the construction grammar framework that are particularly relevant for the analysis of the manner in which clausal information is organized. Secondly, I present results from a cross-linguistic study of the *way*-construction (Section 13.3). Following this (Section 13.4), I put this analysis into perspective by discussing cross-linguistic evidence from other semantic domains, as reflected in both typical and less typical expressions. In Section 13.5, I formulate a hypothesis that enables us to make some cross-linguistic generalizations about the manner in which clausal information may be organized in parallel versions of the *way*-construction, and other construction types. Finally, I draw a link back to Talmy's typology of motion events and discuss some important implications of the analyses presented in this chapter (Section 13.6). Wherever examples in Sections 13.4 and 13.6 are not provided with references, they are made-up or translated examples, checked by native speakers.

13.2 The Construction Grammar Framework

A construction grammar approach to clausal argument structure is partly in conflict with a lexical approach, according to which argument structure is licensed and organized by the verb (e.g. Grimshaw 1990; Levin and Rappaport Hovav 1995; Pinker 1989). In construction grammar, argument structure is encoded by means of schematic form-meaning pairs, that is, schematic constructions, and specified lexically by the verb. Schematic constructions thus play a crucial role in expressions of argument structure, though it is recognized that a semantic specification of the event, or situation, is provided by the verb, in what is understood as a lexical construction.

In Goldberg's version of construction grammar, CONSTRUCTIONS are non-derived form-meaning pairs at different levels of specificity (Goldberg 1995, 2006). Substantial information is encoded as LEXICAL CONSTRUCTIONS, e.g. Spanish [casa] / 'house', or idioms, e.g. Spanish [más vale tarde que nunca] / 'better late than never'. Schematic, more general information is encoded at a taxonomically higher level. ARGUMENT STRUCTURE CONSTRUCTIONS are the most important type, such as the

English ditransitive construction, which may be formalized as [SUBJ, V, OBJ$_1$, OBJ$_2$] / 'X causes Y to receive Z'. Grammatical rules are stored in users' grammar as constructions of even more schematic information, for instance the rule of conjunction reduction, which may be formally represented as [SUBJ, V$_1$, AND, Ø, V$_2$] / 'Conjunction reduction'. Language users constantly analyse and categorize input in different construction types. Therefore, identification is basically a matter of users' categorization (e.g. Croft 2001; Tomasello 2003). A subject is a form-meaning pair,[4] though from a strict theoretical point of view, it is not a construction since the subject can be derived from the more complex argument structure constructions, for instance the transitive construction. Nevertheless, if a derived form-meaning pair, such as the subject, is used with very high frequency, it is also stored as a construction. So, even synchronically derived form-meaning pairs may count as constructions in the grammar (Goldberg and Jackendoff 2004; Goldberg 2006).

13.2.1   Organizing argument structure—a contrastive perspective

In the early 1990s, when linguists started addressing issues of the origin of language and its evolution, a near consensus was being shaped on one important issue associated with the relation between grammar and human conceptual representations (Newmeyer 2003). The basic idea is that grammatical form, that is syntax, is anchored in conceptual structure. Syntax, from this perspective, is grounded in predicate-argument structure, that is, conceptual representations of events, actors, and entities acted upon (e.g. Jackendoff 1990; Newmeyer 1991; Pinker and Bloom 1990). The implication of this insight is that a simple clause, for example with subject, verb, and object, is basically built upon the formation of an argument structure, which represents the core information of the clause. This information is complemented by lexically and morphologically encoded inform-ation, such as modal, temporal, or aspectual information. In a construction grammar framework (e.g. Goldberg 1995, 2006), a typical clausal expression contains in its internal structure, at different levels of specificity, a range of different constructions. In general terms, clausal information is organized by means of two construction types:

- SCHEMATIC CONSTRUCTIONS (SC) that organize information at an abstract level.
- LEXICAL CONSTRUCTIONS (LC) that organize information around a lexical nucleus.

---

[4] On the one hand, a subject may be formally identified by means of, for instance, nominative case marking, agreement, or a specific word order; and on the other hand, it is a marker of prominence.

There are, thus, organizing devices in language at different levels of schematicity. SCHEMATIC SKELETONS and LEXICAL GOVERNMENT are the most important mechanisms.[5] Almost all languages seem to make use of both organizational devices, though in different manners. Croft (2003) nevertheless argues that it is misleading to think about lexical rules versus constructions as a dichotomy of grammatical organization. Croft states that verbs appear to change their meaning when put into particular constructions, for instance, *bake* appears to mean 'A bake B and give B to C' in the ditransitive construction. From one point of view, he argues, this meaning may be derived by a lexical rule, that is, by means of lexical government. Another possibility is that the meaning of *bake* is predictable from the semantics of the construction. According to Croft, there are indications that both analyses are partly right, and that the simplest way to capture these facts is to represent verb-specific constructions in the grammar of English. However, an essential point in Goldberg's and Jackendoff's framework is that ultimately the argument structure is determined by the composite effects of the verb and the construction. The verb does not change its meaning so as to license unexpected arguments of the construction (Goldberg and Jackendoff 2004). For instance, in the ditransitive construction, *bake* is not converted into a transfer-verb in the lexicon. Its contribution to meaning in a ditransitive construction is the same as its contribution to meaning in a transitive construction. In both cases it is 'A bake B'. We will follow Goldberg and Jackendoff (2004) in this matter.

Some construction grammar frameworks emphasize that constructions are LANGUAGE SPECIFIC (e.g. Croft 2001). From this point of view, the following questions are particularly interesting for a contrastive study of clausal organization:

- How is clausal information organized in a specific language, and on the basis of which construction types?
- How is argument structure organized?

A preliminary assumption is that languages may differ systematically according to the level of constructional specificity at which the argument structure is organized.

13.3 The *Way*-construction

According to Goldberg (1995), basic clausal information in English is encoded in SCHEMATIC ARGUMENT STRUCTURE CONSTRUCTIONS (SC). This core information is

---

[5] LEXICAL GOVERNMENT refers to the so-called LEXICAL APPROACH (see e.g. Grimshaw 1990; Levin and Rappaport Hovav 1995; Pinker 1989). It is an organizing device based on principles of lexical (verbal) projection, subcategorization, and valence structure.

specified in LEXICAL ARGUMENT STRUCTURE CONSTRUCTIONS (LC), particularly by the verb. The *way*-construction is a convincing example:

(5)   [Peter [fought] his way out of the restaurant]
      SC: [SUBJ$_i$ V POSS$_i$ *way* OBL]   /   'x moves y by creating a path'
      LC: [SUBJ V]   /   'A in activity of fighting'

In the *way*-construction, whose basic meaning may be paraphrased as 'X moves somewhere (Y) with difficulty by creating a path' (cf. e.g. Goldberg 1995), none of the lexical items have per se a central, organizing role in the encoding of this core meaning. Particularly, the core meaning is not predictable from the lexical meaning of *fought*, but it may not be attributed to the lexical structure of *way* or *out of* either.[6] We have to recognize, instead, that a schematic form, the *way*-construction: [SUBJ$_i$ V POSS$_i$ *way* OBL], carries its characteristic meaning, which cannot be derived from its component constituents. The verb *fought* specifies the means by which this motion event is carried out: the activity of fighting.[7] Notice that given this very specific meaning predicated by the verb, there are strong restrictions on the subject.[8]

The objective of the current study is to analyse, cross-linguistically, counterparts of English expressions, principally the *way*-construction as exemplified in (5), whose basic form-meaning structure can only be accounted for as encoding by means of schematic form and meaning. Example (6), which is parallel to (5), indicates that Spanish may differ systematically from English in this respect:

(6)   Pedro   se   [abrió/hizo]   camino   [a codazos]   para   salir...
      Pedro   REFL.DAT open/make-PRS.3SG   way   by elbows   to   get out
      LC: [SUBJ, REFL/DAT, abrió/hizo, OBJ] / 'x creates himself y (a path)'
      SC: [ADV- construction] / 'specifying information'

In the Spanish version of the *way*-construction, the basic meaning of 'X creates himself a path' is predictable from the inherent meaning and argument structure of the verb: *abrirse camino para salir...* 'open for himself a way in order to move somewhere'; or *hacerse camino para salir...* 'make for himself a way in order to move somewhere'. Specifying information about the means of motion may be added as an adverbial construction (*a codazos*). A verbal expression of the means of motion, as used in English, is not acceptable:

---

[6] In a Cognitive Linguistic framework, the basic meaning of *out* may be understood as 'leaving a container' (Rudzka-Ostyn 2003).

[7] The verb may also denote the manner of motion: *Sam joked his way into the meeting* ('Sam went into the meeting (while) joking') (Jackendoff 1990).

[8] That is, the subject has to be licensed by the substantial lexical meaning of the verb.

(6') * Pedro [pele-ó]   su camino fuera del restaurante
      Pedro   fight-PST.3SG   his way   out   of the restaurant

There are, thus, indications that the Spanish version of the *way*-construction differs systematically from the English source version, when it comes to how the core information and the specifying information are organized. Examples like (6) suggest that Spanish tends to organize the basic meaning of the *way*-construction in LEXICAL ARGUMENT STRUCTURE CONSTRUCTIONS (LC), by means of valence structure and subcategorization. Supplementary information may be provided by means of an added, SCHEMATICALLY ORGANIZED CONSTRUCTION (SC).

13.3.1 Data and methodology

The discussion of the *way*-construction in this section is based on a corpus study. Searches in a parallel corpus have provided different versions of the *way*-construction: the original English version, and Spanish, German, and French versions. The parallel corpus has been constructed by using original English texts and their translations into the three languages. The texts stem from the electronic publications of Project Syndicate (Project Syndicate 2008), which is an international association of 392 newspapers in 146 countries. Project Syndicate delivers commentaries to the world's foremost newspapers on topics ranging from economics and international affairs to science, culture, and philosophy.

The current study can be characterized as semasiological and onomasiological at the same time, in the sense that our objective is to determine how a specific semantic structure ('x moves somewhere with difficulty by creating a path') identified in a specific expression type of one language (the *way*-construction in English) is expressed in other languages. For this purpose, particularly the parallel corpus is a suitable data source. Large monolingual corpora are available on the Internet—regarding Spanish, for example, CREA (approximately 200 million words)—but this corpus type is not suitable for the present study since searches in monolingual corpora require a search string, like '*way*' for English, that we do not have for Spanish and the other non-English languages. The parallel corpus allows us not only to identify the *way*-construction in English, by means of a simple search string, but it also provides us with expressions of the same meaning structure in other languages. There are disadvantages to using parallel corpora as well. Particularly, their relatively limited size rules out the possibility of making use of statistical calculations. Moreover, when using parallel corpora, we have to take into account that the translation process, including individual preferences of the translators, may influence the choices made in the production of the parallel versions.

Our parallel corpus contains relatively short texts (max. two pages), which are divided into clearly marked paragraphs for each version. This enables us to shift easily from one language to another. The actual size of the corpus is 618 texts, available in the four languages. From the corpus, we have extracted a sample of twenty *way*-expressions, each of which is available in four versions. The searches were relatively time-consuming tasks. They were carried out manually as simple lexical searches. We searched for the word *way*, sorting out all irrelevant occurrences, in order to find source expressions of the *way*-construction in English. Moreover, a newspaper corpus is admittedly not the ideal data source, since the *way*-construction is probably more frequent in spoken than in written discourse. However, the easy accessibility of parallel versions of the *way*-construction in different languages has been decisive for the choice of corpus.[9]

13.3.2   Parallel versions of the *way*-construction

In this section, parallel versions of the *way*-construction in English, German, Spanish, and French are analysed. In (7), the core meaning 'x moves y with difficulty by creating a path' is not clearly predictable from the lexical meaning of *making* or the prepositional phrase, though the verb does not provide a specification of the means of motion either:

(7)   a.   *making* its way into the heartland of civil society

b.	ihren	Weg	in	die Mitte	der	Zivilgesellschaft	*antritt.*
	its	way	in	the middle	of	civil society	set out-INF

c.	se	est-á		integr-ando	al	corazón	de	la sociedad civil.
	REFL	be.PROG-PRS.3SG		integrate-GER	to	the heart		of the society civil

The core meaning must be mapped onto the schematic form: [SUBJ$_i$ V POSS$_i$ *way* OBL], which carries the characteristic meaning of the *way*-construction, as argued in the analysis of (5). Regarding the lexical specification of the means by which this metaphoric motion event is realized, the semantic contribution of the verb *making* is relatively neutral. The German version (7b) is a direct parallel to the English *way*-construction. The core meaning cannot be derived from the verb (*antritt* = 'set out') nor from the satellite (= prepositional phrase). It must be attributed to a German counterpart to the *way*-construction. The verb *antritt* provides a lexical specification of the means by which this figurative event of 'moving with difficulty by creating a path' is carried out. In (7c), the corresponding Spanish version is centred in the complex verbal predicate *se está integrando*, which via its valence structure predicts the principal event: 'x creates himself a path'. This event is not specified by a schematically organized, adverbial construction, as it is in (6). This analysis suggests that in the Spanish version, the core

---

[9] In future studies, we will hopefully have at our disposal a tagged source corpora and a digital alignment of the different versions.

information is organized as a lexical, verbal construction, which is also what is found in (6). There is no French version available in the corpus.

In (8), the skeletal argument structure associated with the *way*-marker must also be organized schematically as a *way*-construction: [SUBJ$_i$ V POSS$_i$ *way* OBL] / 'x moves y with difficulty by creating a path':

(8)   a. he *barged* his way past Hillary Clinton

     b. konn-te   er   sich an   Hillary Clinton, . . . ,   vorbei-*drängeln*
        can-PST.3SG he REFL   Hillary Clinton   past-push-INF

     c. logr-ó   super-ar   *a los tumbos*   a   Hillary Clinton
        (he) manage-PST.3SG do better-INF in a clumsy way than Hillary Clinton

     d. il   a pu   dépass-er   Hillary Clinton
        he   can-PRF.3SG pass-INF   Hillary Clinton

The verb *barged* specifies lexically the means by which the subject passed Hillary Clinton. He may have acted in an unceremonious and threatening way, paying little respect, and thereby made his way past H. C. In this case, the German version is not a direct copy of the English *way*-construction; though, interestingly, when it comes to clausal organization, it has the same schematic characteristics. The core meaning cannot be derived from either the verb (*drängeln* = 'pushed') or the satellite (*vorbei* = 'past'). It can only be accounted for by positing the existence of a German reflexive counterpart to the schematic *way*-construction in English. The German version may be formalized as [SUBJ, V$_{aux}$, REFL, OBL, V] / 'x moves y with difficulty by creating a path'.[10] This schematic construction is complemented with a causal specification lexically by the verb *drängeln*.[11] In (8c), the complex verbal predicate *logró superar* organizes lexically, in a valence structure, the encoding of the core meaning ('he managed to do better'). This core meaning is therefore predictable from the verbal predicate. Like (7c), example (8c) suggests that the Spanish version is basically organized as a lexical, verbal construction. In this case, the core meaning is further specified by a schematically organized construction, as suggested in the discussion of (6): *a los tumbos*, indicating that he did it in a clumsy way. The French version appears

[10] In this formalization, for the sake of simplicity, I have not taken into account constructional variation due to word order.

[11] The German version of the *way*-construction has been discussed in more detail in Callies and Szczesniak (2008) and Ludwig (2005). In her study of the Dutch *way*-constructions, van Egmond (2006) suggests that all Germanic languages may have two different versions of the *way*-construction: one which denotes MOTION ALONG A PATH, as in (5), and one which denotes a TRANSITION TO A LOCATION as in (8a)–(8b). In Dutch, and maybe also in German, this distinction also implies a formal distinction, as these languages seem to use two formally different constructions (*weg*-constructions vs reflexive constructions). Conversely, in English (the *way*-construction) and Swedish, Norwegian, and Danish (reflexive constructions), this distinction is not visible in the syntax since the path-variant is formally identical to the transition-variant.

to be organized as the Spanish, though it has no secondary constructional specification.

Also in (9b) and (10b), the German versions of the *way*-construction, the organization of the core meaning may be represented schematically as a reflexive construction [SUBJ, V,..., REFL, OBL, V] / 'x moves Y with difficulty by creating a path', cf. (8b):

(9)   a. if you try to *bob and weave* your way... towards an end game

    b. wenn man versuch-t, sich... auf ein Endspiel *zuzuschlängeln*
       if you try-PRS.3SG REFL.3 to an end game to snake-INF

    c. si se intenta abrir camino... hacia el final del juego.
       if you try-PRS.3SG to open way toward the end of the game

    d. si vous tent-ez de louvoy-er... vers une solution
       if you try-2PL to squeeze-INF toward a solution

(10)   a. We may be able to *manage* our way through it

    b. sind wir vielleicht in der Lage, uns hindurchzu*manövrier-en*
       be-1PL we maybe in a position REFL.1PL around-to-manoeuvre-INF

    c. tal vez pod-amos sorte-ar-la
       maybe (we) may-1PL be able to sort-INF-ACC out

    d. nous allons peut-être nous en sort-ir
       we go-PRS.1PL perhaps we find-INF a way out

In the English as well as the German version, the verbal lexemes provide more specific information on the means by which these motion events take place (*bob and weave / zuzuschlängeln* and *manage / manövrieren*, respectively). In the Spanish versions—see (9c) and (10c)—the core meaning, 'x create a path', is predictable from the complex predicate and its argument structure (*se intenta abrir camino / podamos sortearla*). This is also true in the French version in (9d) (*vous tentez de louvoyer*), while the core meaning of the *way*-construction is not captured in the French translation in (10d) (*nous allons peut-être nous en sortir*). Neither the Spanish nor the French versions of (9) and (10) have further specifications of the core meaning. (11b) appears to be a direct German parallel to the English *way*-construction in (11a):

(11)   a. we have tried to *inch* our way to a settlement...

    b. hab-en wir versuch-t, uns *Zentimeter um Zentimeter*
       AUX-PRS.1PL we try-PART us centimetre by centimetre
       auf unserem Weg zu einer Regelung *vorwärts zu beweg-en*,...
       on our way to a settlement forward to move-INF

c. hemos intent-ado   *arduamente*   lleg-ar   a   un arreglo...
    (we) try-PRF.1PL   hard   reach-INF   to   a settlement

d. nous avons tenté de nous rapproch-er *pas à pas* d'un accord...
    we   try-PRF.1PL   we   get close-INF step by step to a settlement

Interestingly, the core meaning of the German version in (11b) ('reach, with difficulty, a settlement by creating a path') is not centred in a *Weg*-construction that is parallel to the original English *way*-construction (11a). The core meaning is centred in the reflexive construction: '...versucht uns vorwärts zu bewegen'. The verbal specification (*bewegen*) is rather neutral, as compared to the English version (*inch*). Instead, the remainder of the clause provides the details (*Zentimeter um Zentimeter...auf unserem Weg zu einer Regelung*). The core meaning, 'x tries to reach y', is provided by lexical constructions in the Spanish and the French versions. It is organized around the complex predicates *hemos intentado llegar* and *avons tenté de rapprocher*. The verbal valence structure makes predictions about the core meaning, which is similar to the core meaning that characterizes the *way*-construction. In both versions, the core meaning is further specified by schematically organized adverbial constructions (*arduamente, pas à pas*). In (12b), a combination of the reflexive construction and the [...POSS way...] construction characterizes the schematic construction of the core meaning in the German version (*die Bulldozer können sich ihren Weg bahnen*). The core meaning, 'x pulls down y' and 'x not take into account y', is organized around, and predicted by, the verbal predicate in the Spanish version (12c) (*puede derribar cualquier aldea*) and in the French version (12d) (*n'a nullement besoin de tenir aucun compte*), respectively:

(12) a. it can *bulldoze* its way through any village in its path.

b. *könn-en*   *sich*   *die Bulldozer*   ihren   Weg,...,
    could-PRS.3PL   REFL   the bulldozers   their   way,...,
    durch   jedes Dorf   *bahn-en.*
    through   every village   pave-INF

c. pued-e   derribar   *con*   *maquinaria* *pesada*
    (it) could-PRS.3SG topple   with   machinery   heavy
    cualquier   aldea   que   le   estorb-e
    every   village   that   DAT   obstruct-PRS.3SG

d. elle   n'a nullementbesoinde ten-ir   aucun compte des villages
    there is no   need   to take-INF into   account the villages
    qui   se   trouv-ent   sur le   tracé prévu
    that   REFL find-PRS.3PL on   the   route plan-PART

In (13c), (14c), and (15c), the core meaning, 'x find y in z', seems in Spanish, again, to be organized lexically in verbal predicate-argument structure on the basis of valence relations (*buscó en Google la manera de llegar* / *él pudo encontrar la manera de llegar* / *esta liquidez encontrará su destino en el exterior*):

(13) a. he *Googled* his way to the only lawyer in Russia

      b. | fand | | er | *über* | *Google* | den | einzigen | Anwalt | in Russland |
|---|---|---|---|---|---|---|---|---|
| find-PST.3SG | | he | in | *Google* | the | only | lawyer | in Russia |

      c. | busc-ó | | *en* | | *Google* | la manera | de | lleg-ar | al | único |
|---|---|---|---|---|---|---|---|---|---|
| search-PST.3SG | in | | | Google | the manner | of | reach-INF | the only | |
| abogado | (he) | en Rusia | | | | | | | |
| lawyer | | in Russia | | | | | | | |

      d. | (il) | a trouvé | | *sur* | *Google* | les coordonnées | | du | seul |
|---|---|---|---|---|---|---|---|---|
| he | find-PRF.3SG | | in | Google | the address | | of the | only |
| avocat | de Russie | | | | | | | |
| lawyer | in Russia | | | | | | | |

(14) a. he was able to find his way to a lawyer

      b. | es | ihm | gelang, | | einen | Anwalt | zu | find-en. |
|---|---|---|---|---|---|---|---|
| it | DAT | succeed-PST.3SG | a | | lawyer | to | find-INF |

      c. | él | pudo | | encontr-ar | la manera | de lleg-ar |
|---|---|---|---|---|---|
| he | could-PST.PFV.3SG | find-INF | | the manner | to reach-INF |
| a | un | | abogado | | |
| to | a | | lawyer | | |

      d. | il | a réussi | | à contact-er | un avocat. |
|---|---|---|---|---|
| he | succeed-PRF.3SG | to contact-INF | a lawyer | |

(15) a. much of it will find its way abroad

      b. | wird | | ein | großer | Teil | ins Ausland | abfließ-en |
|---|---|---|---|---|---|---|
| will-PRS.3SG | a | | larger | part | abroad | drain-INF |

      c. | gran | parte | de | esta | liquidez | encontr-ará | su destino | en el exterior. |
|---|---|---|---|---|---|---|---|
| large | part | of | this | liquidity | find-FUT.3SG | its destiny | abroad |

      d. | elles | iront | | en grande | partie | à l'étranger. |
|---|---|---|---|---|---|
| they | go-FUT.3PL | in large | | part | abroad |

It cannot be properly translated in the German version (*fand er den einzigen Anwalt*... / *einen Anwalt zu finden* / *wird ins Ausland abfließen*), nor in the French version (*a trouvé les coordonnées*... / *il a réussi à contacter un avocat* / *elles iront partie à l'étranger*).[12]

The contrastive analysis of the *way*-construction indicates that Spanish, as opposed to English, tends to organize the basic clausal meaning lexically by the

---

[12] Notice that in the *way*-construction in (13a), the secondary specification of the core meaning is very precise (*googled*), while it is almost absent in (14a) and (15a) (*find*).

verb, while supplementary information may be provided by means of schematically organized adverbial constructions. German follows the English pattern, as
observed in previous studies (e.g. Toivonen et al. 2006), in the sense that the core
skeletal meaning and the secondary specification are mapped onto a schematic
construction and the verb, respectively. German, though, typically makes use of a
reflexive construction as a counterpart to the *way*-construction in English. French
appears to behave like Spanish.

It may be objected, nevertheless, that the contrastive perspective on the *way*-
construction only shows that some languages (e.g. Spanish and French) do not
have expressions, as do other Germanic languages, that are comparable with the
way-construction in English. Cross-linguistically, different expression types may
provide a similar meaning. This difference, though, is not necessarily due to a
difference in the way this meaning is organized in the clause. The problem is that
verb-predicted core meaning, as we have observed for Spanish, does not prove
that the clausal information is lexically organized by the verb. The expression
might be built upon another schematic construction, such as the transitive
construction, while the meaning that is comparable with the *way*-construction
may be provided by the verbal lexeme. Analyses of the Spanish texts, for example,
might be interpreted as simply indicating that Spanish does not have an expression equivalent with the characteristic meaning of the English *way*-construction,
but that it has other (schematically or lexically organized?) expressions with
similar meanings. Nothing would then be indicated about the potential in
Spanish grammar for organizing clausal argument structure in schematic or
lexical argument structure constructions. Moreover, in some cases, for example
in (13)–(15), we found that the translations into German and French do not
capture the core meaning of the *way*-construction. In these cases, nothing is
indicated about the organizing devices (schematic or lexical) of the language in
question, as compared to English.

The data do seem to show formal regularity in equivalent expressions of the
English *way*-construction. Nevertheless, we may find it preferably to extend our
contrastive analysis to include a range of semantic domains in which we know
that English and Spanish, for example, have common comparable expressions.
Such an analysis is conducted in the next section.

13.4   Evidence from Other Semantic Domains

In this section, we examine Spanish expressions of argument structure that have
direct counterparts in English. When these Spanish expressions are characterized
by having VERB-PREDICTED ARGUMENT STRUCTURE, for example *le dio una tarta* 'she
gave him a cake', the question is whether the same core meaning, volitional
transfer, may be expressed in a NON-VERB-PREDICTED CONSTRUCTION, as in English
examples such as *she baked him a cake* (Goldberg 1995). If only verb-predicted

core meaning is acceptable, this is an indication that Spanish, as opposed to English, organizes argument structure lexically, by means of lexical constructions.

13.4.1   The ditransitive construction

The core meaning transmitted by the English ditransitive construction involves transfer between a volitional agent and a willing recipient ('x caused y to receive z') (Goldberg 1995). The main content of (16), which is a prototypical ditransitive expression, is thus a meaning of transfer, which is reflected in the inherent ditransitive meaning of the verb *gave*. Regarding form as well as meaning, Spanish has a comparable, yet not identical, expression type, as exemplified in (17):

(16)   She gave him a cake

(17)   Le   dio   una   tarta
        DAT   (she) give-PST.PFV.3SG   a   cake

Prototypical expressions of the ditransitive, however, as in (16)–(17), do not indicate whether the transfer-meaning is organized in a lexical argument structure, or whether it is organized in a schematic argument structure construction. In the latter interpretation, the schematic construction is redundantly supported by a verbal specification whose semantic contribution is mostly the same. The 'confusion' is due to the trivalent meaning of the verb. In (16) and (17), the transfer-meaning is perfectly predictable from the trivalent meaning of the verb: 'x gives y to z'. On the other hand, more atypical examples, such as (18), in which the transfer-meaning is not predictable from the verb, suggest that this core meaning is determined independently in a schematic ditransitive argument structure construction (SC), and that the verb (LC) provides a specification of the involved activity:

(18)   She baked him a cake   (Goldberg 1995)
        SC: [SUBJ,V,OBJ$_1$,OBJ$_2$]   / 'x causes y to receive z'
        LC: [SUBJ,V,OBJ]   / 'A bakes B'

The principal argument for this analysis is that the transfer-meaning cannot plausibly be part of the lexical meaning of *bake* (Goldberg 1995). If the core meaning were organized by the verb, the lexical meaning of *bake* should include a special sense of transfer, which is not plausible. The point here is that Spanish does normally not allow such atypical usage.[13] Example (19) would be a typical Spanish version of (18):

---

[13] Expressions like *María le cocinó un asado* ('María cooked him a joint of meat') are possible. But in this case, the use of the dative does not necessarily imply a volitional agent and a willing recipient, which is the central meaning of the ditransitive construction in English. See the analysis in Pedersen (2009b: 247f).

(19) Le   hizo   una tarta
      DAT   make-PST.PFV.3SG   a cake
      'She made him a cake'
      LC: [SUBJ,V,OBJ,IOBJ] / 'complex make-transfer-event'

The transfer-meaning is a frequent meaning pattern in Spanish, as exemplified in (17) and (19), though it does not occur in a non-verb predicted construction (Martínez Vázquez 2003; Pedersen 2009b). This observation indicates that the core meaning in (17) and (19), comparable with the English ditransitive, is a verb-predicted argument structure, and that it is organized in a lexical argument structure construction.

13.4.2 The resultative construction

The same argument applies for expressions of resultative argument structure. Examples (20) and (21) demonstrate that Spanish has resultative expressions comparable with the English resultative:[14]

(20) She painted the house red

(21) Pint-ó   la casa   roja
      (she) paint-PST.PFV.3SG   the house   red

We cannot determine, though, whether the resultative meaning in the two versions is encoded in a lexical argument structure construction, or in a schematic argument structure construction. As for ditransitive expressions, English verbs that do not per se reflect the resultative core meaning, may nevertheless instantiate a schematic argument structure construction that on an independent basis encodes the resultative core meaning (see e.g. Goldberg 1995; Goldberg and Jackendoff 2004). Spanish verbs do not allow such a use, which is exemplified in (22) and (23):

(22) She cried   herself   asleep   (Goldberg 1995)

(23) *Llor-ó   a   sí misma   dorm-ida
      (she) cry-PST.PFV.3SG   to   REFL.3SG   sleep-PART.FEM

---

[14] Some Spanish users reject examples like (21) and prefer a slightly different expression type: *pintó la casa de rojo* ('he painted the house with red'), in which the verbal activity is modified by an adverbial expression. Mendívil Giró (2003) argues, for instance, that the type of resultative expression in (21) is not a genuine resultative construction. Nevertheless, the existence of different types of resultatives in Spanish, such as *la dejó agotada* ('he left her exhausted') and *pintó la casa de rojo*, cannot be denied. The important observation is that the resultative form/meaning structure has to be licensed, and organized in a valence structure, by the verb.

(24) exemplifies a verbally organized expression in Spanish whose meaning is similar to that of (22), but notice that the core meaning is not resultative as in (22):

(24) Se   durm-ió   llor-ando
     REFL   (she) sleep-PST.PFV.3SG   cry-GERUND
     'She fell asleep crying'

Unlike (24), the resultative meaning in (22) is transitive. Spanish allows a similar resultative construction, exemplified in (25), though it is not a typical Spanish expression:

(25) Se   durm-ió   a   sí misma   llor-ando
     REFL   (she) sleep-PST.PFV.3SG   to   REFL.3SG   cry-GERUND
     'She slept herself crying'

This expression type implies mismatch between a schematic argument structure ('x acts on y = x') and the semantics of the verb ('x *dormir*'), but it is by no means unacceptable, since, unlike the English version in (22), the nucleus of the principal resultative meaning is centred in the verb.[15]

In (26)–(27), the English verb *to kiss* and the corresponding Spanish verb *besar* appear in expressions of a transitive argument structure, which is reflected in the verbal lexemes:

(26) She kissed him

(27) Le   bes-ó
     DAT   (she) kiss-PST.PFR.3SG

In English, the same verb may also appear in a non-verb predicted resultative argument structure construction, whose meaning cannot be predicted by the verbal lexeme:

(28) She kissed him unconscious   (Goldberg 1995)

This kind of verbal alternation does not have an equivalent in Spanish:

(29) * Le   bes-ó   inconsciente
     DAT   (she) kiss-PST.PFR.3SG   unconscious

A Spanish version of (28) would organize the resultative argument structure around the verb, in a lexical argument structure construction:

---

[15] This Spanish resultative is an instance of PARTIAL TYPE FRAMING, as defined in Pedersen (to appear, a). When the argument structure is only partly organized by the basic device (schema or lexeme) of the language type in question, this is referred to as partial type framing. See also Section 13.6.

(30) La   desmay-ó   con un beso
      ACC   he faint-PST.PFR.3SG   with a kiss

The different ways of organizing the resultative core meaning in English and Spanish are formalized in the analyses of (31) and (32):

(31) He licked the plate clean
      SC: [SUBJ,V,OBJ, PRED]   /   'x caused y to become z'
      LC: [SUBJ V OBJ]   /   'A lick B'

(32) Limpi-ó   el plato   con   la lengua
      (she) clean-PST.PFR.3SG   the plate   with   the tongue
      LC:[SUBJ V OBJ]   /   'x cleaned y'
      SC:[ADV- form]   /   'specification (of causal activity)'

The findings from (20)–(32) indicate that schematic and lexical argument structure constructions have a privileged role in the clausal organization of resultative meaning in English and Spanish respectively. Resultative argument structure constructions do, thus, exist in Spanish, though it seems that they only combine with verbs that license and predict the resultative argument structure. Expressions of caused motion may be analysed contrastively in a similar manner (see Pedersen 2009a, b).[16]

13.4.3 Constructions of communication

We now turn to the skeletal argument structure of communicative meaning: 'x communicates y'. (33) and (34) exemplify comparable English and Spanish expressions of this core meaning:

(33) He said yes

(34) Dijo   que sí
      he say-PST.PFR.3SG   that yes

Again, we cannot determine whether the communicative argument structure in the two languages is organized lexically by the verb, or whether it is organized skeletally as a schematic argument structure construction, and specified lexically by the verb. More atypical communicative expressions, however, like (35) for English, indicate that the communicative argument structure is organized in a schematic argument structure construction, and that the communicative act is specified by the verb:

---

[16] For a more detailed analysis of English resultatives, see e.g. Goldberg and Jackendoff (2004) and Boas (2003). Resultative expressions in Spanish are discussed in more detail in, e.g., Mendívil Giró (2003).

(35) He nodded yes

(36) * Cabece-ó   sí
      he nod-PST.PFR.3SG   yes

The reason, also in this case, is that the core meaning of communicating some-thing cannot plausibly be part of the lexical meaning of nodding, which is, presumably, the reason why a parallel Spanish version is not possible; see (36). Martínez Vázquez (2003) observed that such mismatches between the semantics of the verb and the communicative meaning are very productive in English, as opposed to in Spanish, which only allows them sporadically. Martínez Vázquez suggests that the low occurrence of this kind of mismatch in Spanish is due to a cognitive preference of Spanish speakers to avoid syntactic metonymies.[17] But why should Spanish speakers prefer to avoid awkward, non-predictable combin-ations of lexical and constructional meaning? Examples like (37) give us a hint. The expression in (37), in which the communicative core meaning is provided lexically by the verbal predicate, would be a typical Spanish version of (35):

(37) Asint-ió   con   la cabeza
      (he) consent-PST.PFR.3SG   with   the head

The nodding-activity is specified by a schematically organized adverbial con-struction (*con la cabeza*). It seems that Spanish, basically, only allows the core meaning (the argument structure) to be organized by the verbal predicate; a principle for organizing clausal information in Spanish for which we have observed indications in a broad range of semantic domains (cf. previous sections of this chapter).

13.5 Hypothesis of Cross-linguistic Variation in Syntax

The cross-linguistic analyses in Sections 13.3 and 13.4 indicate that observed differences of clausal organization between English and Spanish are due to a general pattern. English tends to organize clausal core information, the argument structure, in schematic argument structure constructions, leaving more detailed information for lexical, and further constructional, specification. This explains the fact that mismatches between the semantics of the verb and the core seman-tics of, for example, the *way*-construction, the ditransitive, the resultative, or the communicative construction are licensed, and productive in English. Spanish tends to organize the argument structure lexically by the verb, leaving supportive information for constructionally organized specifications. This constructional

---

[17] Usage is syntactically metonymic when a lexeme, e.g. a verb, is used in expressions whose meaning is not predictable from its lexical meaning.

specification may consist of schematic constructions of different kinds, with different functions. It may be specifying devices that are added to the lexically organized argument structure construction, or it may, for example, be complementary modal, temporal, or aspectual information.

Contrastive patterns are obviously not the same as typological differences. However, the cross-linguistic analysis of the *way*-construction indicates that this pattern not only concerns English and Spanish, but also German and French. Germanic languages seem to behave like English, whereas Romance languages in general seem to behave like Spanish. As pointed out by Schøsler (2008, cited in Noël 2007: 75), in Latin, arguments were first of all identified by means of the lexicon, that is, selectional restrictions imposed by the verb, supplemented by indications of the nominal morphology. In modern Romance languages, there is a larger variety of grammatical devices—schematic constructions—used as a supporting device for identifying the arguments: for instance, word order constructions, or prepositional phrases.[18] Also non- or less-related languages like Turkish and Hindi seem to behave like Spanish (Narasimhan 1998). In many languages, in fact, the verbs are much more restrictive than they are in English, in the sense that they only appear in syntactic configurations that match their meanings (Goldberg 2006). In spite of this observation, Goldberg maintains her position that schematic argument structure constructions have universal status as the basic encoding device by stating that 'it seems unlikely that they fail to form argument structure constructions in such languages . . .' (Goldberg 2006: 120). It seems reasonable to assume that the formation of schematic constructions in grammar, on the basis of generalizations from usage, is universal. But our cross-linguistic analyses of the *way*-construction and other expression types in other semantic domains suggest that schematic argument structure constructions are not universally the principal encoding devices in clausal organization of argument structure.

13.6   Implications for Talmy's Typology of Macro-events

In this section, I discuss some implications of the present proposal for Talmy's typology of MACRO-EVENTS (Talmy 2000).[19] Our proposal argues that there must be

---

[18] Schøsler argues in another recent paper (Schøsler 2007) that schematic argument structure constructions, or what she calls 'specialized valency patterns' (Schøsler, 2010), have developed in French as cases of 'paradigmatisation of valency patterns'. In the present framework, this is a diachronic outcome motivated by constant generalizations from usage. The interesting question that these data raise for the discussion in this chapter is whether schematic constructions in French, in some cases, and maybe progressively, are used as the principal encoding device in clausal organization.

[19] MACRO-EVENTS are complex semantic structures comprising a MAIN EVENT, the framing event, and a CO-EVENT (Talmy 2000). Bohnenmeyer et al. (2007) refer to what they call the MACRO-EVENT PROPERTY (MEP). MEP is a property of clausal expressions that assesses the tightness of packaging of subevents

some deeper principles operating behind the Talmian dichotomy of satellite- vs verb-framed languages. Not only Spanish, but also other Romance languages, and languages like Turkish and Hindi, which, as we have seen, only allow clausal meaning that matches the verbal meaning, are all considered verb-framed languages in the Talmian typology. This apparent correlation between verb-predictive languages and verb-framed languages indicates a connection between the Talmian typology and principles of the organization of argument structure. The existence of such a connection is not a matter of course. In principle it is not difficult to imagine the existence of a Talmian verb-framed language in which some verbs may be used in non-verb-predictive constructions. Recall that, in fact, Talmy's typology only concerns five semantic domains: motion, state change, temporal contour (aspect), action correlation, and events of realization/completion.

Nevertheless, by linking Talmy's typology to principles of clausal organization of argument structure, we may better understand common deviations from the basic patterns in Talmy's typology. For instance, the hypothesized schematic organization of argument structure in Germanic languages enables us in these languages to organize expressions on the basis of different schematic constructions.[20] As we shall see in this section, this may explain some usage patterns that are unpredicted by Talmy's typology. It will also be demonstrated that the hypothesized verbal organization of argument structure in Romance languages may explain the constraints, which are unpredicted by Talmy's typology, on the use of manner of motion verbs with directional satellites in Spanish expressions of motion events.

In Talmy's generalized typology (Talmy 1991, 2000), a change of state in Germanic languages should be mapped onto a satellite, and specified by the verb, as in (38):

(38) Han   puste-de   stearinlyset   ud   Danish
      he   blow-PST   the candle   out
      'He blew the candle out'

However, expressions like (39), in which the main event, the state change, is apparently mapped onto the verb, are acceptable as well:

(39) Han   slukke-de   stearinlyset   Danish
      he   put-PST out   the candle

---

in the expression. An expression has the MEP if it packages event representations such that temporal operators (e.g. tense and time adverbial) necessarily have scope over all subevents.

[20] Pedersen (to appear, a) introduces the term VARIABLE TYPE FRAMING. It captures the idea that within one and the same language, the clausal argument structure may be organized on the basis of a skeleton (of a schematic or lexical kind) of varying complexity.

The acceptability of (39), but precedence of (38) as a macro-event, may be explained by referring to basic principles of clausal organization, as outlined in Section 13.5. (39) may be analysed as a schematic transitive argument structure construction: [SUBJ, V, OBJ] / 'x acts on Y', providing the core meaning, on the basis of which the verbal predication specifies the meaning of state change. This way of organizing the state change meaning, however, does not facilitate a specification of the manner (*pustede*) as in (38). Likewise, example (41) may be an alternative to (40):

(40) Han   sparke-de   bolden   tværs over   banen   Danish
      he   kick-PST   the ball   across   the field
      'He kicked the ball across the field'

(41) Han   send-te   bolden   tværs over   banen   Danish
      he   send-PST   the ball   across   the field
      'He sent the ball across the field'

In (41), a verb with the meaning of caused motion is used, redundantly, in a schematic caused motion construction ('x caused Y to move Z') impeding a substantial verbal specification of the cause ('he kicked the ball...'). Thus, if we assess (38)–(41) as communicated information of specific complex events, the principles of clausal organization for Germanic languages will favour the variants in (38) and (40). The theory predicts that Danish, as well as English, will organize the argument structure of these complex events in a schematic construction, leaving the secondary information for verbal specification. This prediction is best fulfilled in (38) and (40), which are therefore prototypical Danish expressions of these macro-events. The prediction is also fulfilled for (39) and (41), though the verbal specification is in these variants schematic ('A *slukkede* B', 'A *sendte* B...'), in the sense that it completes the basic resultative/caused motion argument structure; it is not substantial (as it is in 'A *pustede* B...', 'A *sparkede* B...'). The analysis of (39) also applies for expressions like (42):

(42) He entered the room

The use of PATH VERBS in English, as exemplified in (42), in Talmian typology, is usually explained with reference to the fact that verbs like *enter* are historically related to Romance languages (Latin) (e.g. Talmy 2000, II: 228; Beavers et al. 2010). However, this does not explain why other verbs also may express the main event in Germanic languages, as exemplified in (39) and (41) for expressions of 'state change' and 'caused motion' in Danish, and by English path verbs such as *rise, fall*, and *sink* (Beavers et al. 2010).

According to the Talmian typology, a typical Romance (Spanish) counterpart of (38) would be (43):

(43) Apag-ó   la vela   de un soplido
      put-PST.PFR.3SG out   the candle   with a blow

in which the main event, the state change, and the co-event, the causal specification, are mapped onto the verb and outside the verb respectively. Spanish,
however, has another variant—exemplified in (44)—that maps the causal specification onto the verb, which runs counter to the Talmian theory:

(44) Sopl-ó   la vela   (*fuera)
      blow-PST.PFR.3SG   the candle   (out)

If we follow the organizational principles for Spanish suggested in this chapter, the
argument structure is organized by the verb and the clausal arguments have to be
licensed by the semantic structure of the verb. First of all, the verb provides a
substantial specification of the activity of blowing (*sopló* = 'blew'). The skeletal
transitive structure of (44) is, however, also licensed lexically by the verb: 'x
transferring energy to y'. In addition, the substantial lexical meaning of the verb
implies a potential, though marginal, associative reading of state change: 'x caused
y to become z', which enables this construction type to be an alternative to the
prototypical one exemplified in (43). The possibility of adding a directional satellite,
as in the Germanic type, is ruled out, since the directional meaning of the satellite is
not licensed by the lexical structure of the verb (*soplar*); see also below. Assessed as
an expression of state change, the corresponding resultative reading is licensed by
the verb, though it is not prominently expressed, neither as the core meaning of
the verb, nor as an added subcategorized satellite. The secondary information, the
substantial causal specification, is unusually encoded as the core meaning of the
verb. The basic prediction for clausal organization in Spanish, that the skeletal
argument structure has to be licensed by the verb, is therefore fulfilled for (44);
though it is an atypical encoding option since the skeletal argument structure is not
provided as the core meaning of the verb. This explains the acceptability of (44), but
precedence of (43), assessed as expressions of state change.

   According to Slobin and Hoiting (1994), Spanish expressions of motion with
atelic manner verbs and a satellite are only acceptable as long as the motion event
does not implicate a process in which a boundary is crossed (e.g. a goal or an end
point; see Aske 1989). This condition is fulfilled in (45), but not in (46):

(45) La botella   flot-ó   hacia   la cueva   (Aske, 1989)
      the bottle   float-PST.PFR.3SG   toward   the cave
      'The bottle floated toward the cave'

(46) * La botella   flot-ó   a   la cueva   (Aske, 1989)
      the bottle   float-PST.PFR.3SG   to   the cave
      'the bottle floated to the cave'

The verb *bailar* makes another good example:

(47) Bail-ó   hacia   la puerta
      (she) dance-PST.PFR.3SG toward   the door
      'She danced toward the door'

(48) * Bail-ó   a   la puerta
      (she) dance-PST.PFR.3SG to   the door
      'She danced to the door'

Considered as a matter of principles for clausal organization in Spanish (cf. the current hypothesis), the essence of the unacceptability of (46) and (48) is that the meaning of *flotar/bailar* ('float'/'dance') does not predict, and thereby not license, a telic action. These verbs may combine with a directional PP, as in (45) and (47), because the activity of *bailar* may have a specific direction. The result, though, is not a telic action. The same principles may explain why (49) and (50) seem to be acceptable in the right context:

(49) La botella   flot-ó   hasta   la cueva
      the bottle   float-PST.PFR.3SG   to   the cave
      'The bottle floated to (it reached) the cave'

(50) Bail-ó   hasta   la puerta
      (she) dance-PST.PFR.3SG   to   the door
      'She danced to (she reached) the door'

The meaning of the verbs (*flotó/bailó*) excludes a reading of a telic action with a goal, but it may license the atelic activity to take place until an end point, marked by a PP. It is unclear how Aske's and Slobin and Hoiting's proposals may account for examples like (49) and (50), since they do seem to implicate somehow a crossed boundary (Beavers 2010).

Interestingly, if we choose atelic manner verbs like *nadar* or *correr*, the principles suggested by Aske and Slobin and Hoiting cannot account for the acceptability of (51) as well as (52):[21]

(51) Nadó   hacia   el borde /   corrió
      (he) swim-PST.PFR.3SG   toward   the edge /   (he) run- PST.PFR.3SG
      hacia   la playa
      toward   the beach
      'He swam toward the edge' / 'He ran toward the beach'

---

[21] Turkmen, a Turkic language spoken primarily in Turkmenistan, also admits certain combinations of manner of motion verbs and goal-oriented satellites, which cannot be accounted for if we adopt the principles suggested by Aske (1989) and Slobin and Hoiting (1994). Like Spanish and Turkish, Turkmen is a verb-framed language. See Word-Allbritton (2004).

(52) Nadó   a-l   borde /   corrió
      (he) swim-PST.PFR.3SG   to-the   edge   /   (he) run- PST.PFR.3SG
      a   la playa
      to   the beach
      'He swam to the edge' / 'He ran to the beach'

In (52), the atelic manner verbs are used in a 'telic action with a goal' context. The reason is that even though the meaning of the verbs *nadar/correr* is atelic, it is still an activity that typically involves directed motion toward a goal (e.g. *he swam across the bay, he ran to the beach*). Therefore, although these verbs in isolation have an atelic meaning, they do license a telic context. Accordingly, they may organize expressions of telic actions marked by a PP, as opposed to other atelic verbs such as *flotar* and *bailar* that may not. The examples (53)–(55), extracted from the corpus CREA, are for the same reason perfectly acceptable:

(53) Corr-ió   a-l   lavabo   (CREA)
      (he) run- PST.PFR.3SG   to-the   toilet
      'He ran to the toilet'

(54) Nad-ó   a   tierra   (CREA)
      (he) swim-PST.PFR.3SG   to   land
      'He swam to the shore'

(55) Nad-ó   de   Dover   a   Calais   (CREA)
      (he) swim-PST.PFR.3SG   from Dover   to   Calais
      'He swam from Dover to Calais'

Even though examples like (53)–(55) are acceptable, they are relatively rare (see Pedersen, to appear, b, for quantitative evidence). The reason seems to be that the lexical basis for the verbal organization of the directed motion event is largely inhomogeneous. The meaning of goal-oriented motion is not represented as the verbal core meaning, but is rather marginal and associative, unlike the expression of directed motion in (56):

(56) Pedro   sali-ó   fuera
      Pedro   go-PST.PFR.3SG out   out
      'Pedro went out'

Comparing (44) with (56), the latter is a completely normal expression, in which the directional meaning is redundantly marked by a satellite, in spite of what is predicted by Talmy's typology (see e.g. Aske 1989). The core meaning of direction and end point (telicity) is mapped onto the verb (as predicted in the present framework), but reinforced by the satellite (*fuera*). The reinforcement is in this case licensed by the lexical meaning of the verb, while the meaning of the satellite in (44) is not thus licensed.

If we adopt the principles for clausal organization, as outlined in Section 13.5, as the typological fundamentals, instead of the more rigid categorization of languages in terms of patterns of lexicalization, as suggested by Talmy (among many others who follow his typology), it is apparent from this section that a broader range of variation may be accounted for in a systematic way. In addition, the proposal makes predictions about which construction types are prototypical as expressions of complex events. In other words, the proposal makes predictions about the typical patterns, but it also accounts for, in a systematic manner, the substantial variation that can be observed.

13.7 Conclusion and Perspectives

In this study, we have explored how the meaning of the *way*-construction, and of other complex predicate constructions, may be expressed in a Romance language, with particular focus on Spanish. We found that Spanish versions of, for instance, the *way*-construction and the resultative do exist, though with the restriction that they have to be licensed and predicted by the verbal predicate. We suggest that this restriction is attributable to a fundamental organizing role of the verbal lexeme in Romance languages, as opposed to Germanic languages, for which a central role of CONSTRUCTIONS has recently been proposed (e.g. Goldberg 1995, 2006; Goldberg and Jackendoff 2004).

The cross-linguistic analysis has thus indicated that there may be typological differences regarding the way clausal argument structure is organized. This insight has led to a new interpretation of Talmy's descriptive typology of macro-events. It accounts, in a systematic manner, for the typical patterns as well as the variation that can be observed. Given the validity of this analysis, the huge amount of data originally meant for attesting or refining Talmy's typology of lexicalization may potentially be converted into evidence for a typology of clausal organization of argument structure.

Such a general typology of organizational principles may prove to be a challenge to the principles of parametric variation in syntax as envisioned in Chomsky (1981) and defended by Snyder (2001), among others, in his important study of parametric variation in syntax. Snyder's principal claim, based on converging evidence from child language acquisition and comparative syntax, is that the theory of parameter setting, in the classical sense of Chomsky (1981), is correct. In some languages, he claims, the compounding parameter is activated, while in other languages it is not. An important implication of Snyder's analysis is that the availability of complex-predicate constructions, such as the English resultatives and the telic expressions of directed motion discussed in this chapter, varies across languages. A Romance language like Spanish, for example, appears, in this approach, to be a strong candidate for a language in which complex predicates of the English type are systematically excluded, since the compounding parameter in Spanish is not activated.

Goldberg and Jackendoff (2004), among others, show convincingly that the CONSTRUCTIONAL VIEW plays an indispensable role in grammatical theory. By accepting this, they argue, the constructional view becomes a serious challenge to the parameter theory. They point out that because certain aspects of various construction types, for instance the *way*-construction, are so rare cross-linguistically, and on occasion peculiar to English, we must question an attempt to characterize them in terms of parameter settings in the sense of Principles and Parameters theory. As we have seen, several other Germanic languages, including Danish, Swedish, Norwegian, German, and Dutch, have a construction with almost the same meaning as the English *way*-construction. However, the three former languages use a reflexive construction instead of the *way*-construction, and the two latter use specific reflexive constructions and different combinations of reflexive constructions and parallels to the *way*-construction (see van Egmond 2006; Ludwig 2005; Seland 2001; Toivonen 2002a, b; Verhagen, 2003). According to Goldberg and Jackendoff, such cross-linguistic differences are stipulations that speakers of each language must learn as schematic constructions. If schematic constructions, they argue, have appeared to be necessary in the theory of grammar to account for, for example, the *way*-construction and cross-linguistic variants of the *way*-construction, there can be no a priori objection to using them to present detailed accounts also for the resultative construction and many other constructions of complex events. This has turned out to be a challenge to the parameter theory since practitioners of this approach have not been able to come up with comparably detailed accounts (Goldberg and Jackendoff 2004: 564).

In the present study, we have followed the CONSTRUCTIONAL VIEW, though recognizing that there are systematic typological differences of the kind pointed out by Snyder (2001). Our position is 1) that typological distinctions made on the basis of lexicalization patterns (Talmy 1991, 2000) are superficial, and not fundamental; 2) that typological distinctions made on the basis of parameter setting (Chomsky 1981; Snyder 2001; among others) lack complexity and are too much focused on grammatical form; 3) that the CONSTRUCTIONAL VIEW (Goldberg and Jackendoff 2004; among others) should recognize that in some languages, lexical constructions have a central role in clausal organization of argument structure, while schematic constructions correspondingly play a more secondary role; and 4) that we should make fundamental typological distinctions on the basis of the relative importance of constructional and lexical constraints in clausal organization of argument structure.

14

Spatial Adjectives in Dutch Child Language: towards a Usage-based Model of Adjective Acquisition

ELENA TRIBUSHININA[*]

14.1 Introduction

Studies of language acquisition can provide particularly useful insights into the intricate relationships between spatial cognition and spatial language. On the one hand, infants enter the language acquisition process already equipped with some fundamental pre-linguistic representations of SPACE. For instance, the fact that humans are vertically oriented beings motivates primacy of the linguistic terms for the vertical axis (Carroll and Becker 1993; Cox and Ryder Richardson 1985; Tribushinina 2008a). On the other hand, a lot of spatial concepts are acquired through exposure to the linguistic input in the target language. As a result, children acquiring typologically different languages may attend to different portions of the conceptual domain of SPACE (Bowerman and Choi 2001). This chapter aims to shed new light onto the development of spatial language by focusing on dimensional concepts associated with adjectival meanings.

Spatial adjectives such as *large, tall,* and *long* are among the first adjectives emerging in child speech (CS). However, there is little agreement in the literature about how exactly these adjectives are used by toddlers. The semantic feature hypothesis (E.V. Clark 1973b) suggests that children master spatial adjectives by adding more specific spatial features (e.g. [+vertical], [+secondary dimension]) to more general ones (e.g. [+physical extent]). This hypothesis predicts that the use of spatial adjectives in child language remains deviant until all relevant features constituting the lexical entry of a word are acquired. An important prediction of this hypothesis is that children will initially interpret *large* as a synonym of either *small* or *tall.*

* This research is supported by the Netherlands Organization for Scientific Research (NWO), grant 447-08-018. I thank two anonymous reviewers and the editors of this volume for helpful comments on an earlier draft of the manuscript.

Carey (1978) proposed an alternative view, called the missing-feature-plus-haphazard-example hypothesis. According to this line of thought, an important part of immature lexical entries is knowledge of object types to which spatial adjectives can be applied. Children may know, for instance, that *tall* is used with reference to buildings and people. On the basis of these specific exemplars, children later make generalizations about common features within various uses of the word. By this view, *large* cannot be synonymous to either *small* or *tall*, because all these adjectives will have their own sets of referents.

Another important approach to the acquisition of spatial adjectives, which I will refer to as the 'best exemplar hypothesis', was proposed by Smith et al. (1986, 1988). This view posits that toddlers initially attach spatial adjectives only to best exemplars of the property. For example, *high* will first apply only to extremely high objects and *low* will be used only for the lowest entities. It is claimed that children do not understand the inverse relations between *high* and *low* and interpret the two terms with respect to two different reference points—the top and the bottom, respectively.

Since Clark (1973b) presented her semantic feature hypothesis, there has been a plethora of experimental studies investigating the acquisition of spatial adjectives (e.g. Eilers et al. 1974; Hallett 1974; Brewer and Stone 1975; Bartlett 1976; Ehri 1976; Daems 1977; Keil and Carroll 1980; Harris and Folsch 1985; Harris et al. 1986; Sera and Smith 1987; Ebeling and Gelman 1994; Ryalls 2000; Barner and Snedeker 2008). Very little attention, by comparison, has been paid to naturalistic longitudinal data (but see Nelson 1976; Murphy 2004; Tribushinina 2008b). This state of affairs is problematic, since we cannot make any definitive conclusions about the development of lexical items in child language without considering developmental patterns in the longitudinal data. The purpose of this chapter is, then, to re-examine the three hypotheses presented above with the longitudinal data from children's spontaneous speech.

Further, the vast majority of studies into the acquisition of spatial adjectives have been performed on English data. Very few attempts have been made to investigate the development of spatial adjectives in languages other than English (but see Daems 1977; Harris and Folsch 1985; Harris et al. 1986; Tribushinina 2008b). It is obvious that we cannot get a proper insight into the acquisition of spatial vocabulary unless data from other languages are also taken into account. To this end, the present chapter studies the development of spatial adjectives in Dutch.

Section 14.2 of this chapter summarizes the main postulates of the three dominant hypotheses. Section 14.3 presents the research questions of this study. Data and methodology are described in section 14.4. Section 14.5 reports the results of the corpus analysis. In Section 14.6, I consider my findings in the light of the usage-based constructivist approach to language acquisition. Conclusions are summarized in Section 14.7.

14.2 **Previous Research**

14.2.1 Semantic feature hypothesis

The semantic feature hypothesis assumes that there is a universal set of semantic primitives and that languages differ primarily in the rules for combining semantic features into lexical entries. A child learns the meaning of a word by gradually adding semantic features to the lexical entry. Cognitive and linguistic development, it is argued, proceed by attaching more specific features to more general ones.

On the basis of these general theoretical prerequisites, the semantic feature theory makes several specific predictions about the acquisition of spatial adjectives.

Firstly, it is argued that adjectives with fewer semantic features will be acquired first. So the terms *big* and *little* (*wee*) which only comprise two semantic features—[physical extent] and [±polarity]—will be fully acquired before all other spatial adjectives. The adjectives *high, low, tall, long,* and *short* which contain an additional feature—[+vertical dimension] or [unspecified single dimension]—will be acquired after *big* and *little,* but before the words *narrow, wide, thick,* and *thin,* which contain the greatest number of features. This claim received experimental support from a number of studies demonstrating that children tend to make more errors with less general pairs (Eilers et al. 1974; Hallett 1974; Brewer and Stone 1975; Bartlett 1976; Daems 1977).

Secondly, unmarked terms such as *large* and *tall* are claimed to be acquired before marked adjectives such as *small* and *short,* because of the greater complexity of marked adjectives. Thirdly, one of the versions of the semantic feature hypothesis assumes that dimensionality is acquired before polarity (H. H. Clark 1970; E. V. Clark 1973b). By this view, early in development children do not understand that *small* is an antonym of *large* and treat these two adjectives as synonyms. According to another version of the theory, polarity is acquired before dimensionality (Brewer and Stone 1975; Bartlett 1976). In this latter case, terms like *long* and *high* are claimed to be initially treated as synonyms of *large.*

14.2.2 Missing-feature-plus-haphazard-example hypothesis

The missing-feature-plus-haphazard-example theory was introduced by Carey (1978) as an elaboration of the semantic feature hypothesis. Following Clark (1973b), the haphazard example hypothesis assumes that lexical development involves the addition of features to lexical entries of words. A crucial departure from Clark's theory is, however, that children are claimed to start by storing haphazard examples of adjectives in actual use. In other words, children learn what kind of objects and what dimensions are described by means of particular adjectives. For instance, they may learn that *tall* applies to buildings and people, whereas *long* is often used with reference to hair and trains. On this view, 'the initial lexical entry for each new word contains the abstract comparative core, including polarity, plus specific examples of contexts in which it is appropriate to use the word' (Carey 1978: 292; cf. Harris et al. 1986: 349). It is on the basis of these specific exemplars that language learners make generalizations and abstract common features within the uses of a word. It is also worth pointing out that the exemplars are taken to be truly haphazard and have an equal status, namely none of the stored exemplars is expected to have a privileged status.

An important prediction of the haphazard example hypothesis is that *tall* will never be taken as a synonym of *large*. Even if the child's representation of dimensionality is immature, the entries for *tall* and *large* will include different privileges of occurrence.

14.2.3   Best exemplar hypothesis

Several psychological studies have shown that younger children attach spatial adjectives only to the extremes of the scale (H. H. Clark 1970, 1973; Ehri 1976; Berndt and Caramazza 1978; Smith et al. 1986, 1988). When presented with a series of same-kind objects incrementally increasing/decreasing in size, three year olds usually agree to label only the highest object *high* and only the lowest object *low*. The objects between the two extremes are said to be neither high nor low. Four year olds agree to extend categories and five year olds were shown to perform like adults, using class-dependent reference points when applying dimensional adjectives to objects.

Clark (1970) argues that this finding is related to the fact that toddlers interpret scalar adjectives nominally, that is in the sense 'having extent'. The best exemplar of a dimension is, then, an object with the most extent. In contrast, Smith and collaborators (Smith et al. 1986; Sera and Smith 1987; Smith et al. 1988) have shown that interpretation of spatial adjectives by younger children is also relativistic in nature. By this view, the reason that three year olds choose the highest object for *high* and the lowest for *low* is that they use two different reference points for *high* and *low* (top and bottom, respectively) and fail to understand that *high* and *low* denote values diverging in the opposite directions from the same reference point in the middle of the scale.

14.3   **Research Questions**

Taking the models reviewed above as a point of departure, this study will pursue the following questions:

1. What is the order of emergence of spatial adjectives in child speech (CS)?
2. Do children understand the relation of opposition between the members of an antonym pair?

3. What are the referents of spatial adjectives early in development?
4. Do children make combinability errors early in development? And if so, how does the combinability pattern change over time?

In the remainder of this section, I will summarize the predictions of the three models regarding the four research questions presented above. The first research question about the order of emergence of spatial adjectives in CS, is important for two reasons. In the first place, it is crucial to start by taking an inventory of spatial adjectives used by children at different stages of early acquisition process before focusing on specific contexts of use. In the second place, although the semantic feature hypothesis makes predictions about the order of acquisition (i.e. arriving at adult semantics) rather than the order of emergence, it is reasonable to assume that words with the same number of semantic features will emerge around the same time, since they will have the same level of complexity.

Second, do children understand the relation of opposition between the members of an antonym pair? According to the best exemplar hypothesis and one of the versions of the semantic feature hypothesis (H. H. Clark 1970; E. V. Clark 1973b), toddlers start using spatial antonyms without understanding that the two terms are opposites of one another. In contrast, the haphazard example view and the second version of the semantic feature theory (Brewer and Stone 1975; Bartlett 1976) argue for early appreciation of polarity.

Third, what are the referents of spatial adjectives early in development? According to the semantic feature hypothesis, a child may initially apply an adjective to any kind of object, since early semantics is very broad and unspecified. For the same reason, this hypothesis predicts a considerable overlap between referents of different spatial adjectives in the first months after the emergence of the word. In contrast, the haphazard example view predicts that there will be very little overlap between the referents of different spatial adjectives early in development, because a child keeps track of objects to which an adjective is applied in child-directed speech (CDS). The best exemplar hypothesis, in its turn, argues that children will start off by attaching adjectives to extreme values. We may therefore expect that early referents of spatial adjectives will be the best exemplars of the described properties. In this scenario, *big* will be applied (primarily) to extremely large objects such as elephants and hippopotamuses.

Fourth, do children make combinability errors early in development? Recall that the semantic feature hypothesis predicts early combinability errors, because early lexical entries contain only few very general semantic features. Therefore, the child is initially expected to apply adjectives to (topologically) wrong referent types (e.g. *large rails*). According to the semantic feature theory, combinability errors are expected to become less frequent when more specific semantic features are added to the lexical entry of a word. The opposite claim is made by the haphazard example hypothesis, which posits that children's early uses of spatial adjectives will be correct in terms of referent types, because combinability with nouns (or applicability to object types) is an indispensable part of early lexical entries. The best exemplar hypothesis does not make any predictions about combinability errors.

14.4 Method

The longitudinal transcripts from the Groningen corpus (Bol 1995) in the CHILDES database (MacWhinney 2000) were selected for analysis. The corpus contains transcripts of 30- to 75-minute audio-recordings of spontaneous speech from seven Dutch-speaking children between one year five months and three seven months. The recordings were made about twice a month in unstructured home settings. The total of 208 recordings resulted in more than 170 hours of spontaneous interaction. Some of the recordings were not transcribed because of technical problems. The Groningen corpus was selected because it covers the period when most spatial adjectives emerge in child language.

All children were from middle-class families residing in the Netherlands. They all attended either a toddler playgroup or a daycare centre. The details of participants are summarized in Table 14.1.

Spatial adjectives were targeted in the search: *groot* 'large', *klein* 'small', *hoog* 'high/tall', *laag* 'low', *lang* 'long', *kort* 'short', *diep* 'deep', *ondiep* 'shallow', *breed* 'wide', *smal* 'narrow', *dik* 'thick/fat', and *dun* 'thin'. Searches were made by means of the Clan program. Both positive and non-positive (comparative and superlative) forms were counted. Table 14.2 lists the frequencies of spatial adjectives in the child tiers of the Groningen corpus. The subsequent analyses were determined by the nature of the research question dealt with and will be described in detail in the corresponding sections.

Before closing this section, I should acknowledge the fact that using corpus data for studying spatial adjectives in child language has both advantages and

TABLE 14.1. *The subjects*

Name	Sex	Age at first recording	Age at last recording	No of transcribed recordings
Abel	male	1;10.30	3;4.01	28
Daan	male	1;7.23	3;3.30	34
Iris	female	2;1.01	3;6.15	22
Josse	male	2;0.07	3;4.17	28
Matthijs	male	1;5.22	3;7.02	42
Peter	male	1;5.02	2;9.26	28
Tomas	male	1;7.05	3;1.02	26

TABLE 14.2. *Spatial adjectives in the CS*

	groot	klein	hoog	laag	lang	kort	smal	breed	diep	ondiep	dik	dun
Abel	140	65	16	0	1	3	0	3	0	0	10	0
Daan	140	38	29	2	12	3	0	3	0	0	2	0
Iris	52	86	7	0	7	0	0	0	2	0	2	1
Josse	162	50	8	0	4	0	0	0	1	0	3	1
Matthijs	188	138	59	0	65	0	0	0	8	0	9	0
Peter	36	44	22	0	0	0	0	0	0	0	4	0
Tomas	51	23	12	0	5	0	0	0	0	0	7	0
Total	769	444	153	2	94	6	0	6	11	0	37	2

disadvantages. A major asset of this approach is that it makes use of the linguistic material that was spontaneously produced in real-life communicative contexts. Naturalistic data are in this sense more reliable than artificially elicited experimental data. Another strong point of this method is its longitudinal character, which gives us an opportunity to pinpoint developmental changes over time. Finally, this method is also valuable because it allows comparision of the speech of a particular child with the speech of her caretakers, thereby establishing the role of the adult input.

However, there are also weaknesses to this methodology. One obvious problem is discontinuity of the recordings. If we do not encounter an adjective in the transcript at a certain age, it does not necessarily mean the child was not using the adjective at the time; its absence in the transcript may simply be explained by sampling error. Therefore, conclusions about the order of emergence should be taken as suggestive only. Another problem of the analysis of spontaneous speech is that production data do not tell us much about the way children understand adjectives. For one, if CS remarkably resembles adult speech, this does not mean that children have the same semantic analysis as adults; they may simply be imitating adult speech and have a non-adult interpretation of the words.

In summary, analysis of longitudinal corpus data is a valuable method which can inform us about the way spatial adjectives are actually used in CS—for instance, in terms of combinatorial patterns—and how these patterns develop over time. Experimental research, on the other hand, is crucial to studying comprehension of adjectives by children. In order to bridge the spontaneous data analysed in this chapter with previous experimental studies, I will compare my results with the findings from the current experimental literature repeatedly throughout this chapter.

14.5 **Results**

14.5.1 Order of emergence

Figure 14.1 shows cumulative frequencies (total frequencies for all subjects) of the spatial adjectives in the CS divided over three-month intervals.

As is evidenced by the figure, the overall-size terms *groot* 'large' and *klein* 'small' are the first spatial adjectives to appear, which is consistent with the semantic feature hypothesis. Furthermore, we do find errors suggesting that children use *groot* and *klein* where adults would use more specific terms. Witness examples (1) and (2):

(1) Child:

| en | die | heef | | grote | benen. |
| and | that | has | | large | legs |
'And that one has large legs.'

   Investigator:

| die | heeft | ontzettend | lange | benen. |
| that | has | terribly | long | legs |
'And that one has terribly long legs.'

(2) Mother:

| dat | zijn | net | stokken, | he. |
| that | are | just | sticks | PART |
'Those are just like sticks.'

   Child:

Ja
'Yes.'

   Investigator:

| hele | lange? |
| very | long |
'Very long ones?'

   Child:

| kleine | lange. |
| small | long |
'Small long ones.'

   Mother:

| kleine | lange? |
| small | long |
'Small long ones?'

   Child:

Ja.
'Yes.'

   Investigator:

hm.
'Hmm.'

   Mother:

| een beetje | dun? |
| a bit | thin |
'A bit thin?'

   Investigator:

| dunne | lange |
| thin | long |
'Thin long ones.'

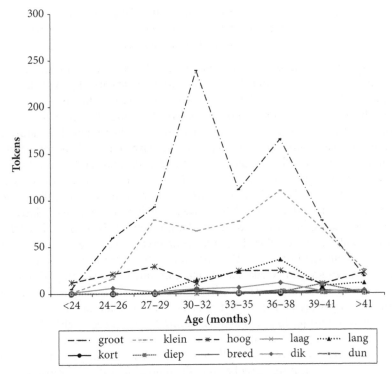

Fig. 14.1. Cumulative frequencies in the CS

In example (1), Iris (3;5.18) erroneously uses *groot* 'large' instead of *lang* 'long' with reference to legs. This error is consistent with the semantic feature hypothesis, which predicts that the 'meaning of *big* first extends over the meanings of the unmarked dimensional terms like *long, high, tall, wide*, and only later does the child learn to apply the other dimensional adjectives to more specific areas of the semantic domain' (E. V. Clark 1973b: 92). Similarly, the semantic feature theory argues that *small* initially functions as a cover term for more specific dimensions such as thinness. This type of error is exemplified by (2), where Matthijs (3;4.09) describes baguettes as *kleine lange* 'small long ones', apparently referring to their diameter.

On the one hand, examples (1) and (2) suggest that children indeed start with more general dimensional adjectives denoting overall size. This is probably due to greater cognitive complexity of notions such as verticality or secondary dimensionality as compared to overall size. Relatedly, in the CDS adults sometimes avoid using more specific dimensional adjectives and substitute them with 'large' or 'small'. Witness the following example from the Peter corpus (1;11.25):

(3)   Investigator: ik zie het konijn met de lange oren... grote oren.
              I see the rabbit with the long ears   big   ears
              'I see the rabbit with long ears... big ears.'

On the other hand, the errors in (1) and (2) are relatively late errors. Iris made the error in (1) at age 3;5.18, after she had been using *groot* correctly for at least nine months and *lang* for almost half a year. Likewise, Matthijs had been using *klein* correctly for at least fifteen months before he made the error in (2). This observation is consistent with the finding from the experimental literature that children between three and five years of age have not yet fully mastered the meaning of the overall-size adjectives *big* and *little*, and tend to use them for objects with the greatest vertical extent. More specifically, four year olds were shown to interpret *big* as 'tall' and *little* as 'short' (Lumsden and Poteat 1968; Maratsos 1973, 1974; Ravn and Gelman 1984; Harris and Folsch 1985; Harris et al. 1986; Coley and Gelman 1989; Sena and Smith 1990). This suggests that *tall* and *short* are fully acquired before *large* and *small*, even though the overall-size terms are first to emerge in the CS. The observation that combinability errors occur relatively late may also be taken as evidence of initial rote-learning of adjective–noun (or adjective–object, since adjectives are not always explicitly combined with nouns) pairings, a point I will return to in subsection 14.5.4.

Further, according to the semantic feature theory, *hoog* 'high/tall' and *lang* 'long' will be acquired about the same time, because they contain the same number of semantic features. Both adjectives denote a single dimension and only differ in one feature: *hoog* has the differentiating feature [+verticality] and *lang* is not specified for dimension. If we agree with the semantic feature hypothesis that *hoog* and *lang* are equally complex and will be acquired about the same time, we may also expect these two adjectives to emerge about the same time. This expectation, however, is not supported by the longitudinal data. The subjects of this study start using *hoog* about the same time as *groot* and *klein* (see Figure 14.1). *Lang*, however, emerges on average eight months later than *hoog*. This observation is compatible with the results from the experimental studies demonstrating that dimensional adjectives (Carroll and Becker 1993) and spatial prepositions (Cox and Ryder Richardson 1985) for the vertical axis are acquired before the terms for the lateral axis. This asymmetry might be related to the intrinsic vertical orientation of the human body, which renders verticality primary in our anthropocentric worldview (cf. H. H. Clark 1973; Maratsos 1973; Moreno et al. 1999). This finding shows that an account in terms of semantic features is too simplistic. Other factors, such as the orientation of the human body, may also constrain the acquisition process.

Notice also that *groot* does not become less frequent after the emergence of *lang* (see Figure 14.1). This might be taken as counterevidence to the claim made by E. V. Clark (1973b) that 'large' initially covers the semantic realm of 'high/tall' and 'long'. If this were the case, *groot* would become less frequent as soon as *lang* enters the CS, which does not happen.

Finally, according to the semantic feature hypothesis, *dik* 'thick/fat' should be one of the last spatial adjectives to appear, since it contains the greatest number of semantic features, including the complex feature [secondary dimension]. However, as shown in Figure 14.1, *dik* emerges quite early (30 months on average). One explanation for the early emergence of *dik* could be that parents often use this adjective in combinations like *dikke buik* 'fat belly', *dikke bult* 'big bump', or *dikke wangen* 'round cheeks'. Since this adjective overwhelmingly applies to the child herself and its use is usually marked by positive emotions, it is not surprising that the children start using *dik* with reference to bellies, cheeks, and the like quite early. This again shows that the world of a human being cannot be framed by a strict arithmetic logic of semantic features and is largely constrained by other factors, such as emotional involvement with the referent.

14.5.2   Antonymy

Both the semantic feature hypothesis and the best exemplar hypothesis argue for late understanding of antonymy. The semantic feature hypothesis posits that children learn to map various dimensions (e.g. verticality, secondary axis) onto spatial adjectives before they understand that, say, *large* and *small* are antonyms, the former being a positive term and the latter its negative counterpart. By this view, both members of the antonym pair are initially interpreted as 'having extent' and are therefore treated as synonyms (cf. Clark 1970; Donaldson and Wales 1970). The best exemplar view, in its turn, claims that children younger than four do not appreciate the inverse relationship between the members of the antonym pair and interpret the two terms with respect to two distinct reference points (e.g. top for *high* and bottom for *low*). In this section, I will assess these claims with the spontaneously produced CS.

In order to find out whether children treat *groot* 'large' and *klein* 'small' as synonyms, I compared the distribution of the two antonyms with the diminutive forms of nouns in the CS and the CDS. This diagnostic was chosen for three reasons. Firstly, one of the basic functions of diminutives is to denote objects of relatively small size (Dressler and Merlini Barbaresi 1994). Secondly, diminutive formation is highly productive in Dutch and is one of the first grammatical morphemes acquired by Dutch children (Gillis 1997). Thirdly, if children understand that *klein* denotes smaller dimensions than *groot*, the former adjective should be significantly more often combined with nouns in the diminutive than the latter. In principle, this analysis could be applied to other spatial antonyms as well. However, the other [−Pol]-adjectives are highly infrequent in my corpus and therefore cannot be analysed in the same way as *groot* and *klein*.

TABLE 14.3. *Head-nouns of* groot *and* klein: *CS vs CDS*

		CS		CDS	
		tokens	%	tokens	%
groot 'large'	diminutive	26	3.7	18	1.9
	non-diminutive	672	96.3	954	98.1
klein 'little'	diminutive	185	48.8	419	49.5
	non-diminutive	194	51.2	428	50.5

Cumulative frequencies of diminutive and non-diminutive head-nouns of *groot* and *klein* are summarized in Table 14.3. By head-nouns, I understand nouns denoting objects described by means of the spatial adjectives.

The figures in the table show that diminutives are more often combined with *klein* than with *groot* in the CS: $\chi^2(1) = 316.9$, p < 0.001; there was no significant difference with the CDS: $\chi^2(1) = 0.04$, p = 0.83. The children, however, combined diminutives with *groot* slightly more often than their adult caretakers (3.7 per cent vs 1.9 per cent): $\chi^2(1) = 5.5$, p < 0.05.

Not only the quantitative, but also the qualitative analysis of the data strongly suggests that children associate *klein* and diminutives with smaller objects. In the corpus, we find numerous examples of switching to or from diminutives depending upon the adjective being used. See examples (4) and (5) from Matthijs (2;7.02) and Josse (2;8.18), respectively:

(4) Child: waren ook giraffen. groot giraf en ə klein girafje.
     were too giraffes big giraffe and a small giraffe-DIM
     'There were also giraffes. A big giraffe and a small giraffe.'

(5) Child: ik kan ook zonnetje maken. is een grote zon.
     I can too sun-DIM make-INF is a big sun
     'I can make a sun too. It's a big sun.'

The prediction that 'large' is treated as a synonym of 'small' is not supported by the results presented in this section. From early on, children use *groot* and *klein* differently: just like adults, they significantly more often combine *klein* with diminutive nouns. This result is consonant with the findings from the experimental studies demonstrating that polarity is acquired quite early in the child's linguistic development (Eilers et al. 1974; Brewer and Stone 1975; Bartlett 1976; Ehri 1976; Daems 1977).

Qualitative analysis of the data also suggests that antonymous adjectives emerge simultaneously and may facilitate each other's acquisition. After all, it is difficult to explain to a child what *large* means without at the same time using *small* and contrasting two objects in terms of size. It is noteworthy that the frequencies of *groot* and *klein* in the CS (Figure 14.1) remarkably parallel each other. This is probably due to the fact that if *groot* is used, it is likely to activate its antonym and vice versa. Therefore, transcripts containing *groot* also contain *klein*. From early on, children, just like their caregivers, use antonymous adject-ives in contrastive contexts, as shown in examples (6) and (7) from Abel (2;6.11) and Iris (2;11.12), respectively:

(6) Child: jij   grote   stoel?   neem   klein   stoeltje?
           you   big   chair   take-2.SG   small   chair
           'You a big chair? Do you take a small chair?'

(7) Investigator: dat   is   een   groot   eendje.
                  that   is   a   big   duck-DIM
                  'That is a big duck.'
    Child: groot   eendje.   klein   eendje.
                 big   duck-DIM   small   duck-DIM
                 'Big duck. Small duck.'

In the same vein, Jones and Murphy (2005), Murphy and Jones (2008), and Murphy (2004) show that children use antonyms in adult-like ways from two years and for mostly the same purposes as in adult speech. This finding runs counter to both the semantic feature theory and the best exemplar view. Both the quantitative and the qualitative analyses indicate that young language learners do not use *klein* as a synonym of *groot* and appreciate the contrary relationship between these antonyms. Additional evidence for this claim will be presented in subsection 14.5.4, where I will show that children apply *groot* and *klein* to the same objects in order to distinguish between members of a category on the basis of size.

14.5.3   Frequencies in the input

Until now I have been discussing cumulative frequencies (i.e. total frequencies for all the subjects) and general tendencies across the seven subcorpora. However, it might also be rewarding to take a closer look at one particular child and to analyse frequencies of the spatial adjectives in his speech in relation to the parental input. In this section, I will zoom in on the Matthijs corpus. As shown in Table 14.1, this corpus contains the greatest number of transcripts and is therefore a better sample.

Table 14.4 shows the frequencies of the spatial adjectives in the speech of Matthijs and his caregivers. The figures are percentages (proportion to the total number of spatial adjectives used by Matthijs).

It is clear from the figures in the table that the relative frequencies in the CS are remarkably similar to the CDS. The descending order of relative frequencies is the same for the CS and the CDS: *groot* 'large', *klein* 'small', *lang* 'long', *hoog* 'high/tall', *dik* 'thick/fat', *kort* 'short', *diep* 'deep'. The least frequent spatial adjectives from the

TABLE 14.4. *Frequencies in the Matthijs corpus: percentages in the CS vs the CDS*

	groot	klein	hoog	laag	lang	kort	smal	breed	diep	ondiep	dik	dun
CS	40	29	13	0	14	0.2	0	0	0.2	0	1.7	0
CDS	37	27	11	0.6	13	2	0.1	1	2	0	7	0.2

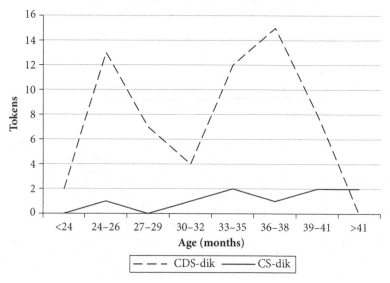

FIG. 14.2. *dik* in the Matthijs corpus

CDS (*laag* 'low', *dun* 'thin', and *smal* 'narrow') were not attested in Matthijs' speech. There might be two reasons for this: either these adjectives have not yet emerged in the CS, or they fell out of the sample due to their infrequency.

The only adjective whose frequency deviates somewhat from the input is *dik* 'thick/fat' (1.7 per cent in the CS vs 7 per cent in the CDS). *Dik* emerges quite early in Matthijs' speech (around age 2), but it does not reach adult frequency, not even at age 3;7 (see Figure 14.2). This is different from *hoog* 'high/tall' and *lang* 'long', whose frequency reaches the adult level around age 2;6 (see Figure 14.3).

The difference between the frequencies of *hoog/lang* and *dik* in the CS and the CDS might be evidence of the relative semantic complexity of *dik* along the lines of the semantic feature hypothesis. *Hoog* and *lang* denote a single dimension, whereas *dik* presupposes at least three dimensions and focuses on a secondary horizontal dimension.

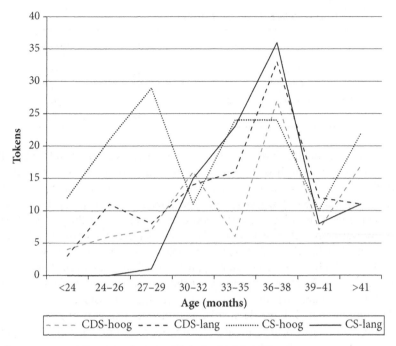

FIG. 14.3. *hoog* and *lang* in the Matthijs corpus

14.5.4 Early referents

A major function of spatial adjectives is to describe objects. Therefore, referents of spatial adjectives should constitute an important part of their semantic description. This subsection will focus on the early referents of spatial adjectives and assess the following three claims against the naturalistic corpus data: a. 'high/tall' and 'long' initially function as synonyms of 'large' (semantic feature hypothesis); b. toddlers initially keep track of objects and dimensions to which an adjective is applied in adult speech (haphazard example hypothesis); c. two and three year olds overwhelmingly apply spatial adjectives to best exemplars (best exemplar hypothesis).

If the semantic entries of *hoog* 'high/tall' and *groot* 'large' were identical early in development, as suggested by one of the versions of the semantic feature hypothesis (Brewer and Stone 1975; Bartlett 1976), then we would expect a significant overlap in referent categories of *groot* and *hoog* in the CS. Table 14.5 shows the number of referents described (a) only by means of *groot*, (b) only by means of *hoog*, and (c) by both *groot* and *hoog* in the CS and the CDS. Direct imitations and recitals were not counted.

TABLE 14.5. *Referent types:* groot *vs* hoog

		groot 'large'	*hoog* 'high/tall'	overlap
CS	tokens	279	42	15
	%	83	12.5	4.5
CDS	tokens	464	72	36
	%	81.1	12.6	6.3

Critically, the degree of overlap between the referents of *groot* and *hoog* in the CS is only 4.5 per cent. It is also important that there is no significant difference with the CDS: $\chi^2(2) = 1.4$, p = 0.5. Thus, even very young children know what types of objects are dubbed *hoog* and what referents are normally described by means of *groot*. Tribushinina (2008b) reports similar results for the pair *groot–lang*. The observation that there is some overlap in referent types in both the CS and the CDS is attributable to the fact that some objects can be described by means of several spatial adjectives, depending upon the profiled dimension. For instance, blocks can be dubbed both *groot* and *hoog*; the former adjective profiles the overall size of the object and the latter focuses on its vertical dimension.

The finding that children distinguish between the referents of *groot* and *hoog* from early on is against the semantic feature theory and in line with the haphazard example theory. These data indicate that a crucial part of early acquisition of spatial adjectives is discovering what kind of objects and which directions of variation are labelled by particular spatial adjectives.

Further, recall that the haphazard example theory also predicts that early lexical entries of spatial adjectives will include not only privileges of occurrence, but also representations of polarity. In other words, young language users are expected to understand that antonyms such as *large* and *small* share the reference point in the middle of the scale and denote opposite directions from this reference point. If this is the case, then the number of overlapping referent types in *groot* 'large' and *klein* 'small' should be larger than in *groot* 'large' and *hoog* 'high/tall', since *groot* and *klein*, unlike *groot* and *hoog*, share common dimensionality and may be applied to contrast same-kind objects. This prediction of the haphazard example theory is confirmed by the distribution of *groot* and *klein* across referent types in the corpus. Compare the results summarized in Tables 14.5 and 14.6.

It is evident that the degree of overlap in terms of referent types is bigger for the pair *groot–klein* than for the pair *groot–hoog*; the difference is highly significant: $\chi^2(2) = 112.7$, p < 0.001. This is fully consistent with the prediction that young children have understanding of polarity from the outset of the acquisition of spatial adjectives (see subsection 14.5.2). Yet again, the proportion of overlapping referent types in the CS precisely mirrors the corresponding frequencies in the CDS; the difference between the CS and the CDS in terms of referent types of *groot* vs *klein* is not significant: $\chi^2(2) = 0.6$, p = 0.75.

TABLE 14.6. *Referent types:* groot *vs* klein

		groot 'large'	*klein* 'little'	overlap
CS	tokens	215	172	79
	%	46.1	36.9	17
CDS	tokens	367	319	132
	%	44.9	39	16.1

TABLE 14.7. *Referents attested in both the CS and the CDS*

	groot 'large'	*klein* 'little'	*hoog* 'high/tall'
Abel	51	59	100
Daan	49	62	39
Iris	58	82	25
Josse	42	29	67
Matthijs	52	22	68
Peter	88	91	86
Tomas	56	63	38

Therefore, the pattern of the obtained results suggests that toddlers pick up ready-made adjective–noun/object pairings from the input. This conclusion is also bolstered by the comparison of referent types in the CS and the CDS for each child. Table 14.7 lists the proportion of referent types from the CS, which were also attested in the CDS, for the adjectives *groot*, *klein*, and *hoog*. The figures indicate percentages.

Importantly, even despite the discontinuous recordings, we observe a large overlap of referent types in the CS and the CDS. This provides additional support to the claim of the haphazard example hypothesis that children keep track of object types described by means of specific dimensional adjectives in the input.

The last point to consider in this connection is the role of best exemplars. On several occasions, it has been pointed out in the literature that spatial adjectives in adult language reveal prototypicality effects qua best exemplars (Dirven and Taylor 1988; Weydt and Schlieben-Lange 1998; Vogel 2004; Tribushinina 2008a). For instance, towers and houses are usually elicited as best exemplars of tallness, elephants are often cited as prototypically large objects, whereas a mouse is a best exemplar of smallness by virtue of being extremely small. If such prototypical referents are frequently described by means of the corresponding spatial adjectives in the CS, it could be taken as an indication of the reference-point status of best exemplars along the lines of Smith et al. (1986, 1988).

Referents of the three most frequent spatial adjectives in the corpus—*groot* 'large', *klein* 'small', and *hoog* 'high/tall'—are summarized in Table 14.8. Only referents that had a frequency greater than 10 in the CS are listed in the table. The overview of the most frequent referents suggests that the best exemplar hypothesis is supported only to a certain extent. On the one hand, *groot* is often applied to very large objects that may serve as best exemplars of largeness (e.g. tower, house, plane, bear). Similarly, *hoog* is most frequently used with reference to towers—well-established prototypes of tallness. In this connection, it should be noticed that prototypically tall objects such as towers are rarely dubbed *hoog* in adult-directed speech due to redundancy of this modification: a tower is tall by virtue of being a tower. Only in 0.08 per cent of occurrences in the Corpus of Spoken Dutch (2004), is *hoog* used with reference to towers. In contrast, tower-related uses of *hoog* in the Groningen corpus account for 36 per cent of the relevant tokens in the CDS. This result reinforces the conclusion that parents intentionally use their knowledge of best exemplars to explain the meaning of *hoog* to their children. In this sense, best exemplars do play an important part in the acquisition of spatial adjectives.

TABLE 14.8. *Referents of* groot, klein, *and* hoog

Adjectives	Referents	Frequency in CS	Frequency in CDS
groot 'large'	car	55	29
	tower	38	12
	block	25	28
	house	17	21
	child	16	103
	plane	15	7
	people	14	14
	fish	13	9
	bear	12	26
	piece	12	15
	ball	11	15
	flower	11	13
	bicycle	11	11
	book	11	9
	snake	11	4
klein 'small'	piece	49	65
	child	28	155
	car	16	25
	boat	13	15
	train	11	13
hoog 'high/tall'	tower	18	51

Table 14.8 also presents counterevidence to the claim of the haphazard example hypothesis that all exemplars have an equal status. The figures in the table demonstrate that some objects are more likely to be described by means of particular spatial adjectives than other types of objects. For instance, towers are by far the most frequent referents of *hoog* in both the CS and the CDS. Thus, some adjective–object pairings are more prototypical than others (cf. Tribushinina 2008b).

On the other hand, as shown in Table 14.8, toddlers often use *groot* to describe objects of very moderate size, such as blocks, balls, and flowers (cf. Nelson 1976: 25). In the same vein, *klein* is applied to large objects such as boats and trains. What is more, children often apply antonymous adjectives to objects of the same class. Recall that the proportion of overlapping referent types of *groot* and *klein* in the CS was not significantly different from the CDS. This result runs counter to the best exemplar hypothesis, in the sense that it shows that children as young as two understand that even very large objects can be dubbed *klein* if they are smaller than other objects of that kind. Although it is reasonable to assume that the child's understanding of inverse relations within antonym pairs is immature, it is not the case that toddlers do not have any understanding of contrariety at all (cf. Sera and Smith 1987).

14.5.5   Combinability errors

Between two and three years children make virtually no combinability errors. At the beginning of the acquisition process they correctly apply spatial adjectives to objects of the corresponding topological type. Combinability errors such as in (1) and (2) emerge relatively late (on average, six months after the emergence of an adjective). Such late errors present strong counterevidence to the semantic feature hypothesis and support the haphazard example view. According to the semantic feature hypothesis, errors should occur primarily at the beginning of the acquisition process, that is at the time children have not yet acquired all the relevant features. In contrast, the haphazard example view suggests that children start by rote-learning specific adjective–noun combinations and later generalize over a number of stored instances. Generalizations occur later and herald the beginning of productive use, which is sometimes accompanied by overgeneralizations of the type illustrated by (1) and (2).

As explained in subsection 14.5.1, Iris had been correctly applying *groot* 'large' for more than half a year before she started making combinability errors such as *grote pen* 'large pen' (3;3.09) and *grote benen* 'large legs' (3;5.18). In a similar fashion, Matthijs started using *groot* at age 1;11, whereas the first combinability errors such as *grote vuilnis* 'big garbage' (3;1.13) and *grote stoom* 'large steam' (3;5.13) were attested in the corpus only after his third birthday. Thus, the longitudinal data are consistent with the prediction of the haphazard example hypothesis that early adjective–noun (or adjective–object) pairings seem to result from rote-learning of ready-made exemplars and that combinability errors come in at a later stage, when children start generalizing over the haphazardly stored instances of an adjective.

14.6   The Usage-based Model

14.6.1   Background

The empirical analysis in the previous section has shown that the existing models of adjective acquisition cannot adequately account for early uses of spatial adjectives. Some of the predictions made by the three approaches considered above were confirmed by the longitudinal data, others not. For instance, the observation that toddlers make few overgeneralization errors is aganist the semantic feature theory, but consistent with the haphazard example view. The haphazard example theory, in its turn, cannot account for the fact that some adjective–noun/object pairings are more prototypical than others and that children are sensitive to this prototypicality. In order to overcome the problems of the existing models, I will introduce a new approach to the acquisition of adjectives in general and spatial adjectives in particular.

The hypothesis I propose arises from the usage-based (cognitive-functional) models of grammar (Langacker 1987; Bybee 1995; Barlow and Kemmer 2000; Goldberg 2006), which assume that knowledge of language includes both item-specific knowledge and generalizations over the stored instances. On this view, all linguistic knowledge of various degrees of abstraction invariably stems from the comprehension and production of specific expressions in specific communicative situations. Usage-based models therefore deal with actual uses of linguistic elements and give particular attention to such facts as type/token frequency, local combinability patterns, and prototypicality effects.

More specifically, I advocate the constructionist approach to language acquisition as developed by Tomasello (2000a, 2000b, 2003), Goldberg (2006), and Dąbrowska (2004). According to this view, language consists of constructions of various levels of abstraction—from fully lexically specific constructions (e.g. idioms) to highly schematic ones (e.g. predicate argument structure). With respect to the acquisition process, it is argued that 'children are both conservative and quick generalizers' (Goldberg 2006: 91). A child's conservativeness involves the finding that early constructions are highly concrete and item-specific; children merely learn them as 'prefabs' (Dąbrowska 2004) from the language they hear around them. Later, children start generalizing over the stored instances; their constructions gradually grow in abstractness 'as more and more relevant exemplars are encountered and assimilated to the construction' (Tomasello 2003: 316).

The existing constructionist approaches have by and large focused on children's syntactic and morphological development. The important contribution that the work reported here makes to this line of research is that it shows that lexical semantic development remarkably mirrors the development of grammar. In what follows, I will show how the usage-based model can neatly account for the findings regarding the acquisition of spatial adjectives reported in Section 14.5.

14.6.2 Frequencies

A crucial factor in the acquisition of language according to the usage-based model is input frequency (e.g. Matthews et al. 2005). The results presented above strongly support this claim. As explained in Section 14.5, input frequency is a very strong predictor of the order of emergence and the frequencies of the spatial adjectives in the CS. Additionally, the pattern of diminutive use with *groot* 'large' and *klein* 'small' and the distribution of adjective instances over various referent classes in the CS present a fairly direct reflection of the frequencies in the CDS.

The only case where we have attested a significant difference between the CS and the CDS was the frequency of *dik* 'thick/fat' in the speech of Matthijs and his caregivers. Given the frequency in the CDS and the time of emergence we would expect a higher frequency of this adjective in the CS, which does not happen. This delay is probably related to the fact that frequency interacts with various cognitive factors. One such factor is degree of complexity (Tomasello 2003: 175). *Dik* is a semantically complex adjective denoting a secondary horizontal dimension (cf. E. V. Clark 1973b). Therefore, input frequency is here constrained by the complexity of the linguistic item, which results in an asymmetric distribution of the adjective in the CS vs the CDS.

14.6.3 Referential conservativeness

The analysis of children's spontaneous productions (Section 14.5) has provided evidence that children pick up their first adjective–noun combinations from the input in the ready-made form (cf. haphazard example hypothesis). More precisely, they learn what objects and what type of dimensional variation can be described by means of a particular adjective. For this reason, there is very little overlap between referent categories of different spatial adjectives even in the speech of very young children; furthermore, the extent of overlap is not significantly different from the CDS. This finding further supports the idea that children's early utterances are prefabs rote-learnt from the input and creative combinations of such prefabs.

14.6.4 Prototypicality effects

As noticed by Goldberg, 'tokens of constructions are typically centered around one or a few specific words, or around a semantic prototype, even when they potentially occur with a much broader range of words or meanings' (Goldberg

2006: 88). In line with this statement, the above analysis has demonstrated that not all of the adjective–noun pairings have an equal status: some of them are more prototypical than others. A specific kind of prototypicality is prototypicality qua best exemplars. Adults commonly apply *hoog* 'high/tall' to extremely tall entities such as towers. Best exemplars are also often used in picture books in order to make the meaning of relative adjectives clear to toddlers. As a result, applications to best exemplars are also very frequent in the CS.

   The constructionist approach to language acquisition predicts that high-frequency items will function as cognitive reference points. This prediction is based on the finding from categorization research that frequency is positively correlated with the likelihood that the learner will categorize the entity as a prototype (see Goldberg 2006: 85–9 for an overview). It is also plausible to assume that holistic similarity to the prototype is more important in the generalization process than isolated semantic features (cf. Gathercole 1983, 1985). It will be a matter for future research to establish whether this is indeed the case.

14.6.5   Acquisition of antonymy

A central mechanism in language acquisition is what Tomasello et al. (1993) term 'cultural learning'. By this view, children do not just parrot the surface structure of adult utterances; rather they understand the communicative intentions of adult speakers and reproduce linguistic sequences they have witnessed for the same communicative function as in the input. It is therefore not surprising that antonymy is acquired early, as demonstrated in subsection 14.5.2. Contrasting is a major communicative function of antonymous adjectives in general and spatial adjectives in particular. And this is something children pick up quite early in development through the mechanism of cultural learning. The analysis of spontaneous productions has shown that toddlers, like adults, often apply antonymous adjectives to same-kind objects in order to contrast them in terms of size (cf. Jones and Murphy 2005; Murphy and Jones 2008). Therefore, the referents of adjectives constituting an antonym pair overlap to a far greater extent than the referents of non-antonymous adjectives. Recall also that the proportion of overlapping referent types of *groot* and *klein* in the CS was not significantly different from the CDS. Thus, lexical contrasts play an important part in child language, because contrast is a central communicative function of relative adjectives in adult speech.

14.6.6   Generalization process

A result of major interest in this study is that overgeneralization errors of the type *grote benen* 'large legs' and *kleine stokbroodjes* 'small baguettes' (referring to diameter) considerably lag behind the first instances of an adjective in the CS. Combinability errors appear at least half a year after a child starts using an adjective. This finding is fully consistent with the constructionist assumption that children start off as conservative learners and simply repeat what they hear in the input; overgeneralization errors come in later, when a child has stored a critical mass of specific exemplars and starts generalizing over them.

It is obvious that this developmental pattern does not confirm the hypothesis that children possess abstract semantic knowledge (as in semantic feature theory). These data are more consistent with the usage-based view in which children start with very concrete representations and gradually construct more abstract grammatical and lexical categories. Similar results are reported for syntactic overgeneralizations such as *She falled me down*. It has been noticed on several occasions that children make very few overgeneralization errors before about three years (see Tomasello 2000b for an overview). Early syntactic constructions are merely learnt as prefabs from the input. Overgeneralizations manifest the outset of the generalization process, in which more abstract grammatical categories arise (see also Lieven et al. 2003; Dąbrowska and Lieven 2005).

Likewise in lexical semantic development, children start off by imitating adult uses of spatial adjectives and therefore apply adjectives to the same objects as adults do. After having stored a critical mass of such combinations, they start extracting general schemas and proceed to productive use. For instance, an abstract schema for *hoog* may include such properties as [canonical vertical orientation], [vertical dimension is the maximal one], and [standing out from the background] (Tribushinina 2008b). The productive stage manifests itself in overgeneralization combinability errors. Since it takes some time to store the critical mass of exemplars, overgeneralization errors are not likely to be produced early, which is fully consistent with the data in this study.

14.7 Conclusion

This chapter evaluated three hypotheses about the acquisition of spatial adjectives (semantic feature hypothesis, haphazard example hypothesis, and best exemplar hypothesis) with the longitudinal data from seven Dutch-speaking children. The predictions of these hypotheses have been confirmed only to a certain degree. Of the three hypotheses considered here, the results are most consistent with the haphazard example view in which toddlers initially apply adjectives only to the objects they have witnessed as the referents of these adjectives in CDS. Later in the developmental process, they start generalizing over the stored adjective–object pairings and arrive at productive use. On this view, overgeneralization errors will be produced relatively late and antonymy will be acquired quite early, which is entirely compatible with the results of this study.

However, the haphazard example hypothesis cannot account for prototypicality effects attested in the longitudinal data. Nor can it give a satisfactory explanation of the order of emergence of spatial adjectives in child language. These aspects are more successfully captured by, respectively, the best exemplar hypothesis and the semantic feature theory.

I have advanced an alternative hypothesis which provides a more realistic account of spatial adjectives in child language. This new hypothesis—a constructionist hypothesis—combines the strong points of the three existing models assessed in the chapter and is rooted in the usage-based paradigm. I have argued that children acquire spatial adjectives by rote-learning of specific adjective–noun combinations and/or adjective–object pairings (cf. haphazard example view); this explains the considerable overlap of referent categories in the CS and the CDS. After having stored a critical mass of concrete adjective–noun/object pairings, a child starts making generalizations and proceeds to productive use. This stage is characterized by overgeneralization errors.

A crucial factor in language acquisition, according to a usage-based theory, is frequency. Input frequencies in this study were directly reflected in the CS frequencies, unless a more general cognitive constraint interfered (e.g. complexity of *dik* 'thick/fat'). I have also suggested that antonymy is acquired early due to the crucial developmental mechanism of cultural learning. Children are particularly good at reading communicative intentions of other people and are therefore able to grasp a basic communicative function of antonymous adjectives (contrast) very early in development. Spontaneous child–parent interactions provide ample evidence of this.

Finally, the usage-based constructivist approach can also account for prototypicality effects. Spatial adjectives are overwhelmingly applied to best exemplars of the corresponding property in both CS and CDS. The constructivist approach predicts that these frequent applications will gain a reference-point status and will steer the development of the semantic category. I will leave this point for future investigation.

15

Negation and Approximation of Antonymic Meanings as Configuration Construals in SPACE

CARITA PARADIS and CAROLINE WILLNERS*

15.1 Introduction

Paradis and Willners (2006) investigated the interpretation of twenty UNBOUNDED (SCALAR) antonymic adjectives with and without negation, for example '(not) thin'—'(not) thick', and ten BOUNDED antonymic adjectives with and without negation, for example '(not) dead'—'(not) alive', as well as their interpretations with approximating degree modifiers: 'fairly' and 'almost'. The investigation was based on Swedish data and designed to test whether the negator was sensitive to the configuration of the adjective in terms of BOUNDEDNESS. The results of the experiments showed that negated UNBOUNDED adjectives did not evoke the interpretation of their antonyms; that is, 'not thin' did not equal 'thick', but rather had an attenuating function similar to that of the degree modifier 'fairly'. For instance, 'fairly thin' was interpreted as similar to 'not thick'. The results for the UNBOUNDED adjectives were robust and the individual test items all behaved in the same way. The results of the experiments with BOUNDED adjectives, however, were more complex and inconclusive. Of the five pairs included in the experiment, four different types of interpretational patterns of the antonym pairs emerged. Only a couple of the negated adjectives were interpreted as synonyms of their antonyms—for example 'not alive' equalled 'dead'—while others readily lent themselves to be laid out on a scale. Due to the fact that there were only five pairs in the experiment with BOUNDED test items, the conclusions were necessarily cautious.

This chapter revisits the issue of the semantics of negation and approximation of antonymic adjectives in Swedish. It brings forth three issues. Firstly, it takes another look at language users' interpretations of BOUNDED antonymic adjectives in order to confirm or disprove Paradis' and Willners' (2006) findings and thereby, hopefully, arrive at a more comprehensive and conclusive picture of

* With the usual disclaimer, we would like to thank two reviewers and Joost van de Weijer (Lund University) for helpful and generous comments on an earlier version of this chapter.

how these adjectives are interpreted with and without negation and with 'almost'. It presents the results of a psycholinguistic experiment investigating the inter-pretation of BOUNDED antonymic adjectives and the role of negation and 'almost' with these adjectives. Two questions are central to the study (x and y are assumed to be opposite values):

 (i) Is BOUNDED (x) the same as *not* BOUNDED (y), and vice versa?
 (ii) Is *not* BOUNDED (x) the same as *almost* BOUNDED (y), and vice versa?

Our hypothesis concerning the reading of the negator is semantic in nature and states that, when *not* combines with BOUNDED antonymic meanings, its function is to express the absolute opposite meaning, for example *not dead* equals *alive*, and the interpretations of *not*, as in *not alive*, and *almost*, as in *almost dead*, differ significantly. Secondly, the results from Paradis and Willners (2006) are assessed in relation to the outcome of the present study and the interpretation of the negator as a configuration construal of content structures in conceptual SPACE is discussed both with reference to sentential negation, morphological negation, and the combination of the two in double negation, such as *not impossible* and *not unofficial*. Thirdly, broadly within the framework of Cognitive Semantics (Langacker 1987; Talmy 2000; Cruse 2002), this chapter addresses the motivations and mechanisms behind various different interpretations of negation in the light of the theoretical implications of the results for meaning in language. It argues that the negator in combination with antonymic adjectives is a degree modifier. Negation is expressive of either totality with BOUNDED meanings or attenuation with UNBOUNDED SCALAR meanings.

15.2 Lexical Meaning as Ontologies and Construals

The cognitive approach to meaning advanced in this chapter takes concepts to form the ontological basis of lexical knowledge, which involves both encyclo-paedic and linguistic knowledge (Croft and Cruse 2004; Paradis 2005). The meaning of a lexical item is its use potential in conceptual SPACE (see also Allwood 2003 and Zlatev 2003 for similar ideas). Actual contextual readings of lexical expressions in language use are relevant portions of the meaning potential construed on the occasion of use.[1] Conceptual space comprises to two types of ontological structure: *contentful structures* and *configurational structures* (Cruse

---

[1] The model is usage-based, which is to be understood both in terms of the importance of different kinds of observational techniques in linguistic inquiry that focus on how human beings make use of language (Paradis et al. 2009), as well as the assumption that linguistic knowledge is usage-based in the sense that knowledge and use of words and constructions in discourse is based on generalizations over usage events (e.g. Langacker 1987: 46; Tomasello 2003: 1–8; Croft and Cruse 2004: 3–4; Verhagen 2005: 24; Goldberg 2006: 215).

and Togia 1996; Paradis 1997, 2001). Contentful meaning structures host encyclo-paedic knowledge, for example THING, EVENT, PROPERTY, and configurational struc-tures provide various configurational templates for the construal of meaning in human communication, for example BOUNDEDNESS and SCALE. In addition to these conceptual pre-meaning structures, there is an operating system consisting of different types of *construals*, which are imposed on the pre-meanings by speakers and addressees at the time of use (Paradis 2004/2011, 2005, 2008a). Their role is to fix the final reading of lexical items in context. In our model, antonymy is treated as a construal that makes use of boundaries and scales in order to structure various content domains as opposites (Paradis and Willners 2011). A great deal of flexibility is built into our modelling of meaning in that configurational concepts such as BOUNDEDNESS and SCALE are considered to be free structures that are mapped onto different content domains. The advantage in the context of anto-nymic meanings is that it is a highly dynamic model in which we are able to treat both conventionalized and more ad hoc form–meaning couplings between configuration and content.

15.3   Antonymy, BOUNDEDNESS, and Degree

A characteristic of antonyms is that they are construals of binary opposition. The members of the pairs are at the same time minimally different from one another, by way of content, and maximally different, by way of configuration (Willners 2001: 17; Murphy 2003: 43–5; Paradis 2008b). They denote the same contentful property, but they occupy opposite poles/parts of that structure. For instance, adjectives such as *long–short*, *good–bad*, and *dead–alive* are considered to be typical members of the category and denote properties in the content spaces LENGTH, MERIT, and EXISTENCE, respectively (Paradis et al. 2009; Willners and Paradis 2010).[2]

Adjectival antonyms are thus basically of two kinds: UNBOUNDED (SCALAR) or BOUNDED antonyms (Paradis 2001; Croft and Cruse 2004: 164–92; Paradis and Willners 2007). UNBOUNDED antonyms such as *long* and *short* occupy opposite

---

[2] Following Gärdenfors (2000: 137), we define the term property as a region in one domain in conceptual space. In our case, the region is located in the contentful domain. Concepts, on the other hand, are regions based on several separable domains in conceptual space. In other words, properties are seen as special cases of concepts. They are independently defined and not only seen as parts of more complex concepts. Gärdenfors does not distinguish between content structures, such as LENGTH and configurational structures such as SCALE. He conflates the two and does not model schematic structures as free structures. He sees schematic structures as integral dimensions (2000: 24), since they do not occur on their own. Paradis (2005) models content structures and configurational structures separately and sees configurations as free structures that may apply to content structures more or less freely in different contexts, as this study will show.

poles of a scale, which in this case is a scale of SIZE, and hence they are in the possession of more or less of the conceptual content of that particular conceptual SPACE. They are counter-directional, which means that when intensified they move away from one another in opposite directions of the scale. Extreme values of *long* and *short* only tend towards the extreme, but actually never reach an end point. This characteristic of being construed according to an UNBOUNDED SCALE is highlighted by the fact that *completely long* and *completely short* are infelicitous.

BOUNDED antonyms such as *dead* and *alive*, on the other hand, represent another type of configurational construal. They are complementary in the sense that they are absolute and divide some conceptual domain into two distinct parts. *She is dead* entails that *she is not alive*, and *she is alive* entails that *she is not dead*. Because of this absolute divide, the expression *she is neither alive nor dead* comes across as paradoxical. It should be noted, however, that it is a general feature of most BOUNDED adjectives that they can for more or less ad hoc purposes be played around with and laid out on a scale (Paradis 1997: 48–66, 2008a). For instance, *very dead* comes across as less conventional than *wide open*. Because of this flexibility that language offers, an alternative interpretation of *she is neither alive nor dead* could be 'almost dead' or 'half alive'. These interpretations presuppose both a scale and a boundary (Paradis 1997: 65; Holleman and Pander Maat 2009). Scalar adjectives, however, are normally not associated with a boundary and do not bisect a domain in an 'either–or' fashion. They are laid out on a scale, and there is a pivotal area between the two sides which makes the expression *this road is neither wide nor narrow* perfectly acceptable and natural.

Scalar readings of adjectives combine with UNBOUNDED, scaling degree modifiers such as '*very* wide' or '*fairly* wide', while BOUNDED readings expressing a notion of 'either–or' go with BOUNDED and absolute modifiers such as '*totally* dead' or '*almost* dead'. It should be noted that when the antonymic relation between two adjectives is made salient, some pairs appear to map onto both a BOUNDED and a SCALE structure. Such double configurations may be basically BOUNDED, but with a scale attached to the boundary—for example *(totally/almost) empty* and *(completely/almost) full*. These meanings are objective in the sense that they can be calibrated and language users would agree on their application: 'an empty glass' would be empty for everyone (Warren 1992: 19). When the focus is on one meaning of a pair of antonyms, say either 'empty' or 'full', they are both BOUNDED in the sense that they are associated with a definite limit, but when they are combined, a scale is construed between the two boundaries.

Furthermore, there are also items that are basically scalar but located at the very end of the extreme of the scale, for example *(absolutely) terrific* and *(totally) disgusting*. They are primarily scalar and evaluative–subjective meanings for which language users may disagree as to their application. A terrific meal for one speaker might very well be a disgusting experience for somebody else. The term that has been used for these adjectives is 'extreme adjectives'. Unlike primarily BOUNDED meanings such as 'empty', these basically scalar meanings are infelicitous with *almost* (Paradis 1997: 56). As in Paradis and Willners (2006), we take the individual adjective as the point of departure for the categorization of adjectives as BOUNDED meanings and disregard the antonymic construal, and the criterion for inclusion in the test set is that it harmonizes with BOUNDED degree modifiers.

In sum, the constraints underlying the construals of boundaries or absence of boundaries, and indeed of all linguistic production and interpretation, are multi-farious and varying in strength and stability across uses (Cruse 2002). One very basic constraint is that of human cognitive capacities in terms of conceptualiza-tion and cognitive processing (outlined in our model of meaning above); and there are constraints related to memory and attention. Secondly, construals are constrained by the nature of reality. Some experiences more naturally lend them-selves to certain construal configurations than others: 'dead' and 'alive' as BOUNDED or 'long' and 'short' as UNBOUNDED, for instance. Thirdly, there are contextual constraints of various kinds on linguistic processing, such as previous discourse, cultural and personal knowledge, communicative and situational aspects. Finally, there are constraints of conventionalization of linguistic expression: how certain content structures (situations and entities) are habitually construed in a linguistic community and the patterns of routinized form–meaning pairings. Again, all such constraints affect all aspects of linguistic expression. Our focus in this chapter, however, is restricted to the interpretation, in terms of BOUNDEDNESS, of antonyms with and without negation and with 'almost'.

15.4 Negation of Antonyms

Turning now to the negator as a polarity item, we note that in traditional literalist semantics, negation is an operator expressing the absolute opposite proposi-tion: given the truth of p, $\neg p$ is false. If we see negation as an absolute operator, we may argue that its role is to apply a definite boundary to the meaning of the element within its scope. Negated antonymic adjectives differ from adjectives qualified by degree modifiers in that the oppositeness relation is in focus. Negated propositions are assumed to evoke two contrasting spaces, a factual space and the counterfactual space, which makes interpretations of negated expressions more complex (Fauconnier and Turner 2002; Verhagen 2005; Hasson and Glucksberg 2006). For instance, if we compare *totally dead* and *not dead*, it is obvious that the focus in *totally dead* is on 'total death' as opposed to some kind of partial death, while *not dead* is 'life' as opposed to 'death'. This means that if the negated BOUNDED adjective is antonymic, the interpretation of the expression is in some sense synonymous to the lexically coded antonym—that is, *not alive* equals 'dead' and *not dead* equals 'alive'.

Paradis and Willners (2006) criticize the literalist account and claim that the function of negation is crucial for our understanding of negation in natural discourse.[3] It is obvious from Paradis' and Willners' (2006) treatment of the negator that it has the potential to operate on both BOUNDED and UNBOUNDED meaning structures, and as has already been discussed, adjectival meanings are, strictly speaking, not *either* BOUNDED *or* UNBOUNDED. True, some meanings have a strong bias towards one or the other—for instance 'identical' is strongly BOUNDED and 'long' is strongly UNBOUNDED. Expressions such as ?'very identical' and ?'totally long' come across as infelicitous or strange. But, it is also true that there are very many meanings that do not have a strong bias for one or the other reading. On the occasion of use, coercion of an adjective with a weak bias towards a BOUNDED reading into a scalar reading is readily at hand. These BOUNDED or UNBOUNDED readings become fixed when adjectives are qualified by degree modifiers—for instance 'absolutely clear' with an 'either–or' reading of clear and 'very clear' with an UNBOUNDED SCALAR reading of *clear*. When weakly biased adjectival meanings are modified by *quite*, which is a degree modifier that may take on either a scaling function similar to that of 'fairly' or an 'either–or' reading similar to 'totally', contextual cues are crucial to the interpretation. This means that out of context, the interpretation of *quite clear* is vague.[4]

Like *quite*, *not* has been shown to be capable of invoking BOUNDEDNESS as well as UNBOUNDEDNESS in the adjectives it modifies, and like *quite*, *not* is both possible and natural with either UNBOUNDED or BOUNDED readings of adjectives. In combination with UNBOUNDED adjectives, *not* gives rise to various different interpretations along the scale in question. For instance, along the scale of LENGTH: *not long* may not necessarily mean 'short', but may position itself somewhere in between 'long' and 'short', for example as near synonyms of 'fairly long' or perhaps 'fairly short'. However, since scalarity may be eliminated in favour of a BOUNDED reading with the aid of negation, *not long* may also very well be interpreted as synonymous with its antonym 'short' occupying the opposite end of the scale of WIDTH. It is precisely to these problems that the present chapter is devoted. We question the literalist view that negation functions as a logical operator. The explicit questions are: how do speakers interpret BOUNDED antonyms with and without negation, as well as with 'almost'?

Negation is a powerful instrument in natural discourse as a hedging device (Tottie and Paradis 1982; Colston 1999; Holleman 2000), a metaphorization

---

[3] For a criticism of *the standard pragmatic view*, which proposes that people must analyse the literal meaning of 'indirect' utterances before the pragmatic information is called upon to infer the non-literal content, see e.g. Gibbs (2002), Giora (2003), and the untenability of disregarding encyclopaedic meaning in semantic analysis, e.g. Paradis (2003, 2005).

[4] Various studies of totality modifiers highlight aspects of change from totality modification to scalar modification. For instance, *all* (Buchstaller and Traugott 2006), *helt* in Swedish (Ekberg 2007) and *helemaal* in Dutch (Tribushinina and Janssen 2011).

trigger, and an implicature facilitator: for example *I am not your maid* (Giora et al. 2009; Giora et al. 2010). Verhagen (2005: 1) points out that although the expressions *it is possible* and *it is not impossible* logically entail one another, they are not functionally equivalent in language use. He deals with negated constructions in a communicative model of perspectivization and intersubjectivity. Similarly to Paradis' (2005, 2008a) model of lexical meaning, Verhagen (2005: 22) treats linguistic expressions as triggers of contextualized meaning structures. Lexical items do not 'have' meanings, and understanding is not primarily a process of decoding but an interactive course of events of (invited) inferencing and negotiation that lead to adequate cognitive and conversational moves. Thus the meanings of linguistic expressions are not completely fixed, but can be adapted to their contexts in order to support the purposes of the interlocutors. The meanings of linguistic entities are established via 'meetings of minds' (Gärdenfors, this volume).

Verhagen's (2005) socio-cognitive communicative model of intersubjectivity is of particular interest to a usage-based treatment of negation. He argues that the primary function of negation in natural language has to be seen in terms of cognitive coordination, not primarily in terms of the relation between language and the world, or the language user and the world, but in view of systematic aspects of its use in regulating relations between different mental spaces rather than between language and the world. Moreover, within this model Verhagen is able to formulate an important difference between sentential and morphological negation that we will return to in the discussion of the individual test items. In order to demonstrate the difference, Verhagen coordinates a negated construction with a contrasting construction using *on the contrary* to guarantee the opposition. Consider examples (1) and (2) (i.e. examples (3) and (5) in Verhagen 2005: 31–5).

(1)   Mary is not happy. On the contrary, she is feeling really depressed.

(2)   *Mary is unhappy. On the contrary, she is feeling really depressed.

In both (1) and (2) the function of *on the contrary* is to reinforce the setting up of opposing conceptual spaces. In (1) *she is feeling really depressed* is contrasted to *Mary is not happy* in a coherent and well-formed construction. The contrast is made possible because *Mary is not happy* evokes two distinct mental spaces, both p and $\neg p$, for which *Mary is not happy* is the opposite of *she is feeling really depressed*. In (2), however, only one space is opened up: the affirmation that *Mary is unhappy*. From these facts, Verhagen concludes that (1) is coherent because two different mental spaces with two different epistemic stances towards the same proposition are evoked. Morphological negation reverses the scale associated with *happy*, but it does not invite the addressee to consider-and-abandon the thought of applying the scale with the non-negated orientation. Verhagen's take on sentential negation is that it operates primarily in the dimension of intersubjective coordination. Sentential negation is used by the speaker to direct the addressee's inferences in the direction that the speaker wants, while morphological negation operates at the propositional, ideational level.

15.5   Aim and Hypothesis

The aim of this study is to account for the role of the negator of BOUNDED antonyms as well as to match the role of the negator *inte* 'not' with the role of the degree modifier *nästan* 'almost'. Subsequently, we compare the results with a similar experiment of BOUNDED antonyms as well as the role of the negator and *ganska* 'fairly' with UNBOUNDED antonyms in Swedish. Our main hypotheses and its corollary predictions are as follows.

15.5.1   Hypotheses

Negation and approximation are sensitive to BOUNDEDNESS. When they combine with a BOUNDED antonym, they operate on the boundary configuration. Negation results in an absolute opposite construal and approximation falls short of the boundary. Negation and modification of the adjectives will take significantly longer to assess than bare adjectives.

15.5.2   Predictions

- There will be consistency within the group of BOUNDED antonyms with respect to the participants' judgments that 'x' = 'not y' and 'y' = 'not x'.
- The negated BOUNDED antonyms 'not dead' and 'not alive' will not correspond to 'almost alive' and 'almost dead', respectively.
- The response times for 'not' + antonym as well as 'almost' + antonym will be longer than the response times for bare antonyms.

15.6   Experiment Design and Procedure

Twenty-nine participants, twenty women and nine menaged between nineteen and seventy-three took part in a judgment experiment. All were native speakers of Swedish. The experiment was carried out online. The real purpose of the study was not revealed to the participants, who instead were asked to participate in a readability test. The experimental software was E-prime, which is a commercially available Windows-based presentation program with a graphical interface, a scripting language similar to Visual Basic, and response collection.[5] E-prime conveniently logged the ratings as well as the response times in separate files for each of the participants. The information and the tasks were presented on the computer screen in the following order:

- questions about personal data (name, age, sex, occupation, native language, and parents' native language)
- practical instructions such as how to use the mouse to proceed
- two practice trials
- the judgment experiment: 60 test items + 48 distracters = 108 items

The screen layout is shown in Figure 15.1. The sentence at the top of the screen is the test sentence that contains the test item to be assessed by the participants—*Dörren till köket var inte stängd* 'The door to the kitchen was not closed', and *inte stängd* 'not closed' is the test item in this case.

All test sentences consisted of a noun phrase followed by a copula and an adjective with or without negation. The statement was followed by a question, for example *Hur var dörröppningen?* 'How was the gap?', as shown in Figure 15.1. The task of the participants was to make a judgment of interpretation of the test item on an eleven-point scale. We deliberately avoided using either of the antonyms—so in

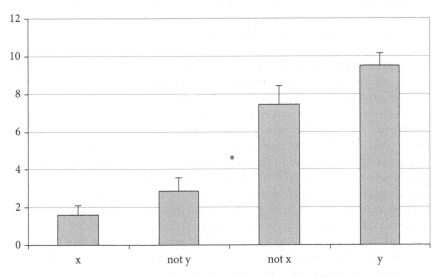

FIG. 15.1. An example of a task from the experiment (screen dump)

[5] For more information about E-prime see http://www.pstnet.com/products/e-prime/.

this case neither *closed* nor *open*—in the question or as end points of the scale. The scale end points were designated with tags such as *obefintlig* 'non-existent' and *maximal* 'maximal'. None of the end points was numerical. No global context was provided, and no attempt was made to control individual contextual interpretations. The participants were asked to respond to the out-of-global-context statements expressed by the top sentence in combination with the two end points on the eleven-point scale. In other words, the participants had to imagine a more specific context themselves, which means that the contexts were bound to differ across the individual participants. The structure of the distracters was not the same as for the test set, because we did not want to make the experiments monotonous. *Selma hatar Otto* 'Selma hates Otto' is an example of a distracter. The question asked was *Hur är Selmas känslor för Otto?* 'What are Selma's feelings for Otto?', and the end points of the scale were *kalla* 'cold' and *varma* 'hot'.

The test set included ten pairs of antonyms, all of which were different from the ones used in Paradis' and Willners' (2006) experiment. The experiment was self-paced, but the procedure was constrained in the sense that the participants could only move forward and never go back and change their judgments.

Table 15.1 lists all the test items and phrases used as end points for each pair. The test items were tested across six conditions: (*inte*/*nästan*/∅) ADJECTIVE X and (*inte*/*nästan*/∅) ADJECTIVE Y; that is ADJECTIVE X and ADJECTIVE Y with and without negation and with 'almost'. All the X items are items that are seen as 'lacking' in the property asked about in the question on the screen, and all the Y items are items that express maximally 'having' the property. For instance, 'The statement made by the politician was false.' 'How trustworthy was it?': at either end of the eleven-point scale were 'not at all' and 'totally'. 'False' is lacking in trustworthiness, while 'true' expresses trustworthiness. The test items are all natural and compatible with totality modifiers, such as *helt* 'totally', and some of them are natural in combination with *nästan* 'almost', for example *nästan sant* 'almost true', while others are less good and sometimes contrived, for example *nästan falskt* 'almost false', but possible given an appropriate contextual construal (Paradis 2001: 50). Apart from the sixty test sentences (10*6) with non-negated and negated BOUNDED adjectives and with modification by *nästan* 'almost', there were forty-eight distracters. See Appendix A for the full list of sentences used as test items. Henceforth only the English equivalents will be used. The overall differences of the ratings and the response times across the conditions were tested in two separate analyses of variance using repeated-measures ANOVA: one by item and one by subject followed by Post Hoc comparisons, using Bonferroni's procedure. The same procedure was used for the response times.

TABLE 15.1. *Ten Swedish* BOUNDED *adjectives and their antonyms in the left columns.* X *corresponds to meanings 'lacking' in the designated property and* Y *for adjectival meanings 'having' the designated property. Their corresponding end points are given in the right column*[6]

		End points	
X	Y	X	Y
falsk 'false'	*sann* 'true'	*inte alls* 'not at all'	*helt* 'totally'
olika 'different'	*likadana* 'identical'	*inte alls* 'not at all'	*helt* 'totally'
nyktra 'sober'	*onyktra* 'non-sober'	*inte alls* 'not all'	*totalt* 'totally'
urusla 'lousy'	*perfekta* 'perfect'	*botten* 'the worst'	*toppen* 'the best'
hela 'whole'	*trasiga* 'torn'	*botten* 'the worst'	*toppen* 'the best'
stängd 'closed'	*öppen* 'open'	*obefintlig* 'non-existent'	*maximal* 'maximally'
inofficiell 'unofficial'	*officiell* 'official'	*inte alls* 'not at all'	*helt* 'totally'
omöjligt 'impossible'	*möjligt* 'possible'	*inte alls* 'not at all'	*helt* 'totally'
torr 'dry'	*genomblöt* 'soaking wet'	*minimalt* 'minimally'	*maximalt* 'maximally'
frusen 'frozen'	*upptinad* 'defrosted'	*stenhård* 'hard as brick'	*helt mjuk* 'totally soft'

15.7   Results

The averages of the ratings are shown in Table 15.2. The mean rating of the 'x' member of the antonym pair is 1.6, and the rating for its negated antonym 'not y' is 2.8, 'not x' is 7.4 and 'y' is 9.5. In between are 'almost x' with the mean 3.7 and 'almost y' with 6.8.

It is clear from Table 15.2 that the standard deviations across the conditions are low. They range from 0.5 to 1.[7] The overall differences across the six conditions

---

[6] The English equivalents are rough and ready translations and should be considered as glosses. For instance, the Swedish word *hela* is notoriously difficult to translate. Idiomatically, it corresponds to something like *alright, whole, in perfect shape,* or *like new.* We opted for *whole* because it is a single word translation. *Whole* in English is contextually more restricted than *hela.* The antonym pairs in Swedish are all natural opposites in everyday language, and the members of the pairs are symmetrical and stylistically similar.

[7] Again, it deserves to be pointed out that *nästan* 'almost' combines more naturally with some of the test items than with others, but all of them are possible to construe given an appropriate context. Like in English, some of the test items are more natural with *knappast* 'barely' or 'hardly', but *knappast* has the effect of orienting the addressee towards negative conclusions, while *nästan* 'almost' has positive orientation (e.g. Horn 2011; Verhagen 2005: 45–50). We decided to use *nästan* for all test items for two reasons. Firstly, we wanted to be consistent across the test items and, secondly, we wanted to be able to compare with Paradis' and Willners' (2006) results for *ganska* 'fairly' as the

TABLE 15.2. *Ratings of the six conditions of* BOUNDED *adjectives*

Condition	Mean	Std. deviation
X	1.6	0.5
not Y	2.8	0.7
almost X	3.7	0.8
almost Y	6.8	0.9
not X	7.4	1.0
Y	9.5	0.7

FIG. 15.2. Ratings of the antonymic adjectives with and without negation

were significant in both the subject analysis ($F_1[5,140]=430.429$, $p < 0.001$) and the item analysis ($F_2[5,50]=66.989$, $p < 0.001$). The Post Hoc comparisons, however, showed that 'x', 'not y', 'not x' and 'y' should be regarded as two different subgroups, as is shown in Figure 15.2.

The Post Hoc analysis also showed that there were significant differences between 'x', 'almost x', 'almost y', and 'y', as shown in Figure 15.3.

The relative locations of all six conditions on the scale are shown in Figure 15.4. There were no significant differences between 'x' and 'not y', 'not x' and 'y', 'not y'

modifier of UNBOUNDED antonymic meanings. Like their English counterparts *almost* and *fairly*, neither *nästan* nor *ganska* has negative orientation. The potentially contrived readings of combinations such as 'almost lousy' and 'almost unofficial' may however have the effect of prolonging the response times. This issue is brought up again in the discussion in Section 15.7.

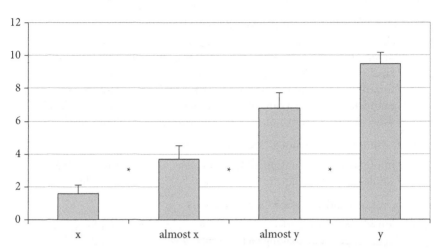

FIG. 15.3. Ratings of the antonymic adjectives with and without the modifier 'almost'

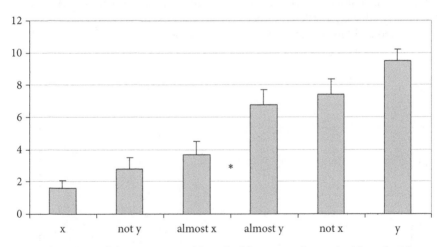

FIG. 15.4. Ratings of the antonyms with and without negation and with and without 'almost'

and 'almost x', 'almost y' and 'not x', but significant differences between 'almost x' and 'almost y'.

However, when we carried out a repeated-measures ANOVA by subject followed by Post Hoc comparisons using Bonferroni's procedure for each individual pair across the conditions, three different negated types emerged from the results of the experiment:

(i)   x = not Y and Y = not x (see Figure 15.5)

'closed'	=	'not open'	'open'	=	'not closed'
'different'	=	'not identical'	'identical'	=	'not different'
'false'	=	'not true'	'true'	=	'not false'
'frozen'	=	'not defrosted'	'defrosted'	=	'not frozen'
'unofficial'	=	'not official'	'official'	=	'not unofficial'
'sober'	=	'not non-sober'	'non-sober'	=	'not sober'

(ii) x = not y and y ≠ not x (see Figure 15.6)

| 'impossible' | = | 'not possible' | 'possible' | ≠ | 'not impossible' |
| 'whole' | = | 'not torn' | 'torn' | ≠ | 'not whole' |

(iii) x ≠ not Y and Y ≠ not x (see Figure 15.7)

| 'lousy' | ≠ | 'not perfect' | 'perfect' | ≠ | 'not lousy' |
| 'dry' | ≠ | 'not soaking wet' | 'soaking wet' | ≠ | 'not dry' |

While 'x' and 'not Y' were judged to be in the boxes on the left side of the screen as viewed by the participants, and 'Y' and 'not x' on the right side of the screen for the test items in groups (i) and (ii) (see Figures 15.5 and 15.6), the test items in group (iii) display a different order. 'x' and 'not x' were placed on the left side of the screen and 'not Y' and 'Y' on the right side (see Figure 15.7).[8]

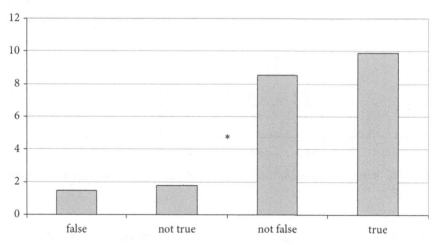

Fig. 15.5. Ratings for group (i) and their negated antonyms

[8] The 'not x' – 'x' order is true of 'open' and 'closed' and 'official' 'unofficial', but not of the other members of the group, which have the order 'x' – 'not x'. The difference between the two conditions 'not x' and 'x' is not statistically significant, which means that sequencing is irrelevant.

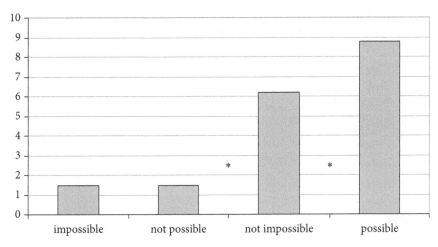

FIG. 15.6. Ratings for group (ii) and their negated antonyms

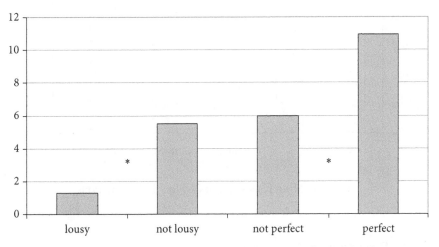

FIG. 15.7. Ratings for group (iii) and their negated antonyms

Furthermore, Table 15.3 and Figure 15.8 show the response times for the six conditions. The Post Hoc analysis reveals that there are no significant differences between any of the neighbouring conditions except between 'Y' and 'almost Y'.

The response times for the modified and negated adjectives were significantly longer than for the bare antonyms. The experiment was not designed to put pressure on the participants to respond as quickly as possible, and as a result of that the response times are long across the board.

TABLE 15.3. *Mean response times (in s) for the six conditions*

Condition	Mean	Std. deviation
X	6.99	3.27
Y	7.14	2.10
almost Y	8.67	2.32
not Y	8.99	3.08
almost X	9.20	3.20
not X	9.58	3.36

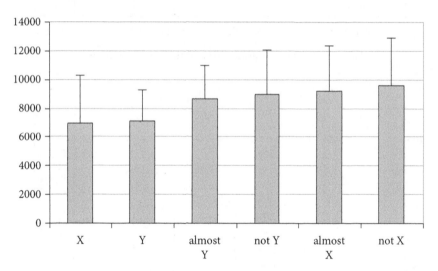

FIG. 15.8. Mean response times (s) for all six conditions

15.8   Discussion

The goal of this study was to repeat and extend Paradis' and Willners' (2006) study of BOUNDED antonyms in order to test the BOUNDEDNESS hypothesis, which predicts that negation will be sensitive to the configuration construal of BOUNDEDNESS of the element it combines with: (i) BOUNDED (ADJECTIVE X) will have the same reading as the 'not' BOUNDED (ADJECTIVE Y), and vice versa, and (ii) 'not' BOUNDED (ADJECTIVE X) will have a different reading from 'almost' BOUNDED (ADJECTIVE Y), and vice versa. The third prediction under investigation stated (iii) that the response times for 'not' + ADJECTIVE as well as for 'degree modifier' + ADJECTIVE will be longer than the response time for bare antonyms. In Paradis and Willners (2006), results of the readings of the UNBOUNDED adjectives were robust and consistent across the test items, but the BOUNDED test set was relatively small, and for that reason the results were not as consistent and reliable as for the UNBOUNDED ones. From now onwards, the results of the present study are assessed in relation to the results from Paradis and Willners (2006).

15.8.1   Negation in combination with BOUNDED meanings

The BOUNDEDNESS hypothesis was corroborated in the overall results of this study: BOUNDED (ADJECTIVE X) has the same reading as the *not* BOUNDED (ADJECTIVE Y), and vice versa. The results for the individual BOUNDED adjectives in Paradis and Willners (2006) fall into four subgroups, three of which are consistent with the groups in the present study. They also obtain a group with the 'x ≠ not Y and Y = not x' pattern for 'bound'–'free'. All the test items from Paradis and Willners (2006) and the test items of this study are presented in Table 15.4. Group (ii) holds all members with both = and ≠, which means that we disregard whether the adjectives are x or Y adjectives.

Recall that the members of group (III) were differently distributed on the eleven-point scale than all other antonyms. On the surface it looks like they behaved in the same way as the UNBOUNDED adjectives did, that is, 'short' ≠ 'not long' and 'long' ≠ 'not short'. This was not the case, however, since neither 'not empty' nor 'not full' was located on the opposite side of the scale by the participants and thus were given very different scores. The order of the four conditions on the eleven-point scale for the UNBOUNDED meanings was 'x' – 'not Y' – 'not x' – 'Y' for all of the test items both in this study and in Paradis' and Willners' (2006) study, except for the test items in (III) where the order was 'x' – 'not x' – 'not Y' – 'Y' with

TABLE 15.4. *The participants' interpretations of the non-negated and the negated antonyms*

I	II	III
	x = not Y : Y ≠ not x (i)x ≠	
x = not Y : Y = not x	not Y : Y = not x (ii)	x ≠ not Y : Y ≠ not x
closed – open	impossible – possible (i)	lousy – perfect
identical – different	whole – torn (i)	dry – soaking wet
false – true	wrong – right (i)	empty – full
frozen – defrosted	sterile – fertile (i)	
unofficial – official	bound – free (ii)	
sober – non-sober		
dead – alive		

TABLE 15.5. *The lists of individual adjectives in relation to their negated antonyms*

ADJECTIVE = *not* ANTONYM	ADJECTIVE ≠ *not* ANTONYM
closed	right
open	possible
false	bound
true	perfect
unofficial	empty
official	soaking wet
non-sober	torn
free	fertile
whole	lousy
sterile	dry
identical	full
different	
frozen	
defrosted	
sober	
dead	
alive	
impossible	
wrong	

significant differences between the conditions.[9] It also deserves to be mentioned that there was no significant difference between 'not lousy' and 'not perfect', and 'not dry' and 'not soaking wet', while 'not empty' and 'not full' differed significantly. The same results may also be presented in terms of the individual test items rather than the pairings as in Table 15.5.

The left column in Table 15.5 contains adjectives which obtained the same scores as their negated antonyms in terms of identity or lack of resistance of being laid out on a scale; that is, 'closed' was interpreted as being synonymous with 'not open', while the test items in the right columns do not—for example 'right' was not understood to be synonymous with 'not wrong'. In other words, the prediction that ADJECTIVE = *not* ANTONYM was borne out for the majority of the test items. That is, the nineteen test items in the left columns were interpreted as BOUNDED meanings. The eleven test items in the right columns, however, were not interpreted as BOUNDED meanings. On the contrary, the participants interpreted them as SCALAR meanings.

---

[9] As was mentioned before, for two of the test items in this experiment (none in Paradis and Willners 2006), 'not Y' preceded 'x': 'not official' received lower scores than 'unofficial', and the same was true of 'not open' and 'closed'. The differences were however not significant.

15.8.2   Modification by 'almost'

Our second prediction stated that the negation of BOUNDED adjectives would be different from modification by 'almost', that is, 'not dead' ≠ 'almost alive' and 'not alive' ≠ 'almost dead'. This prediction was not borne out. For all the test items taken together, there were no significant differences between 'not Y' and 'almost X', and 'almost Y' and 'not X'. This should be compared to the interpretations of UNBOUNDED meanings, which showed that 'not X' was judged to equal 'fairly Y': 'not narrow' = 'fairly wide' and 'not wide' = 'fairly narrow'. However, in the case of the UNBOUNDED meanings, the negated adjectives differed significantly from the bare adjectives, which was not the case for the BOUNDED antonyms.

15.8.3   Response times

Our final prediction stated that the response times for antonyms modified by the negator or by the degree modifier 'almost' would be longer than the response times for the bare antonyms. Part of the prediction was proven right in that there was a significant difference between the bare test items on the one hand and the test items with 'almost' and 'not' on the other. However, there was no significant difference between the test items modified by 'almost' or 'not'. The results for the response times in Paradis and Willners (2006: 1073) showed a similar pattern: the bare antonyms were judged faster than the antonyms modified by 'fairly', 'almost', which in turn were judged faster than the negated antonyms, but like in the present study only the differences between the bare test items and the negated ones were significant. These tendencies for response times have also been confirmed by Kaup and Zwaan (2003), MacDonald and Just (1989), Giora et al. (2005), Hasson and Glucksberg (2006), and Kaup et al. (2006). The response times for the adjectives negated by 'not' were also shown to be significantly longer than the morphologically negated antonyms, which is a result that may be interpreted to support Verhagen's (2005: 32–5) claim that sentential and morphological negation are functionally different. The longer response times in both these studies for negated antonyms may be explained by the necessity for the language user to construe both a factual and a counterfactual space (Langacker 1991; Fauconnier and Turner 2002; Verhagen 2005). This investigation examines the resulting interpretations only, and does not in any way attempt at explanations of reasoning or reasoning strategies.

15.8.4   Functional–communicative explanations for speaker interpretations

The results of Paradis and Willners (2006) and of the present investigation support an analysis of the negated meanings in terms of BOUNDEDNESS, which is a general type of configuration applicable to all kinds of meaning construals in language (Paradis 2001). It has a particularly clear effect on combinations of 'not' + adjectives and 'degree modifiers' + adjectives. In the case of UNBOUNDED meanings of adjectives, the role of the negator is to point up a range on a scale. The function of 'not' is to attenuate the force of the modified adjective in a similar way to that of the attenuating degree modifier 'fairly'. In combination with strongly BOUNDED antonymic meanings, on the other hand, the negator is interpreted in the same way as a logical operator in formal literalist approaches to meaning: expressing the absolute opposite p versus $\neg\ p$. However, on closer inspection, the results for the individual test items are not at all as robust and straightforward as the results for the UNBOUNDED meanings. There is quite a lot of variation across the individual test items.

There are at least three different types of functional–communicative explanations of conventionalized usage patterns for some of the BOUNDED–SCALAR asymmetries of the adjectival antonyms. Firstly, for the 'bound' – 'free' type, as in *The horse was not bound = The horse was free* but *The horse was not free ≠ The horse was bound*, the explanations for the participants' interpretations may be that a horse is 'not free' because it is in a field with a fence or it is in fact free when it is in a field because it is not tied to a pole, much in the same way as free-range chickens are free but fenced in. Secondly, there are BOUNDED meanings such as 'empty' – 'full', 'lousy' – 'perfect', 'dry' – 'soaking wet' that are absolutives but when they are opposed their configuration construal is one of a SCALE with two BOUNDED end points. Horn (1989: 242) says that '[t]wo expressions may denote the same objective reality but differ in terms of the conclusions they can be used to argue for; cf. *The glass is half empty* (→ we should fill it, or buy another) vs *The glass is half full* (→ we should, or can, empty it). This difference [. . .] is brought out on the scale reversal: a glass which is not half empty is more full than a glass that is not half full, since *not* here [. . .] equates "less than".' It has been empirically demonstrated by Holleman and Pander Maat (2009) that it is possible to create situations that promote different perspectives on 'emptiness' and 'fullness'. The third type of explanation concerns people's tendency to express themselves using hedged positive evaluative items for pairs such as 'wrong' – 'right' and 'impossible' – 'possible'. A plausible explanation for the judgments of 'right' and 'wrong' may be that speakers use the positive alternative for a more negative fact (Colston 1999; Holleman 2000). This is part of speakers' knowledge of the interpretations of subjective–evaluative words such as 'right' and 'wrong'. Speakers use 'not right' instead of 'wrong' to be less offensive. The same is true of 'impossible' = 'not possible', but 'possible' ≠ 'not impossible', in which case the double negative 'not impossible' expresses a cautious but optimistic attitude to the possibility of something.

In order to investigate the effect of double negation—not unofficial', 'not impossible'—a number of antonym pairs, each with one morphologically negated member, were included as test items in the present study: 'different' – 'identical', 'sober' – 'non-sober', 'unofficial' – 'official', 'impossible' – 'possible'.[10] This analysis provides preliminary evidence for further analysis of double negation. The result of the present investigation shows that the four morphologically negated antonyms are not members of the same subtypes of negated antonyms: 'different' – 'identical', 'sober' – 'non-sober', 'unofficial' – 'official' all behave as predicted for BOUNDED antonyms, that is, neither is 'x' $\neq$ 'not y' nor is 'y' $\neq$ 'not x', while that is not the case for 'impossible' – 'possible' whose patterning is: 'x' = 'not y' but 'y' $\neq$ 'not x', that is, 'impossible' = 'not possible' but 'possible' $\neq$ 'not impossible'. The former three doubly negated antonymic adjectives were interpreted in the same way as most of the BOUNDED adjectives, but 'impossible' was not. We interpret this as an indication of functional differences in language use between 'impossible' and the other morphologically negated adjectives.

Strictly speaking, it is correct to say that the expressions *it is possible* and *it is not impossible* entail one another. However, as has been shown in many of the studies mentioned in this chapter, 'x' and 'not y' are not functional equivalents in language use. There are various socio-cognitive and communicative reasons why we use *not impossible* instead of *possible* in communication. *Not impossible* invites further discussion than the more definite *possible* both in Swedish and English and is vaguer and lower in speaker commitment. The use of *not impossible* can be compared to the use of *not bad* instead of *good* in response to *How are you? Not bad* is vaguer and invites further small talk compared with the more definite *good*, and the use of understatement is a conventionalized way of responding to questions that concern health and state of mind. There are ample examples in natural conversation where negation is not employed to discard the affirmation, but has totally different functions. Consider examples (3)[11] and (4):

(3) A time for tea # would you like some#
     B yes# yes#
     A thanks for your invitation you throwing a party#
     B yes# ... well#
     A that's good#
     B I don't know# I don't know whether I drink coffee or tea at this time of
        day# if there were any tea

                                                           (S.1.4 – TUs 7–18)

---

[10] Note that in Swedish one of the members is morphologically negated by *o-* or *in-* as in *olika, onyktra, inofficiell,* and *omöjlig* (see Table 15.1).

[11] The example is from the London–Lund Corpus of English Conversation. These texts are also available in print in Svartvik and Quirk (1980). S.1.4. is the text identification, TU is the tone unit identification. For information about the London Lund Corpus, see Greenbaum and Svartvik (1990) and http://khnt .hit.uib.no/icame/manuals/LONDLUND/INDEX.HTM.

(4)   Garth   No way, Wayne
       Wayne   Way, Garth

(Giora 2006)

In (3), the negated sequence serves to soften the decline of the offer and *I know* is not the corresponding affirmative opposite (Tottie and Paradis 1982). Similarly, in (4), there is not a conventionalized opposite for the function of *no way* that is just *way*. It is however possible to derive an opposite for effect. The differences in function of a large number of negated expressions are not derived or functionally related to their affirmative equivalents. For instance, the opposite of *I don't give a shit* is not *I give a shit* (Giora et al. 2007), the opposite of *don't worry!* is not *worry!* (Stefanowich and Gries 2003) and the function of *not to mention...* is not *to mention* but has the function of introducing an explicit list of all that is advisable for the addressee to note rather than to ignore, and its function is one of reinforcement (Giora et al. 2007). It is commonly considered that negation is derived from affirmation: that the default is that a negated meaning presupposes an affirmative counterpart. It should be clear from the above examples that this is far from always the case.

This also raises a question about another difference between morphological negation and sentential negation. As already mentioned, Verhagen (2005: 31–2) argues that there is an important difference between sentential negation and morphological negation, in that the former opens up two mental spaces while the latter does not. This claim can be taken to be supported by the longer response times for negated antonyms in Paradis and Willners (2006) and in the present study. Antonyms formed by a negating prefix such as the ones included in this study do not invoke a counterfactual construal of the consider-and-abandon type. Unlike Horn (1989: 304), who seeks the answer to the puzzle about double negation in Gricean pragmatic principles, Verhagen (2005: 70–7) seeks the answer to the question of why the double-negation constructions are not redundant in the specific properties of sentential negation as the configurational construal of two mental spaces and two distinct epistemic stances to the same idea. He argues that the function of sentential negation is to invalidate inferences through a consider-and-abandon process of contrasting mental spaces rather than invalidating the idea itself. Verhagen presents a thought-provoking analysis of sentential negation as coordination at the intersubjective level, while the primary dimension for morphological negation (and antonyms based on different roots) is at the objective level (Verhagen 2005: 76).

Our model of meaning accords with Verhagen (2005: 22) in that linguistic expressions are primarily cues for making inferences, and understanding is not primarily a process of decoding and decomposing the exact content of expressions. Much more important is inference-making that promotes adequate reasoning and communicative behaviour. Like Verhagen, we argue that this approach to meaning in language frees the expressions from being completely conventionally fixed. In fact, like quite a few other scholars (e.g. Cruse 2002; Traugott and Dasher 2005), we argue that meanings are negotiated in context. Lexical meanings do not 'have' meanings, but function as triggers of meaning that evoke the relevant portions of conceptual structure that support the implicational purposes and the inferential reasoning by speakers and addressees in the communicative situation (Paradis 2005, 2008a).

15.9   Conclusion

This study set out to extend Paradis' and Willners' (2006) study and synthesize the results of the present study with their findings in order to be able to present a more comprehensive and reliable analysis of language users' interpretations of negation in the context of UNBOUNDED (SCALAR) and BOUNDED antonymic meanings and in relation to moderating 'fairly' and approximating 'almost'. The same two questions were posed in both studies: (i) Is 'x' the same as 'not y', and vice versa? and (ii) Is 'not x' the same as 'fairly/almost y', and vice versa?, and the conclusions are drawn on the basis of the findings in both studies.

First, the results for the UNBOUNDED antonyms were very robust, showing that 'x' is not the same as 'not y' and vice versa, that is, 'short' was not judged to be synonymous with 'not long' and 'long' was not synonymous with 'not short' (Paradis and Willners 2006). In the case of the BOUNDED antonyms, a more complex scenario emerged. For most of the antonyms 'x' was interpreted as 'not y' and 'y' as 'not x': 'dead' and 'not alive' were judged to be synonyms and so were 'alive' and 'not dead'. Yet, a fair number of the BOUNDED antonymic test items were laid out on a scale and interpreted in the same way as the test items in the UNBOUNDED test set. With focus on the test items as antonym pairings, three different types of pairs emerged from the experiments: (i) x = not y : y = not x; (ii) x = not y : y ≠ not x or x ≠ not y : y = not x; and (iii) x ≠ not y : y ≠ not x.[12]

Second, 'not' in combination with antonymic adjectives is a degree modifier of scalarity or totality depending on the configuration construal of the modified adjectival meaning. Just like *quite*, it can perform both these functions. The result for the UNBOUNDED test set in Paradis and Willners (2006) revealed no significant difference between the antonymic adjectives modified by 'not' or by 'fairly'. This means that the function of negation in combination with UNBOUNDED meanings is to moderate the grading force of the adjectival meaning with the same force as 'fairly'. The interpretations of the negator and 'almost' in the context of the BOUNDED meanings do not differ significantly either. There is, however, a difference between the two meaning types in that the negated antonyms equal the bare antonyms in the BOUNDED set, which is not the case for the

---

[12] This division of dimensional meanings into one UNBOUNDED type and three BOUNDED types has recently been shown to hold in Bianchi et al. (2011).

UNBOUNDED meanings, and, more importantly, the BOUNDED results are not as reliable as the UNBOUNDED ones because of the combinatorial infelicities for some of the BOUNDED test items due to the polarity effect of 'almost'.

On a more general note, we have given evidence that indicates that interpretations of linguistic expressions on all occurrences of use are shaped both by competing constraints and constraints working in unison. Interpretations are shaped by the human cognitive system of conceptual representations and cognitive processes, as modelled in Section 15.3, by the nature of reality, by their pragmatic function in a particular context and by conventionalization in language. The strength and the stability of these constraints vary across uses. It was shown that the interpretations of negated adjectival meanings are sensitive to whether these meanings are based on BOUNDED or UNBOUNDED configuration construals and that negation operates differently on those structures in conceptual SPACE.

The results also highlight the flexibility of language in use and the varying strength and stability of the constraints as revealed by the participants' willingness to interpret some of the negated test items in the BOUNDED test set as partial meanings, which we interpret as an indication of there being competing constraints. For instance, contextual constraints compete with conceptual constraints when participants choose to view 'not perfect' as closer to 'perfect' than to 'lousy', or conventional constraints such as the possible preference for 'not impossible' over 'possible' in language use. It was also shown through the response times that it takes longer to judge negated sentences than non-negated sentences. Moreover, judgments of sentences with negator and adjective, for example 'not official', 'not possible', 'not sober', took longer to judge than morphological negation such as 'unofficial' and 'impossible'. Yet, in order to be able to draw any strong conclusions based on response times, more sophisticated methods using strict time control are needed. The strength and the stability of the judgments of the individual test items varied both at the level of configurational types in that all the test items in the UNBOUNDED test set were judged in the same way, while the test items in the BOUNDED test set fell into three subtypes.

Finally, meaning differences such as the ones evoked by the combination of opposite meanings expressed through lexicalized antonyms as well as negated antonyms can best be explained through a comprehensive model of meaning which takes language users' constructs of meanings seriously, in preference to ill-founded assumptions about the appropriateness of the notion of literalness. Our model has the advantage of being capable of explaining meaning flexibility. Alternating readings of lexical items are formed in context through configuration construals of contentful meanings in conceptual SPACE. In the context of gradable adjectives, this means that on the occurrence of use, meanings may be construed on the basis of scales and/or boundaries due to the contextual requirements that form the current readings. Contextual readings are construed on the basis of the relevant portion of the meaning potential of the lexical items shaped by context, conventionalization, and communicational demands. The negator does not have two meanings or two functions, one literal and one non-literal. It gives rise to different readings in combination with UNBOUNDED meaning structures and BOUNDED meaning structures. The negator is best seen as a pragmatically motivated configuration construal of a SPACE structure, whose differences cannot simply be explained away as 'marked' vs 'un-marked' or 'default' vs 'non-default', but have clear repercussions on meaning modelling, with the consequence that a definite boundary between semantics and pragmatics cannot be maintained in any strict sense.

Appendix: The Test Sentences

Statements	Questions
Påståendet från politikern var falskt/sant.	*Hur pålitligt var det?*
'The statement from the politician was false/true.'	'How trustworthy was it?'
Gardinerna i fönstren var olika/likadana.	*Hur väl överensstämde gardinerna?*
'The curtains in the windows were different/identical.'	'How well did the curtains match?'
Passagerarna i Volvon var nyktra/onyktra.	*Hur alkoholpåverkade var de?*
'The passengers in the Volvo were sober/non-sober.'	'How alcohol-affected were they?'
Svaren på mattetentan var urusla/perfekta.	*Hur var standarden på svaren?*
'The answers in the maths exam were lousy/perfect.'	'What was the standard of the answers?'
Byxorna på stolen var trasiga/hela.	*I vilket skick var byxorna?*
'The trousers on the chair were torn/whole.'	'In what condition were the trousers?'
Dörren till köket var stängd/öppen	*Hur var dörröppningen?*
'The door to the kitchen was closed/open.'	'How was the gap?'
Diskussionen om ordförandens avgång var inofficiell/officiell.	*Hur känd var diskussionen?*
'The discussion about the chairperson's resignation was unofficial/official.'	'How open was the discussion?'
Köpet av bilen var omöjligt/möjligt.	*Hur tänkbart var köpet?*
'The purchase of the car was impossible/possible.'	'How likely was the purchase?'
Handduken på strecket var torr/genomblöt.	*Hur mycket vatten var det i handduken?*
'The towel on the clothes line was dry/soaking wet.'	'How much water was there in the towel?'
Sockerkakan på diskbänken var frusen/upptinad.	*Hur var kakan?*
'The sponge cake on the counter was frozen/defrosted.'	'How was the cake?'

References

Alexander, R. M. (1989). *Dynamics of Dinosaurs and Other Extinct Giants*. New York: Columbia University Press.

Alexander, R. M. (1996). *Optima for Animals*. Princeton: Princeton University Press.

Alibali, M. W., Heath, D. C., and Myers, H. J. (2001). 'Effects of visibility between speaker and listener on gesture production: some gestures are meant to be seen'. *Journal of Memory and Language*, 44, 169–88.

Allwood, J. (1976). *Linguistic Communication as Action and Cooperation*. (Gothenburg Monographs in Linguistics 2). Göteborg University, Department of Linguistics.

Allwood, J. (2001a). *Dialog Coding – Function and Grammar*. Gothenburg Papers in Theoretical Linguistics, 85. Göteborg University, Department of Linguistics.

Allwood, J. (2001b). 'The Structure of Dialog'. In M. Taylor, D. Bouwhuis, and F. Nel (eds), *The Structure of Multimodal Dialogue II*. Amsterdam: John Benjamins, 3–24.

Allwood, J. (2003). 'Meaning potentials and context: some consequences for the analysis of variation in meaning'. In Hubert Cuyckens, René Dirven, and John Taylor (eds), *Cognitive Approaches to Lexical Semantics*. Berlin: Mouton de Gruyter, 29–65.

Allwood, J., Cerrato, L., Jokinen, K., Navarretta, C., and Paggio, P. (2007). 'The MUMIN Coding Scheme for the Annotation of Feedback, Turn Management and Sequencing Phenomena'. In J. C. Martin, P. Paggio, P. Kuenlein, R. Stiefelhagen, and F. Pianesi (eds), *Multimodal Corpora for Modelling Human Multimodal Behaviour*. Special issue of the *International Journal of Language Resources and Evaluation*, 41(3–4), 273–87. Springer. SpringerLink Online: http://www.springerlink.com/content/x77r37881706/?p=8ce2b63b499242b5a926ac1bb2f78ed6andpi=1

Altmann, H. (2011). *Prüfungswissen Wortbildung*. Göttingen: Vandenhoeck and Ruprecht.

Andreichin, L. [et al]. (2004). *Bulgarski tulkoven rechnik* (Dictionary of the Bulgarian Language), 4th edn. Sofia: Nauka i Izkustvo.

Ashley, A. and Carlson, L. A. (2007). 'Encoding direction when interpreting proximal terms'. *Language and Cognitive Processes*, 22(7), 1021–44.

Aske, J. (1989). 'Path predicates in English and Spanish: a closer look'. In K. Hall, M. Meacham, and R. Shapiro (eds), *Proceedings of the Fifteenth Annual Meeting of the Berkeley Linguistics Society*. Berkeley, CA: Berkeley Linguistics Society, 1–14.

Ballard, H. D., Hayhoe, M., Pook, P. K., and Rao, R. P. (1997). 'Deictic codes for the embodiment of cognition'. *Behavioral Brain Sciences*, 20, 723–67.

Bally, C. (1965). *Linguistique générale et linguistique francaise*, 4th edn. Bern: Franke.

Bamberg, M. (1994). 'Development of linguistic forms: German'. In R. Berman and D. I. Slobin (eds), *Relating events in Narrative: a Cross-linguistic Development Study*. Hillsdale, NJ: Erlbaum, 189–284.

Banville, J. (2005). *The Sea*. London: Picador.

Barlow, M. and Kemmer, S. (2000). *Usage-based Models of Grammar*. Stanford, CA.: CSLI Publications.

Barner, D. and Snedeker, J. (2008). 'Compositionality and statistics in adjective acquisition: 4 year olds interpret tall and short based on the size distributions of novel noun referents'. *Child Development*, 4, 747–52.

Barsalou, L. W. (1999). 'Perceptual symbol systems'. *Behavioral and Brain Sciences*, 22, 577–660.

Bartlett, E. J. (1976). 'Sizing things up: the acquisition of the meaning of dimensional adjectives'. *Journal of Child Language*, 3, 205–19.

Bates, E. (1976). *Language and Context: the Acquisition of Pragmatics*. New York: Academic Press.

Bates, E., Camaioni, L., and Volterra, V. (1975). 'The acquisition of performatives prior to speech'. *Merrill-Palmer Quarterly*, 21, 205–24.

Bavelas, J. B., Chovil, N., Lawrie, D. A., and Wade, A. (1992). 'Interactive Gestures'. *Discourse Processes*, 15, 469–89.

Bavelas, J. B., Gerwing, J., Sutton, C., and Prevost, D. (2008). 'Gesturing on the telephone: independent effects of dialogue and visibility'. *Journal of Memory and Language*, 58, 495–520.

Beattie, G. and Shovelton, H. (2006). 'When size really matters: how a single semantic feature is represented in the speech and gesture modalities'. *Gesture*, 6(1), 63–84.

Beavers, J., Levin, B., and Shiao Wei, T. (2010). 'The typology of motion expressions revisited'. *Journal of Linguistics*, 46, 331–77.

Bejan, A. and Marden, J. (2006). 'Unifying constructal theory for scale effects in running, swimming and flying'. *The Journal of Experimental Biology*, 209, 238–48.

Benveniste, É. (1966). *Problèmes de linguistique générale*. Paris: Gallimard.

Berman, R. A. and Slobin, D. I. (eds) (1994). *Different Ways of Relating Events in Narrative: a Crosslinguistic Developmental Study*. Hillsdale, NJ: Erlbaum.

Berndt, R. S. and Caramazza, A. (1978). 'The development of vague modifiers in the language of pre-school children'. *Journal of Child Language*, 5(2), 279–94.

Bertel, S. (2007). 'Towards attention-guided human–computer collaborative reasoning for spatial configuration and design'. In D. D. Schmorrow and L. M. Reeves (eds), *Augmented Cognition*, HCII 2007, LNAI 4565, 337–45.

Bertel, S., Barkowsky, T., Engel, D., and Freksa, C. (2006). 'Computational modeling of reasoning with mental images: basic requirements'. In Danilo Fum, Fabio del Missier, and Andrea Stocco (eds), *Proceedings of the 7th International Conference on Cognitive Modeling*, ICCM, Trieste, 2006. Trieste: Edizioni Goliardiche, 50–5.

Berthele, R. (2004). 'The typology of motion and posture verbs: a variationist account'. In B. Kortmann (ed.), *Dialectology Meets Typology: Dialect Grammar from a Cross-linguistic Perspective*. Berlin: Walter de Gruyter, 93–126.

Blanchi, I., Sarardi, U., and Kubory, M. (2011). 'Dimensions and their poles: a metric and topological approach to opposites'. *Language and Cognitive Processes*, 26(8), 1232–65.

Blaser, E, and Sperling, G. (2008). 'When is motion "motion"?' *Perception*, 37(4), 624–7.

Bloomfield, L. (1933). *Language*. New York: Holt, Rinehart and Winston.

Boas, H. (2003). *A Constructional Approach to Resultatives*. Stanford, CA: CSLI Publications.

Bohnemeyer, J., Enfield, N. J., Essegbey, J., Ibarretxe-Antuñano, I., Kita, S., Lüpke, F., and Ameka, F. K. (2007). 'Principles of event segmentation in language: the case of motion events'. *Language*, 83(3), 495–532.

Bokmål and Nynorsk Dictionary online (http://www.dokpro.uio.no/ordboksoek.html)

Bol, G. W. (1995). 'Implicational scaling in child language acquisition: the order of production of Dutch verb constructions'. In M. Verrips and F. Wijnen (eds), *Papers from The Dutch–German Colloquium on Language Acquisition*. Amsterdam: Institute for General Linguistics, 1–13.

Boroditsky, L. and Ramscar, M. (2002). 'The roles of body and mind in abstract thought'. *Psychological Science*, 13, 185–9.

Borst, Alexander. (2000). 'Models of motion detection'. *Nature Neuroscience*, 3, 1168.

Bourdieu, P. (1980). *Le sens pratique*. Paris: Les Éditions de Minuit.

Bowerman, M. (1996). 'The origins of children's spatial semantic categories: cognitive versus linguistic determinants'. In J. J. Gumperz and S. C. Levinson (eds), *Rethinking Linguistic Relativity*. Cambridge: Cambridge University Press, 145–76.

Bowerman, M. (2007). 'Containment, support, and beyond: constructing topological spatial categories in first language acquisition'. In M. Aurnague, M. Hickmann, and L. Vieu (eds), *Spatial Entities in Language and Cognition*. Amsterdam/Philadelphia: John Benjamins, 177–203.

Bowerman, M. and Choi, S. (2001). 'Shaping meanings for language: universal and language-specific in the acquisition of spatial semantic categories'. In M. Bowerman and S. C. Levinson (eds), *Language Acquisition and Conceptual Development*. Cambridge: Cambridge University Press, 475–511.

Bowerman, M. and Choi, S. (2003). 'Space under construction: language-specific categorization in first language acquisition'. In D. Gentner and S. Goldin-Meadow (eds), *Language in Mind: Advances in the Study of Language and Thought*. Cambridge, MA: MIT Press, 387–427.

Boye, K. (2001). 'The force-dynamic core meaning of Danish modal verbs'. *Acta Linguistica Hafniensia*, 33, 19–66.

Boye, K. and Harder, P. (2007). 'Complement-taking predicates. Usage and linguistic structure'. *Studies in Language*, 31(3), 569–606.

Brandt, S. A. and Stark, L. W. (1997). 'Spontaneous eye movements during visual imagery reflect the content of the visual scene'. *Journal of Cognitive Neuroscience*, 9, 27–38.

Brewer, W. and Stone, J. B. (1975). 'Acquisition of spatial antonym pairs'. *Journal of Experimental Child Psychology*, 19, 299–307.

Brinck, I. (2001). 'Attention and the evolution of intentional communication'. *Pragmatics and Cognition*, 9(2), 255–72.

Brinck, I. (2004a). 'The pragmatics of imperative and declarative pointing'. *Cognitive Science Quarterly*, 3(4), 429–46.

Brinck, I. (2004b). 'Joint attention, triangulation and radical interpretation: a problem and its solution'. *Dialectica*, 58(2), 179–205.

Brinck, I. (2008). 'The role of intersubjectivity for the development of intentional communication'. In J. Zlatev, T. Racine, C. Sinha, and E. Itkonen (eds), *The Shared Mind: Perspectives on Intersubjectivity*. Amsterdam: John Benjamins, 115–140.

Brinck, I. and Gärdenfors, P. (2003). 'Co-operation and communication in apes and humans'. *Mind and Language*, 18, 484–501.

Brown, A. and Gullberg, M. (2008). 'Bidirectional crosslinguistic influence in L1-L2 encoding of manner in speech and gesture'. *Studies in Second Language Acquisition*, 30, 225–51.

Brown, L. (ed.) (1993). *The Shorter Oxford English Dictionary on Historical Principles*, 4th edn. Oxford: Clarendon Press.

Buchstaller, I. and Traugott E. (2006). 'The lady was al demonyak: historical aspects of adverb *all*'. *English Language and Linguistics*, 10(2), 345–70.

Bühler, K. (1982). *Sprachtheorie: Die Darstellungsfunktion der Sprache*. Stuttgart: Fischer.

Bühler, K. (1990) [1934]. *Theory of Language. The Representational Function of Language.* (Foundations of Semiotics 25). D. F. Goodwin (trans.). Amsterdam: John Benjamins.

Butterworth, B. and Hadar, U. (1989). 'Gesture, speech, and computational stages: a reply to McNeill'. *Psychological Review*, 96(1), 168–74.

Butterworth, G. and Jarret, N. L. M. (1991). 'What minds share in common is space: spatial mechanisms serving joint visual attention in infancy'. *British Journal of Developmental Psychology*, 9, 55–72.

Bybee, J. L. (1995). 'Regular morphology and the lexicon'. *Language and Cognitive Processes*, 10, 425–55.

Callies, M. and Szczesniak, K. (2008). 'Europa meisterschaft zu erdribbeln. Manner of obtainment constructions in sports reporting'. In E. Lavric, G. Pisek, A. Skinner, and W. Stadler (eds), *The Linguistics of Football*. (Language in Performance 38). Tübingen: Narr, 23–34.

Cambridge Advanced Learner's Dictionary (http://dictionary.cambridge.org/)

Carey, S. (1978). 'The child as word learner'. In M. Halle, J. Bresnan, and G. A. Miller (eds), *Linguistic Theory and Psychological Reality*. Cambridge, MA and London: MIT Press, 264–93.

Carroll, M. and Becker, A. (1993). 'Reference to space in learner varieties'. In C. Perdue (ed.), *Adult Language Acquisition: Cross-linguistic Perspectives. Vol. II: the Results.* Cambridge: Cambridge University Press, 119–49.

Cassell, J., McNeill, D., and McCullough, K.-E. (1999). 'Speech-gesture mismatches: evidence for one underlying representation of linguistic and nonlinguistic information'. *Pragmatics and Cognition*, 7(1), 1–33.

Chafe, W. (1994). *Discourse, Consciousness, and Time. The Flow and Displacement of Conscious Experience in Speaking and Writing.* Chicago, IL: University of Chicago Press.

Chan, T. T. and Bergen, B. (2005). 'Writing direction influences spatial cognition'. In *Proceedings of the Twenty-Seventh Annual Conference of the Cognitive Science Society.* Mahwah, NJ: Erlbaw, 412–17.

Choi, S. and Bowerman, M. (1991). 'Learning to express motion events in English and Korean: the influence of language-specific lexicalization patterns'. *Cognition*, 41, 83–121.

Chomsky, N. P. (1981). *Lectures on Government and Binding*. Dordrecht: Foris.

Cifuentes Férez, (2007). 'Human locomotion verbs in English and Spanish'. *International Journal of English Studies*, 7(1), 117–36.

Clark, E. V. (1972). 'Some perceptual factors in the acquisition of locative terms by young children'. *Proceedings of the Chicago Linguistic Society*, 8, 431–9.

Clark, E. V. (1973a). 'Nonlinguistic strategies and the acquisition of word meanings'. *Cognition*, 1, 161–82.

Clark, E. V. (1973b). 'What's in a word? On the child's acquisition of semantics in his first language'. In T. E. Moore (ed.), *Cognitive Development and the Acquisition of Language.* New York and London: Academic Press, 65–110.

Clark, E. V. (1980). 'Here's the top: nonlinguistic strategies in the acquisition of orientational terms'. *Child Development*, 51, 329–38.

Clark, E. V. (2001). 'Emergent categories in first language acquisition'. In M. Bowerman and S. Levinson (eds), *Language Acquisition and Conceptual Development*. Cambridge: Cambridge University Press, 379–405.

Clark, H. H. (1970). 'The primitive nature of children's relational concepts'. In J. R. Hayes (ed.), *Cognition and the Development of Language*. New York, etc.: John Wiley, 269–77.

Clark, H. H. (1973). 'Space, time, semantics and the child'. In T. E. Moore (ed.), *Cognitive Development and the Acquisition of Language*. New York: Academic Press, 27–63.

Clark, H. H. (1996). *Using Language*. Cambridge: Cambridge University Press.

Cohen, A. A. and Harrison, R. P. (1973). 'Intentionality in the use of hand illustrators in face-to-face communication situations'. *Journal of Personality and Social Psychology*, 28, 276–9.

Coley, J. D. and Gelman, S. A. (1989). 'The effects of object orientation and object type on children's interpretation of the word *big*'. *Child Development*, 60, 372–80.

Colston, H. (1999). '"Not good" is "bad" but "not bad" is not "good": an analysis of three accounts of negation asymmetries'. *Discourse Processes*, 28, 237–56.

Coventry, K., Greer, J., Smailles, D., Vulchanova, M., Eshuis, R., and Bester, A. (in preparation). 'Fat runners and tall walkers: object form affects descriptions of object motion'.

Cox, M. V. and Ryder Richardson, J. (1985). 'How do children describe spatial relationships?' *Journal of Child Language*, 12, 611–20.

Croft, W. (2001). *Radical Construction Grammar*. Oxford: Oxford University Press.

Croft, W. (2003). 'Lexical rules vs. constructions: a false dichotomy'. In H. Cuyckens, T. Berg, R. Dirven, and K.-U. Panther (eds), *Motivations in Language*. Amsterdam/New York: John Benjamins, 49–68.

Croft, W. and Cruse, A. (2004). *Cognitive Linguistics*. Cambridge and New York: Cambridge University Press.

Croft, W., Barðdal, J., Hollmann, W., Sotirova, V., and Taoka, C. (2010). 'Revising Talmy's typological classification of complex event constructions'. In H. Boas (ed.), *Contrastive Studies in Construction Grammar*. Amsterdam and New York: John Benjamins, 201–36.

Cruse, A. (2002). 'The construal of sense boundaries'. *Revue de sémantique et pragmatique*, 12, 101–19.

Cruse, A. and Togia, P. (1996). 'Towards a cognitive model of antonymy'. *Journal of Lexicology*, 1, 113–41.

Crystal, D. and Davy, D. (1969). *Investigating English Style*. London: Longmans.

D'Entremont, B. (2000). 'A perceptual–attentional explanation of gaze following in 3 and 6 month olds'. *Developmental Science*, 3, 302–11.

Dąbrowska, E. (2004). *Language, Mind, and Brain: Some Psychological and Neurological Constraints on Theories of Grammar*. Edinburgh: Edinburgh University Press.

Dąbrowska, E. and Lieven, E. (2005). 'Developing question constructions: lexical specificity and usage-based operations'. *Cognitive Linguistics*, 16, 437–74.

Daems, F. (1977). 'Markeringstheorie: Een empirisch onderzoek bij tweeënhalf- en vijfjarige kinderen'. In M. Spoelders (ed.), *Pedagogische Psycholinguïstiek*. Gent: Rijksuniversiteit Gent, 101–18.

Damasio, A. (1994). *Descartes' Error: Emotion Reason, and the Human Brain*. New York: Grosset/G. P. Putnam's Sons.

Damasio, A. (1999). *The Feeling of What Happens: Body and Emotion in the Making of Consciousness*. New York etc.: Harcourt Brace.

de Ruiter, J. P. (2000). 'The production of gesture and speech'. In D. McNeill (ed.), *Language and Gesture*. Cambridge: Cambridge University Press, 284–311.

de'Sperati, C. (2003). 'Precise oculomotor correlates of visuo-spatial mental rotation and circular motion imagery'. *Journal of Cognitive Neuroscience*, 15, 1244–59.

Deignan, Alice (2005) *Metaphor and Corpus Linguistics*. Amsterdam and Philadelphia: John Benjamins.

Demarais, A. and Cohen, B. H. (1998). 'Evidence for image-scanning eye movements during transitive inference'. *Biological Psychology*, 49, 229–47.

Den Danske Ordbog (The Danish Dictionary), Vol. I–VI (2003–5). Copenhagen: The Danish Society for Language and Literature and Gyldendal.

Dimitrova-Vulchanova, M. (1996/99). *Verb Semantics, Diathesis and Aspect*. München and Newcastle: Lincom.

Dimitrova-Vulchanova, M. (2004a). 'Verbs of motion and their conceptual structure'. Motion Encoding Workshop, Åbo Akademi, Turku.

Dimitrova-Vulchanova, M. (2004b). 'Paths in Verbs of Motion'. Invited talk at Argument Structure CASTL Conference, Tromsø University, 4–6 November 2004.

Dimitrova-Vulchanova, M. and Dąbrowska, E. (in preparation). 'Motion encoding across languages'.

Dimitrova-Vulchanova, M. and Martinez, L. (in preparation). 'Motion naming in Atcan: a serial lexicalization pattern'. Ms., NTNU (Norwegian University of Science and Technology).

Dimitrova-Vulchanova, M. and van der Zee, E. (in preparation). 'Run, walk, and crawl: a forced-choice motion experiment'.

Dimitrova-Vulchanova, M. and Weisgerber, M. (2007). 'Integrating context in semantic representation'. SKY Symposium, Tampere 2007.

Dirven, R. and Taylor, J. (1988). 'The conceptualisation of vertical space in English: the case of tall'. In B. Rudzka-Ostyn (ed.), *Topics in Cognitive Linguistics*. Amsterdam and Philadelphia: John Benjamins, 379–402.

Dodge, E. and Lakoff, G. (2005). 'Image Schemas: from linguistic analysis to neural grounding'. In Beate Hampe (ed.), *From Perception to Meaning: Image Schemas in Cognitive Linguistics*. Berlin: Mouton de Gruyter, 57–91.

Donaldson, M. and Wales, R. (1970). 'On the acquisition of some relational terms'. In J. Hayes (ed.), *Cognition and the Development of Language*. New York: Wiley, 235–68.

Dörnyei, Z. and Scott, M. L. (2001). 'Communication strategies in a second language: definitions and taxonomies'. *Language Learning*, 47 (1), 173–210.

Dowty, D. (1979). *Word Meaning and Montague Grammar: the Semantics of Verbs and Times in Generative Semantics and Montague's PTQ*. (Synthese Language Library 7). Dordrecht: Reidel.

Dressler, W. U. and Merlini Barbaresi, L. (1994). *Morphopragmatics. Diminutives and Intensifiers in Italian, German, and Other languages*. Berlin: Mouton de Gruyter.

Durst-Andersen, P. (1992). *Mental Grammar. Russian Aspect and Related Issues*. Columbus, Ohio: Slavica.

Durst-Andersen, P. (1997). 'De russiske bevægelsesverbers leksikalske og grammatiske struktur'. *Svantevit*, 19, 25–48.

Durst-Andersen, P. (2000). 'The English progressive as picture description'. *Acta Linguistica Hafniensia*, 32, 45–103.

Durst-Andersen, P. (2002). 'Russian and English as two distinct subtypes of accusative languages'. *Scando-Slavica*, 48, 103–26.

Durst-Andersen, P. (2006). 'Location in Danish as opposed to English and Russian'. In H. Nølke, I. Baron, H. Korzen, I Kori and H.H. Müller (eds), *Grammatica. Festschrift in Honour of Michael Herslund*. Bern: Peter Lang, 69–84.

Durst-Andersen, P. (2008a). 'The two aspectual systems of French'. In M. Birkelund, M-B. Mosegaard Hansen, and C. Norén (eds), *L'énonciation dans tous ses états: mélanges offerts à Henning Nølke à l'occasion de ses soixante ans*. Bern: Peter Lang, 473–94.

Durst-Andersen, P. (2008b). 'Linguistics as semiotics. Saussure and Bühler revisited'. *Signs*, 2, 1–29.

Durst-Andersen, P. (2011). *Linguistic Supertypes. A Cognitive-semiotic Theory of Human Communication*. Berlin/New York: De Gruyter Mouton.

Durst-Andersen, P. and Herslund, M. (1996). 'The syntax of Danish verbs'. In E. Engberg-Pedersen, M. Fortescue, P. Harder, L. Heltoft, and L. F. Jakobsen (eds), *Content, Expression and Structure. Studies in Danish Functional Grammar*. Amsterdam and Philadelphia: John Benjamins, 65–102.

Durst-Andersen, P. and Nedergaard Thomsen, O. (to appear). 'The social contract-making function of language. Evidence from gesture, child language, and adult communication'.

Ebeling, K. S. and Gelman, S. A. (1994). 'Children's use of context in interpreting "big" and "little"'. *Child Development*, 65, 1178–92.

Efron, D. (1972). *Gesture, Race and Culture*. Paris and the Hague: Mouton (Originally published in 1941 as *Gesture and Environment*. New York: King's Crown Press).

Ehri, L. C. (1976). 'Comprehension and production of adjectives and seriation'. *Journal of Child Language*, 3, 369–84.

Eilers, R. E., Oller, D. K., and Ellington, J. (1974). 'The acquisition of word-meaning for dimensional adjectives: the long and short of it'. *Journal of Child Language*, 1, 195–204.

Ekberg, L. (2007) 'Språket hos ungdomar i en flerspråkig miljö i Malmö'. *Nordlund*, 27.

Ekman, P. and Friesen, W. V. (1969). 'The repertoire of nonverbal behavior: categories, origins, usage, and coding'. *Semiotica*, 1, 49–97.

Emmorey, K. and Casey S. (2001). 'Gesture, thought and spatial language'. *Gesture*, 1(1), 35–50.

Engel, D., Bertel S., and Barkowsky T. (2005). 'Spatial principles in control of focus in reasoning with mental representations, images, and diagrams'. *Spatial Cognition*, 4, 181–203.

Falck-Ytter, T., Gredebäck. G. and von Hofsten, C. (2006). 'Infants predict other people's action goals'. *Nature Neuroscience*, 9, 878–9.

Falk, H. and Torp, A. (1900). *Dansk-Norskens Syntax*. Kristiania: Aschehoug.

Fauconnier, G. and Turner, M. (2002). *The Way We Think*. New York: Basic Books.

Ferreira, F., Apel, A., and Henderson, J. M. (2008). 'Taking a new look at looking at nothing'. *Trends in Cognitive Science*, 12(11), 405–10.

Feyereisen, P. (1991). 'Communicative behavior in aphasia'. *Aphasiology*, 5, 323–33.

Feyereisen, P. and de Lannoy, J.-D. (1991). *Gestures and Speech: Psychological Investigations*. Cambridge and Paris: Cambridge University Press, Éditions de la Maison des Sciences de l'Homme.

Feyereisen, P., Barter, M., Goossens, M., and Clerebaut, N. (1988). 'Gestures and speech in referential communication by aphasic subjects: channel use and efficiency'. *Aphasiology*, 2, 21–32.

Fillmore, C. J. (1971). 'Toward a theory of deixis'. Paper read at Pacific Conference on Contrastive Linguistics and Language Universals, January 1971, University of Hawaii. Mimeographed.

Finke, R. A. (1989). *Principles of Mental Imagery*. Cambridge, MA: MIT Press.

Foley, W. A. and Van Valin, Jr., R. D. (1984). *Functional Syntax and Universal Grammar*. Cambridge: Cambridge University Press.

Foote, I. (1967). 'Verbs of Motion'. In D. Ward (ed.), *Studies in the Modern Russian Language*. Cambridge: Cambridge University Press, 4–33.

Freksa, C. and Bertel, S. (2007). 'Eye movements and smart technology'. *Computers in Biology and Medicine*, 37, 983–8.

Frisson, S. and Pickering, M. (1999). 'The processing of metonymy: evidence from eye movements'. *Journal of Experimental Psychology: Learning, Memory, and Cognition*, 25, 1366–83

Ganis, G., Thompson, W. L., and Kosslyn, S. M. (2004). 'Brain areas underlying visual mental imagery and visual perception: an fMRI study'. *Cognitive Brain Research*, 20, 226–41.

Gärdenfors, P. (2000). *Conceptual Spaces. The Geometry of Thought*. Cambridge, MA: MIT Press.

Gärdenfors, P. (2004). 'Cooperation and the evolution of symbolic communication'. In K. Oller and U. Griebel (eds), *The Evolution of Communication Systems*. Boston: MIT Press, 237–56.

Gärdenfors, P. (2007). 'Evolutionary and developmental aspects of intersubjectivity'. In H Liljenström and P. Århem (eds), *Consciousness Transitions: Phylogenetic, Ontogenetic and Physiological Aspects*. Amsterdam: Elsevier, 281–305.

Gärdenfors, P. and Osvath, M. (2010). 'Prospection as a cognitive precursor to symbolic communication'. In R. K. Larson, V. Déprez, and H. Yamakido (eds), *Evolution of Language: Biolinguistic Approaches*. Cambridge: Cambridge University Press, 103–14.

Gathercole, V. C. (1983). 'Haphazard examples, prototype theory, and the acquisition of comparatives'. *Folia Linguistica*, 4, 169–96.

Gathercole, V. C. (1985). 'More and more and more about more'. *Journal of Experimental Child Psychology*, 40, 73–104.

Geeraerts, D. and Cuyckens, H. (2007). 'Introducing Cognitive Linguistics'. In D. Geeraerts and H. Cuyckens, *Handbook of Cognitive Linguistics*. Oxford: Oxford University Press.

Gennari, S. P., Sloman, S. A., Malt, B. C., and Fitch, W. T. (2002). 'Motion events in language and cognition'. *Cognition*, 83, 49–79.

Gentner, D. and Stevens, A. L. (eds) (1983). *Mental Models*. Hillsdale, NJ: Erlbaum.

Geuder, W. and Weisgerber, M. (2006). 'Manner and causation in movement verbs'. In Chr. Ebert and C. Endriss (eds), *Proceedings from Sinn und Bedeutung* 10, Berlin, ZAS Papers in Linguistics, 125–38.

Gibbs, R. W. Jr. (1994). *The Poetics of Mind: Figurative Thought, Language, and Understanding*. New York: Cambridge University Press.

Gibbs, R. W. Jr. (2002). 'A new look at literal meaning in understanding what is said and implicated'. *Journal of Pragmatics*, 34, 457–86.

Gibbs, R. W. Jr. (2006a). *Embodiment and Cognitive Science*. New York: Cambridge University Press.

Gibbs, R. W. Jr. (2006b). 'Metaphor interpretation as embodied simulation'. *Mind and Language*, 21, 434–58.

Gibbs, R. W. Jr., Lima, P., and Francuzo, E. (2004). 'Metaphor is grounded in embodied experience'. *Journal of Pragmatics*, 36, 1189–210.

Gibbs, R. W. Jr. and Perlman, M. (2006). 'The contested impact of cognitive linguistic research on psycholinguistic theories of metaphor understanding'. In G. Kristiansen, M. Achard, R. Dirven, and F. Ruiz de Mendoza (eds), *Cognitive Linguistics: Foundations and Fields of Application*. Berlin: Mouton.

Gibson, J. (1979). *The Ecological Approach to Visual Perception*. Boston: Houghton Mifflin.

Giese M. A. and Poggio, T. (2003). 'Neural mechanisms for the recognition of biological movements and action'. *Nature Reviews Neuroscience*, 4, 179–92.

Giese, M. (2004). 'Learning as principle of action recognition in visual cortex'. Second Summer School for Cognitive Vision, Bonn, 16–20 August 2004.

Gillis, S. (1997). 'The acquisition of diminutives in Dutch'. In W. U. Dressler (ed.), *Studies in Pre- and Protomorphology*. Vienna: Österreichische Akademie der Wissenschaften, 165–79.

Giora, R. (2003). *On our Mind: Salience, Context and Figurative Language*. New York: Oxford University Press.

Giora, R. (2006). 'Anything negatives can do affirmatives can do just as well, except for some metaphors'. *Journal of Pragmatics*, 38(7), 981–1014.

Giora, R., Balaban, N., Fein, O., Alkabets, I. (2005). 'Negation as positivity in disguise'. In H. Colston and A. Katz (eds), *Figurative Language Comprehension*. Mahwah, NJ: Erlbaum, 233–58.

Giora, R., Fein, O., Ganzi, J., Alkeslassy Levi, N., and Sabah, H. (2005). 'On negation as mitigation: the case of negative irony'. *Discourse Processes*, 39(1), 81–100.

Giora, R., Fein, O., Aschkenazi, K., and Alkabets-Zlozover, I. (2007). 'Negation in context: a functional approach to suppression'. *Discourse Processes*, 43, 153–72.

Giora, R., Heruti, V., Metuki, N. and Fein, O. (2009). 'When we say no we mean no: on negation in vision and language'. *Journal of Pragmatics*, 41(11), 2222–2239.

Giora, R., Fein, O., Metuki, N., and Stern, P. (2010). 'Negation as a metaphor-inducing operator'. In L. Horn (ed.), *The Expression of Negation*. Berlin: Mouton de Gruyter.

Glenberg, A. and Kaschak, M. (2002). 'Grounding language in action'. *Psychonomic Bulletin and Review*, 9, 558–65.

Goldberg, A. E. (1995). *A Construction Grammar Approach to Argument Structure*. Chicago: University of Chicago Press.

Goldberg, A. E. (1996). 'Making one's way through the data'. In M. Shibatani and S. A. Thompson, *Grammatical Constructions – Their Form and their Meaning*. New York: Oxford University Press, 29–53.

Goldberg, A. (2006). *Constructions at Work: The Nature of Generalization in Language*. Oxford: Oxford University Press.

Goldberg, A. E. and Jackendoff, R. (2004). 'The English resultative as a family of constructions'. *Language*, 80, 532–68.

Goldin-Meadow, S. (2007). 'Pointing sets the stage for learning language—and creating language'. *Child Development*, 78, 741–5.

Gomez, J.-C. (2007). 'Pointing behaviors in apes and human infants: a balanced interpretation'. *Child Development,* 78(3), 729–34.

Goodwin, C. (1986). 'Gestures as a resource for the organization of mutual orientation'. *Semiotica,* 62(1/2), 29–49.

Goodwin, C. (2003a). 'Introduction'. In C. Goodwin (ed.), *Conversation and Brain Damage.* Oxford: Oxford University Press, 3–20.

Goodwin, C. (2003b). 'Conversational frameworks for the accomplishment of meaning in aphasia'. In C. Goodwin (ed.), *Conversation and Brain Damage.* Oxford: Oxford University Press, pp. 90–116.

Goodwin, C. (2003c). 'Pointing as situated practice'. In S. Kita (ed.), *Pointing: Where Language, Culture and Cognition Meet.* Mahwah, NJ: Erlbaum, pp. 217–41.

Goodwin, C. (2007). 'Environmentally coupled gestures'. In S. Duncan, J. Cassell, and E. Levy (eds), *Gesture and the Dynamic Dimensions of Language.* Amsterdam and Philadelphia: John Benjamins, 195–212.

Grady, Joseph (2005). 'Primary metaphors as inputs to conceptual integration'. *Journal of Pragmatics,* 37, 1595–614.

Greenbaum, S. and Svartvik, J. (1990). 'The London–Lund Corpus of spoken English'. In J. Svartvik (ed.), *The London–Lund Corpus of Spoken English* (Lund Studies in English 82). Lund: Lund University Press, 11–17.

Grice, H. P. (1975). 'Logic and conversation'. In P. Cole and J. Morgan (eds), *Syntax and Semantics:* Vol. 3. New York: Academic Press, 41–58.

Gries, S. Th. (2006). 'Corpus-based methods and cognitive semantics: the many senses of to run'. In S. Gries, and A. Stefanowitsch (eds), *Corpora in Cognitive Linguistics: Corpus-based Approaches to Syntax and Lexis.* Berlin and New York: Walter de Gruyter, 57.

Grimshaw, J. (1990). *Argument Structure.* Cambridge, MA: MIT Press.

Gullberg, M., Hendriks, H., and Hickmann, M. (2008). 'Learning to talk and gesture about motion in French'. *First Language,* 28(2), 200–36.

Hadar, U. and Butterworth, B. (1997). 'Iconic gestures, imagery and word retrieval in speech'. *Semiotica,* 115, 147–72.

Haggblade, E. (1994). 'Die Lexikalisierung von semantischen Komponenten in den Bewegungsverben'. Berlin: Microfiche-Edition.

Hallett, S. H. (1974). 'Over-extension phenomena in children's acquisition of spatial adjectives'. Paper presented at the Annual Convention of the American Speech and Hearing Association, Las Vegas, November 1974.

Halliday, M. A. K. (1985). *An Introduction to Functional Grammar.* London: Arnold.

Halliday, M. A. K. and Matthiessen, Chr. M. I. M. (1999). *Construing Experience through Meaning. A Language-based Approach to Cognition.* London and New York: Continuum.

Hanks, W. F. (1996). *Language and Communicative Practices.* Boulder, CO and Oxford: Westview Press.

Hansen, E. (1980). 'Motorik und Lokalbestimmung einiger hochfrequenter verba ponendi im Dänischen'. In M. Dyhr, K. Hyldgaard-Jensen, and J. Olsen (eds), *Kopenhagener Beiträge zur Germanistischen Linguistik,* Sonderband 1. Copenhagen: Institut für germanische Philologie der Universität Kopenhagen, 189–98.

Harder, P. (2007). 'Shaping the interactive flow. Language as input, process and product'. *Acta Linguistica Hafniensia,* 37, 7–36.

Harder, P., Heltoft, L., and Nedergaard Thomsen, O. (1996). 'Danish directional adverbs. Content syntax and complex predicates: a case for host and co-predicates'. In E. Engberg-Pedersen, M. Fortescue, P. Harder, L. Heltoft, and L. F. Jakobsen (eds), *Content, Expression and Structure. Studies in Danish Functional Grammar.* Amsterdam and Philadelphia: John Benjamins, 159–98.

Harnad, S. (ed.) (1987). *Categorical Perception: the Groundwork of Cognition.* New York: Cambridge University Press.

Harper, L. D., Loehr, D. D., and Bigbee, A. J. (2000). 'Gesture is not just pointing'. Presented at and published by the International Natural Language Generation Conference. Retrieved 10 October 2003, from http://www.lisaharper.org/pubs/gesture_is_not_just_p%23663B7.pdf

Harr, A-K. (2012). *Language-specific Factors in First Language Acquisition: The Expression of Motion in French and German.* (Studies on Language Acquisition). Berlin: Mouton de Gruyter.

Harris, P. L. and Folsch, L. (1985). 'Decrement in the understanding of *big* among English- and Spanish-speaking children'. *Journal of Child Language,* 12, 685–90.

Harris, P. L., Morris, J. E., and Terwogt, M. M. (1986). 'The early acquisition of spatial adjectives: a cross-linguistic study'. *Journal of Child Language,* 13(2), 335–52.

Hasson, U. and Glucksberg, S. (2006). 'Does understanding negation entail affirmation? An examination of negated metaphors'. *Journal of Pragmatics,* 38(7), 1015–32.

Haviland, J. (1996). 'Pointing, gesture spaces, and mental maps. Language and culture': Symposium 3. Retrieved 14 May 1999, from http://www.language-culture.org/archives/subs/haviland-john/1.html

Haviland, J. B. (2000). 'Pointing, gesture space and mental maps'. In D. McNeill (ed.), *Language and Gesture,* Cambridge: Cambridge University Press, 13–46.

Hebb, D. O. (1968). 'Concerning imagery'. *Psychological Review,* 75, 466–77.

Hedden, T., Ketay, S., Aron, A., Markus, H. R., and Gabrieli, J. D. E. (2008). 'Cultural influences on neural substrates of attentional control'. *Psychological Science,* 19, 12–17.

Hegarty, M. (1992). 'Mental animation: inferring motion from static displays of mechanical systems'. *Journal of Experimental Psychology: Learning, Memory and Cognition,* 18, 1084–102.

Hellberg, S. (2007). 'Polysemy across image schemas: Swedish *fram'. Studia Linguistica,* 61(1), 20–58.

Heltoft, L. (1998). 'Det danske morfologiske system' (The Danish morphological system). In *Selskab for Nordisk Filologi. Årsberetning 1996–1997.* Copenhagen: Selskab for Nordisk Filologi, 85–99.

Hendriks, H., Hickmann, M., and Demagny, A.-C. (2008). 'How adult English learners of French express caused motion: a comparison with English and French natives'. *Aile,* 27, 15–41.

Herskovits, A. (1986). *Language and Spatial Cognition: an Interdisciplinary Study of the Prepositions in English.* Cambridge: Cambridge University Press.

Hesslow, G. (2002). 'Conscious thought as simulation of behaviour and perception'. *Trends in Cognitive Science,* 6, 242–7.

Hickmann, M. (2003). *Children's Discourse: Person, Space and Time across Languages.* Cambridge: Cambridge University Press.

Hickmann, M. (2006). 'The relativity of motion in first language acquisition'. In M. Hickmann and S. Robert (eds), *Space across Languages: Linguistic Systems and Cognitive Categories*. Amsterdam: John Benjamins, 281–308.

Hickmann, M. (2007). 'Static and dynamic location in French: developmental and cross-linguistic perspectives'. In M. Aurnague, M. Hickmann, and L. Vieu (eds), *Spatial Entities in Language and Cognition*. Amsterdam and Philadelphia: John Benjamins, 205–31.

Hickmann, M. (2010). 'Linguistic relativity in first language acquisition: spatial language and cognition'. In M. Kail and M. Hickmann (eds), *Language Acquisition across Linguistic and Cognitive Systems*. Amsterdam: John Benjamins, 125–46.

Hickmann, M. and Hendriks, H. (2006). 'Static and dynamic location in French and in English'. *First Language*, 26(1) 103–35.

Hickmann, M., Taranne, P., and Bonnet, Ph. (2009). 'Motion in first language acquisition: Manner and Path in French and English child language'. *Journal of Child Language*, 36(4) 705–41.

Hirsch, R. (1995). 'The act of speaking: spoken language and gesture in the determination of definiteness of intention'. In C. Pankow (ed.), *Indexicality Papers from the Symposium 'Indexikala tecken' and Annual Meeting of the Swedish Society of Semiotics*. (University of Göteborg, November 2005), 14–30. Retrieved 24 March 2000, from http://www.sskkii.gu.se

Hockett, C. F. (1960). 'The origin of speech'. *Scientific American*, 203(3), 88–96.

Holleman, B. (2000). *The Forbid/Allow Asymmetry: on the Cognitive Mechanisms Underlying Wording Effects in Surveys*. Amsterdam and Atlanta, GA: Rodopi.

Holleman, B. and Pander Maat, H. L. W. (2009). 'The pragmatics of profiling: framing effects in text interpretation and text production'. *Journal of Pragmatics*, 41, 2204–21.

Holmqvist, K. (1993). *Implementing Cognitive Semantics. Image schemata, valence accommodation and valence suggestion for AI and computational linguistics*. Lund University Cognitive Studies, 17.

Holsanova, J. (2001). *Picture viewing and picture description: two windows on the mind*. Lund University Cognitive Studies, 83.

Holsanova, J. (2006). 'Dynamics of picture viewing and picture description'. In L. Albertazzi (ed.), *Visual Thought: The Depictive Space of the Mind, Part Three: Bridging Perception and Depiction of Visual Spaces*. Amsterdam and Philadelphia: John Benjamins, 233–54.

Holsanova, J. (2008). *Discourse, Vision and Cognition*. Amsterdam and Philadelphia: John Benjamins.

Holsanova, J. (2011). 'How we focus attention in picture viewing, picture description, and during mental imagery'. In K. Sachs-Hombach and R. Totzke (eds), *Bilder, Sehen, Denken*. Köln: Herbert von Halem Verlag, 291–313.

Holsanova, J., Hedberg, B., and Nilsson, N. (1999). 'Visual and verbal focus patterns when describing pictures'. In W. Becker, H. Deubel, and T. Mergner (eds), *Current Oculomotor Research: Physiological and Psychological Aspects*. New York, London and Moscow: Plenum.

Holsanova, J., Johansson, R., and Holmqvist, K. (2008). 'To tell and to show: the interplay of language and visualisations in communication'. In P. Gärdenfors and A. Wallin (eds), *A Smorgasbord of Cognitive Science*. Nora: Nya Doxa, 215–29.

Hörberg, T. (2006). 'Influences of form and function on spatial relations. Establishing functional and geometrical influences on projective prepositions in Swedish'. (Master's thesis, Stockholm University). Available: www.diva-portal.org/diva/getDocument? urn_nbn_se_su_diva-6867-1__fulltext.pdf –2006

Horn, L. (1989). *A Natural History of Negation.* Chicago and London: University of Chicago Press.

Horn, L. (2004). 'Implicature'. In Laurence Horn and Gregory Ward (eds), *The Handbook of Pragmatics.* Oxford: Blackwell, 3–28.

Horn, L. (2011). 'Almost forever'. In E. Yuasa, T. Bagchi, and K. Beals (eds), *Pragmatics and Autolexical Grammar.* Amsterdam and Philadelphia: John Benjamins, 3–21.

Hovmark, H. (2007). *Danske retningsadverbier og rumlig orientering* (Danish directional adverbs and spatial orientation) (PhD thesis). Copenhagen: University of Copenhagen.

Huber, S. and Krist, H. (2004). 'When is the ball going to hit the ground? Duration estimates, eye movements, and mental imagery of object motion'. *Journal of Experimental Psychology: Human Perception and Performance,* 30(3), 431–44.

Ibarretxe-Antuñano, I. (2004a). 'Motion events in Basque narratives'. In S. Strömqvist and L. Verhoeven (eds), *Relating Events in Narrative: Typological and Contextual Perspectives.* NJ: Erlbaum, 89–111.

Ibarretxe-Antuñano, I. (2004b). 'Dicotomías frente a continuos en la lexicalización de los eventos de movimiento' [Dichotomies vs. continua in the lexicalization of motion events]. *Revista Española de Lingüística,* 34(2), 481–510.

Ibarretxe-Antuñano, I. (2005). 'Interview: A windowing to conceptual structure and language: Part 1: Lexicalisation and typology.' Annual Review of Cognitive Linguistics. Vol 3, 325–47.

Israel, M. (1996). 'The way constructions grow'. In A. Goldberg (ed.), *Conceptual Structure, Discourse and Language.* Stanford, CA: CSLI Publications, 217–30.

Itkonen, E. (2005). 'Analogy as structure and process: approaches in linguistics, cognitive psychology and philosophy of science'. *Human Cognitive Processing,* 14. Amsterdam and Philadelphia: John Benjamin.

Jackendoff, R. (1983). *Semantics and Cognition.* Cambridge, MA: MIT Press.

Jackendoff, R. (1990). *Semantic Structures.* Cambridge, MA: MIT Press.

Jackendoff, R. (1992). 'Babe Ruth homered his way into the hearts of America'. In T. Stowell and E. Wehrli (eds), *Syntax and the Lexicon. Syntax and Semantics,* 26. New York: Academic Press, 155–78.

Jackendoff, R. (1997). 'Twistin' the night away'. *Language,* 73, 534–89.

Jackendoff, R. (2002). *Foundations of Language. Brain, Meaning, Grammar, Evolution.* Oxford: Oxford University Press.

Jastorff, J., Kourtzi, Z., and Giese, M. (2006). 'Learning to discriminate complex movements: biological versus artificial trajectories'. *Journal of Vision,* 6, 791–804 (http://journalofvision.org/6/8/3/).

Johansson, G. (1973). 'Visual perception of biological motion and a model for its analysis'. *Perception and Psychophysics,* 14, 201–11.

Johansson, R., Holsanova, J., and Holmqvist, K. (2005). 'What do eye movements reveal about mental imagery? Evidence from visual and verbal elicitations'. *Proceedings of the Cognitive Science Conference. Stresa, Italy.*

Johansson, R., Holsanova, J., and Holmqvist, K. (2006). 'Pictures and spoken descriptions elicit similar eye movements during mental imagery, both in light and in complete darkness'. *Cognitive Science*, 30(6), 1053–79.

Johansson Falck, M. (2005). 'Technology, language and thought: extensions of meaning in the English lexicon'. Luleå: Luleå University of Technology, Dept. of Languages and Culture. Available online at http://epubl.ltu.se/1402-1544/2005/31/LTU-DT-0531-SE.pdf

Johansson Falck, M. (2010). 'Are metaphorical paths and roads ever paved? Corpus analysis of real and imagined journeys'. *Review of Cognitive Linguistics*, 8, 93–122.

Johnson, M. (1987). *The Body in the Mind: the Bodily Basis of Meaning, Imagination, and Reason*. Chicago, IL: University of Chicago Press.

Johnson-Laird, P. N. (1983). 'Comprehension as the construction of mental models'. *Philosophical Transactions of the Royal Society of London. Series B. Biological Sciences*, Vol. 295, No. 1077, 353–74.

Johnston, J. R. (1988). 'Children's verbal representation of spatial location'. In J. Stiles-Davis, M. Kritchevsky, and U. Bellugi (eds), *Spatial Cognition: Brain Bases and Development*. Hillsdale, NJ: Erlbaum, 195–205.

Jokinen, K. (2009). *Constructive Dialogue Management—Speech Interaction and Rational Agents*. Chichester, UK: John Wiley and Sons.

Jokinen, K. and Ragni, A. (2007). 'On the annotation and analysis of multimodal corpus'. *Proceedings of the 3rd Baltic Conference on Human Technology*. Kaunas, Lithuania.

Jokinen, K. and Vanhasalo, M. (2009). 'Stand-up gestures—annotation for communication management'. In C. Navarretta, P. Paggio, J. Allwood, E. Ahlsén, and Y. Katagiri (eds), *Proceedings of the NoDaLiDa Workshop on Multimodal Communication—from Human Behaviour to Computational Models*. NEALT Proceedings Series, Vol. 6, 15–20.

Jokinen, K., Paggio, P., and Navarretta, C. (2008). 'Distinguishing the communicative functions of gestures—an experiment with annotated gesture data'. In A. Popescu-Belis and R. Stiefelhagen (eds), *Machine-Learning for Multimodal Interaction*. Berlin/Heidelberg: Springer, 38–49, http://www.springerlink.com/content/48120k4582616082/

Jones, S. and Murphy, M. L. (2005). 'Using corpora to investigate antonym acquisition'. *International Journal of Corpus Linguistics*, 10(3), 401–22.

Kaller, C. P., Rahm, B., Bolkenius, K., and Unterrainer, J. M. (2009). 'Eye movements and visuospatial problem solving: identifying separable phases of complex cognition'. *Psychophysiology*, 46(4), 818–30.

Kaup, B. (2001). 'Negation and its impact on the accessibility of text information'. *Memory and Cognition*, 29(7), 960–7.

Kaup, B. and Zwaan, R. (2003). 'Effects of negation and situational presence on accessibility of text information'. *Journal of Experimental Psychology: Learning, Memory and Cognition*, 29(3), 439–46.

Kaup, B., Lüdtke, J., and Zwaan, R. (2006). 'Processing negated sentences with contradictory predicates: is a door that is not open mentally closed?' *Journal of Pragmatics*, 38(7), 1033–50.

Keil, F. C. and Carroll, J. J. (1980). 'The child's acquisition of "tall": implications for an alternative view of semantic development'. *Papers and Reports on Child Language Development*, 19, 21–8.

Kendon, A. (1972). 'Some relationships between body motion and speech. An analysis of an example'. In A. Siegman and B. Pope (eds), *Studies in Dyadic Communication*, Elmsford and New York: Pergamon Press, 177–210.

Kendon, A. (1980). 'Gesticulation and speech: two aspects of the process of utterance'. In M. R. Key (ed.), *The Relationship of Verbal and Nonverbal Communication*. The Hague: Mouton, 207–27.

Kendon, A. (1983). 'Gesture and speech: how they interact'. In J. M. Wiemann and R. P. Harrison (eds), *Nonverbal Interaction*. Beverly Hills: Sage, 13–43.

Kendon, A. (1986). 'Current issues in the study of gesture'. In J.-L. Nespoulous, P. Perron, and A. Roch Lecours (eds), *The Biological Foundations of Gestures*. Hillsdale NJ: Erlbaum, 23–48.

Kendon, A. (1988). 'How gestures can become like words'. In F. Poyatos (ed.), *Cross-cultural Perspectives in Nonverbal Communication*. Toronto: Hogrefe, 131–41.

Kendon, A. (1991). 'Implications of recent research on gesture and sign languages for the gesture theory of language origins'. Retrieved 10 February 2000, from http://welcome.to/LOS

Kendon, A. (1994). 'Do gestures communicate? A review'. *Research on Language and Social Interaction*, 27(3), 175–200.

Kendon, A. (1995). 'Gestures as illocutionary and discourse structure markers in Southern Italian conversation'. *Journal of Pragmatics*, 23(3), 247–79.

Kendon, A. (1998). 'An agenda for gesture studies'. *The Semiotic Review of Books*, 7(3), 9–12.

Kendon, A. (2004). *Gesture. Visible Action as Utterance*. Cambridge: Cambridge University Press.

Kita, S. (2004). 'Speech-accompanying gestures as window into event conceptualization at the moment of speaking in adults and children'. Plenary presentation at the conference Language, Culture and Mind. Integrating Perspectives and Methodologies in the Study of Language, Portsmouth, UK, 18–20 July 2004.

Kita, S. and Lausberg, H. (2008). 'Generation of co-speech gestures based on spatial imagery from the right-hemisphere: evidence from split-brain patients'. *Cortex*, 44, 131–9.

Kita, S. and Özyürek, A. (2003). 'What does cross-linguistic variation in semantic coordination of speech and gesture reveal?: Evidence for an interface representation of spatial thinking and speaking'. *Journal of Memory and Language*, 48(1), 16–32.

Kita, S., de Condappa, O., and Mohr, C. (2007). 'Metaphor explanation attenuates the right-hand preference for depictive co-speech gestures that imitate actions'. *Brain and Language*, 101, 185–97.

Kita, S., van Gijn, I., and van der Hulst, H. (forthcoming). 'The non-linguistic status of the Symmetry Condition in signed languages: evidence from a comparison from signs and speech-accompanying representational gestures'.

Klatzky, R. L., Pellegrino, J. W., McCloskey, B. P., and Doherty, S. (1989). 'Can you squeeze a tomato? The role of motor representations in semantic sensibility judgments'. *Journal of Memory and Language*, 28, 56–77.

Koch, W. A. (2002). 'Consciousness, communication, speech: a condensed view of the origins of language'. In F. Brisard and T. Mortelmans (eds), *Language and Evolution*. Antwerp Papers in Linguistics, 101, 39–70, Retrieved 15 March 2011 from http://webh01.ua.ac.be/apil/apil101/koch.pdf

Kopecka, A. (2004). 'Étude typologique de l'expression de l'espace: localisation et déplacement en français et en polonais'. Doctoral dissertation, Université Lumière Lyon 2.

Kopecka, A. (2006). 'The semantic structure of motion verbs in French: typological perspectives'. In M. Hickmann and S. Robert (eds), *Space in Languages. Linguistic Systems and Cognitive Categories* (Typological Studies in Language 66). Amsterdam and Philadelphia: John Benjamins, 83–101.

Kosslyn, S. M. (1973). 'Scanning visual images: some structural implications'. *Perception and Psychophysics*, 14, 90–4.

Kosslyn, S. M. (1980). *Image and Mind*. Cambridge, MA and London: Harvard University Press.

Kosslyn, S. M. (1994). *Image and Brain*. Cambridge, MA: MIT Press.

Kosslyn, S. M., Thompson, W. L., Kim, I. J., and Alpert, N. M. (1995). 'Topographical representations of mental images in primary visual cortex'. *Nature*, 378, 496–8.

Kosslyn, S. M., Thompson, W. L. and Ganis, G. (2006). *The Case for Mental Imagery*. New York: Oxford University Press.

Kövecses, Z. (2002). *Metaphor: a Practical Introduction*. New York: Oxford University Press.

Krauss, R. M., Dushay, R., Chen, Y., and Rauscher, F. (1995). 'The communicative value of conversational hand gestures'. *Journal of Experimental Social Psychology*, 31, 533–52.

Laeng, B. and Teodorescu, D. S. (2002). 'Eye scanpaths during visual imagery re-enact those of perception of the same visual scene'. *Cognitive Science*, 26, 207–31.

Lakoff, G. and Johnson, M. (1980). *Metaphors We Live By*. Chicago, IL: University of Chicago Press.

Lakoff, G. and Johnson, M. (1999). *Philosophy in the Flesh: the Embodied Mind and Its Challenge to Western Thought*. New York: Basic Books.

Lakusta, L. and Landau, B. (2005). 'Starting at the end: the importance of goals in spatial language'. *Cognition*, 96, 1–33.

Lambrecht, K. (1994). *Information Structure and Sentence Form*. Cambridge: Cambridge University Press.

Landau, B. and Jackendoff, R. (1993). '*What* and *where* in spatial language and spatial cognition'. *Behavioral and Brain Sciences*, 16, 217–65.

Lander, Y., Maisak, T., and Rakhilina, E. (2012). 'Verbs of aqua-motion: semantic domains and lexical systems'. In M. Vulchanova and E. van der Zee (eds), *Motion Encoding in Language and Space*. Oxford: Oxford University Press, 67–83.

Langacker, Ronald, W. (1982). 'Space grammar, analysability, and the English passive'. *Language*, 58(1), 22–80.

Langacker, R. W. (1987). *Foundations of Cognitive Grammar, Vol. I: Theoretical Prerequisites*. Stanford, CA: Stanford University Press.

Langacker, Ronald W. (1991a). *Foundations of Cognitive Grammar. Vol. II. Descriptive Application*. Stanford, CA: Stanford University Press.

Langacker, R. W. (1991b). *Concept, Image, and Symbol. The Cognitive Basis of Grammar*. Berlin and New York: Mouton de Gruyter.

Langacker, R. W. (1997). 'The contextual basis of cognitive semantics'. In J. Nuyts and E. Pederson (eds), *Language and Conceptualization* (Language, Culture, and Cognition 1). Cambridge: Cambridge University Press, 229–52.

Langacker, R. W. (1998). 'On subjectification and grammaticization'. In J.-P. Koenig (ed.), *Discourse and Cognition. Bridging the Gap*. Stanford, CA: CSLI Publications, 71–89.

Langacker, R. W. (2006). 'Subjectification, grammaticization, and conceptual archetypes'. In A. Athanasiadou, C. Canakis, and B. Cornillie (eds), *Subjectification. Various Paths to*

Subjectivity (Cognitive Linguistics Research 31). Berlin and New York: Mouton de Gruyter, 17–40.

Lautenschütz, A.-K. et al. (2007). 'The influence of scale, context and spatial preposition in linguistic topology'. In T. Barkowsky et al. (eds), *Spatial Cognition V, LNAI 4387.* Berlin and Heidelberg: Springer-Verlag, 439–52.

Leavens, D. A. and Hopkins, W. D. (1999). 'The whole-hand point: the structure and function of pointing from a comparative perspective'. *Journal of Contemporary Psychology*, 113(3), 417–25.

Lécuyer, R., Streri, A. and Pêcheux, M.-G. (1996). *Le développement cognitif du nourrisson.* Paris: Nathan.

Lemmens, M. (2005). 'Motion and location: toward a cognitive typology'. In G. Girard-Gillet (ed.), *Parcours linguistiques: domaine anglais.* [CIEREC Travaux 122], Publications de l'Université de Saint-Etienne, 223–44.

Levin, B. and Rappaport Hovav, M. (1995). *Unaccusativity: At the Syntax-lexical Semantics Interface.* Cambridge, MA: MIT Press.

Levinson, S. C. (1996). 'Relativity in spatial conception and description'. In J. J. Gumperz and S. C. Levinson (eds), *Rethinking Linguistic Relativity.* Cambridge: Cambridge University Press, 177–202.

Levinson, S. C. (1997). 'From outer to inner space: linguistic categories and non-linguistic thinking'. In J. Nuyts and E. Pederson (eds), *Language and Conceptualization.* Cambridge: Cambridge University Press, 13–45.

Levinson, S. C. (2003a). *Space in Language and Cognition—Explorations in Cognitive Diversity.* New York: Cambridge University Press.

Levinson, S. C. (2003b). 'Language and mind: let's get the issues straight!' In D. Gentner and S. Goldin-Meadow (eds), *Language in Mind: Advances in the Study of Language and Thought.* Cambridge, MA: MIT Press, 25–46.

Levinson, S. and Wilkins, D. (eds) (2006). *Grammars of Space.* Cambridge: Cambridge University Press.

Levy, E. T. and Fowler, C. A. (2000). 'The role of gestures and other graded language forms in the grounding of reference'. In D. McNeill (ed.), *Language and Gesture* (Language, Culture and Cognition 2). Cambridge: Cambridge University Press, 215–34.

Lieven, E., Behrens, H., Speares, J., and Tomasello, M. (2003). 'Early syntactic creativity: a usage-based approach'. *Journal of Child Language*, 30, 333–70.

Lindsey, T. (2008). 'The balkanization of motion verbs'. Talk given at the XVI Balkan and South Slavic Conference, Banff, 1–4 May 2008.

Lindstedt, J. (1985). *On the Semantics of Tense and Aspect in Bulgarian.* University of Helsinki, Dept. of Slavonic Languages.

Liszkowski, U., Carpenter, M., Henning, A., Striano, T., and Tomasello, M. (2004). 'Twelve month olds point to share attention and interest'. *Developmental Science*, 7, 297–307.

Liszkowski, U., Carpenter, M., and Tomasello, M. (2007). 'Reference and attitude in infant pointing'. *Journal of Child Language*, 34, 1–20.

Liszkowski, U., Schäfer, M., Carpenter, M., and Tomasello, M. (to appear). 'Prelinguistic infants, but not chimpanzees, communicate about absent entities'. *Psychological Science.*

Lotman, M. (2002). 'Atomistic versus holistic semiotics'. In P. Torop, M. Lotman, and K. Kull (eds), *Sign Systems Studies*, 30(2) Tartu: Tartu University Press, 513–27.

Loucks, J. and Baldwin, D. (2009). 'Sources of information for discriminating dynamic human actions'. *Cognition*, 111, 84–97.

Ludwig, I. (2005). 'The *way*-construction in German'. Honours paper, Department of Linguistics, University of Canterbury.

Lumsden, E. A. and Poteat, B. W. S. (1968). 'The salience of the vertical dimension in the concept of "bigger" in five and six year olds'. *Journal of Verbal Learning and Verbal Behavior*, 7, 404–8.

Lurija, A. R. (1961). *The Role of Speech in the Regulation of Normal and Abnormal Behaviour*. Oxford: Liveright.

Lurija, A. R. (1969). 'Speech development and the formation of mental processes'. In J. Cole and I. Maltzman (eds), *A Handbook of Contemporary Soviet Psychology*. New York: Basic Books, 121–62.

Lyons, J. (1977). *Semantics* (2 vols) Cambridge: Cambridge University Press.

MacDonald, M. and Just, M. (1989). 'Changes in activation levels with negation'. *Journal of Experimental Psychology*, 1(4), 633–42.

MacWhinney, B. (2000). *The CHILDES Project: Tools for Analyzing Talk*. Mahwah, NJ: Erlbaum.

Mahl, G. F. (1961). 'Sensory factors in the control of expressive behavior: an experimental study of the function of auditory self-stimulation and visual feedback in the dynamics of vocal and gestural behavior in the interview situation'. *Acta Psychologica*, 19, 497–8.

Majid, A., Gullberg, M., van Staden, M., and Bowerman, M. (2007). 'How similar are semantic categories in closely related languages? A comparison of cutting in four Germanic languages' *Cognitive Linguistics*, 18(2), 179–94.

Malt, B., Gennari, S., Imai, M., Ameel, E., Tsuda, N., and Majid, A. (2008). 'Talking about walking: biomechanics and the language of locomotion'. *Psychological Science*, Vol. 19(3), 232–40.

Malt, B., Gennari, S., and Imai, M. (2010). 'Lexicalization patterns and the world-to-words mapping'. In B. Malt and P. Wolff (eds), *Words and the World: How Words Capture Human Experience*. New York: Oxford University Press.

Mandler, J. M. (1988). 'How to build a baby: on the development of an accessible representational system'. *Cognitive Development*, 3, 113–36.

Mandler, J. M. (1991). 'Prelinguistic primitives'. In L. Sutton and C. Johnson (eds), *Proceedings of the Seventeenth Annual Meeting of the Berkeley Linguistic Society*, Berkeley, CA, 414–25.

Mandler, J. (1996). 'Preverbal representation of language'. In P. Bloom, M. Peterson, L. Nadel, and M. Garrett (eds), *Language and Space*. Cambridge, MA: MIT Press.

Mandler, J. (2004). *The Foundations of Mind: Origins of Conceptual Thought*. New York: Oxford University Press.

Mandler, J. (2006) 'Actions organize the infant's world'. In K. Hirsh-Pasek and R. Golinkoff (eds), *Action Meets Word: How Children Learn Verbs*. Cary, NC: Oxford University Press, 128–49.

Mandler, J. M. and McDonough, L. (2000). 'Advancing downward to the basic level'. *Journal of Cognition and Development*, 1(4), 379–403.

Maratsos, M. P. (1973). 'Decrease in the understanding of the word "big" in pre-school children'. *Child Development*, 44, 747–52.

Maratsos, M. P. (1974). 'When is a high thing the big one?' *Developmental Psychology*, 10, 367–75.

Markman, K. D., Klein, W. M. P., and Suhr, J. A. (2009). *The Handbook of Imagination and Mental Simulation*. New York: Psychology Press.

Martin, J. R. and Matthiessen, Chr. M. I. M. (1990). 'Systemic typology and topology'. In F. Christie (ed.), *Literacy in Social Processes*. Darwin: Centre for Studies of Language in Education, Northern Territory University, 345–83.

Martínez Vázquez, M. (ed.). (2003). *Gramática de construcciones. Contrastes entre el inglés y el español* [Construction Grammar. Contrasts between English and Spanish]. Huelva: University of Huelva.

Mast, F. W. and Kosslyn, S. M. (2002). 'Eye movements during visual mental imagery'. *Trends in Cognitive Sciences*, 6, 271–2.

Mateu Fontanals, J. (2000). 'Path and telicity in idiomatic constructions. A lexical-syntactic approach to the *way*-construction'. Paper presented at the ESSLLI Workshop on Paths and Telicity in Event Structure, University of Birmingham, 2000.

Mateu Fontanals, J. and Rigau, G. (2002). 'A minimalist account of conflation processes: parametric variation at the lexicon-syntax interface'. In D. A. Alexiadou (ed.), *Theoretical Approaches to Universals*. Amsterdam and Philadelphia: John Benjamins, pp. 211–36.

Matlock, T. (2004). 'Fictive motion as cognitive simulation'. *Memory and Cognition*, 32, 1389–400.

Matlock, T. (2006). 'Depicting fictive motion in drawings'. In J. Luchenbroers (ed.), *Cognitive Linguistics: Investigations across Languages, Fields, and Philosophical Boundaries*. Amsterdam: John Benjamins.

Matlock, T. and Richardson, D. C. (2004). 'Do eye movements go with fictive motion?' In K. Forbus, D. Gentner, and T. Regier (eds), *Proceedings of the 26th Annual Conference of the Cognitive Science Society*. Mahwah, NJ: Lawrence Erlbaum Ass., 909–914.

Matthews, D., Lieven, E., Theakston, A., and Tomasello, M. (2005). 'The role of frequency in the acquisition of English word order'. *Cognitive Development*, 20, 121–36.

Mayo, R., Schul, Y., and Burnstein, E. (2004). '"I am guilty" vs. "I am innocent": successful negation may depend on the schema used for its encoding'. *Journal of Experimental Social Psychology*, 40(4), 443–9.

McCullough, K.-E. (2005). 'Using gestures in speaking: self-generating indexical fields'. Unpublished PhD dissertation, University of Chicago.

McDonough, L., Choi, S., and Mandler, J. (2003). 'Understanding spatial relations: flexible infants, lexical adults'. *Cognitive Psychology*, 46, 229–59.

McNeill, D. (1985). 'So you think gestures are nonverbal?' *Psychological Review*, 92(3), 350–71.

McNeill, D. (1992). *Hand and Mind: What Gestures Reveal about Thought*. Chicago, IL: University of Chicago Press.

McNeill, D. (1999). 'One ontogenetic universal and several cross-linguistic differences in thinking for speaking'. Plenary presentation at the 6th International Cognitive Linguistics Conference, Stockholm, 13 July 1999.

McNeill, D (2000). 'Analogic/analytic representations and cross-linguistic differences in thinking for speaking'. *Cognitive Linguistics*, 11, 43–60.

McNeill, D. (2005). *Gesture and Thought*. Chicago, IL: University of Chicago Press.

McNeill, D. and Pedelty, L. (1995). 'Right brain and gesture'. In K. Emmorey and J. S. Reilly (eds), *Language, Gesture, and Space*. Hillsdale, NJ: Erlbaum, 63–85.

Melinger, A. and Levelt, W. (2004). 'Gesture and the communicative intention of the speaker'. *Gesture*, 4, 119–41.

Mendívil Giró, J. L. (2003). 'Construcciones resultativas y gramática universal'. *Revista Española de Lingüística*, 33(1), 1–28.

Merriam-Webster Online (http://www.merriam-webster.com/)

Michaelis, L. A. (2004). 'Type shifting in Construction Grammar: an integrated approach to aspectual coercion'. *Cognitive Linguistics*, 15, 1–67.

Mora Gutiérrez, J. P. (2001). 'Directed motion in English and Spanish'. *Estudios de Lingüística del Español*, 11. Available online at http://elies.rediris.es/elies11

Moreno, M. A. G., Adrados, H. P., and Ponce, E. C. (1999). 'Adult performance in naming spatial dimensions of objects'. *The Spanish Journal of Psychology*, 2(1), 39–54.

MSN Encarta Dictionary (http://encarta.msn.com/encnet/features/dictionary/dictionary-home.aspx)

Murphy, G. (1996). 'On metaphoric representations'. *Cognition*, 60, 173–204.

Murphy, M. L. (2003). *Semantic Relations and the Lexicon: Antonyms, Synonyms and Other Semantic Paradigms*. Cambridge: Cambridge University Press.

Murphy, M. L. (2004). 'The development of size adjective meaning: what antonym use reveals'. Paper presented at the Seminar on Child Language, Bristol, 12–14 July 2004.

Murphy, M. L. and Jones, S. (2008). 'Antonyms in children's and child-directed speech'. *First Language*, 28(4), 403–30.

Narasimhan, B. (1998). 'The encoding of complex events in Hindi and English'.: Boston University: Doctoral dissertation.

Nedergaard Thomsen, O. (1991). 'Unit accentuation as an expression device for predicate formation in Danish?' *Acta Linguistica Hafniensia*, 23, 145–96.

Nedergaard Thomsen, O. (1992). 'Unit Accentuation as an expression device for predicate formation. The case of syntactic noun incorporation in Danish'. In M. Fortescue, P. Harder, and L. Kristoffersen (eds). *Layered Structure and Reference in a Functional Perspective*. Amsterdam and Philadelphia: John Benjamins, 173–229.

Nedergaard Thomsen, O. (1994). 'Dyirbal ergativity and embedding. A functional–pragmatic approach'. *Studies in Language*, 18(2) 411–88.

Nedergaard Thomsen, O. (1995). 'Discourse, grammar, and prosody in a corpus of spoken Danish—a functional–pragmatic account'. In J. Rischel and H. Basbøll (eds), *Aspects of Danish Prosody*. [= Rask Supplement Vol. 3]. Odense: Odense University Press, 129–213.

Nedergaard Thomsen, O. (1998). 'Retningsadverbialer og komplekse prædikater i dansk' (Directional adverbials and complex predicates in Danish). In *Selskab for Nordisk Filologi. Årsberetning 1996–1997*. Copenhagen: Selskab for Nordisk Filologi, 66–84.

Nedergaard Thomsen, O. (2002a). 'Complex predicates and processing in Danish'. In O. Nedergaard Thomsen and M. Herslund (eds), *Complex Predicates and Incorporation. A Functional Perspective*. [Travaux du Cercle Linguistique de Copenhague XXXII]. Copenhagen: C.A. Reitzel, 120–74.

Nedergaard Thomsen, O. (2002b). 'Complex predicate formation and incorporation. Towards a typology'. In O. Nedergaard Thomsen and M. Herslund (eds), *Complex Predicates and Incorporation. A functional perspective*. [Travaux du Cercle Linguistique de Copenhague XXXII]. Copenhagen: C.A. Reitzel, 288–381.

Nedergaard Thomsen, O. (2003). 'Danish'. In T. Roelcke (ed.), *Variationstypologie. Ein sprach-typologisches Handbuch der europäischen Sprachen in Geschichte und Gegenwart.* Berlin and New York: Walter de Gruyter, 199–249.

Nedergaard Thomsen, O. (2008). 'Funktionel diskurs grammatik—og funktionel pragmatik'. *Nydanske Sprogstudier*, 36, 63–119.

Nedergaard Thomsen, O. and Herslund, M. (2002). 'Complex predicates and incorporation'. In O. Nedergaard Thomsen and M. Herslund (eds), *Complex Predicates and Incorporation. A Functional Perspective.* [Travaux du Cercle Linguistique de Copenhague XXXII]. Copenhagen: C.A. Reitzel, 7–47.

Nelson, K. (1976). 'Some attributes of adjectives used by young children'. *Cognition*, 4, 13–30.

Nesset, T. (2007). 'The Path to neutralization: Image Schemas and prefixed motion verbs'. *Poljarnyj Vestnik*, 10, 61–71.

Newell, A. and Simon, H. (1972). *Human Problem Solving.* Englewood Cliffs, NJ: Prentice Hall.

Newman, J. (ed.) (2002). *The Linguistics of Sitting, Standing, and Lying.* Amsterdam and Philadelphia: John Benjamins.

Newman, J. and Rice, S. (2004). 'Patterns of usage for English SIT, STAND, and LIE: a cognitively inspired exploration in corpus linguistics'. *Cognitive Linguistics*, 15(3), 351–96.

Newmeyer, F. J. (1991). 'Functional explanation in linguistics and the origins of language'. *Language and Communication*, 11, 3–28.

Newmeyer, F. J. (2003). 'Grammar is grammar and usage is usage'. *Language*, 79(4), 682–707.

Nikanne, U. and van der Zee, E. (2005). 'The grain levels in the linguistic expressions of motion'. Talk at 21 Scandinavian Conference of Linguistics, Trondheim.

Nikanne, U. and van der Zee, E. (2012). 'Grain levels in linguistic expressions of motion: a three-level hypothesis'. In M. Vulchanova and E. van der Zee (eds), *Motion Encoding in Language and Space.* Oxford: Oxford University Press, pp. 187–2.

Nisbett, R. E. (2003). *The Geography of Thought. How Asians and Westerns Think Differently, and Why.* New York: The Free Press.

Nisbett, R. E., Peng, K., Choi, I., and Noronzayan, A. (2001). 'Culture and systems of thought: holistic versus analytic cognition'. *Psychological Review*, 108, 291–310.

Noël, D. (2007). 'Verb valency patterns, constructions and grammaticalisation'. In T. Herbst and K. Götz-Votteler (eds), *Valency. Theoretical, Descriptive and Cognitive Issues.* Berlin: Mouton de Gruyter, 67–83.

Nordqvist, S. (1990). *Kackel i trädgårdslandet.* Bromma: Bokförlaget Opal.

Osgood, C. E., Suci, G. J., and Tannenbaum, P. H. (1957). *The Measurement of Meaning.* Urbana, IL: University of Illinois Press.

Osimo, B. (2002). 'On psychological aspects of translation'. In P. Torop, M. Lotman, and K. Kull (eds), *Sign Systems Studies*, Vol. 30.2. Tartu: Tartu University Press, 607–27.

Oxford English Dictionary (http://www.oed.com/). Oxford: Oxford University Press.

Özçalişkan, S. (2005). 'Metaphor meets typology: ways of moving metaphorically in English and Turkish'. *Cognitive Linguistics*, 16, 207–46.

Özçalişkan, S. (2007). 'Metaphors we move by: children's developing understanding of metaphorical motion in typologically distinct languages'. *Metaphor and Symbol*, 22, 147–68.

Öztürk, P., Vulchanova, M., Tumyr, Chr., Martinez, L., and Kabath, D. (2011). 'Assessing the feature-driven nature of similarity-based sorting of verbs'. *Polibits*, 43, Thematic issue: computational linguistics and intelligent text processing, 15–22.

Paradis, C. (1997). *Degree Modifiers of Adjectives*. Lund: Lund University Press.

Paradis, C. (2000a). 'It's well weird. Degree modifiers of adjectives revisited: the nineties'. In J. Kirk (ed.), *Corpora Galore: Analyses and Techniques in Describing English*. Amsterdam and Atlanta, GA: Rodopi, 147–60.

Paradis, C. (2000b). 'Reinforcing adjectives: a cognitive semantic perspective on grammaticalization'. In R. Bermúdez–Otero, D. Denison, R. Hogg, and C. B. McCully (eds), *Generative Theory and Corpus Studies*. Berlin: Mouton de Gruyter, 233–58.

Paradis, C. (2001). 'Adjectives and boundedness'. *Cognitive Linguistics*, 12(1), 47–65.

Paradis, C. (2003). 'Is the notion of linguistic competence relevant in Cognitive Linguistics?' *Annual Review of Cognitive Linguistics*, 1, 247–71.

Paradis, C. (2004/2011). 'Where does metonymy stop? Senses, facets and active zones'. *Metaphor and Symbol*, 19, 245–64. [Reprinted in P. Hanks and R. Giora (eds) (2011). *Metaphor and Figurative Language*. London: Routledge.]

Paradis, C. (2005). 'Ontologies and construals in lexical semantics'. *Axiomathes*, 15, 541–73.

Paradis, C. (2008a). 'Configurations, construals and change: expressions of DEGREE'. *English Language and Linguistics*, 12(2), 317–43.

Paradis, C. (2008b). 'What kind of meanings form conventionalized antonym pairings?' Paper given at Colloquium on Lexico-Semantic relations from theoretical and practical perspectives at the Institut für Deutsche Sprache in Mannheim, 5–6 June 2008.

Paradis, C. and Willners, C. (2006). 'Antonyms and negation: the boundedness hypothesis'. *Journal of Pragmatics*, 38(7), 1051–80.

Paradis, C. and Willners, C. (2007). 'Antonyms in dictionary entries: selectional principles and corpus methodology'. *Studia Linguistica*, 61(3) 261–77.

Paradis, C. and Willners, C. (2011). Antonymy: from convention to meaning-making. *Review of Cognitive Linguistics*, 9(2), 367–9.

Paradis, C., Willners, C., and Jones, S. (2009). Good versus bad antonyms: using textual and experimental methods to measure canonicity. *The Mental Lexicon* 4, 380–429.

Pavlova, M., Krageloh-Mann, I., Sokolov, A., and Birbaumer, N. (2001). 'Recognition of point-light biological motion displays by young children'. *Perception*, 30, 925–33.

Pavlova, M., Sokolov, A., Staudt, M., Marconato, F., Birbaumer, N., and Krägeloh-Mann, I. (2005). 'Recruitment of periventricular parietal regions in processing cluttered point-light biological motion'. *Cerebral Cortex*, 15, 594–601.

Pedersen, J. (2009a). 'The construction of macro-events. A typological perspective'. In C. Butler and J. M. Arista (eds), *Deconstructing Constructions*. Amsterdam and New York: John Benjamins, 25–62.

Pedersen, J. (2009b). 'Lexical and constructional organization of argument structure. A contrastive analysis'. In J. Zlatev, M. Andrén, M. Johansson Falck, and C. Lundmark (eds), *Studies in Language and Cognition*. Cambridge: Cambridge Scholars Publishing, 241–56.

Pedersen, J. (to appear, a). 'Spanish expressions of directed motion—variable type framing'. In H. C. Boas and F. G. García (eds), *Constructional Approaches to Romance Languages.* (Constructional Approaches to Language). Amsterdam and Philadelphia: John Benjamins.

Pedersen, J. (to appear, b). 'Typological prototypes and variation—measuring lexicalization patterns in a constructional environment'. In S. Gries and J. Yoon (eds), *CxG beyond English: Observational and Experimental Approaches.* (Constructional Approaches to Language). Amsterdam and Philadelphia: John Benjamins.

Pedersen, K. M. (2001). Præpositioner med statisk og dynamisk form' (Prepositions with static and dynamic form). In P. Jarvad, F. Gregersen, L. Heltoft, J. Lund, and O. Togeby (eds), *Sproglige åbninger.* Copenhagen: Hans Reitzels Forlag, 164–71.

Peirce, C. S. (1931–58). *Collected Papers of Charles Sanders Peirce.* C. Hartshorne, P. Weiss, and A. W. Burks (eds), Vol. 1–8. Cambridge, MA: Harvard University Press.

Pelc, J. (1986). 'Iconicity: iconic signs or iconic uses of signs?' In P. Bouissac, R. Posner, and M. Herzfeld (eds), *Iconicity: Essays on the Nature of Culture. Festschrift for Thomas A. Sebeok on his 65th birthday.* (Problems in Semiotics 4). Tübingen: Strauffenburg-Verlag, 7–16.

Perniss, P. M. (2007). 'Space and Iconicity in German Sign Language (DGS)'. Doctoral dissertation (MPI Series in Psycholinguistics 45). University of Nijmegen.

Piaget, J. (1954). *The Construction of Reality in the Child.* New York: Basic Books.

Piaget, J. and Inhelder, B. (1947). *La représentation de l'espace chez l'enfant.* Paris: Presses Universitaires de France.

Pickering, M. J. and Garrod, S. (2004). 'Toward a mechanistic psychology of dialogue'. *Behavioral and Brain Sciences,* 27, 169–90.

Pinker, S. (1989). *Learnability and Cognition: the Acquisition of Argument Structure.* Cambridge, MA: MIT Press.

Pinker, S. and Bloom, P. (1990). 'Natural language and natural selection'. *Behavioral and Brain Sciences,* 13, 707–84.

Polunin, O., Holmqvist, K., and Johansson, R. (2008). 'The time line is mapped onto the visual field'. *International Journal of Psychology,* 43(3–4), 610.

Pourcel, S. and Kopecka, A. (2005). 'Motion expression in French: typological diversity'. *Durham and Newcastle Working Papers in Linguistics* 11, 139–53.

Pragglejaz Group (2007). 'MIP: A method for identifying metaphorically used words in discourse'. *Metaphor and Symbol,* 22, 1–39.

Preacher, K. J. (2001). 'Calculation for the chi-square test: an interactive calculation tool for chi-square tests of goodness of fit and independence' [Computer software]. Available from http://www.quantpsy.org

Preacher, K. J. and Briggs, N. E. (2001). 'Calculation for Fisher's Exact Test: an interactive calculation tool for Fisher's exact probability test for 2 × 2 tables' [Computer software]. Available from http://www.quantpsy.org

Project Syndicate (2008). 'Text-corpora'. http://www.project-syndicate.org/

Pulverman, R., Hirsh-Pasek, K., Golinkoff, R., Pruden, S., and Salkind, S. (2006). 'Conceptual foundations of verb learning: celebrating the event'. In K. Hirsh-Pasek and R. M. Golinkoff (eds), *Action Meets Word: How Children Learn Verbs.* Oxford: Oxford University Press, 134–59.

Pulverman, R., Golinkoff, R., Hirsch-Pasek, K., and Buresh, J. (2008). 'Infants discriminate manners and paths in non-linguistic dynamic events'. *Cognition*, 108, 825–30.

Pustejovsky, J. (1995). *The Generative Lexicon*. Cambridge, MA: MIT Press.

Pylyshyn, Z. W. (2002). 'Mental imagery: in search of a theory'. *Behavioral and Brain Sciences*, 25(2), 157–238.

Radden, G. (1996). 'Motion metaphorical: the case of "coming" and "going"'. In E. Casad (ed.), *Cognitive Linguistics in the Redwoods*. Berlin: Mouton, 423–58.

Rasche, C. (2005). *The Making of a Neuromorphic Visual System*. Berlin: Springer.

Ravn, K. E. and Gelman, S. A. (1984). 'Rule usage in children's understanding of "big" and "little"'. *Child Development*, 55, 2141–50.

Reed, C. L., Stone, V. E., Bozova, S., and Tanaka, J. (2003). 'The body-inversion effect'. *Psychological Science*, 14, 302–8.

Richardson, D. C., Spivey, M. J., McRae, K., and Barsalou, L. W. (2003). 'Spatial representations activated during real-time comprehension of verbs'. *Cognitive Science*, 27, 767–80.

Richardson, D. C., Altmann, G. T. M., Spivey, M. J., and Hoover, M. A. (2009). 'Much ado about eye movements to nothing: a response to Ferreira et al.: taking a new look at looking at nothing'. *Trends in Cognitive Science*, 13(6), 235–6.

Rimé, B. (1982). 'The elimination of visible behaviour from social interactions: effects on verbal, nonverbal and interpersonal behaviour'. *European Journal of Social Psychology*, 12, 113–29.

Rizzolatti, G. and Arbib, M. A. (1998). 'Language within our grasp'. *Neuroscience*, 21(5), 188–94.

Rosch, E., Mervis, C. B., Gray, W. D., Johnson, D. M., and Boyes-Braem, P. (1976). 'Basic objects in natural categories'. *Cognitive Psychology*, 8, 382–439.

Rossini, N. (2007). '"Unseen gestures" and speaker's mind: an analysis of co-verbal gestures in map-task activities'. In A. Esposito, M. Bratanic, E. Keller, and M. Marinaro (eds), *Fundamentals of Verbal and Nonverbal Communication and the Biometric Issue*. (NATO Security through Science Series E: Human and Societal Dynamics, Vol. 18. Amsterdam: IOS Press, 58–64).

Rossini, N. (2012). *Reinterpreting Gesture as Language—Language 'in Action'*. Amsterdam: IOS Press.

Rossini, N. and Gibbon, D. (2011). 'Why gesture without speech but not talk without gesture?' *Online Proceedings of the GESPIN 2011 Conference, Bielefeld*.

Rozik, E. (1992). 'Metaphorical hand gestures in the theatre'. In E. Rozik (ed.), *Assaph: Studies in the Theatre*, 8, Tel Aviv University: Faculty of Visual and Performing Arts, 127–52.

Rudzka-Ostyn, B. (2003). *Word Power: Phrasal Verbs and Compounds. A Cognitive Approach*. Berlin: Mouton de Gruyter.

Rummo, I. and Tenjes, S. (2011). 'AJA möistestamine Patau sündroomiga subjekti suhtluses' (Conceptualization of TIME in the context of Patau syndrome). In H. Metslang, M. Langemets, and M.-M. Sepper (eds), *Eesti Rakenduslingvistika Ühingu aastaraamat (Estonian Papers in Applied Linguistics)* 7. Tallinn: Eesti Keele Sihtasutus, 231–47.

Rundell, M. and Fox, G. (eds) (2007). *Macmillan English Dictionary for Advanced Learners*, 2nd edn. Oxford: Macmillan Education.

Ryalls, B. O. (2000). 'Dimensional adjectives: factors affecting children's ability to compare objects using novel words'. *Journal of Experimental Child Psychology*, 76, 26–49.

Sacks, H., Schegloff, E. A., and Jefferson, G. (1974). 'A simplest systematics for the organization of turn-taking for conversation'. *Language*, 50, 696–735.

Saeed, J. I. (2003). *Semantics*, 2nd edn. Oxford: Blackwell.

Sampaio, W., Sinha, C., and da Silva Sinha, V. (2008). 'Mixing and mapping: Motion, Path and Manner in Amondawa'. In J. Guo, E. Lieven, N. Budwig, S. Ervin-Tripp, K. Nakamura, and Ş. Özçalişkan (eds), *Crosslinguistic Approaches to the Study of Language: Research in the Tradition of Dan Isaac Slobin*. New York: Psychology Press.

Schegloff, E. A. (1984). 'On some gestures' relation to talk'. In J. M. Atkinson and E. J. Heritage (eds), *Structures of Social Action: Studies in Conversation Analysis*. Cambridge: Cambridge University Press, 266–96.

Schøsler, L. (2007). 'The status of valency patterns'. In T. Herbst and K. Götz-Votteler (eds), *Valency. Theoretical, Descriptive and Cognitive Issues*. Berlin: Mouton de Gruyter, 51–66.

Schøsler, L. (2008). 'Argument marking from Latin to modern Romance languages: an illustration of "combined grammaticalization processes"'. In Þ. Eyþórsson (ed.), *Grammatical Change and Linguistic Theory: the Rosendal Papers*. Amsterdam: John Benjamins, 411–438.

Schultheis, H. (2007). 'A Control Perspective on Imaginal Perspective Taking'. *Proceedings of the 8th International Conference on Cognitive Modelling 2007*.

Searle, J. (1979). 'Metaphor'. In A. Ortony (ed.), *Metaphor and Thought*. New York: Cambridge University Press, 92–123.

Seland, G. (2001). 'The Norwegian reflexive caused motion construction. A Construction Grammar approach'. Oslo: Department of Linguistics, University of Oslo.

Sena, R. and Smith, L. B. (1990). 'New evidence on the development of the word *big*'. *Child Development*, 61, 1034–52.

Sera, M. and Smith, L. B. (1987). 'Big and little: "nominal" and relative uses'. *Cognitive Development*, 2, 89–111.

Shallice, T. (1988). *From Neuropsychology to Mental Structure*. Cambridge: Cambridge University Press.

Shepard, R. N. and Metzler, J. (1971). 'Mental rotation of three-dimensional objects'. *Science*, 171, 701–3.

Shipley, T. F. (2003). 'The effect of object and event orientation on perception of biological motion'. *Psychological Science*, 14(4), 377–80.

Simion, F., Regolin, L., and Bulf, H. (2008). 'A predisposition for biological motion in the newborn baby'. *Proceedings of the National Academy of Sciences in the United States*, 105/2, 809–13 (http://www.pnas.org/content/105/2/809.abstract).

Sinha, C. (1999). 'Grounding, mapping and acts of meaning'. In T. Janssen and G. Redeker (eds), *Cognitive Linguistics: Foundations, Scope and Methodology*. Berlin and New York: Mouton de Gruyter, 223–55.

Sinha, C. (2005). 'Biology, culture and the emergence and elaboration of symbolization'. In A. P. Saleemi, O.-S. Bohn, and A. Gjedde (eds), *Search of a Language for the Mind-Brain: Can the Multiple Perspectives be Unified?* Aarhus, Denmark: Aarhus University Press, 311–35.

Sinha, C. and Kuteva, T. (1995). 'Distributed spatial semantics'. *Nordic Journal of Linguistics*, 18, 167–99.

Slobin, D. I. (1987). 'Thinking for speaking'. *Proceedings of the Thirteenth Annual Meeting of the Berkeley Linguistics Society*, 435–44.

Slobin, D. I. (1996a). 'Two ways to travel: verbs of motion in English and Spanish'. In M. Shibatani and S. A. Thompson (eds), *Grammatical Constructions: Their Form and Meaning*. Oxford: Oxford University Press, 195–219.

Slobin, D. I. (1996b). 'From "thought and language" to "thinking for speaking"'. In J. J. Gumperz and S. C. Levinson (eds), *Rethinking Linguistic Relativity*. Cambridge: Cambridge University Press, 70–96.

Slobin, D. I. (1997). 'Mind, code and text'. In J. Bybee, J. Haiman, and S. Thompson (eds), *Essays on Language Function and Language Type*. Amsterdam: John Benjamins, pp. 437–68.

Slobin, D. I. (2000). 'Verbalized events: a dynamic approach to linguistic relativity and determinism'. In S. Niemeier and R. Dirven, *Evidence for Linguistic Relativity*. Amsterdam: John Benjamins, 107–38.

Slobin, D. I. (2001). 'Form-function relations: how do children find out what they are?' In M. Bowerman and S. Levinson (eds), *Language Acquisition and Conceptual Development*. Cambridge: Cambridge University Press, 406–49.

Slobin, D. I. (2004). 'The many ways to search for a frog: linguistic typology and the expression of motion events'. In S. Strömquist and L. Verhoeven (eds), *Relating events in narrative: Typological Contextual Perspectives*. Mahwah, NJ: Erlbaum 219–57.

Slobin, D. I. (2005). 'Relating narrative events in translation'. In D. D. Ravid and H. B.-Z. Shyldkrot (eds), *Perspectives on Language And Language Development: Essays in Honor of Ruth A. Berman*. Dordrecht: Kluwer, 115–29.

Slobin, D. I. (2006a). 'Typology and usage: explorations of motion events across languages'. Paper given at the V International Conference of the Spanish Cognitive Linguistics Association, Universidad de Murcia, Spain.

Slobin, D. I. (2006b). 'What makes manner of motion salient? Explorations in linguistic typology, discourse, and cognition'. In M. Hickmann and S. Robert (eds), *Space across Languages: Linguistic Systems and Cognitive Categories*. Amsterdam and Philadelphia: John Benjamins, 59–81.

Slobin, D. I. and Hoiting, N. (1994). 'Reference to movement in spoken and signed languages: typological considerations'. In S. Gahl, A. Dolbey, and C. Johnson (eds), *Proceedings of the Twentieth Annual Meeting of the Berkeley Linguistic Society*. Berkeley, CA: Berkeley Linguistics Society, 487–505.

Smith, L. (2005). 'Shape: a developmental product'. In L. Carlson and E. van der Zee (eds), *Functional Features in Language and Space*. Oxford: Oxford University Press pp. 235–55.

Smith, L. B., Cooney, N. J., and McCord, C. (1986). 'What is "high"? The development of reference points for "high" and "low"'. *Child Development*, 57, 583–602.

Smith, L. B., Rattermann, M. J., and Sera, M. (1988). '"Higher" and "lower": comparative and categorical interpretations by children'. *Cognitive Development*, 3, 341–57.

Smith, T. (2006). 'Bulgarian motion verbs: Manner and Path in a Balkan context'. Talk given at the First Meeting of the Slavic Linguistic Society, Indiana University, Bloomington, IN.

Smith, V. (2003). 'Talking about motion in Danish, French, and Russian: some implications for LSP in theory and practice'. *LSP and Professional Communication*, 2, 66–90.

Smith, V. (2005). 'Modeling the semantics of relocation: for SugarTexts and beyond'. In B. Nistrup Madsen and H. Erdmann Thomsen (eds), *Terminology and Concept Development*, 226–36.

Smith, V. (2006). 'Talking about motion in Danish, French, and Russian: typological, methodological, and translational considerations'. In H. Nølke, I. Baron, H. Korzen, I. Korzen, and H. H. Müller (eds), *Grammatica. Festschrift in Honour of Michael Herslund*. Bern: Peter Lang, 461–75.

Smith, V. (2009). 'Telling the SugarStory in 7 Indo-European languages: what may and what must be conveyed?' In I. Korzen and C. Lavinio (eds), *Lingue, culture e testi istituzionali. Seminario italo-danese* (Halo-Danish seminar, Cagliari, 13–14 November 2007). Firenze: Franco Cesati.

Smith, V. and Nedergaard Thomsen, O. (2009). 'SugarTexts—Telling the SugarStory in diverse languages'. Available at http://www.sugartexts.dk/

Snyder, W. (2001). 'On the nature of syntactic variation: evidence from complex predicates and complex word-formation'. *Language*, 77(2), 324–42.

Sonesson, G. (1996). 'Indexicality as perceptual mediation'. In C. Pankow (ed.), *Indexicality. Papers from the Symposium "Indexikala Tecken"*. November 1995. University of Göteborg, pp. 127–37. Retrieved 7 January 2001, from http://www.sskkii.gu.se/Publications/Documents/html/Indexikality/

Sonesson, G. (2001). 'De l'iconicité des images à l'iconicité des gestes'. In C. Cavé, I. Guïtelle, and S. Santi (eds), *Oralité est gestualité: interactions et comportements multimodaux dans la communication*. Actes du Colloque ORAGE, Aix-en-Provence, 18–22 June 2001. Paris: L'Harmattan, 47–55.

Spelke, E. S. (1994). 'Initial knowledge: six suggestions'. *Cognition*, 50, 431–45.

Spelke, E. S. (2003). 'What makes us smart? Core knowledge and natural language'. In D. Gentner and S. Goldin-Meadow (eds), *Language in Mind: Advances in the Study of Language and Thought*. Cambridge, MA: MIT Press, 277–311.

Spivey, M. and Geng, J. (2001). 'Oculomotor mechanisms activated by imagery and memory: eye movements to absent objects'. *Psychological Research*, 65, 235–41.

Spivey, M., Tyler, M., Richardson, D., and Young, E. (2000). 'Eye movements during comprehension of spoken scene descriptions'. *Proceedings of the 22nd Annual Conference of the Cognitive Science Society*, Mahwah, NJ: Erlbaum, 487–92.

Stanfield, R. A. and Zwaan, R. A. (2001). 'The effect of implied orientation derived from verbal context on picture recognition'. *Psychological Science*, 12, 153–6.

Stefanowitsch, A. (2008). 'Covarying Manner–Path collexemes in German and Spanish motion clauses'. Invited talk presented at the workshop 'Human Locomotion across Languages, Max Planck Institute for Psycholinguistics', Nijmegen, June 2008.

Stefanowitsch, A. and Gries, S. T. (2003). 'Collostructions: investigating the interaction of words and constructions'. *International Journal of Corpus Linguistics*, 8, 209–43.

Stefanowitsch, A. and Gries, S. T. (2007). *Corpus-based Approaches to Metaphor and Metonymy*. New York and Berlin: Mouton de Gruyter.

Stern, D. N. (1985). *The Interpersonal World of the Infant: a view From Psychoanalysis and Developmental Psychology*. New York: Basic Books.

Streeck, J. (1988). 'The significance of gesture: how it is established'. *IPRA Papers in Pragmatics*, 2(1), 60–83.

Streeck, J. and Knapp, M. L. (1992). 'The interaction of visual and verbal features in human communication'. In F. Poyatos (ed.), *Advances in Nonverbal Communication*. Amsterdam and Philadelphia: John Benjamins, 3–24.

Strömquist, S. and Verhoeven, L. (eds) (2004). *Relating Events in Narrative: Typological and Contextual Perspectives*. Mahwah, NJ: Erlbaum.

Svartvik, J. and Quirk, R. (eds), 1980. *A Corpus of English Conversation*. Lund: Gleerups.

Swinney, D. (1979). 'Lexical access during sentence comprehension: (re)consideration of context effects'. *Journal of Verbal Learning and Verbal Behavior* 18, 645–59.

Tabossi, P. and Zardon, F. (1993). 'Processing ambiguous words in context'. *Journal of Memory and Language* 32, 359–72.

Talmy, L. (1975). 'Semantics and syntax of motion'. In J. Kimball (ed.), *Syntax and Semantics*, 4, 181–238. New York: Academic Press.

Talmy, L. (1983). 'How language structures space'. In H. Pick and L. Acredolo (eds), *Spatial Orientation*. New York: Plenum, 225–82.

Talmy, L. (1985). 'Lexicalization patterns. Semantic structure in lexical forms'. In T. Shopen (ed.), *Language Typology and Syntactic Description. Vol. 3: Grammatical Categories and the Lexicon*. Cambridge: Cambridge University Press, 57–149.

Talmy, L. (1991). 'Path to realization: a typology of even conflation'. In L. A. Sutton, C. Johnson and R. Shields (eds), *Proceedings of the Seventeenth Annual Berkeley Linguistics Society*, 480–519.

Talmy, L. (2000). *Toward a Cognitive Semantics. Vols I–II*. Cambridge, MA: MIT Press.

Talmy, L. (2006). 'The fundamental system of spatial schemas in language'. In B. Hampe (ed.), *From Perception to Meaning: Image Schemas in Cognitive Linguistics*. Berlin: Mouton, 199–234.

Tasmowski, L. (coordinator) (2010). *A Concise Comparative Grammar of Modern Balkan Languages*. Brussels: KVAB-VLAC.

Teleman, U., Hellberg, S., and Andersson, E. (1999). *Svenska Akademiens grammatik vol. I–IV*. Stockholm: Svenska Akademien.

Tenjes, S. (2001a). 'Gestures in communication and their use for pointing and referring in space: Estonian examples'. In I. Tragel (ed.), *Papers in Estonian Cognitive Linguistics*, (Tartu Ülikooli üldkeeleteaduse õppetooli toimetised 2/ Publications of the Department of General Linguistics 2, University of Tartu.). Tartu: Tartu University Press, 216–48.

Tenjes, S. (2001b). 'Gestures as pre-positions in communication'. *Trames*, 5(55/50)(4), 302–20.

Tenjes, S. (2003). 'Gestures and spatial relationships in Estonian'. In M. Rector, I. Poggi, and N. Trigo (eds), *Gestures. Meaning and Use* (Proceedings). Oporto: Edições Universidade Fernando Pessoa, 169–73.

Tenjes, S., Rummo, I., and Praakli, K. (2009). 'Kommunikatiivse situatsiooni dünaamiline dimensioon'. In H. Metslang, M. Langemets, M.-M. Sepper, and R. Argus, *Eesti Rakenduslingvistika Ühingu aastaraamat* 5 / Estonian Papers in Applied Linguistics 5. Tallinn: Eesti Keele Sihtasutus, 267–85.

Tesnière, L. (1976 [1959]). *Éléments de syntaxe structurale*. 2nd edn. Paris: Klincksieck.

Thelen, E. and Smith, L. B. (1994). *A Dynamic Systems Approach to the Development of Cognition and Action*. Cambridge, MA: MIT Press.

Thomas, L. E. and Lleras, A. (2007). 'Moving eyes and moving thought: on the spatial compatibility between eye movements and cognition'. *Psychonomic Bulletin and Review*, 14, 663–8.

Thomas, N. J. T. (1999). 'Are theories of imagery theories of imagination? An active perception approach to conscious mental content'. *Cognitive Science*, 23, 207–45.

Thornton, I. and Vuong, Q. C. (2004). 'Incidental processing of biological motion'. *Current Biology*, 14, 1084–9.

Thornton, I., Resnik, R., and Shiffrar, M. (2002). 'Active versus passive processing of biological motion'. *Perception*, 31, 837–53.

Toivonen, I. (2002a). 'The directed motion construction in Swedish'. *Journal of Linguistics*, 38, 313–45.

Toivonen, I. (2002b). 'Particles and results in Swedish and Finnish'. In L. Mikkelsen and C. Potts, *Proceedings of the 21st West Coast Conference on Formal Linguistics* (WCCFL 21) 457–70.

Toivonen, I., van Egmond, M.-E., and Ludwig, I. (2006). 'A cross-Germanic comparison of the *way*-construction. Collocations and Idioms 1'. Paper presented at the First Nordic Conference on Syntactic Freezes. Joensuu, Finland.

Tomasello, M. (1999). *The Cultural Origins of Human Cognition*. Cambridge, MA: Harvard University Press.

Tomasello, M. (2000a). 'Do young children have adult syntactic competence?' *Cognition*, 74, 209–53.

Tomasello, M. (2000b). 'The item-based nature of children's early syntactic development'. *Trends in Cognitive Sciences*, 4(4), 156–63.

Tomasello, M. (2001). 'Perceiving intentions and learning words in the second year of life'. In M. Bowerman and S. Levinson (eds), *Language Acquisition and Conceptual Development*. Cambridge: Cambridge University Press.

Tomasello, M. (2003). *Constructing a Language. A Usage-Based Theory of Language Acquisition*. Cambridge, MA and London: Harvard University Press.

Tomasello, M. (2008). *Origins of Human Communication*. Cambridge and London, MA: MIT Press.

Tomasello, M., Kruger, A., and Ratner, H. (1993). 'Cultural learning'. *Behavioural Brain Sciences*, 16, 495–511.

Tomasello, M., Carpenter, M., and Liszkowski, U. (2007). 'A new look at infant pointing'. *Child Development*, 78, 705–22.

Torreano, L., Cacciari, C., and Glucksberg, S. (2005). 'When dogs can fly: level of abstraction as a cue to metaphorical use of verbs'. *Metaphor and Symbol*, 20, 59–274.

Tottie, G. and Paradis, C. (1982). 'From function to structure. Some pragmatic determinants in impromptu speech'. In N. -E. Enkvist (ed.), *Impromptu Speech*. Åbo: Publications of the Research Institute of Åbo Akademi Foundation, 78, 307–17.

Traugott, E. and Dasher, R. (2005). *Regularity in Semantic Change*. Cambridge: Cambridge University Press.

Tribushinina, E. (2008a). 'Cognitive reference points: semantics beyond the prototypes in adjectives of space and colour'. Utrecht: LOT.

Tribushinina, E. (2008b). 'Do small elephants exist?: Prototypicality effects in the acquisition of dimensional adjectives'. *Toegepaste Taalwetenschap in Artikelen*, 79(1), 31–41.

Tribushinia, E. and Janssen, T. (2011). 'Reconceptualizing scale boundaries: the case of Dutch *helemaal'. Journal of Pragmatics* 43(7), 2043–56.

Troje, N. (2002). 'Decomposing biological motion: a framework for analysis and synthesis of human gait patterns'. *Journal of Vision*, 2, 371–87.

Tversky, A. (1977). 'Features of similarity'. *Psychological Review*, 84 (4), 327–52.

Tversky, B. (1999). 'What does drawing reveal about thinking?' In J. S. Gero and B. Tversky (eds), *Visual and Spatial Reasoning in Design*. Sydney, Australia: Key Centre of Design Computing and Cognition, 93–101.

van Egmond, M.-E. (2006). 'Two *way*-constructions in Dutch: motion along a path and transition to a location'. Australasian Digital Theses Program 2006. Master's thesis. University of Canterbury.

Van Oosten, J. (1984). 'Sitting, standing and lying in Dutch: a cognitive approach to the distribution of the verbs *zitten, staan*, and *liggen'*. In J. van Oosten, and J. Snapper (eds), *Dutch Linguistics at Berkeley*. Berkeley: UCB, 137–60.

van Staden, M. and Narasimhan, B. (2012). 'Granularity in the cross-linguistic encoding of motion and location'. In in M. Vulchanova and E. van der Zee (eds), *Motion Encoding in Language and Space*. Oxford: Oxford University Press, 134–48.

Vandeloise, C. (1986). *L'espace en français*. Paris: Éditions du Seuil.

Varela, F. J., Thompson, E., and Rosch, E. (1991). *The Embodied Mind: Cognitive Science and Human Experience*. Cambridge, MA: MIT Press.

Vendler, Z (1967). *Linguistics in Philosophy*. Ithaca, NY: Cornell University Press.

Verhagen, A. (2003). 'The Dutch way'. In A. Verhagen and J. van de Weijer (eds), *Usage-based Approaches to Dutch*. Utrecht: LOT, 27–57.

Verhagen, A. (2005). *Constructions of Intersubjectivity: Discourse, Syntax and Cognition*. Oxford: Oxford University Press.

Verkuyl, H. (1993). *A Theory of Aspectuality: the Interaction between Temporal and Atemporal Structure*. Cambridge: Cambridge University Press.

Verkuyl, H. (1999). *Aspectual issues: studies on time and quantity*. Stanford, Calif.: CSLI Publications.

Verkuyl, H. (2008). *Binary Tense*. Stanford: CSLI Publications. (Distributed by Chicago University Press.)

Viberg, Å. (2006). 'Towards a lexical profile of the Swedish verb lexicon'. *Sprachtypologie und Universalienforschung*, 59(1), 103–26.

Vogel, A. (2004). *Swedish Dimensional Adjectives*. Stockholm: Almqvist and Wiksell.

Vulchanova, M. and van der Zee, E. (eds) (2012). *Motion Encoding in Language and Space*. Oxford: Oxford University Press.

Vulchanova, M., Martinez, L., and Vulchanov, V. (2012). 'Distinctions in the linguistic encoding of motion: evidence from a free naming task'. In M. Vulchanova and E. van der Zee (eds), *Motion Encoding in Language and Space*. Oxford: Oxford University Press, 11–43.

Vygotskij, L. S. (1962). *Thought and Language*. Cambridge, MA: MIT Press.

Vygotskij, L. S. and Lurija, A. R. (1930). 'The function and fate of ego-centric speech'. *Proceedings of the 9th International Congress of Psychology*. Princeton: The Psychological Review, 464–5.

Warglien, M. and Gärdenfors, P. (to appear). 'Semantics, concep;tual spaces and the meeting of minds'. *Synthese*. DOI 10. 1007/s11229-011-963.

Warren, B. (1992). *Sense Developments*. (Stockholm Studies in English 80). Stockholm: Almqvist and Wiksell.

Weber, G. (1983). *Untersuchungen zur mentalen Repräsentation von Bewegungsverben: Merkmale, Dimensionen und Vorstellungsbilder*. Doctoral thesis: Technische University Braunschweig.

Wei, C. Y. (2006). 'Not crazy, just talking on the phone: gesture and mobile phone conversations'. In *Proceedings of the 2006 International professional Communication Conference, saratoga springs, NY*. Piscatawn NJ: IEEE, 299–307.

Weisgerber, M. (2008). 'Where lexical semantics meets physics: towards a three-level framework of modelling Path'. Manuscript, Konstanz University.

Weisgerber, M. and Geuder, W. (2007). 'Force antagonism in the semantics of movement verbs'. Talk given at the conference FiGS 2007: Forces in Grammatical Structures, Paris, January 2007. Journal article in preparation.

Weissenborn, J. and Klein, W. (1982). *HERE and THERE: Cross-linguistic Studies in Deixis and Demonstration*. Amsterdam and Philadelphia: John Benjamins.

Weydt, H. and Schlieben-Lange, B. (1998). 'The meaning of dimensional adjectives. Discovering the semantic process'. *Lexicology*, 4(2), 199–236.

Whorf, B. L. (1956). *Language, Thought and Reality: Selected Writings of Benjamin Lee Whorf*. Cambridge, MA: MIT Press.

Wilcoxon, F. (1945). 'Individual comparison by ranking methods'. *Biometrics*, 1, 80–3.

Wilkins, D. P. and Hill, D. (1995). 'When "go" means "come": questioning the basicness of basic motion verbs'. *Cognitive Linguistics*, 6(2/3), 209–59.

Willners, C. (2001). 'Antonyms in context. A corpus-based semantic analysis of Swedish descriptive adjectives'. *Travaux de l'Institut de Linguistique de Lund* 40. Dept. of Linguistics, Lund University.

Willners, C. and Paradis, C. (2010). 'Swedish antonyms—a multimethod approach to goodness of antonymy'. In P. Storjohan (ed.), *Semantic Relations: Theoretical and Practical Perspectives*. Amsterdam: John Benjamins.

Wilson, N. and Gibbs, R. (2007). 'Real and imagined body movement primes metaphor comprehension'. *Cognitive Science* 31, 721–31.

Word-Allbritton, A. (2004). 'The Turkmen verb system: Motion, Path, Manner and Figure'. *IULC Working Papers Online*, 1–11.

Yamanashi, M. (2000). 'Negative inference, space construal, and grammaticalization'. In L. and Y. Kato (eds), *Negation and Polarity. Syntactic and Semantic Perspectives*. Oxford: Oxford University Press, 243–54.

Yoon, D. and Narayanan, N. H. (2004a). 'Mental imagery in problem solving: an eye tracking study'. *In Proceedings of the Third ACM Symposium on Eye Tracking Research and Applications, Association for Computing Machinery*, ACM Press, pp. 77–83.

Yoon, D. and Narayanan, N. H. (2004b). 'Predictors of success in diagrammatic problem solving'. *In Diagrammatic Representation and Inference: Proceedings of the Third International Conference on the Theory and Application of Diagrams. Lecture Notes in Artificial Intelligence*, Vol. LNAI 2980, Springer-Verlag, 301–15.

Yu, N. (1998). *The Contemporary Theory of Metaphor: Perspectives from Chinese*. Amsterdam: John Benjamins.

Zacks, J. and Tversky, B. (2001). 'Event structure in perception and conception'. *Psychological Bulletin*, 127(1), 3–21.

Zacks, J. and Tversky, B. (2012). 'Granularity in taxonomy, time and space'. In M. Vulchanova and E. van der Zee (eds), *Motion Encoding in Language and Space*. Oxford: Oxford University Press, 123–31.

Zangemeister, W. H. and Liman, T. (2007). 'Foveal versus parafoveal scanpaths of visual imagery in virtual hemianopic subjects'. *Computers in Biology and Medicine*, 37(7), 975–82.

Zheng, M. and Goldin-Meadow, S. (2002). 'Thought before language: how deaf and hearing children express motion events across cultures'. *Cognition*, 85, 145–75.

Zinken, J. (2007). 'Discourse metaphors: the link between figurative language and habitual analogies'. *Cognitive Linguistics*, 18, 445–66.

Zlatev, J. (2003). 'Polysemy or generality?' In H. Cuyckens, R. Dirven, and J. Taylor (eds), *Cognitive Approaches to Lexical Semantics*. Berlin: Mouton de Gruyter, 445–94.

Zlatev, J. (2005). 'What is a schema? Bodily mimesis and the grounding of language'. In B. Hampe and J. E. Grady (eds), *From Perception to Meaning: Image Schemas in Cognitive Linguistics*. Berlin and New York: Walter de Gruyter, 313–342.

Zlatev, J. and Yangklang, P. (2004). 'A third way to travel: the place of Thai (and other serial verb languages) in motion event typology'. In S. Strömquist and L. Verhoeven, *Relating Events in Narrative: Typological Perspectives*. Mahwah, NJ: Erlbaum, 159–90.

Zlatev, J., Persson, T., and Gärdenfors, P. (2005). 'Bodily mimesis as "the missing link" in human cognitive evolution'. (Lund University Cognitive Studies, 121, Lund University).

Zlatev, J., Blomberg, J., and David, C. (2010). 'Translocation, language and the categorization of experience'. In V. Evans and P. Chilton (eds), *Space, Language, and Experience*. London: Equinox, 389–418.

Index of Names

Subject Index